Material
Events

# Material
# Events

PAUL DE MAN
AND
THE AFTERLIFE
OF
THEORY

Tom Cohen
Barbara Cohen
J. Hillis Miller
Andrzej Warminski
Editors

University of Minnesota Press   Minneapolis — London

"How Can I Deny That These Hands and This Body Are Mine?" first appeared in abbreviated form in *Qui Parle* 11, no. 1 (1998); the essay is reprinted here by permission of the author, Judith Butler.

"Anthropomorphism in Lyric and Law" first appeared in a slightly longer form in *Yale Journal of Law and the Humanities* 10 (1998): 549–74; the essay is reprinted by permission of the author, Barbara Johnson, and *Yale Journal of Law and the Humanities.*

Published by the University of Minnesota Press
111 Third Avenue South, Suite 290
Minneapolis, MN 55401-2520
http://www.upress.umn.edu

Library of Congress Cataloging-in-Publication Data

Material events : Paul de Man and the afterlife of theory / Tom Cohen . . . [et al.], editors.
   p. cm.
Includes bibliographical references and index.
   ISBN 0-8166-3613-3 (alk. paper) — ISBN 0-8166-3614-1 (pbk. : alk. paper)
   1. De Man, Paul—Contributions in criticism. 2. Criticism—History—20th century. 3. Deconstruction. I. Cohen, Tom, 1953– II. Title.
   PN75.D45 M38 2000
   801'.95'092—dc21

                                             00-009996
Printed in the United States of America on acid-free paper

The University of Minnesota is an equal-opportunity educator and employer.

11 10 09 08 07 06 05 04 03 02 01       10 9 8 7 6 5 4 3 2 1

# Contents

# A "Materiality without Matter"?

Tom Cohen, J. Hillis Miller, and Barbara Cohen

Why de Man today? What if any claim might a project so linked to a "theory" that seems out of fashion—that is, rightly or not, to literary preoccupations and close reading—have in an era, say, moving beyond "cultural studies" to a reworking of technology, of technicity, of concerted political imaginaries and revived notions of materiality? Such questions were deferred not only in the overdetermined violence of de Man's occlusion following discussions of the wartime journalism but in the artificially delayed and seemingly *untimely* publication of the last essays, collected in *Aesthetic Ideology* (1996). Is it in these texts, primarily, that de Man moves away from preoccupations with tropological displacements to what perhaps precedes figuration itself, to inscription, a certain "materiality," the mnemonic, the historial "event"—or does it still anticipate that as work "to come"? What value is this most "literary" of microtextual projects to a time undergoing the transformations of the electronic archive and political and terrestrial impasses concerned with anything but textual reading (ecoterrestrial catastrophes, the homogenizations dictated by global capital, resurgent genocidal sidebars, the "University in ruins")? What, after all, has a riddle that haunts the history of the "aesthetic"—and, for that matter, "materiality"—to do with world history or today's critical aporia? This would only be true, say, if the former were attempting in fact to access and alter the program and definition of the "human" itself, and the epistemo-aesthetic regime that shapes and participates in these "impasses" as well.[1] Here, on the far side of the era of "cultural studies," and at a time of increasing preoccupation with the politics of the (electronic) archive, with mnemotechnics and with the posthuman, is there again reason to ask this?

What was de Man doing with "materiality" (what Derrida reminds us is a materiality without "matter"), with inscription, mnemotechnics, the "event"? One might address these late texts today not as relentless pursuits of the "linguistics of literariness," if we still have an ear for such a phrase, but as something pragmatic in the extreme. Here the terms necessary for any mnemotechnic intervention in the historial are examined, put in play, performatively tested?[2] At stake in de Man's late writings, we might say, is the gamble of a transformation within the conceptual programming of the historial, of agency and event, of the "human" (a preoccupation of these essays).[3] That presumed "passage" seems linked to one of the older and more metaphysical terms in the tradition, to a redefinition of the "material." Given the competing idioms, today, that would claim the term *materialism* in order to authorize themselves, what is at stake in this usage—this "materialism" without matter?

We will take the position for the sake of argument and because it is interesting to consider, that what remains unengaged in de Man's text addresses the possibility of intervention in the mnemonic, the programming of the "historial," and a treatment of "materiality" that compels a rethinking of technicity and the "sensorium" on the basis of inscription. Among other things it would be an approach, given the "materiality of inscription," to the notion of the "virtual" and toward a rendering virtual—and hence, toward alternative histories to those programmed by inherited regimes of definition and perception.

Of course, in referencing an *other* "materiality" to inscription, we are left with one that inverts the usual promise of the term that includes in its genealogy the promise of reference, the irreducible real, the prefigural and nonlinguistic. Whatever *inscription* designates, it conjures sheer anteriority. It does not deliver us to any immediacy of reference, to any historical narrative that presumes to encode such, but to mnemonic programs that appear to precede and legislate these— together, necessarily, with reading models, the "senses" for that matter, the "human" as fiction or category, perhaps the humanities as an institution situated over (and against) a disturbance he finds within the "aesthetic" as routinely defined. The "materiality of inscription" as phrase invokes a prefigural domain, the domain of the event and the "performative." To alter this domain, to intervene in the historial and thus allow for the possibility of alternative futures to those now prescribed entails a recasting (the figure of chance must remain a part of this calculation) of inscription. Behind de Man's relentless turn toward inscription and away from "tropological systems" of substitution lies the rather banal but imponderably necessary task not only of the "translator" but of the *engineer*. To alter the archive, the prerecordings out of which experience is projected and semantic economies policed is at issue (one term for this, in de Man, is the "aesthetic state," the manner in which hermeneutic and humanistic programs function in a repressively epistemo-political and statist fashion). De Man speaks here of a movement or passage that can go only in "one direction." One cannot simply go back from having entered the problematics of inscription. This passage is, in Benjamin's terms, a one-way street, "irreversible."

Perhaps one way of laying out or momentarily caricaturing this project for the sake of today's readership is as an appropriation and precision of Benjamin's own "materialistic historiography." The last is one term or conceit that redistributes (and voids) the inherited uses of each term to designate how a rewriting of the archive stands to intervene in received narratives, with the aim of optioning alternative pasts, and hence futures. In the essays of *Aesthetic Ideology* there appears a rather open subtext that we are pointlessly warned not to be distracted by: an appropriation and effacement of Benjamin—darting, violent, dismissed, but marked. Most explicit in the one essay of de Man's overtly on Benjamin, significantly that on the "translation" essay, this is also heard in the recurrence of Benjaminian preoccupations to the point of being a kind of white noise ("shock," a movement "beyond" mourning, recurrent exploitation of terms such as *passage,* of course *allegory* and *translation,* and a use of "materiality" that is at least informed by Benjamin's "materialistic historiography").[4] It may be useful to hypothesize for the moment, as one can do, that we see de Man as working out the means and mechanics of the sort of interventionist machine Benjamin proposed much too metaphorically and elliptically— a fact responsible for traditional misappropriations of Benjamin— under the term *materialistic historiography* in the *Theses on History.* If "materiality" as differently redeployed by Benjamin and de Man entails both a radical displacement of the term (most explicitly, for Benjamin, in Marxist tradition) and a strategic or nomadic reinscription, in both instances we witness not a "theorization" but a performative attempting to disperse a political-referential regime or archive that Benjamin terms *historicism* and that he allies, despite its intents, with what he terms epistemo-political "fascism."[5] De Man's performances may be read perhaps as explorations in how such intervention in received programs of history prepares for and theorizes itself as an event—associated with the mnemonic suspension or "shock" that Benjamin would, across his work, ally with allegory, caesura, translation, and cinema. Since, as Benjamin observes, the "past" must also be altered, anteriority itself reconfigured, the segue into de Man's interrogations of inscription and disinscription appear as other than supplementary. What is infrequently grasped about the violent rewriting of "allegory" in the hands of Benjamin and, very technically and obsessively, de Man—as with "materiality," undergoing semantic evisceration—is that it, *allegory,* is not redefined to function even as a sophisticated representational redescription of a reflexive system of "meanings," even if these include its own scene of production (however defined). Rather, it emerges from the *katabasis* of "literary history" and philosophical aesthetics as a kind of technical apparatus that tracks and aims at a virtual disruption, and alteration, of *anteriority* itself.[6] It is a performative apparatus in the domain of inscription out of which, necessarily, various "futures" are projected as well. The powers accorded *allegory* in Benjamin migrate into other terms such as cinema, translation, or "materialistic historiography"—where this trajectory finds an ultimate articulation as a radical (re)programming of the (historial) archive out of which the "sensorium" would be alternatively produced. Thus de Man reads Hegel's remark in the *Aesthetics* that "art is a thing of the past" as in fact referencing the sheer anteriority of all inscription, all marking systems as a *technē* of writing.[7] Benjamin's figure of a historically mutating "sensorium" is, again, given relentless precision in de Man's attribution of "phenomenality" to the domain of signification, and hence to inscriptions that program perception (which is to also say, the body, agency, the definition of the political, interpretation, and so on). What is not immediately apparent perhaps is that "aesthetic ideology" as a phrase in de Man's use circumscribes the domain of this encounter with memory, blending it with the politics of hermeneutic regimes and epistemo-aesthetic programming. Moreover, he does so by positing what might be termed a *mnemotechnics.* In Benjamin, the "monad" is the name for a site on the textual grid or switchboard at which such an intervention is possible, such an event, and de Man aims, it seems at times, at little more (except this is immense) than clearing the terms in which such a translation may be pursued performatively, microtextually. Between the flaneur and the engineer something occurs.[8]

The term *materiality* in de Man's recitation conjures a locus through which sheer anteriority is in transit, both accessed and preceded as the facticity of inscription out of which human perception forgetfully is staged. Since that is also in this model where "ideology" appears generated—that is, as a relapse and regression from the facticity of the event—de Man observes several things. Among them, that this "relapse" recurs routinely as an artificial humanization, effacement, and interpretive inversion of what the (textual) event performed—that is, everything that is associated with the parabolic figure of "Schiller" in the latter's reading and transposition of "Kant" ("Kant and Schiller"). However long this inversion persists in historical or academic terms, it does not amount to history so long as a reactive hermeneutic program legislates the terms of self-narration.[9] The "one direction" marked by the event—say, by what is implied by Kant's "materiality," as de Man calls it—is irreversible regardless of the evasive parenthesis marked by our inevitable Schillerian relapse, which testifies to it. That is, by the strategies of historicism, or identity politics, or cultural studies that evade the problematic and programming of inscription. What is focused upon here is that which precedes and partakes of the very mnemotechnic site of archival politics out of which the categories of politics, the human, and the aesthetic appear organized, interest in which de Man's text shares with emergent concerns with "posthuman" technicity, the animal, and epistemo-political media today. From de Man's perspective, "aesthetic ideology" suggests not only how the traditional, marginalized construction of "the aesthetic"—dominant today still, certainly—is a model of ideology more generally, or that the latter is designed to conceal, among other things, that "aesthetics" (the word echoes the Greek *aisthanumai,* for perception) names an ancient problematic surrounding the phenomenalization of signifying orders. Our Schillerian attempts to return from the inscriptive order of mnemonic programming to rhetorics of historicism (a move away from the "performative"), of practicality (neopragmatism), of descriptive forms and empiricisms, or to retro-humanist appeals to representation, the subject (identity politics), or experience more generally (metaphorical work on the "body"), are examples of this relapse. If the domain of inscription suggests a palpable horizon of the material and the real (a sort of *magical* "realism" with the virtual potential to alter the latter's program), the list of recent "pragmatic" turns reveals evasive idealisms of various sorts.[10] Their "ideological" signature, we might say, occurs when a model of reference is imposed upon the same conceptual space whose impulse is to fabricate an organizing ground or immediacy (the subject, experience, history) that effaces the problematic of inscription.

Ideology is always mimetic ideology. Hence "ideology" as a term re-calls still the *eidos* and how visibility and "light" remain metaphysi-cally configured as guarantors—a promise monumentalized in the sphinx-like event called "the Enlightenment." It is systematized in an aesthetico-political regime, an occlusion of the order of inscription (on this a certain definitional closure of the "human" depends) in favor of tropes guarding the claims of human immediacy and perception. This, suggests de Man, renders imperceptible the mistaking for percep-tion or phenomenality of a linguistic and mnemonically programmed effect.[11]

The logics emanating from the phrase "phenomenality of the sign"—which references perception to signification—name not only a secret that has organized, by repression and inversion, the marginalized field only recently (that is, in the last several centuries formalized under the concept of aesthetics). The "phenomenality of the sign" calls, as hy-pothesis, for a microtextual response, a mechanics of performative in-tervention at the site of prerecordings (to use a Burroughsian trope), of what precedes "anteriority" so encountered. Since inscription is per definition visible and public, the very site of phenomenalization, its logic precludes relapse into familiar models of *interiority* and content (or reference). It is the site of sheer *exteriority* and what cannot even be contained by that term.[12] This "materiality" without matter takes for granted a coming (and always the case) posthumanist and posthuman horizon by noting that the "human," as we constitute it, *never quite existed other than as an epistemo-political phantasm,* the alibi of the Schillerian relapse. If the economy of the "human" is enforced through a division from its others—various exclusions of gender, the animal, allomimetic agency and, de Man would say, history—the term *post-*human cannot be taken any more literally than postmodern or post-theory. We now see that, in de Man's confabulation, "irony" ceases to be a rhetorical trope and operates as a *technē* of suspension prepara-tory to the possibility of an event. Alternately a decoy figure such as prosopopoeia emerges not as a lyric trope, but as a *technē* for render-ing virtual all that a given historical arrangement of marks encodes as real, or "fact." The precession of face or *prosopos* registers a preces-sion of the subject and of the contemporary models of reference. A rendering *virtual* of what is taken as fixed, as reified, as immediate, as "experience" from within an operation of *disinscription.*

De Man's work might no longer be caricatured as a "literary" diva-gation into the refinements of close-reading, since the latter becomes the portal for a wide-ranging interrogation into how the "event" operates in history, and what intervention in the order of inscription entails. By way of de Man's late work on "materiality" a project emerges that relates less to a "seventies" venture in theory than to still future and proactive investigations of and interventions in the hypertextual relay systems and programs out of which the "human" (and nonhuman) appears constituted, temporalization produced and managed, the "sensorium" altered, the virtuality of the present and the technicity of inscription brought to a point of passage or crossing.

This "one direction" or passage which de Man's text calls "irreversible" is not inimical to a coming politics that may address less that of globalization than of the terrestrial and the nonhuman (species, resources, "life"). Perhaps. For the moment, this passage remains once virtual *and* already testified to. If in the early Hitchcock thrillers Britain served as the Schillerian or "aesthetic state," so that all the political villains aiming to undermine it were also stand-ins for Hitchcock's cinemallographic project, the knowledge de Man's text implies can be likened to that of Mr. Memory in *The 39 Steps*—a walking allegory of a machine of inscription, whose memorized formula for a silent warplane he would *cross* the border with as if en route to an unnamed enemy state. Mr. Memory only records unembellished "facts," snapshots of information, which he can only repeat unaltered— registered in the law of exteriorization[13] which compels Memory to all too publicly explain his intrigue before the crowd at the Palladium when asked "What are 'the 39 steps'?" But that, too, is the title of the film: what Mr. Memory would bring across the border in a way that imperils the "aesthetic state" is a knowledge of being a machine of inscription (like, and as, cinema). That this banality always was the case is marked by the film's opening invocation of Hesiod's Mnemosyne, whom Mr. Memory seems less a modernist revision of, that is, as though fallen from some interior pathos into an externally determined machine, than merely a figure who exposes his predecessor as always having been just this, which is to say, memory has always been this site of inscription without aura. The epic or sublime—if utterly banal— formula is recited, and is nothing but unintelligible numbers and letters (what de Man calls "the materiality of the letter"). It is linked, nonetheless, to sublime flight, the imperceptible or soundless flight of an attacking warplane. While the Schillerian audience would be expected to identify with the "state," with "home" or Britain, which of course always wins or seems to, the mystery of Memory's exteriorization had been outed from the beginning, from the first frame caught in its own material loop of repeated projections, from the moment a hand pays for entry into the Music Hall (spelled out, sequentially, in luminous letters).

This formulaic or McGuffinesque knowledge of "the materiality of inscription" wars with the "aesthetic state's" police and hermeneutic regimes. It does so, in every case and with Hitchcock's insignia, in the name of an alternative epistemo-political model to come. Mr. Memory, a performer in a music hall, in a low-mimetic Hall of the Muses, records "facts" voided of sense by their standardized or mechanical formality. It is through repetition that their mimetic pretense to be "facts" (pictures) is converted into signifying marks and remarks (Mr. Memory is called by his Impresario a "re-markable" man). What is interesting is not that Hitchcock's practice is the closest thing to what we might call a Benjaminian cinema, but that this crossing, this passage of Mr. Memory as if "out" of Britain is both impossible (there is no enemy-other state) and yet presented in vaguely Mosaic terms as is echoed, perhaps, in the academically inflected name of Professor Jordan. What would Jordan, the site of crossing, profess? This passage, which may also be that de Man calls from language as trope to "another conception of language" and the performative, aims at projects getting under way in today's "posthuman" horizon. Moreover, it seems allied to political battles to come over the very definition of the "human" and the animal, of "life" and temporalization, of archival politics and mnemotechnics. Benjamin's recourse, at one point, to calling upon a "natural history" for a nonhuman perspective names a technicity operating within the "natural" which is not that of human history or its recent narration.

What, then, is the "afterlife" of theory—if this term does not name something contrasted to the practical, as it never did? There might be two competing histories that today's critical perspectives wrestle with here. The first is that which finds a "death of theory" to have preceded the repoliticization of critical interests and a supposed "return" to history, to all variety of identity politics, and to divergent definitions of cultural studies. What is interesting is not the implicit labeling of "theory" as the nonhuman, but the persistent reinstatement of a sort of humanism in many of the latter's defining projects. According to this narrative, there has been a more or less steady progress toward the light of a universalized critical practice, departing from a multipositional "cultural studies." An alternative history is that a partial regression occurs in many of these trajectories, a relapse, in a narrative anything but linear or progressive. Do the obvious limitations of these impending impasses, mimetic methodologies today, varieties of "relapse" if we are to take the domain of inscription as inescapable, return us to the utterly pragmatic "theorization" of the impasse in de Man?

We return to the opening question: is there a "program" present in *Aesthetic Ideology*, in "de Man," that is possible to read according to "today's" own needs and impasses? At a time when the untimely might feel at home, when the aporias not of theory but of mimetic, historicist, and cultural criticism are becoming transparent in all issues pertaining to institutional politics and agency, *Material Events* would pose this question. To do so, the present volume invited a variety of contemporary critical writers usually associated with different domains— Marxism and post-Marxism, law and gender studies, science and psychoanalysis, literary and visual and cinematic theory—to address how different discourses of "materiality" function, today, in relation (or nonrelation) to this preoccupation of the culminating essays of de Man. The title, *Material Events: Paul de Man and the Afterlife of Theory*, evokes the promise of this "other" reading of de Man's "materiality" and situates it as if in something called theory's "afterlife." Readers are left to interpret this afterlife in numerous ways—as an identifiable period clocked almost to the death of de Man or as a rather anachronistic and presumptuous trope. The writers gathered in this volume represent an attempt, without any agenda, to explore whether de Man's "materiality" does or does not impact on or collude with various projects associated with the term *materialism* today. De Man's recent abjection in critical studies may not only have been an exceptional way of marking and encrypting "theory" but evidence of policing as well. Whether referenced to assaults on "de Man" following the revelation of the wartime journalism, the delay in publication itself, or the desire to contain the import of what de Man is addressing as inscription, it marked an exceptional episode and lingers as a sort of black hole, numbness, or effaced trauma within literary and critical studies in America. If it is a tomb or crypt—like the meanings of "materiality" itself—worth inspection, that would be less out of curiosity or nostalgia than for a continuing need of strategies to address impasses "today" in a posthuman(ist) epistemo-political landscape.

The originating germ of this project was Tom Cohen's idea that the publication in 1996 of Paul de Man's last posthumous book, *Aesthetic*

*Ideology,* might be the occasion of a conference and then a possible book on the role of de Man's work in present-day theory and practice. Enough time has perhaps passed, we thought, since the revelation of de Man's wartime writings to allow a balanced assessment of his legacy. More particularly, we asked the participants to respond in one way or another to what is perhaps the most enigmatic word in *Aesthetic Ideology*: *materiality*. We have used the word *legacy* twice. Nothing could be more overdetermined, unpredictable, nonlinear, and even mysterious than the notion of a writer's "legacy." No one inherits de Man's work as one might inherit a watch from a deceased friend (or enemy). As Jacques Derrida comments in his essay in this volume, "As a possible legacy from what is above all an event, *l'œuvre* [in this case Paul de Man's oeuvre, especially *Aesthetic Ideology*] has a virtual future only by surviving or cutting itself off from its presumed responsible signatory. It *thereby* supposes that a logic of the machine is in accordance, however improbable that may seem, with a logic of the event." Just what Derrida means by "a logic of the machine" must be found out by reading his essay. What he says does not mean that de Man should not be posthumously held responsible for all he said, wrote, published, and did, but it does mean that what we make of de Man's work now, after the event, is our own responsibility. Just as a careful reader must conclude that de Man twisted the word *materiality,* anasemically, in a performative speech act, to name something different from the legacy of its previous meanings and uses, that is, to name, in Derrida's formulation, a "mechanistic materiality without materialism and even perhaps without matter," so each contributor to this volume has appropriated de Man's work in his or her own way, in an active intervention, or performative reading, that cannot be fully justified in the straight line of a verifiable cognitive, hermeneutic interpretation. What Derrida in *Specters of Marx* says of his relation to the Marxian heritage might be said of the strongest moments in all the essays in this volume in their relation to the "legacy" of de Man's work. Each is a "performative interpretation, . . . an interpretation that transforms the very thing it interprets." Only such a faithful-unfaithful appropriation can be a responsible reception of such a legacy. This means a diffusion of de Man's work in different and to some degree incompatible directions that constitutes the true "afterlife" of that work, sometimes by refusal of it or by radical disagreement with it. You can always refuse, for one reason or another, to accept the watch that has been bequeathed to you. "We" (meaning, at the least, all who work in humanistic study today) are not just de Man's survivors. We are also, for better or for worse, his inheritors. Of course, you can always refuse an inheritance, sign a deposition that you do not want that watch, because it does not keep good time, is ugly or old-fashioned, or was already broken by the one who bequeathed it into a heap of unrelated useless pieces, or whatever.[14]

In spite of the diversity and heterogeneity of the essays included here, each does in one way or another at least touch on the question of what de Man might have meant by "materiality" and on how that might be appropriated for present uses. De Manian materiality is what might be called the "irreducibly other" within his thought. It would be invidious to try to characterize the various contributors as "Marxist," "feminist," "deconstructionist," "Gramscian," "psychoanalytic," "art-historical," and so on, since each of those terms is itself overdetermined and names a heterogeneous nontotality. It would also be absurd to try to summarize in this introduction each essay in a collection that is so rich and in which each essay has its particularity or singularity even in the context of other work by its author. The category names of the different sections of this book (from "Ideologies of/and the Aesthetic" to "Materiality without Matter") are to some degree playful, or at least open-ended. The heterogeneity of the whole book is present within each section too, for example, in the gathering of T. J. Clark, Tom Cohen, and Laurence Rickels together under the rubric of "Deadly Apollo: 'Phenomenality,' Agency, the Sensorium." Nevertheless, as we have said, each essay touches on de Manian "materiality" in one way or another.

The term *materiality* appears in three different, complex, and interrelated registers in de Man's late work: as the "materiality" involved in a certain way of seeing, a way de Man calls, following Kant, seeing "as the poets do it (wie die Dichter es tun)"; as "the materiality of the letter"; and as "the materiality of actual history." One or another of these registers is reregistered, or more than one, in all of the essays here. Moreover, these versions of de Manian materiality are closely associated with de Man's rethinking, in his last essays, of the relation between performative and constative language. Since each of the essays in this volume is exigent, sui generis, and complex, even what each says directly or indirectly about de Manian "materiality" cannot be adequately encapsulated in a sentence or two. Much less can that be done with the whole argument of any of these essays. These introductory notes are an invitation to you, dear reader, to read each essay for yourself and to decide for yourself its import.

Andrzej Warminski's paper presents a detailed and authoritative reading of one crucial passage where the notion of materiality appears in de Man's work. This is the passage where de Man reads Kant on seeing nature "as the poets do it" in "Phenomenality and Materiality in Kant." It might seem that Warminski's essay is simply subordinated to de Man's, focused on reading it accurately, but Warminski also here reads Kant for himself. Moreover, he has his own inimitable vocabulary and rhythm of exposition that makes his essay an appropriation of de Man for his own uses.

In Michael Sprinker's essay Althusser and de Man are juxtaposed and read side by side in relation to their ideas about art and ideology. Although "ideology" is the name both de Man and Althusser give to what it is in human perception and understanding that obscures a vision of "materiality," in the end Sprinker sees Althusser as offering a program for positive political action that, according to Sprinker, was never worked out by de Man.

In an extremely rich and original essay, Arkady Plotnitsky juxtaposes de Man's essays, the nonclassical epistemology of twentieth-century quantum mechanics, and Romantic literature/philosophy (Kant, Shelley, Kleist, Blake). Plotnitsky employs each of these to read the others. He uses de Man, for example, as much to read quantum mechanics as he uses quantum mechanics as a new vocabulary for talking about de Man, Kant, or Shelley. A distinction between "formalism" and "formalization" is essential to Plotnitsky's essay, as is the claim that for de Man and Romanticism, as well as for quantum theory, individual events are irreducibly singular and lawless, only collectively (or phenomenally) lawful or ordered configurations. "Ultimately," writes Plotnitsky, speaking of all three of his juxtaposed subject matters, "every event, specific configuration, or historical trajectory will prove to be unique—irreducibly singular and lawless. Or else each can always be nonclassically reconfigured as comprised of certain singular, lawless individual elements, on the one hand, and of certain lawful collectivities on the other."

T. J. Clark's "Phenomenality and Materiality in Cézanne" takes its title from the title of the same de Man essay on Kant that is Warminski's focus. Clark's interest is not only in the materiality of canvas and paint in Cézanne's work, but also in Cézanne's representation by way of "wedges and commas of color" of an interaction between phenomenality, prosopopoeia, and sheer materiality in Cézanne's paintings, especially *Mont Sainte-Victoire Seen from Château Noir* in the Edsel and Eleanor Ford House museum.

Tom Cohen's essay reads with subtle attention Hitchcock's films in the light of a penetrating understanding of de Manian "materiality." Cohen, however, unlike most of the other contributors, is especially interested in what de Man called "the materiality of the letter" as it was manipulated in Hitchcock's films.

Laurence A. Rickels's "Resistance in Theory" finds de Manian materiality in the concrete circumstances of the act of transference as it occurs, for example, on the analyst's couch. In the context of a fascinating account of the effect on psychoanalysis and on belief in communication with the dead of new technologies—telegraph, telephone, and, especially, the tape recorder—Rickels interprets from the perspective of transference the only one of de Man's major essays whose original exists only on tape: "Kant and Schiller." *Transference* is the key word in Rickels's essay. Since transference takes place during the "in-session materiality of analytic discourse," and since it escapes to some degree the theoretical formulations that would contain it, "transference" is, it could be argued, Rickels's name for what de Man calls "materiality."

J. Hillis Miller's "Paul de Man as Allergen" seeks to identify those aspects of de Man's notions of materiality that arouse the most resistance in readers. His essay explains, at least tentatively and hypothetically, why the resistance is so strong, why de Man is so allergenic to some readers.

Barbara Johnson's "Anthropomorphism in Lyric and Law" returns to a de Man essay published prior to *Aesthetic Ideology* ("Anthropomorphism and Trope in the Lyric," in *The Rhetoric of Romanticism* [1984]) to investigate the problematic of personification in the law. In United States law, a group or association may be "counted as a juridical 'person' under the law." Johnson recognizes, however, that "Anthropomorphism and Trope in the Lyric" in its concluding sentences anticipates, in speaking of "the materiality of actual history," de Man's thought of materiality in the *Aesthetic Ideology* essays and at the same time uses an anthropomorphism of its own, as though anthropomorphism were the one trope that cannot, at least by de Man, be expunged. "True 'mourning,'" says de Man, "is less deluded."

Ernesto Laclau's "The Politics of Rhetoric" sets an astute understanding of de Man's theory of tropological systems (especially focusing on "Pascal's Allegory of Persuasion" in *Aesthetic Ideology*) against his own Gramscian notion of what he calls "hegemony" as it may allow for emancipatory political action. Although Laclau does not make this point, it might be argued that the Pascalian "zero," in its escape from any tropological recuperation, a situation highlighted by de Man in his essay, and analogized by Laclau to the "contingent hegemonic articulations" that he sees as essential to emancipatory political action, is "another name" for what de Man calls "materiality."

Judith Butler's name for materiality is "the body," also stressed, though in a different way, in Derrida's essay. In the context of a reading of Descartes's *Meditations,* somewhat against the grain of what she calls de Man's "literalization of the trope of performativity," Butler negotiates her own resolution of the conflict within contemporary feminism between constructivist and anticonstructivist notions of sexual difference. Her presumption is that, somewhat as in the case of de Man's materiality, "although the body depends on language to be known, the body also exceeds every possible linguistic effort of capture."

Jacques Derrida's "Typewriter Ribbon: Limited Ink (2): ('within such limits')," finally, is a major reconfrontation of de Man's reading of Rousseau in *Allegories of Reading* and a major reconfrontation of Rousseau, Derrida's first extended one since *Of Grammatology.* Challenging and altering de Man's reading of the "purloined ribbon" episode in Rousseau's *Confessions,* while at the same time paying it homage as "an admirable reading, in fact a paradigmatic interpretation of a text that it poses as paradigmatic," Derrida works toward a deeper understanding, if anything like understanding is in this case possible, of "what might be a thinking of machinistic materiality without materialism and even perhaps without matter." Derrida concludes his essay by contradicting something de Man once wrote about Derrida: "He doesn't need Rousseau. He doesn't need anybody else." To which Derrida replies: "De Man was wrong. I needed Paul de Man." He needed him, we can be sure, to get on with his own work. This can be said of all of "us," not just about the authors of the essays in this volume. Whether we know it or not, or are willing to confess to it or not, we need Paul de Man to get on with our own work. The essays here testify to some of the many ways a response to that need can be made.

With a few variations, most of these essays derive from papers originally presented at the conference,[15] announced to the prospective participants in a deliberately open, challenging, and paradoxical formulation: "Culture and Materiality: A post-millenarian conference—apropos of Paul de Man's *Aesthetic Ideology*—to consider trajectories for 'materialist' thought in the afterlife of theory, cultural studies, and Marxist critique." At first glance, the conference site, the University of California's Davis campus, located in the heart of California's agricultural Central Valley and founded as the "University Farm" of the University of California system in 1908, is a long distance from Paul de Man's—and theory's—Yale/East Coast roots. However, the conference was never intended as a retrospective, but, as earlier stated, a "postmillenarian" focus on the *afterlife* of de Man and of theory. Although East to West Coast may not be what first leaps to mind, visions of afterlife tend to evoke geographic, as well as temporal, relocations, and Paul de Man's afterlife in Davis, if fleeting (April 23–25, 1998), was antecedent to more serious thoughts of a theoretical afterlife in the conference papers. Further, as perceptions of the West as frontier territory removed from the Eastern establishment still linger, it seems fitting that a conference with its eye to the future be situated in a western city. In fact, almost half of the two hundred to four hundred attendees (the number varied daily) were students and junior faculty from relatively small and isolated California, Oregon, and Washington colleges and universities, for whom this particular assemblage of critics was a stated first. In his essay, Jacques Derrida underscores the re-location, or travel, from East Coast theoretical roots to this conference when he refers in his essay to himself, Carla Freccero, and Hillis Miller as "three immigrants from Yale." Not only the West Coast (of the United States), but the West, still faces the endangered frontier of an uncertain future or afterlife.

Derrida also refers in his essay to the conference poster which he calls a "*jeu de l'oie* for a Californian science fiction (a French board game that is . . . a cross between Chinese checkers and Monopoly)." The focus of the poster is a tarot card that itself represents the travel "theme." Although not specifically centered on travel to the West, in this case California, as suggested by Derrida, most viewers assumed it a California piece, perhaps because of its psychedelic, or 1960s, quality often associated with northern California.[16] Named "Chariot," its palette of disquieting blues, oranges, and yellows draws one into a phantasmal hodgepodge of travel icons. An airport runway at the card's bottom center leads the eye to an ancient shield inscribed with horse and chariot. At the card's center is a Roman bust, one of its eyes manifested as a hollow of flame, and head adorned with the victor's symbol of the laurel wreath. Around the perimeter are a mélange of travel/transportation images—rocket ship; hot-air balloon; moon-landing shuttle; falcon poised for flight; superhighway; and the diaphanous figure of a surfer—while the card's extreme left reveals a contemporary male face reflected in a rearview mirror. In sum, a travel card of time and place juxtaposing past, present, and future in a whirl of images, some more discernible than others—a "trip" in itself.

We are grateful to many for their contributions to both the conference and this volume. For the conference, we thank the University of California Humanities Research Institute and the Office of the President, the UCI Humanities Center, and the UC Davis Humanities Center, Critical Theory Institute, and Dean of Humanities, Arts, and Cultural Studies for their important conference support. The UCI Humanities Center generously extended its support to the volume as well. We are indebted to Georges Van Den Abbeele as the guiding spirit behind much of this funding and as our gracious conference host. Ron Saufley helped us successfully manage the conference with his enthusiastic and logistical guidance. The tireless energy, valuable insights, and conscientious attentiveness to detail of Brook Haley, Jessica Haile, Erin Ferris, Jim Zeigler, Francie Krebs, and their fellow UCI graduate students transformed the conference from concept to event. We would like to thank Carla Freccero, Ned Lukacher, Mark Poster, and again Georges Van Den Abbeele for their provocative conference papers, and Fred Jameson, whose presence illumined many discussions. For this volume, we thank Geoffrey Manaugh for his diligent and timely work on the index, and Doug Armato, Gretchen Asmussen, Mike Stoffel, and David Thorstad at the University of Minnesota Press for their unfailing patience and professionalism.

We remember with warmth and admiration Michael Sprinker, whose death too soon followed his contribution to *Material Events*. His esprit— intellectual and personal—was his hallmark, which we find stamped on both conference and volume.

**NOTES**

1. After the Schillerian adjustment of Kant, de Man observes: "The human, the needs of the human, the necessities of the human are absolute and are not open to critical attack. . . . The human is defined as a certain principle of closure which is no longer accessible to rational critical analysis" (*Aesthetic Ideology*, ed. Andrzej Warminski [Minneapolis: University of Minnesota Press, 1996], 150–51; hereafter *AI*). And: "there is entirely ignored the possibility of a language that would not be definable in human terms, and that would not be accessible to the human will at all—none—of a language that would to some extent not be—in a very radical sense, not be human. So that we would at least have a complication, an initial complication, in which the principle of closure is not the human—because language can

always undo that principle of closure—and is not language either, because language is not a firm concept, is not a concept of an entity which allows itself to be conceptualized and reified in any way" (*AI* 151–52).

2. For de Man the "epistemological critique of tropes," as he calls the bracketing of totalized systems of substitution or metaphoric thought, is the premise for, if itself preparatory to, epistemo-political intervention. It precipitates what is called a movement, passage, or translation: "And this passage, if it is thus conceived, that is, the passage from trope to performative—and I insist on the necessity of this, so the model is not the performative, the model is the passage from trope to performative—this passage occurs always, and can only occur, by way of an epistemological critique of trope. . . . [Here] certain linguistic elements will remain which the concept of trope cannot reach, and which then can be, for example—though there are other possibilities—performative. That process . . . is irreversible. That goes in that direction and you cannot get back from the one to the one before" ("Kant and Schiller," in *AI* 133).

3. De Man will observe in his discussion of Benjamin's essay "Translation" in *The Resistance to Theory* (Minneapolis: University of Minnesota Press, 1986), hereafter *RT*: "there is, in a very radical sense, no such thing as the human" (96).

4. The encounter between de Man and Benjamin, Benjamin as "hypogram," is also a subtext of de Man's "Anthropomorphism and Trope in Lyric," in *The Rhetoric of Romanticism* (New York: Columbia University Press, 1984), 239–62; hereafter *RR*). We might posit that the relation of Baudelaire's text "Obsession" to "Correspondances"—referenced by Benjamin's theorization of allegory—touches on de Man's reading of Benjamin (259–60).

5. De Man, in "Shelley Disfigured," speaks generically of "the recuperative and *nihilistic* allegories of historicism" (*RR* 122; emphasis added).

6. Allegory reaches into the scene of pre-inscription with the power to reflexively alter that program, a memory or referential system's own "past." As Benjamin puts it in the *Trauerspiel*: "(Allegory) means precisely the *non-existence* of what it (re)presents" [Und zwar bedeutet es genau das Nichtsein dessen, was es vorstellt]." See Walter Benjamin, *The Origin of German Tragic Drama*, trans. John Osborne (London: NLB, 1977), 233; *Ursprung des deutschen Trauerspiels* (Frankfurt: Suhrkamp, 1963), 265.

7. "Sign and Symbol in Hegel's *Aesthetics*": "The art, the *technē*, of writing which cannot be separated from thought and from memorization can only be preserved in the figural mode of the symbol, the very mode it has to do away with if it is to occur at all" (*AI* 102).

8. In the historical conceptualization and institutionalization of the "aesthetic"—whose symptoms pervade the "crises" of the humanities in academia today—de Man believes he has located, in Benjaminian terms, a *master-monad* whose alteration brings with it shudders and alteration throughout the transtemporal switchboard.

9. "[T]he regression from the event, from the materiality of the inscribed signifier in Kant, . . . is no longer historical, because that regression takes place in a temporal mode and it is as such not history. One could say, for example, that . . . in the whole reception of Kant from then until now, nothing has happened, only regression, nothing has happened at all" (*AI* 134). Since this relapse is constitutive not only of

hermeneutics generally but functional and programmatizable communities, missing in de Man is any calculation of how this inversion may be constitutive of reference and the programming of perception within a socio-aesthetic analysis.

10. De Man: "The important thing is that this apparent realism, this apparent practicality, this concern with the practical, will result in a total loss of contact with reality, in a total idealism" (*AI* 142).

11. This "materiality" is so effaced that to think with it or in its direction is itself to risk sanctions: "if you ever try to do something in the other direction and you touch on it you'll see what will happen to you" (*AI* 142).

12. Of Hegel we are told symptomatically: "In order to have memory one has to be able to forget remembrance and reach the machinelike exteriority, the outward turn, which is retained in the German word for learning by heart, *aus-wendig lernen*" (*AI* 102). This leads to the retirement of the figure itself: "The spatial metaphor of exteriority *(Äußerlichkeit)* is not adequate to describe the knowledge that follows from the experience of the sublime. The sublime, it turns out, is self-destroying in a manner without precedent at any of the other stages of the dialectic" (*AI* 116).

13. De Man: "This *Gesetz der Äußerlichkeit* implies that the principle of signification is now itself no longer animated by the tensions between its dual poles, but that it is reduced to the preordained motion of its own position. As such, it is no longer a sign-producing function (which is how Hegel valorized the sign in the *Encyclopedia*), but the quotation or repetition of a previously established semiosis. Neither is it a trope, for it cannot be closed off or replaced by the knowledge of its reduced condition" (*AI* 116).

14. The example is J. L. Austin's, near the beginning of *How to Do Things with Words*, 2d ed. (Cambridge: Harvard University Press, 1975), 5: "'I give and bequeath my watch to my brother'—as occurring in a will." Later Austin recognizes that this act of bequeathing may be in various ways "infelicitous": "it is hardly a gift if I *say* 'I give it to you' but never hand it over" (9). Among Austin's examples of "the type of infelicity which we have called Misapplications," with a characteristic Shakespearean allusion, is "'I give,' said when it is not mine to give or when it is a pound of my living and non-detached flesh" (34). Were the readings de Man performed his to give and bequeath to us, his inheritors? That is a knotty and perhaps undecidable question, especially in the light of what de Man had to say of the machinal and of the way, in reading, what happens is what is bound to take place. As for the watch broken into a thousand unrelated pieces, so that time is put out of joint, see what de Man says in the last paragraph of "Shelley Disfigured": "*The Triumph of Life* warns us that nothing, whether deed, word, thought, or text, ever happens in relation, positive or negative, to anything that precedes, follows, or exists elsewhere, but only as a random event whose power, like the power of death, is due to the randomness of its occurrence. It also warns us why and how these events then have to be reintegrated in a historical and aesthetic system of recuperation that repeats itself regardless of the exposure of its fallacy" (*RR* 122).

15. Of the essays included in this volume, Barbara Johnson's is the only one not delivered at the conference. In addition to the essays herein, our generous Davis host, Georges Van Den Abbeele, as well as Ned Lukacher, Carla Freccero, and Mark Poster, presented papers of significant contribution to the conference.

16. Indeed, the tarot card publisher is a northern California group (Julie King/Merrill-West Publishing, Carmel, California). We think the illustrator (Ken Kenutson) is a local California artist, but we have not succeeded in our attempts to reach this group and wonder if they are off on their own travels. However, the poster designer, Roger Gordon, is, we know, well grounded in southern California.

# I. Ideologies of/and the Aesthetic

# "As the Poets Do It": On the Material Sublime

Andrzej Warminski

The entrance of "the poets" onto the scene of Kant's attempt to ground aesthetic reflexive judgments of the sublime as a transcendental principle—in his phrase "as the poets do it" *(wie die Dichter es tun)*—could hardly be more peculiar and more enigmatic.[1] Paul de Man's reading of this moment in the third *Critique* is no less enigmatic and, if anything, even more peculiar, not least of all because the vision of the ocean "as the poets do it"—"merely by what appears to the eye" *(bloß . . . nach dem, was der Augenschein zeigt*—"merely according to what the appearance to the eye shows," to put it more "literally," or "according to what meets the eye")—is termed by him a "*material* vision" whose "materiality" is linked to what de Man calls Kant's "materialism" (or "formal materialism"): "The critique of the aesthetic," he writes, "ends up, in Kant, in a formal materialism that runs counter to all values and characteristics associated with aesthetic experience, including the aesthetic experience of the beautiful and of the sublime as described by Kant and Hegel themselves" (*AI* 83).[2] That it might be better not to assume anything about our understanding of de Man's difficult "materiality" and "materialism" is certainly confirmed by the *way* the term gets introduced in "Phenomenality and Materiality in Kant." After characterizing the architectonic vision of the heavens and the ocean—"The heavens are a vault that covers the totality of earthly space as a roof covers a house," writes de Man—as being neither "a trope or a symbol" nor "literal, which would imply its possible figuralization or symbolization by an act of judgment," de Man writes that "The only word that comes to mind is that of a *material* vision, but how this materiality is then to be understood in linguistic terms is not,

3

as yet, clearly intelligible" (*AI* 82). Since "material" is a word, the *only* word, that comes to mind here, one can already suspect that its intelligibility will indeed have a lot to do with its being understood "in linguistic terms." We will get to those terms soon enough, but it is already worth remarking that the word *material* is one that merely "comes to mind," as though on account of the *lack* of a word, the proper word, to designate the peculiarly unfamiliar nature of this vision. I say "unfamiliar" advisedly, for de Man goes to some pains— both before and after the word that comes to mind—to explain at length what this material vision is not and is not like. It is a vision entirely devoid of teleological interference, it is *not* a metamorphosis, *not* a trope or a symbol, heavens and ocean as building are a priori, previous to *any* understanding, to *any* exchange or anthropomorphism, there is *no* room for address in Kant's flat third-person world, this vision of the natural world is in no way solar, it is not the sudden discovery of a true world as an unveiling, as the a-letheia of Heidegger's *Lichtung,* "we are not to think of the stars as suns moving in circles," nor are we to think of them as the constellation that survives at the apocalyptic end of Mallarmé's *Coup de Dés,* and so on. The list of what this vision and its materiality are *not* (and are not *like*) could be extended; as de Man says, "It is easier to say what the [Kant] passage excludes and how it is different from others than to say what it is." Indeed, since "*no mind* is involved in the Kantian vision of ocean and heaven," it is no wonder that the only word to characterize it (apparently) nonnegatively can only "come to mind"—as though "by accident," as one says, no doubt simultaneously utterly random and yet completely determined, that is, *over*determined like the nightmarish hypograms of Ferdinand de Saussure.[3]

But what is most striking (for the "mind" or the "eye" or whatever) about de Man's elegiac-sounding and yet nonelegiac enumeration of what the poets' material vision of heaven and ocean is *not* and not *like* is his going out of his way to insist that it is *not* like the poet Wordsworth's, for example, apparently similar intuitions in passages like the nest-robbing episode of *The Prelude* where the destabilized sky is nevertheless still a sheltering sky. "Kant's passage is *not* like this," asserts de Man, "because the sky does not appear in it as associated in any way with shelter." Dwelling poetically in Kant's architectonic world would seem to mean precisely *not* dwelling in the building constructed of heavens and ocean when it is seen merely as the poets do it, according to what the *Augenschein* shows:

The poet who sees the heavens as a vault is clearly like the savage [in Kant's *Logic*],[4] and unlike Wordsworth. He does not see prior to dwelling, but merely sees. He does not see in order to shelter himself, for there is no suggestion made that he could in any way be threatened, not even by the storm—since it is pointed out that he remains safely on the shore. The link between seeing and dwelling, *sehen* and *wohnen*, is teleological and therefore absent in pure aesthetic vision. (*AI* 81)

Nor, de Man insists, is the Kantian vision like the "sense sublime" in the famous passage of Wordsworth's "Tintern Abbey," which is "an instance of the constant exchange between mind and nature, of the chiasmic transfer of properties between the sensory and the intellectual world that characterizes [Wordsworth's] figural diction." No mind being involved in the Kantian vision, "to the extent that any mind, any judgment intervenes, it is in error." And since Kant's architectonic world is not a metamorphosis, not a trope, not a symbol, and prior to any exchange or anthropomorphism, it cannot be addressed the way the poet Wordsworth does it in book 5 of *The Prelude* as "the speaking face of nature." (Actually, in Wordsworth it is "the speaking face of earth and heaven" [and not the "speaking face of nature"] and it is not, at that moment, addressed!)[5] So: *not* a sheltering sky or earth, *not* in an economy or tropology of exchange in relation to the mind, and *not* anthropomorphized or to be addressed. Such would be the materiality of what the *Augenschein* shows in Kant's, for lack of a better word, material vision.

I recapitulate de Man's examples here in order to give some sense of how far he goes in his insistence that what the poets do in Kant is *not* (like) what the exemplary poet Wordsworth does. What are we to make of this apparently stark divergence between a material vision "as the poets do it," according to Kant, *and* a figuralized aesthetic vision and a sublime that are everything the material vision is *not,* as one poet, Wordsworth, does it, according to de Man? And we do not have to know all *that* much about the special status of "Wordsworth" in de Man's private "canon" to know better than to think that Wordsworth is somehow being given as an example of an insufficient or "inauthentic" poet! The fact that Wordsworth comes back still later in the essay to serve quite different purposes—this time as an example of other texts in which there is a "blank" *like* the "blank" de Man reads between sections 27 and 28, that is, between the accounts of the mathematical and the dynamic sublime, in Kant's third *Critique*—should be enough for those who can read. But *how* Wordsworth comes back here is certainly telling. This time it is not so much what Wordsworth wrote, what is there on the page, as what he did *not* write but was nevertheless able to articulate: that is, "the blank between stanzas 1 and 2 of the Lucy poem 'A slumber did my spirit seal . . .' or between parts 1 and 2 of the Boy of Winander poem."[6] As it happens, what he articulates here is an example of a moment when "articulation is threatened by its undoing," when there is "a shift from a tropological to a different mode of language," as in the case of the "blank" between mathematical and dynamic sublimes, where "one could speak of a shift from trope to performance" (*AI* 89). Given that Wordsworth, of all poets, is able to do this, to do what Kant, or at least Kant's (formal materialist) text, does, it would be worse than premature to relegate him to merely aestheticist status as though he were only another aesthetic ideologist, only another Schiller.[7] It would be more helpful perhaps to recall that de Man's insistence that what the poets do in Kant is not what the poet Wordsworth does is very much like his equally stark declaration in "Anthropomorphism and Trope in the Lyric" that whatever Baudelaire's "Correspondances" may be, "it is, emphatically, *not* a lyric" but rather something of "an infra-text, a hypogram" underneath lyrics like "Obsession" (or "odes," "idylls," or "elegies") or, for that matter, pseudohistorical period terms such as *romanticism* or *classicism,* which are "always terms of resistance and nostalgia, at the furthest remove from the materiality of actual history" (*RR* 262). If Wordsworth can be both *un*like "the poets" of Kant—in seeing the sky as a sheltering sky and nature in terms of phenomenal figures that enter into a tropological system of exchange with the mind or the Imagination and that can be anthropomorphized and addressed—and yet also *like* them, in being able to articulate, if not to say, the moment of disruption, "the material disarticulation not only of nature but of the body" and thus "the undoing of the aesthetic as a valid category," then "Wordsworth" is very much also "like" the Baudelaire, or one could better say, the Baudelaire*s* of de Man's "Anthropomorphism and Trope in the Lyric." As the "author"—or rather the signatory—of both the "lyric" "Obsession" and the emphatic *non*lyric "Correspondances" that is legible like an infratext or a hypogram "underneath" it, Baudelaire clearly both does and does not do what the poets are supposed to do in de Man's account of Kant's material vision. And he does and does not do it because he writes *two* texts: the lyric "Obsession" and the emphatic *non*lyric "Correspondances." By writing the latter,

Baudelaire writes a text of "true mourning," as de Man puts it at the end of "Anthropomorphism and Trope," that allows for noncomprehension and enumerates "non-anthropomorphic, non-elegiac, non-celebratory, non-lyrical, non-poetic, that is to say, prosaic, or, better, *historical* modes of language power" (*RR* 262). In doing so, "Correspondances" constructs something like that architectonic world of Kant's material vision—in this case, not so much a building that is not for dwelling and does not shelter as a temple in which no sacrifice that could transport us from the world of the senses to the world of the spirit takes place. Yet by writing the second text, "Obsession," Baudelaire also writes a lyric of recollection and elegiac mourning that adds remembrance to the flat surface of time in "Correspondances" and that engages the full panoply of lyric tropes and devices—anthropomorphism, apostrophe, exclamation, a *je–tu* structure, specular symmetry along an axis of assertion and negation, and so on—to result in "the reconciliation of knowledge with phenomenal, aesthetic experience" (*RR* 258), which, historicized, issues in "the aesthetic ideologization of linguistic structures" (*RR* 253). In writing *both* texts, Baudelaire is indeed like Wordsworth the phenomenalizing "romantic" poet *and* like Wordsworth the formal materialist who would be as nonlyrical and nonpoetic as those most prosaic poets of Kant. (So: the more "poetic" Wordsworth and Baudelaire, the less they are like "the poets" of Kant; the more "prosaic," the more material and historical.)

But, of course, we should not take the doubleness of the two here—*two* texts, *two* Baudelaires, *two* Wordsworths—too literally, as though these Wordsworths and Baudelaires were Schillerian aesthetic ideologists in some "poetic" poems and Kantian formal materialists in some other, rather "prosaic," poems. No, insists de Man, "whenever we encounter a text such as 'Obsession'—that is, whenever we read—there always is an infra-text, a hypogram like 'Correspondances' underneath" (*RR* 262). In other words, again, "There always are at least two texts, regardless of whether they are actually written out or not; the relationship between the two sonnets, obligingly provided by Baudelaire for the benefit, no doubt, of future teachers invited to speak on the nature of the lyric, is an inherent characteristic of any text" (*RR* 260–61). This is certainly borne out by de Man's reading of "Correspondances"—a text that turns out to be as thoroughly double and duplicitous as the double register of the articulating (and disarticulating) word *comme* in its function as both a term of comparison and metaphorical transport based on substances and their properties *and* a more metonymical syntactical marker of aimless enumeration—as a "metaphor aspiring to transcendental totality" gets stuck in "an enumeration that never goes anywhere" (*RR* 250). In other words, the infratext or hypogram of "Correspondances" has already (and always again) produced the lyric "Obsession"—whether or not "Obsession" were ever actually written out. And, one should quickly add, whether "Correspondances" were ever actually written out or not! Clearly enough, the "materiality" of the infratext, or the hypogram, or of what de Man calls the "prosaic materiality of the letter" or "material inscription" (or, for that matter, "the materiality of actual history"), is not accessible in phenomenal experience and what appears in empirical space and time. Materiality—or the infratext or hypogram or the letter or the inscription or actual history or the prosaic language power of the poets—is not something we are going to put our finger on. It is also not something that we can give more than inadequate, provisional, names to. Just as the "material" of "material vision" is "the only word that comes to mind," so "In the paraphernalia of literary terminology, there is no term available to tell us what 'Correspondances' might be" (*RR* 261), and the terms *infratext* and *hypogram* are clearly also makeshift stand-ins. All the same, this does not mean that de Man's "materiality"—however difficult and even enigmatic it may be—is as mysterious as all that. The various formulations of what it is not and what it is *like*, both in the Kant essays and in "Anthropomorphism and Trope in the Lyric" (and in other essays of the 1980s), indicate where to look for it, or at least how to read it. And that it has indeed everything to do with reading should already be plenty clear. For what else is one going to do to understand the "disruption" or the "blank"—whether between stanzas or parts of Wordsworth poems or between the mathematical and dynamic sublimes or in the juxtaposition of seeing according to what the *Augenschein* shows with an allegorical narrative of how the imagination sacrifices itself for reason—except to try to read them? And how read these moments in Kant (or Wordsworth or Baudelaire or whatever) where "articulation is threatened by its undoing" *except* by making them intelligible "in linguistic terms," as de Man puts it, if at these moments we encounter passages "that could be identified as a shift from a tropological to a different mode of language"? The poets can help us here again—in this case, de Man's compact account of how we are (and, as always, are *not*) to understand the *relation* between the always two texts that there always are whenever we encounter *a* text, that is, whenever we read. Going over this account should make it easier for us finally to go back to Kant's sublime and to read the poets and their purportedly material vision in the context of de Man's reading of the mathematical, the dynamic, and the—for lack of a better word—"material" sublimes.

As it happens, the relation between the two texts that there always are whenever there is text—between an intelligible lyric like "Obsession" and its infratext or hypogram like the forever unintelligible "Correspondances"—is far from simple. And the question of the *order* of their relation—its reversibility or irreversibility—is especially difficult, which is perhaps not surprising since it is the same question as that of the relation between critical and ideological discourse: in shorthand, like the paradigmatic relation between Kant and Schiller or, in this case, between "Correspondances" and "Obsession" in relation to one another *and* in relation to themselves (as, say, "Correspondances"/ "Obsession" and "Obsession"/"Correspondances"). How does it work? On the one hand, the relation is clear: whenever we encounter a text like "Obsession," there is always an infratext, a hypogram, like "Correspondances" underneath. The lyric "Obsession" and its entire tropological system of devices—that is nothing so much as the "defensive motion of understanding, the possibility of a future hermeneutics" (*RR* 261)—is a *reading,* what de Man calls here "a lyrical reading-motion" and "a lyrical reading" of "Correspondances." "Obsession" would be the Schiller to "Correspondances"'s Kant. De Man spells out the one hand:

> We all perfectly and quickly understand "Obsession," and better still the motion that takes us from the earlier to the later text. But no symmetrical reversal of this lyrical reading-motion is conceivable; if Baudelaire, as is eminently possible, were to have written, in empirical time, "Correspondances" after "Obsession," this would change nothing. "Obsession" derives from "Correspondances" but the reverse is not the case. Neither does it account for it as its origin or cause. "Correspondances" implies and explains "Obsession" but "Obsession" leaves "Correspondances" as thoroughly incomprehensible as it always was. (*RR* 261)

Nevertheless, however irreversible this defensive motion of understanding and its lyrical reading-motion, it would be an error and, indeed, a similar phenomenalizing ideologization to understand this order and its irreversibility in phenomenal (spatial or temporal) terms:

> Whenever we encounter a text such as "Obsession"—that is, whenever we read—there always is an infra-text, a hypogram like "Correspondances" underneath. Stating this relationship, as we just did, in phenomenal, spatial terms or in phenomenal, temporal terms—"Obsession," a text of recollection and elegiac mourning, *adds* remembrance to the flat surface of time in "Correspondances"—produces at once a hermeneutic, fallacious lyrical reading of the unintelligible. The power that takes one from one text to the other is not just a power of displacement, be it understood as recollection or interiorization or any other "transport," but the sheer blind violence that Nietzsche, concerned with the same enigma, domesticated by calling it, metaphorically, an *army* of tropes. (*RR* 262)

As far as the materiality of the actual history, that is, whatever it is that *happens* "between" "Correspondances" and "Obsession," is concerned, the spatial or temporal phenomenality of which text is "underneath" which and which text comes after which does not matter and changes nothing, that is, does not happen—and understandably enough at that, for, as I said, it also does not matter whether the two texts were ever actually written out or not! Indeed, even if the "lyrical" reading-motion can go only from "Correspondances" to "Obsession," it is also the case that a reading-motion like de Man's of "Correspondances" goes *from* the all-too-poetic lyric of historicizing literary history that declares, performs (in its synaesthesia), and values sheer aesthetic ideology *to* an infratext underneath that threatens to disarticulate the poem's transcendentalizing tropes and end up in "the stutter, the *piétinement* of aimless enumeration" (*RR* 254). In other words, de Man's own (material? what shall we call it?) "reading-motion" goes *from* trope to another mode of language and thus, in a sense, *from* the lyric "Obsession" to the hypogram "Correspondances." This does not mean, of course, that "Correspondances" and "Obsession" are in fact, materially, historically reversible. What is reversible is only the order of which precedes which and which follows which in the temporality of reading (whether lyric or otherwise), that is, in the temporality of an act of understanding and its inevitable temporalization in an allegory that narrates this act (which involves an inevitable phenomenalization—as de Man remarks in his own language when he says that the infratext or hypogram is "underneath" the lyric or that the lyric *adds* remembrance to the flat surface of time in "Correspondances"). What is *not* reversible, however, is the power "that takes one from one text to the other" in these reading-motions, whether they go from the saturation and emptying out of tropes as the text moves from a tropological to another mode of language—from trope to performance, say—or from the material inscription of the hypogram in a defensive lyrical reading-motion to phenomenalizing aesthetic ideologizations of a celebratory or elegiac, apostrophizing and anthropomorphizing, poetic lyric. Both are inevitable, irreversible, what happens. What happens is the *power* that, as de Man puts it, "takes one from one text to the other"—whether there are empirically one or two or more or fewer texts, or whether they "exist," that is, were ever actually written out, or not!—the sheer blind violence of the inaugural act that put the tropological system into place in the first place and that gets repeated whenever we necessarily and inevitably go from one text to the other—that is, whenever we *read*.

De Man's account of the always two texts of Baudelaire and of reading takes us back to his reading of Kant and helps us to understand, in particular, the itinerary, the *order*, of that reading—that is, the reading of the mathematical and dynamic sublimes and their issuing in the "material sublime" of the poets. Needless to say, understanding this reading, its order, and how the "materiality" of "material vision" emerges from it depends a great deal on making it intelligible "in linguistic terms." "Linguistic" because it turns out that all three moments of Kant's sublime—mathematical, dynamic, and, for lack of a word, material—are to be understood not as philosophical (transcendental or even metaphysical) principles but as what de Man calls a "linguistic principle." In order: the mathematical sublime becomes intelligible—all too intelligible (like Baudelaire's "Obsession")—and can "work," but to a formal extent only, as a linguistic principle. The "linguistic model" of this principle is that of discourse as a tropological system—a very familiar metaphorico-metonymical system of subsitution and exchange on the axes of selection and combination, paradigmatic and syntagmatic. In brief, this system would articulate "the infinity of number" with "the totality of extension"—which is the burden of "proving" the mathematical sublime—in terms of two acts of the imagination: apprehension and comprehension, *Auffassung* and *Zusammenfassung*. "Apprehension proceeds successively, as a syntagmatic, consecutive motion along an axis, and it can proceed ad infinitum without difficulty. Comprehension, however, which is a paradigmatic totalization of the apprehended trajectory, grows increasingly difficult as the space covered by apprehension grows larger" (*AI* 77). This amounts to a system of exchange and substitution: "As the paradigmatic simultaneity substitutes for the syntagmatic succession, an economy of loss and gain is put in place which functions with predictable efficacy" but, adds de Man, "only within certain well-defined limits" (*AI* 77). The limits are clear. Although the power of number can indeed progress to infinity on the level of apprehension—that is, logically, in terms of numerical concepts—the imagination which is to totalize this infinity in *one* comprehension soon reaches a point at which it is saturated and can no longer make additional apprehensions: "it cannot progress beyond a certain magnitude which marks the limit of the imagination." It is at this privileged point which "avoids both excessive comprehension and excessive apprehension" that the imagination makes its stand, as it were, and takes as a trope an impossible trope that is in fact not a metaphor but a catachresis, of a totalized, bordered-off infinity, as though it *could* comprehend it in *one* intuition. (Kant's example of Savary's account of one's experience of pyramids is well known.) What this means is that the mathematical sublime, as such a tropological system of substitution, is in fact *not* a judgment of the "absolutely large" but rather a somewhat subrepetitious displacement, transposition (Kant's German in fact says *versetzen* here), and substitution of the "almost too large" that is not yet "the too large"—in Kant's terms, of the "colossal" that is not yet the "monstrous"—*for* the "absolutely large."[8] It would be an impossible phenomenal trope of infinity, of that which is, by definition, not susceptible to being exhibited *(dargestellt)* in *one* sensory intuition. (In terms of de Man's reading of the zero in Pascal, this would be once again the substitution of *one* as a trope of the *zero,* in that case a substitution of number as trope for that which marks the limit of number, that is the beyond-number, the zero as pure sign.)[9] It is right for de Man to say that this certain magnitude "marks" the limit of the imagination, for what is going on here is indeed the phenomenalization of a mere *marker* of infinity (like, say, a zero) in a perceptible, imaginable, conceivable trope (like, say, a one). If the articulation of number and extension seems to take place, it does so as a tropological system of substitutions that are impossible except in terms of such a purely formal system. De Man summarizes:

> The desired articulation of the sublime takes place, with suitable reservations and restrictions, within such a purely formal system. It follows, however, that it is conceivable only within the limits of such a system, that is, as pure discourse rather than as a faculty of the mind. When the

sublime is translated back, so to speak, from language into cognition, from formal description into philosophical argument, it loses all inherent coherence and dissolves in the aporias of intellectual and sensory appearance. It is also established that, even within the confines of language, the sublime can occur only as a single and particular point of view, a privileged place that avoids both excessive comprehension and excessive apprehension, and that this place is only formally, and not transcendentally, determined. The sublime cannot be grounded as a philosophical (transcendental or metaphysical) principle, but only as a linguistic principle. Consequently, the section on the mathematical sublime cannot be closed off in a satisfactory manner and another chapter on the dynamics of the sublime is needed. (*AI* 78)

So: if the mathematical sublime is "possible" only within the confines of such a purely formal tropological system, it is no wonder that the epistemological and the eudaemonic proofs of the mathematical sublime—that de Man treats *before* his discussion of *Auffassung* and *Zusammenfassung* and Kant treats *after*—end up in the assertions of the possibility of the sublime by dint of its impossibility and failure: "The sublime cannot be defined as the failure of the sublime, for this failure deprives it of its identifying principle" (*AI* 75). The "section on the mathematical sublime cannot be closed off in a satisfactory manner" because its (linguistic) principle of discourse as a tropological system cannot itself be closed off. For what happens is this: in its purely positional transposition of number into extension, of inscribed markers into phenomenal tropes, of catachreses into impossible metaphors, the tropological system of the mathematical sublime introduces into itself an excess or a lack that cannot be mastered or controlled or accounted for by the resources—by the principles of substitution and combination—*of* that system and therefore prevents itself from ever being able to close itself off *as* a system. (This is an *excess*—of marking, of substitutions other than trope, purely differential relations and entities; and a *lack*—of the one metaphor that could complete the tropological system and allow it to close itself off.)[10] De Man's way of putting it is that "the transition from the mathematical to the dynamic sublime, a transition for which the justification is conspicuously lacking in the text, . . . marks [again, *marks*] the saturation of the tropological field as language frees itself of its constraints and discovers within itself a power no longer dependent on the restrictions of cognition" (*AI* 79). In other words, it is precisely the impossible tropes of the infinite—of that which is overdeterminately exterior to the tropological system of *Auffassung* and *Zusammenfassung*—that prohibit the tropological system of the mathematical sublime to close itself off, that is, prevent it from being able to account for its own principles of substitution and exchange *in terms of* principles internal to its (tropological) system; meaning that the one thing this tropological system cannot account for is its own production, the "principle" according to which it was put into place in the first place. Hence this system opens up radically, and empties out in the *force, violence,* and *power* of the dynamic sublime—which force, violence, and power in the end (as at the beginning) are only the repetition of the inaugural act that put the tropological system into place "in the first place." According to de Man, this is "the only way to account for . . . the extension of the linguistic model beyond its definition as a system of tropes": "From the pseudocognition of tropes, language has to expand to the activity of performance, something of which language has been known to be capable well before Austin reminded us of it" (*AI* 79). Hence the "linguistic model" of the dynamic sublime—where the mind overpowers the might of nature and discovers itself independent of nature—would be that of discourse as performative.

Although the passage, the transition—which is in fact a "break" and a "discontinuity" and hence *not* a transition at all—*from* mathematical *to* dynamic sublime, *from* cognition *to* act, *from* trope *to* performative, is called "irreversible" in de Man's sense (as he elaborates at the beginning of "Kant and Schiller"), there is no doubt that to the extent that this passage is something that happens, an event, and thus truly (and, as we know, materially) *historical,* it is indeed also a "repetition," as I have already put it, a repetition "in the Kierkegaardian sense," as de Man might put it, of the inaugural act that put the tropological system into place, again, "in the first place." This is most vividly legible right away at the outset of the discussion of number, of numerical concepts, as Kant writes that "the *power* of numbers progresses to infinity"—*die Macht* [the same word that abruptly begins section 28 on the dynamic sublime: "Macht *ist ein Vermögen, welches großen Hindernissen überlegen ist* (*Power* is an ability that is superior to great obstacles")] *der Zahlen geht ins Unendliche.*[11] If numbers have this power, then there was something of a "dynamic sublime" always already (and always not yet) there in the mathematical sublime and its attempt to border off and exhibit this unimaginable and nonphenomenal power in one intuition (which it cannot do except in impossible, catachrestic tropes that are more markers than metaphors). And, of course, that "power" of number to progress to infinity is its entirely mechanical, automatic ability to "designate" the infinite by writing it, inscribing it, in an arbitrary differential mark. In short, the mathematical sublime too has at its "origin" a power that is itself put into place by an inaugural act of material inscription—minimally, the (aesthetic reflective) judgment that determines the magnitude of the measure by, say, dividing up the extension of a ruler into inches by marking and inscribing them; but, again of course, that the three "linguistic models" of the sublime—tropological, performative, and, call it, inscriptional—are intricated together and in a sense already "there" at the outset becomes legible only if de Man's (and, indeed, Kant's own) "reading-motion" and its narration in what can only be called an allegory (of reading and unreadability, yes) are allowed to unfold in order. It is telling that the order of de Man's presentation is not exactly, not quite, the same as Kant's. Indeed, there is something like a "logic of the sublime"—or, better, a sublime *program, pro-gramma*— at work in de Man's own presentation as he first recounts the epistemological and the eudaemonic (failed) proofs of the sublime, identifies them as "subreptions" in which a metaphysical principle mistakes itself for a transcendental principle, and summarizes the difficulty by reference to the passage on "thinking" *(denken)* the impossibility of an exhibition of ideas in section 29 of the *Critique* (i.e., the section that contains the passage on material vision)—and all this *before* going back to the opening paragraphs of section 26 and the discussion of *Auffassung* and *Zusammenfassung*. No wonder that de Man's transition reads a little oddly; the first sentence of the paragraph begins: "*Still in the mathematical sublime,* in section 26, *next to* the epistemology and the eudaemony of the sublime, appears another description" (*AI* 77; emphasis added), which sounds like "Meanwhile, back in the mathematical sublime. . . ." This is odd because Kant's description of *Auffassung* and *Zusammenfassung* and the tropological system they constitute is not "next to" but rather *before* the epistemology and the eudaemony of the sublime. De Man's getting to it only after he has discussed them as well as *denken* and thus reordering Kant's presentation follows a certain "logic" of the sublime in that it provides a certain "privileged place" that itself allows an easier "comprehension" of his own reading-motion's difficult apprehensions and renders his reading of the mathematical sublime "intelligible in linguistic terms"; that is, de Man's passage on the tropological system itself serves as something like a "metaphor" of comprehension that makes what precedes and follows in his reading of Kant easier to understand. That the one figure of the double operation of *Auffassung* and *Zusammenfassung* de Man provides should be what he calls a "simple phenomenology of reading" is, as one says, no accident:

> The model reminds one of a simple phenomenology of reading, in which one has to make constant syntheses to comprehend the successive unfolding of the text: the eye moves horizontally in succession whereas the mind has to combine vertically the cumulative understanding of what has been apprehended. The comprehension will soon reach a point at which it is saturated and will no longer be able to take in additional apprehensions: it cannot progress beyond a certain magnitude which marks the limit of the imagination. (*AI* 77)

Once this "simple *phenomenology* of reading" is understood in linguistic terms as precisely a tropological system that cannot close itself off—that is, that can account for everything except its own principles of constitution and therefore *cannot read itself*—the *phenomenology* of reading turns into a veritable *allegory* of reading. And when this happens, the "eye" that cooperates with the "mind" so readily in the *phenomenology* of reading turns out to be completely dis-junct from any mind whatsoever and not unlike the eye of the savage or the poets who see only according to the pure optics of what the *Augenschein* shows or what only meets the eye.

I linger with the rhetorical structure of de Man's own essay only to indicate how deep the "deep, perhaps fatal, break or discontinuity" that de Man reads at the center of the third *Critique* runs. Its depending "on a linguistic structure (language as a performative as well as a cognitive system) that is not itself accessible to the powers of transcendental philosophy" (*AI* 79) is just one such "break." It recurs (in section 29) in the stark juxtaposition of the passage on material vision with a story of how the imagination sacrifices itself for the reason, and, indeed, has always already occurred (as recurrence) whenever articulation is threatened by its undoing. The break or discontinuity, the disruption or disarticulation, gets repeated, happens, *occurs*—and is legible, in the order of reading, as "a shift from a tropological to a different mode of language"—whether it be the disarticulation of Kant's sublime (as an aesthetic reflexive judgment), or of aesthetic judgment as such, or of the category of the aesthetic (as philosophical category), or of the articulating project of the third *Critique* to serve as a "bridge" between the supersensuous underlying nature and the supersensuous underlying freedom, or, ultimately, the disarticulation of the critical philosophy itself when it turns out that the transcendental discourse, and thus the critical subject itself, cannot ground itself transcendentally (which is the ultimate project of the mere "appendix" *(Anhang)* on the sublime, according to de Man).[12] In any event, all this is at stake in the sublime and in de Man's reading of the sublime as not a transcendental but rather a "linguistic" principle. And this means that what happens in this reading is not at all a "reduction" of Kant's analytic to "language" or "linguistic models." For these models turn out to be not models at all, as each one fails to account either for itself or for its other—as cognition (and its tropological system) can never account for the act (and least of all for the act that put its tropological system of substitutions and exchanges of meaning into place in the first place), and the power of the act can never be strong enough to verify (i.e., to *make true*) that it took place, happened, was in fact an event. The point is rather that the transcendental discourse needs to have recourse to (always defective) linguistic models precisely at the moment when it would claim to be able to ground itself transcendentally—and thereby complete and close off the critical philosophy—and that this self-grounding project therefore fails, and has to fail, like any and every attempt to define and determine "language" as a theoretical object of study. So: perhaps we are now in a better position to go back to what the poets do when they see only that which the *Augenschein* shows. Let's look again at what de Man calls "our question":

> Our question, then, becomes whether and where this disruption, this disarticulation, becomes apparent in the text, at a moment when the aporia of the sublime is no longer stated, as was the case in the mathematical sublime and in the ensuing general definitions of the concept, as an explicit paradox, but as the apparently tranquil, because entirely unreflected, juxtaposition of incompatibles. Such a moment occurs in the general remark or recapitulation (section 29) that concludes the analytics of the sublime. (*AI* 79)

At first glance, what de Man has in mind by "such a moment" seems relatively straightforward: namely, the curious and unexpected passage on "material vision" that occurs in section 29. The "purely formal" and thus "purely material" vision of heaven and ocean would indeed be the "apparently tranquil, because entirely unreflected, juxtaposition of incompatibles" insofar as it would be the tranquil vision "devoid of any reflexive or intellectual complication" in which "no mind" at all is involved. The judgment of the sublime here would be precisely nonreflective and nonaesthetic (or other than reflective and other than aesthetic). And it would be the juxtaposition of incompatibles at least in the sense that the architectonic vision of nature as a building—the heavens as a vault and the ocean as bounded by the horizon as by the walls of a building—that is not for dwelling and that does not shelter would be the mere juxtaposition (and utter disjunction) of nature and its purposiveness, as though the eye that sees only according to what the *Augenschein* shows were reading a figure or a trope (i.e., nature as a building) completely emptied out of its meaning. "No mind is involved in the Kantian vision of ocean and heaven," de Man writes. "To the extent that any mind, that any judgment, intervenes, it is in error—for it is not the case that heaven is a vault or that the horizon bounds the ocean like the walls of a building. That is how things are to the eye, in the redundancy of their appearance to the eye and not to the mind" (*AI* 82). But perhaps the "unreflected juxtaposition of incompatibles" refers most directly not so much to the *thematics* of the passage on material vision as to the juxtaposition of the passage itself with the allegorical tale of how the imagination sacrifices itself for reason—where we deal, says de Man, not "with mental categories but with tropes" (*AI* 87). The diction of de Man's summary would suggest that *this* is "such a moment" in section 29: "What makes this intrusion of linguistic tropes particularly remarkable is that it occurs in close proximity, almost in *juxtaposition* to the passage on the material architectonics of vision, in the poetic evocation of heaven and ocean, with which it is entirely *incompatible*" (*AI* 87; emphasis added). This would indeed be another version of the break or discontinuity, disruption or disarticulation, where there is "a shift from a tropological to a different mode of language." Still, perhaps one should not hurry quite so much to accept de Man's characterization of this vision as purely formal, purely material, devoid of intellectual complication and semantic depth, and utterly nontropological. After all, as a number of commentators have pointed out, Kant's evocations of the heavens as a vault that encompasses everything *(alles befaßt)* and borders off *(begrenzt)* the ocean, and the ocean as an abyss that threatens to swallow up everything (including, presumably, the sky) are clearly figures, tropes. Tropes, first of all, for the mathematical and dynamic sublimes, respectively, with the bordered-off infinitude of the starry sky an apt figure for the mathematical sublime and the over-

powering natural force of the turbulent ocean (that needs to be over-
powered in turn by the power of the mind) an appropriate figure of the
dynamic sublime. And the passage's proliferating tropology does not
stop there. As more than one commentator has also pointed out, the
sky as a bow- or arch-shaped "vault" (*Gewölbe,* from *wölben*) is a
kind of bridge, in this case a bridge over an abyss figured by the ocean,
and thus a strangely allegorical sign for the project of the critical philosophy and its dominant architectonic figures: the immense gulf between the domains of the concept of nature and the concept of freedom that is to be, that *must* be, bridged and articulated so that the
latter can have, as it should, an influence on the former, and that there
be a "ground of unity" *(Grund der Einheit)*—and not an abyss—for
the supersensible that underlies nature and the supersensible that
underlies freedom.[13]

However neat this tropology, it does leave out the ocean when it is
at rest and seen, according to what the *Augenschein* shows, as a clear
water-mirror *(als einen klaren Wasserspiegel).* Between the all-framing
starry sky and the all-engulfing abyss of ocean, there is the flat, placid,
sheer surface of a mirror without depth. "The sea is called a mirror,"
writes de Man, "not because it is supposed to reflect anything, but to
stress a flatness devoid of any suggestion of depth" (*AI* 83). This placid
flatness does not fit so easily into the tropologies that can account for
sky and sea as mathematical and dynamic sublimes or as the bridge of
the third *Critique* over the abyss between the first and second
*Critique*s. But it does indeed provide a nice figure for the mere juxtaposition of incompatibles—like the mathematical and the dynamic sublime or the understanding and reason, or first and second *Critique*'s,
and so on—the purely formal, purely material, vision of what the
*Augenschein* shows, or, even better, the phlegmatic, a-pathetic vision
of a calculating, counting Dutchman. In other words, legible here are
de Man's three linguistic "models" of Kant's sublime, with the vaulted
sky a figure of the mathematical sublime as tropological system (that
would border off infinity), the abyssal ocean a figure of the dynamic
sublime as performative force, and the clear water-mirror a figure of
the "material sublime" whose model would be that of language as material inscription. But, needless to say, this is all too figural, too tropological; there is all too much purposiveness and too much mind in such
a reading. Such a reading would not be how the poets do it. If we ask,
in the spirit of de Man's reading, what is the equivalence on the level of
language, in linguistic terms, of this placid, flat water-mirror as seen by

the apathetic Dutchman—"described as a phlegmatized kind of German interested only in the dreariest of commercial and moneymaking activities" (*AI* 85) in Kant's precritical (1764) "Observations on the Feeling of the Beautiful and the Sublime"[14]—we get some direction from de Man's own account of how "meaning-producing tropes are replaced by the fragmentation of sentences and propositions into discrete words, or the fragmentation of words into syllables or finally letters." Where to find, how to read, such a "dismemberment of language" in Kant's text? Another hint from de Man helps: "But just try to *translate* one single somewhat complex sentence of Kant, or just consider what the efforts of entirely competent translators have produced, and you will soon notice how decisively determining the play of the letter and the syllable . . . is in this most unconspicuous of stylists" (*AI* 89; emphasis added). And, indeed, if we go back one more time to the sentence on the poets and try to translate it, we find very quickly that it does not in fact say what we and all the translators I have—Bernard, Pluhar, Philonenko—want to see there. For the sentence does *not* say "we must be able to view the ocean as poets do . . . and yet find it sublime" (Pluhar), nor does it say, "To call the ocean sublime we must regard it as poets do" (Bernard), nor does it say, "il faut parvenir à voir l'océan seulement, comme le font les poètes, selon le spectacle qu'il donne à l'œil, soit, lorsqu'il est contemplé au repos tel un clair miroir d'eau qui n'est limité que par le ciel et, lorsqu'il est agité, soit comme un abîme menaçant de tout engloutir, qu'il nous est quand même possible de trouver sublime" (Philonenko).[15] Without exception, the translators want to link what we *must* do to *seeing*—we must see as the poets do—and invariably relegate our nevertheless being able to find the ocean sublime to secondary, subordinate status by supplying a linking or a transitional word: Pluhar an "and," Bernard a "to" (in the sense of "in order to"), and Philonenko the relative pronoun *que*. In doing so, the translations link what is in fact *not* bridged in the German—that is, *must* and *seeing* according to what the *Augenschein* shows—and conversely dis-join (by means of their supplementary linking words) what in fact *is* linked in the German: namely, *must* and *nevertheless be able to find sublime*. Stripped of the subordinate clauses and phrases, the sentence actually reads as follows: "rather, one must nevertheless be able to find sublime [that is, find the ocean sublime] only, as the poets do it, according to what meets the eye, for instance." In short, one, we, must not *see* (as the poets do it, etc. etc.) but rather *must be able to find sublime*. The link between what we *must* do—that is, be able to find sublime—and seeing only according to the *Augen-schein* may indeed be there, as it were "understood," in the sentence, but, if so, it is there only in subordinated, mediated form. Indeed, the sentence never even says that we must do what we must do as the poets *see* it but rather as the poets *do* it, that is, only according to what the *Augenschein* shows (and not what they or we see). The only actual, explicit *seeing* in the passage is in the sub-subordinate phrase "for example, when it [the ocean] is regarded at rest" *(etwa, wenn er in Ruhe betrachtet wird)!* The shift and, indeed, slippage from "must be able to find sublime" to "must see"—and its concomitant relegation of "be able to find sublime," grammatically the main verb of the sentence, to a mere adjunct, a mere appendix—may appear slight. After all, isn't this what the passage *means,* and aren't the translators just helping Kant out a bit? Not quite and not just. For in linking *seeing* to the *must,* the translators are making things far too easy for us and helping out Kant by turning him into something of a Schiller! That is, they introduce the figures of the poets, of the *Augenschein,* and of the ocean precisely *as* figures, as phenomenalizing tropes that can make the difficult task easier: that is, having, "must-ing," as it were, to nevertheless find sublime, *having to have* the "faculty," as it were, of judgments of the sublime. In doing so, the trans-lators, as is their job, carry over and throw up a bridge where there isn't one in the Kant. In the Kant, what we must do is to be able to find sublime despite, whatever, the *Augenschein* shows, and the bridge between our *must* and our *being able to find sublime* is indeed a purely formal, only prosthetic bridge. This would mean, or, better, only mark or inscribe, that what the poets do is not even so much to *see* according to the *Augenschein* as to read an inscription, dismembered sentences, words, syllables, letters—like the illegible letter (or all too interpretable hieroglyph?) of the arching line of the sky on top of the straight or squiggly line of the ocean. Indeed, it would perhaps not be too perverse to suspend Kant's sentence in the middle and identify the antecedent of "it" in "as the poets do it" as neither seeing nor being able to find sublime but rather "must": one must (only) as the poets must (nevertheless be able to find sublime) as one must as the poets must. (I've tried out the German: "Man muß bloß, wie die Dichter es tun, müssen"; "Man muß müssen"; "One, we, *must must.*") Which amounts to saying that what one must do to be able to find sublime is, above all, introduce, inter-ject, "the poets" between the moral imperative and the sublime judgment. The supplying of the poets, as in *Dichter* or *dictare*—the only word that comes to mind, as it were—would be the always necessary and always impossible grammatical, *gramma*-tical, bridge, the bottom line of the prosaic materiality of the letter.

## Postscriptum: On the Super-performative

> *The Triumph of Life* warns us that nothing, whether deed, word, thought, or text, ever happens in relation, positive or negative, to anything that precedes, follows, or exists elsewhere, but only as a random event whose power, like the power of death, is due to the randomness of its occurrence. It also warns us why and how these events then have to be reintegrated in a historical and aesthetic system of recuperation that repeats itself regardless of the exposure of its fallacy.[16]

As is legible in several places, Paul de Man's title for what turned out to be his last book was *Aesthetics, Rhetoric, Ideology*. How and why the book ultimately came to be called *Aesthetic Ideology* is a long and, at times, comical story. In the end, and as always, the matter was decided by a combination of contingency and necessity: the "random event" of de Man's death and the (quite legitimate) preferences of "marketing" at the University of Minnesota Press. The difference between the two titles, however, does invite a question: what difference would it make? Would the (re)insertion of the word *rhetoric* between *aesthetics* and *ideology* make any difference at all? Would it not be, at worst, trivial, and would it not, at best, merely reconfirm the suspicion or assumption that de Man's notions of ideology and of the political never get beyond the analysis of purely linguistic phenomena and their reduction to rhetorical structures?

Even beginning an answer to this question—and explaining the difference that rhetoric makes—is not a simple task, but it is always worth noting that de Man was certainly very aware of the question and in response always maintains that "one could approach the problems of ideology and by extension the problems of politics *only on the basis of critical-linguistic analysis*," which has to be done in its own terms, and that such analysis is "truer" to Marx's own procedures (for example and exemplarily, in *The German Ideology*) than what generally passes for "critique of ideology."[17] Rather than repeating or summarizing arguments made elsewhere,[18] let us instead focus on just one moment of de Man's project and his "critical-linguistic" readings—the moment when and the sense in which something, an event, an occurrence, something happens, something occurs and, *as* an event, is genuinely historical with a "materiality" all its own. As always in the case of de Man, it turns out that rhetoric, the rhetoric of tropes, tropological systems and their attempt and inability to close themselves off, is what makes all the difference.

After de Man's readings—after reading *tout court*—what always happens and is thus predictable and inevitable (like death's "random event" and its inevitable reintegration and recuperation?) is some version of the question "What now?" or "What next?"—"Now that we know the text is unreadable, its meaning indeterminate if not undecidable, what do we *do*? How do we take the next step, the step beyond merely linguistic analysis of merely linguistic phenomena, to what really matters, to political stands and political programs and political power, to what really matters out there, beyond the confines of text and language, to us?" This is, of course, the wrong question. And it is wrong not only because it presumes to know ahead of time what "language" and "linguistic" mean, as though the reference of *these* words were stable and knowable above and beyond all other words— as though, in short, the referent of "language" and "linguistic" could be phenomenalized, could appear, as an object of consciousness and its phenomeno-logic *without* the inevitable interference of the rhetorical dimension of "language," without its being turned into a trope. It is the wrong question above all because it is (always already) inscribed *within* the workings of reading and de Man's "critical-linguistic" analyses, for these are precisely analyses of how it is that something can, does, happen, how the "next step" actually occurs. But a word of precaution is necessary here: those who have read de Man (even a little) should not anticipate too much, for de Man's next step, what actually occurs in (and *as*) de Man is *not* the performative, it is not the performative speech act or the "performative rhetoric" that seems to be the issue of so many of de Man's readings (from *Allegories of Reading* on) and their reception and use in the work of others. It is true that a correct enough but ultimately untrue or at least not "true enough" account of the typical "de Manian" reading and what it does with the relation between knowledge and act, the cognitive and the performative dimensions of a text—that is, trope and performative—would run as follows: de Man's readings start out by *first* setting up, reconstructing, the text as trope, as a tropological system (of substitutions and transformations of meaning)—or, most directly put, by interpreting the text as to be understood on the basis of (and *as*) a tropological system that would be closed, in the sense that its intelligibility is *grounded* in some ultimately stable meaning, an ultimately stable hermeneutic horizon of meaning. (In such a setup, the rhetoric of tropes would be continuous with, homogeneous with, logic—the possibility of universal and hence extratextual [and hence extralinguistic] meaning.) All this means is: de Man begins by interpreting the meaning of the text, figuring out what the text means and how its figural language works to produce that meaning (once one takes even a small step beyond sheer literal-mindedness). De Man's readings, in this account, proceed by, second, demonstrating how it is that the text as tropological system, as system of tropes, in fact cannot close itself off and remains "open." The reason this happens, most directly and succinctly put, is that the tropo-logical system of the text (i.e., that *is* the text) cannot close itself off (in a final stable meaning) because that system cannot account *for its own production,* that is, cannot account for the inaugural act that put it into place in the first place in its own terms, that is, according to prin-ciples internal to itself as system. Hence, third, the text makes a sort of jump—it stutters, as it were—into another textual and linguistic model, that of the performative, of text as *act,* a model that diverges from the text as trope, as cognitive rhetoric, indeed, disrupts the cogni-tive dimension of the text. The upshot being that the text issues in the performative and that the text as performative disrupts the text as cog-nitive, as trope.

This account is correct enough, and many of de Man's readings—from the early 1970s to the early 1980s—would seem to authorize it. For instance, the end of the famous (or infamous) concluding essay of *Allegories of Reading*—"Excuses *(Confessions)"*—would certainly seem to fit: "the linguistic model cannot be reduced to a mere system of tropes," writes de Man, since its "(negative) cognitions fail to make the performative function of the discourse predictable" (*AR* 300)[19] and thus we find that "we are restating the disjunction of the performative from the cognitive" (*AR* 299–300). Or, for another example, one could adduce de Man's reading of the Kantian sublime in "Phenomenality and Materiality in Kant": in the end, it turns out that the mathematical sublime is grounded not as a transcendental (or even a metaphysical) principle but rather as a "linguistic principle" whose model is that of a familiar metaphorico-metonymical tropological system which, because it (is purely formal and) cannot close itself off, issues in the dynamic sublime whose linguistic model is that of language as performative. Nevertheless, even a cursory look at what actually happens in de Man's readings cannot help but notice that something else, something more difficult, is going on and that the account above is so partial and so selective as to constitute a *mis*reading of de Man. Indeed, it is a misreading that leads to all kinds of predictable aberrations, in particular a certain inflation and overvaluation of the performative—as though one could go to the text as *act* directly, immediately, and while bypassing the moment in the reading when the text's tropological system gets reconstructed, in short, while bypassing *the actual act of understanding the text,* in other words, the text itself! In the case of de Man's reading of the Kantian sublime, for instance, the correct enough focus on the disjunction between trope and performative as the "linguistic principle" underneath the mathematical and dynamic sublimes overlooks one rather prominent fact: namely, de Man's reading of the mathematical and dynamic sublimes takes up only and exactly one-half of his essay! After a typographical break, the entire second half of "Phenomenality and Materiality in Kant" is devoted to an attempt to identify whether and where the disruption or disarticulation at the center of the third *Critique*—between cognitive and performative and thus, by extension, between pure and practical reason ultimately— "becomes apparent in the text . . . as the apparently tranquil, because entirely unreflected, juxtaposition of incompatibles" (*AI* 79). And such a moment occurs, according to de Man, in the uncanny "material vision" of the sky and the ocean "as the poets do it," a vision utterly devoid of reflection, internality, or mind, a purely formal "vision" reducible to the formal mathematization or geometrization of pure optics. This means, in short, that the radical "formal materialism" of Kant's text and its strange "materiality"—a "materiality," Derrida writes, "without materialism and even perhaps without matter"—as an event, an occurrence, what happens, is very explicitly *not* to be identified with the performative or the performative dimension or "model" of the text. Rather, whatever it is that happens in, and *as,* "Kant" happens at the point of the "transition" or the "intersection" of the disarticulation of two divergent systems, two divergent models, cognitive and performative.

The same is true of "Excuses *(Confessions)*" and its complicated reading of Rousseau. The fact that Rousseau's *Confessions* is not primarily a confessional text (i.e., the overcoming of guilt and shame in the name of truth and thus "an epistemological use of language" [*AR* 279]), but also and rather a text of excuse (and thus "a complex instance of what [Austin] termed performative utterances" [281–82]), does *not* disrupt the text's intelligibility because both knowledge and action, cognitive and performative, are incorporated in "a general economy of human affectivity, in a theory of desire, repression, and self-analyzing discourse in which excuse and knowledge converge" (*AR* 287). Or, as de Man underlines, "Knowledge, morality, possession, exposure, affectivity (shame as the synthesis of pleasure and pain), *and the performative excuse* are all ultimately part of one system that is epistemologically as well as ethically grounded and therefore available as meaning, in the mode of understanding" (*AR* 287; emphasis added). In short, rather than interfering with or disrupting the figural logic of the text, the "performative excuse" confirms it and is in fact part of it. But what does disrupt this system because it is outside of, foreign and heterogeneous to, the system of intelligibility and understanding is the radicalization of the excuse that takes place in Rousseau's utterly random, contingent, utterance of the name "Marion"—an anacoluthon that "stands entirely out of the system of truth, virtue, and understanding (or of deceit, evil, and error) that gives meaning to the passage" (*AR* 289). It's this "foreign element," continues de Man, "that disrupts the meaning, the readability of the apologetic discourse, and reopens what the excuse seemed to have closed off" (*AR* 289–90). If this truly disruptive random utterance of the name "Marion" is still to be taken as an "excuse," then it would have to be an "excuse" in a way radically different from "the performative excuse" that was, according to de Man, still within the system of causes and effects, desires and repressions, hiding and revealing, and so on. And, in any case, it would *not* be its "performativity" that makes it foreign, radically exterior to and disruptive of the system of understanding. Or, if one still wants to speak of "performative" at all in relation to the random utterance "Marion," then one would have to think of it as something of a "super-performative"—that is, not one that functions *within* an established juridico-political system (within which it can come off or not), but rather one that itself is the inaugural act of positing that puts such a system into place in the first place. In any case, what disrupts the figural chain and the text as system of tropes is not the performative dimension, not language as act, but rather the (impossible and yet necessary) moment of radical excuse, radical "fiction" (as de Man will call it after reading the *Fourth Rêverie*), at which two "systems" heterogeneous to one another—like meaning and grammar—"intersect." It's at the point of the intersection that the text as system of intelligibility and understanding gets disrupted. But, once this "textual event" happens, occurs, it inevitably gets disseminated throughout the text, all along the narrative line, and turns into a permanent parabasis that de Man, following Friedrich Schlegel, calls *irony*—"the systematic undoing, in other words, of understanding" (*AR* 301). In other words, a certain radicalization of the disjunction or divergence between cognitive and performative, trope and performative, takes place in the course of de Man's reading—which suggests that already in the case of "the performative excuse" that would be continuous with and part of the system of intelligibility, there was (always already) a trace of the radicalized "performative," the pure positing power of language whose position—as in the case of the random utterance "Marion"— as an "excuse" is radically disjunct from, has nothing to do with, the "excuse" as linked to the affective feeling of shame and the understanding it makes possible.

That what happens is *not* the performative is very explicitly and directly corroborated by de Man's remarks at the beginning of his spoken lecture "Kant and Schiller." Using his Kant reading to articulate what he means by history as event, as occurrence, as what happens, de Man says that the model for such "historicity a priori" is

> not the performative in itself . . . but the transition, the passage from a conception of language as a system, perhaps a closed system, of tropes, that totalizes itself as a series of transformations which can be reduced to tropological systems, and then the fact that you *pass* from that conception of language to *another* conception of language in which language is no longer cognitive but in which language is performative. (*AI* 132)

And this is important enough for him to repeat it and insist on it: "and I insist on the necessity of this, so the model is not the performative, the model is the passage from trope to performative—this passage occurs always, and can only occur, by ways of an epistemological critique of trope" (*AI* 133). In other words, there is no passage, no occurrence, no event, no *history*—nothing happens—*except as* (or "by ways of") an epistemological critique of trope. What happens—if it happens—does so thanks to the (self-)critical power of the text as tropological system that would want to account for its own production (the only thing worth knowing, as de Man says at the end of "Excuses")[20] in terms internal to its system. Because the text *cannot* do this, cannot account for its own production, for the inaugural instituting act that put it into place, what happens instead is the "passage" to the performative, to language not as cognition but as act. In this emergence of a language of power out of a language of cognition, what emerges is in fact the very "origin" of the text, the material trace or the material inscription that would be the condition of possibility and the condition of impossibility of the text "itself." In Kant's "Analytic of the Sublime" the attempt to ground the critical discourse, to found the very subject of the critical philosophy and transcendental method, instead un-grounds, un-founds, itself in the disarticulation of tropological and performative linguistic models by, ultimately, the "last" linguistic "model": the prosaic materiality of the letter, material inscription. In Rousseau's autobiographical project, the attempt to ground the confessional/apologetic discourse, to found the confessional subject, instead disarticulates itself and founders on the random utterance "Marion"—which, of course, is the material trace at the very "origin" of Rousseau's autobiography, the reason, as he says explicitly, for his writing the *Confessions* in the first place (i.e., to confess the shameful act).[21] Among other things, such an account helps to put the performative into better perspective. For what happens when the text "passes" from trope to performative—which is not a temporal progression but an event, an occurrence (as in "comes to *pass*")—is a certain "repetition" of the violent, groundless and ungrounded, inaugural act that, again, put it into place in the first place. The event of this repetition is what gets disseminated all along the narrative line and thus renders the text an allegory of its inability to account for its own production (an allegory of unreadability, to coin a phrase)—with Rousseau's autobiographer doomed to mindlessly, mechanically, repeating "Marion" over and over again, and Kant's critical philosopher "I *must* be able to bridge pure reason and practical reason," "I *must* exhibit the ideas of reason," "I *must* be able to find sublime," "I *must must*," "Ich *muß müssen, muß müssen, muß müssen . . .*"[22]

So: that's the difference the reinsertion of *rhetoric* between *aesthetics* and *ideology* makes. Without *rhetoric*, without the epistemological critique of trope, as de Man puts it, nothing happens. There is no direct, immediate, royal road to the performative, to action and the act, political or otherwise. Pretending that one can go to it directly is sheer delusion and a guarantee that nothing can happen, nothing will ever happen.[23]

**NOTES**

1. It may be helpful to provide the passage from section 29 of Kant's third *Critique* that de Man reads in the second half of his "Phenomenality and Materiality in Kant." In Werner Pluhar's uncorrected (a point that is dicussed toward the end

of my essay) translation, it reads: "Therefore, when we call the sight of the starry sky *sublime*, we must not base our judgment upon any concepts of worlds that are inhabited by rational beings, and then [conceive of] the bright dots that we see occupying the space above us as being these worlds' suns, moved in orbits prescribed for them with great purposiveness; but we must base our judgment regarding it merely on how we see it, as a vast vault encompassing everything, and merely under this presentation may we posit the sublimity that a pure aesthetic judgment attributes to this object. In the same way, when we judge the sight of the ocean we must not do so on the basis of how we *think* it, enriched with all sorts of knowledge which we possess (but which is not contained in the direct intuition), e.g., as a vast realm of aquatic creatures, or as the great reservoir supplying the water for the vapors that impregnate the air with clouds for the benefit of the land, or again as an element that, while separating continents from one another, yet makes possible the greatest communication among them; for all such judgments will be teleological. Instead we must be able to view the ocean as poets do, merely in terms of what manifests itself to the eye—e.g., if we observe it while it is calm, as a clear mirror of water bounded only by the sky; or, if it is turbulent, as being like an abyss threatening to engulf everything—and yet find it sublime" (Immanuel Kant, *Critique of Judgment,* trans. Werner S. Pluhar [Indianapolis/Cambridge: Hackett Publishing Company, 1987], 130).

2. All references to Paul de Man, *Aesthetic Ideology,* ed. Andrzej Warminski (Minneapolis: University of Minnesota Press, 1996), will be indicated by *AI* followed by the page number. All references to de Man's "Anthropomorphism and Trope in the Lyric," in *The Rhetoric of Romanticism* (New York: Columbia University Press, 1984), will be indicated by *RR* followed by the page number.

3. See de Man's brief but packed reading of Saussure's ana-(and para- and hypo-)grams in "Hypogram and Inscription," in *The Resistance to Theory* (Minneapolis: University of Minnesota Press, 1986), 36–38.

4. De Man quotes Kant on the "savage" in the preceding sentence: "In a lesser-known passage from the *Logic* Kant speaks of 'a wild man who, from a distance, sees a house of which he does not know the use. He certainly observes the same object as does another, who knows it to be definitely built and arranged to serve as a dwelling for human beings. Yet in formal terms this knowledge of the selfsame object differs in both cases. For the first it is mere intuition *[bloße Anschauung],* for the other both intuition and concept'" (*AI* 81).

5. This is no doubt an overdetermined misquotation. See de Man's many texts on (faces in) Wordsworth now in *The Rhetoric of Romanticism* and *Romanticism and Contemporary Criticism,* ed. E. S. Burt, Kevin Newmark, and Andrzej Warminski (Baltimore: Johns Hopkins University Press, 1993). See also my "Facing Language: Wordsworth's First Poetic Spirits," *Diacritics* 17:4 (winter 1987): 18–31; reprinted in *Romantic Revolutions,* ed. Kenneth R. Johnston, Gilbert Chaitin, Karen Hanson, and Herbert Marks (Bloomington: Indiana University Press, 1990), 26–49.

6. It is worth remembering that the "blank" between stanzas 1 and 2 of the Lucy poem and between parts 1 and 2 of "The Boy of Winander" marks the transition from living Lucy and living Boy to dead Lucy and dead Boy. For de Man on "A Slumber Did My Spirit Heal," see his "The Rhetoric of Temporality," now in the

second edition of *Blindness and Insight* (Minneapolis: University of Minnesota Press, 1983), 223–25. De Man's most extensive reading of "The Boy of Winander" is in his "Time and History in Wordsworth," in *Romanticism and Contemporary Criticism,* but see also the discussions in "Heaven and Earth in Wordsworth and Hölderlin" in the same volume and "Wordsworth and Hölderlin" in *The Rhetoric of Romanticism.*

7. For de Man on "Schillerizing" and "re-Kantizing," see "Kant and Schiller" in *Aesthetic Ideology.*

8. Although the reading of Kant's mathematical sublime in terms of such a subreptitious substitution—calling "sublime" what is in fact only "colossal"—is Derrida's (in "Le colossal," in *La Vérité en peinture* [Paris: Flammarion, 1978], 136–68), de Man's own reading is very close to Derrida's here. That de Man had read Derrida's "Le colossal" is clear in the earlier "Kant's Materialism," also in *Aesthetic Ideology.*

9. On de Man's reading of Pascal's zero, see my Introduction, "Allegories of Reference," in *Aesthetic Ideology,* 1–33.

10. The locus classicus for understanding such "economies of the supplement" is, of course, Jacques Derrida, "La mythologie blanche," in *Marges* (Paris: Minuit, 1972). See also my reading of Derrida and catachresis as the "syntax of tropes" in "Prefatory Postscript: Interpretation and Reading," in *Readings in Interpretation: Hölderlin, Hegel, Heidegger* (Minneapolis: University of Minnesota Press, 1987), liv–lxi.

11. Immanuel Kant, *Kritik der Urteilskraft* (Frankfurt am Main: Suhrkamp, 1974), 184.

12. And not just according to de Man. There are remarkable similarities between de Man's understanding of the stakes of Kant's "Analytic of the Sublime" and Jean-François Lyotard's. Indeed, however different their terms, de Man's and Lyotard's readings coincide in many respects. See Jean-François Lyotard, *Lessons on the Analytic of the Sublime,* trans. Elizabeth Rottenberg (Stanford, Calif.: Stanford University Press, 1994).

13. Although he does not explicitly read the vaulted sky as a figure for the bridge between the supersensuous underlying nature and the supersensuous underlying freedom, Derrida does link the ocean in this passage to the abyss between them. See *La Vérité en peinture,* 148.

14. But whose phlegmaticity is then judged sublime in the *Critique of Judgment*! For more on de Man and the Dutchman, see "Kant's Materialism" in *Aesthetic Ideology,* 124–25. It is worth noting that de Man's joke in "Kant's Materialism" about Kant's characterization of the Dutch in the precritical text—"I have never felt more grateful for the hundred or so kilometers that separate Antwerp from Rotterdam" (*AI* 125)—undergoes a slight arithmetical transposition in the later "Phenomenality and Materiality in Kant": "I have never felt more grateful for the *fifty or so* kilometers that separate the Flemish city of Antwerp from the Dutch city of Rotterdam" (*AI* 85; emphasis added). The Dutch—those "phlegmatized Germans"—seem to have been moved closer to Antwerp by the time of the later essay!

15. J. H. Bernard's and Alexis Philonenko's translations are: *Critique of Judgment* (New York: Hafner Press, 1951), 110–11; *Critique de la faculté de juger* (Paris: Vrin, 1984), 107.

16. Paul de Man, "Shelley Disfigured," in *RR* 122.

17. See Stefano Rosso's interview with de Man in Paul de Man, *The Resistance to Theory*, 121.

18. See my "Introduction: Allegories of Reference" to *Aesthetic Ideology*; "Ending Up/Taking Back (With Two Postscripts on Paul de Man's Historical Materialism," in *Critical Encounters*, ed. Cathy Caruth and Deborah Esch (New Brunswick, N.J.: Rutgers University Press, 1995), 11–41; and "'As the Poets Do It': On the Material Sublime" in this volume.

19. *AR* with a page number refers to *Allegories of Reading* (New Haven: Yale University Press, 1979).

20. See "Excuses": "we are restating the disjunction of the performative from the cognitive: any speech act produces an excess of cognition, but it can never hope to know the process of its own production (the only thing worth knowing)" (*AR* 299–300). It's worth noting that de Man here is *restating* the disjunction between performative and cognitive, which would support my contention that a *radicalization* of the performative takes place in the course of his reading.

21. Cf. "Excuses": "Rousseau singled out the episode of Marion and the ribbon as of particular affective significance, a truly primal scene of lie and deception strategically placed in the narrative and told with special *panache*. We are invited to believe that the episode was never revealed to anyone prior to the privileged reader of the *Confessions* 'and . . . that the desire to free myself, so to speak, from this weight has greatly contributed to my resolve to write my confessions.' When Rousseau returns to the *Confessions* in the later *Fourth Rêverie*, he again singles out this same episode as a paradigmatic event, the core of his autobiographical narrative" (*AR* 278–79).

22. See the end of my "'As the Poets Do It': On the Material Sublime" in this volume.

23. In working on Georg Lukács's *History and Class Consciousness*, I was pleased to find that in Lukács too, what he calls "the next step," the step to action, to revolution if one likes, the step that is taken by the class consciousness of the proletariat, turns out in fact to be the passage to the step—indeed, the step to the step. The action of the proletariat is the step to action. The step is the step to the step. That this "next step" emerges out of the system of bourgeois thought—that is, classical German philosophy from Kant to Hegel—that is, out of the inability of the (tropological) system to close itself off, is an indication that the class consciousness of the proletariat and the action that is the step to action, for Lukács as for de Man, emerges out of an epistemological critique of trope—or, if you like, a rhetorical "deconstruction" of the tropological system that is bourgeois thought. See my forthcoming "Next Steps: Lukács, Jameson, Post-dialectics." (That de Man's late work on the philosophical category of the aesthetic is at least somewhat informed by his 1960s reading of Lukács's early reflections on aesthetics is legible in his "Ludwig Binswanger and the Sublimation of the Self," in *Blindness and Insight*, especially 41–44.)

# Art and Ideology: Althusser and de Man

Michael Sprinker

My title refers to a conceptual problematic with a long and complex heritage in Western philosophy. Given its classic formulation in the eighteenth century (most notably in Schiller's *Aesthetic Letters*), it has continued to trouble the theory and practice of art to the present day. For Marxism, it poses special difficulties, not least because of Marx's own tantalizingly brief comments on Greek art in the Introduction to the *Grundrisse,* where the problem of the relationship between the ideological and aesthetic dimensions is posed with great clarity, but left unresolved.

A somewhat less enigmatic account of the art/ideology relation appears in Althusser's "Letter on Art in Reply to André Daspre." The passage in question has provoked a good deal of skeptical commentary (e.g., from Terry Eagleton), but Althusser's formulation remains the necessary point of departure for any serious theory of art understood as a social practice with specific features distinguishing it from other social practices:

> I believe that the peculiarity of art is "to make us see" *(nous donner à voir),* "make us perceive," "make us feel" something which "alludes" to reality. . . . What art makes us *see,* and therefore gives to us in the form of *"seeing," "perceiving"* and *"feeling"* . . . is the ideology from which it is born, in which it bathes, from which it detaches itself as art, and to which it *alludes. . . .* Balzac and Solzhenitsyn give us a "view" of the ideology to which their work alludes and with which it is constantly fed, a view which presupposes a *retreat,* an *internal distanciation* from the very ideology from which their novels emerged. They make us "per-

ceive" . . . in some sense *from the inside,* by an *internal distance,* the very ideology in which they are held.[1]

The burden of the passage (slightly, but not innocently truncated here) is to establish the special modality of art that distinguishes it from ideology. We need not tarry over the rather clumsy term *allusion (faire allusion),* which is meant to conjure up conventional (i.e., non-Althusserian) theories of ideology as pure *il*lusion, focusing instead on the more frequently deployed Althusserian concept of "internal distanciation" *(une prise de distance intérieure).* The passage, then, can be construed as a schematic effort to establish the necessary concept for a properly materialist theory of art, what may be called its particular modality, as distinct from the different modality of ideology (which, it will be recalled from the essay on Ideological State Apparatuses (ISAs), also has a material existence).

In his later writings, Paul de Man came to focus on this same conceptual problematic, projecting a full-scale engagement with Marxism via a reading of *The German Ideology* (a work he did not live to complete). It would of course be perilous to predict the exact form de Man's reading would have assumed, particularly in the light of his own confession that "[w]hat will come out of it, I just do not know."[2] Nonetheless, I shall risk certain conjectures in the direction of de Man's unfinished engagement with Marxism, but in the appropriately critical spirit that de Man himself always exemplified. The long-awaited publication of *Aesthetic Ideology* gives some grounds for speculating, however tentatively, about the shape that engagement would probably have assumed. The points of entry, in any event, seem clear enough.

## TROPOLOGICAL COERCION

In a decisive passage on the nature of tropes in the essay "Pascal's Allegory of Persuasion," de Man quotes Pascal on the relation between signs and things:

> It is not the nature of these [indefinable] things which I declare to be known by all, but simply *the relationship between the name and the thing,* so that on hearing the expression *time,* all turn (or direct) the mind toward the same entity *[tous portent la pensée vers le même objet].*

De Man then comments:

> Here the word does not function as a sign or a name, as was the case in the nominal definition, but as a vector, a directional motion that is

manifest only as a turn, since the target toward which it turns remains unknown. In other words, the sign has become a trope, a substitutive relationship that has to posit a meaning whose existence cannot be verified, but that confers upon the sign an unavoidable signifying function.[3]

It is the coercive but nonrational power of this operation that is significant. Tropes are perforce meaningful, but their meanings can never be equated with that which is true, in the sense of being rationally demonstrable or justifiable; they "posit a meaning whose existence cannot be verified." And yet the tropological imperative is "unavoidable," the turn toward the same mental entity (in the Pascal passage "time") something that "all" *(tous)* are bound to perform. It would not be stretching a point to say that the account of the operation of tropes here contains *in nuce* the de Manian conception of ideology, which is a property of language, or more precisely, of the figural or tropological aspects of language that, pace Locke and a certain tendency in the Enlightenment, cannot be eliminated or controlled in any linguistic science, least of all in contemporary semiotics.[4] De Man's stipulative definition of ideology as "the confusion of linguistic with natural reality, of reference with phenomenalism"[5] restates what in many places he identifies as the seductively mystifying power of tropes, as in the classic instance of catachresis: referring to the legs of a table implicitly confers sentience on an inanimate object by attributing to it features of an animate being. Or, to adopt a slightly different terminology, ideology can be defined as that which "represents the imaginary relationship of individuals to their real conditions of existence."[6]

Tropes or figures enforce an "imaginary relationship" to things; they, as it were, "interpellate individuals [e.g., the table] as subjects *[interpelle les individus en sujets]*" (LP 170; SR 302).[7] And lest it be thought that I myself am engaged in an illicit transposition from one discursive regime to another, that the comparison between de Man on tropes and Althusser on ideology is an abuse of language, another tropological illusion,[8] consider the following passage glossing the thesis on interpellation just quoted:

> As St. Paul admirably put it, it is in the "Logos," meaning in ideology, that we "live, move and have our being." It follows that, for you and for me, the category of the subject is a primary "obviousness" *[évidence]* . . . : it is clear that you and I are subjects (free, ethical, etc. . . .). Like all obviousnesses, including those that make a word "name a

thing" *[désigne une chose]* or "have a meaning" *[possède une significa-tion]* (therefore including the obviousnesses of the "transparency" of language), this "obviousness" that you and I are subjects . . . is an ideological effect, the elementary ideological effect. It is in effect in the very nature of ideology that it imposes (without appearing to do so, since these are "obviousnesses") obviousnesses as obviousnesses, which we cannot *fail to recognize* and before which we have the inevitable and natural reaction of crying out to ourselves (aloud or in the "silence of conscience"): "That's obvious! That's right! That's true!" (*LP* 171–72; *SR* 303–4; translation modified)

In the Pascal passage cited by de Man, moreover, the tropological power of language specifically constitutes (or interpellates) individuals as subjects—a universal subject in fact: "tous [all or everyone] portent la pensée vers le même objet." All hold the same object in thought (time); all respond to the call of this object and recognize it as the same thing, though this recognition be illusory, the necessary consequence of *"the relationship between the name and the thing,"* rather than a true understanding of the nature of the thing itself.

## THE PERFORMATIVE POWER OF IDEOLOGY

As it happens, Pascal also surfaces, somewhat unexpectedly, in the ISAs. Althusser's recourse to the Pascalian account of religious faith discloses yet another point of contact with de Man's conception of ideology. Referring to what he terms "Pascal's defensive 'dialectic,'" Althusser asserts the priority of actions (or, more technically, *practices*) over ideas in the functioning of ideology. He writes: "Pascal says more or less: 'Kneel down, move your lips in prayer, and you will believe'" (*LP* 168; *SR* 301). If ideology is produced by the irresistible tropological potential of language, which carries or directs thought *(porte la pensée)* toward its object, it can be said to exercise a coercive power that moves individuals to act, even against what we conventionally term their will. The existence and the effectivity of ideology are anterior to and cannot be resisted by the individuals it hails as subjects. Of the individual so determined, Althusser asserts:

> *his ideas are his material actions inserted into material practices governed [réglées] by material rituals which are themselves defined by the material ideological apparatus from which derive [relèvent] the ideas of that subject.* (*LP* 169; *SR* 301; emphasis in the original)

Ideology is a performative; as such, it is not regulated according to a regime of truth and falsehood, but by its sheer power to move.

De Man exemplifies this ultimate performative power of ideology in his analysis of Pascal's famous Pensée on justice and power, which concludes on an uncompromisingly Machiavellian note:

> Justice is subject to dispute. Power [la force] is easily recognizable and without dispute. Thus it has been impossible to give power to justice, because power has contradicted justice and said that it is unjust, and said that it is itself just.
>
> And thus, not being able to make the just strong, one has made the strong to be just. (AI 67)

Justice functions here in classical ideological fashion: it instances an imaginary relation to real conditions of existence. But it works, that is to say, it successfully appeals to and governs the actions of individuals, to the extent that it already possesses power. Justice is neither a concept nor an idea; it is a set of practices, as in the decisions of courts and the procedures that lawyers and judges are bound to observe—a seemingly paradoxical notion. The ideology of justice is an effect of the force of law. It is, to quote de Man once more, a "modal statement" that "perform[s] what [it] enunciate[s] regardless of considerations of truth and falsehood" (AI 68).

### AESTHETIC ILLUSION

So much for ideology; what about art? In what sense can we say that art is material for de Man, and to what extent is de Man's materialism comparable (or not) to that of Althusser and the Marxist tradition more generally?

It will hardly come as a surprise to those familiar with de Man's corpus if I say at the outset that the term *aesthetic* is a complex one in the lexicon of de Man's later essays. It can refer, as the title of the posthumous collection *Aesthetic Ideology* indicates, to the protective, sheltering function of art, which allows us to experience as fiction what would threaten us in reality. De Man comments on this usage in his exegesis of Schiller's essay "Of the Sublime" ("Vom Erhabenen"): "one plays at danger as in a fiction or as in a play, but one is sheltered by the figurative status of the danger. It is the fact that the danger is made into a figure that shelters you from the immediacy of the danger" (AI 144). Nor is this aspect of the aesthetic alien to the Marxist theory of art. Marcuse's now generally neglected essay, "The Affirmative

Character of Culture," elaborates the compensatory function of aesthetic pleasure with great lucidity. Even Lukács acknowledges this positive valorization of the noncritical aspects of art in his exegeses of Goethe and Schiller's aesthetic theory. But it may come as something of a surprise that Althusser, the notorious exponent of the ubiquity of ideology and the theoretician of antihumanism, would hold much the same view.

## CATHARSIS AND CRITICISM

In a little-known text of 1968, "Sur Brecht et Marx," Althusser comments on the nature of aesthetic play, virtually repeating what de Man terms the protective or "sheltering" function of the aesthetic in the passage cited in the preceding section. Althusser insists on the essential role in theatrical presentation of what Schiller termed *Schein,* that is, illusion, or better, aesthetic illusion. But Althusser gives this commonplace of aesthetic theory a slight twist that both acknowledges the comforting notion of aesthetic illusion and disrupts it at the same time, turning aesthetic illusion back upon itself in such a way as to provoke a rather different response from the audience than sheer comfort. Here is the passage, quoted in extenso, including the very un-Schillerian sentences that bring Althusser's essay to a close:

> The theater is a catharsis, said Aristotle and Freud: art is a fictive triumph. Translation: a fictive triumph is a fictive risk. In the theater the spectator is given the pleasure of seeing fire played with, in order to be quite sure that there is no fire, or that the fire is not with him, but with others, in any event in order to be quite sure that the fire is not with him.
>
> If we wish to know why the theater diverts, it is necessary to account for this type of very special pleasure: that of playing with fire absent any danger stipulated by this twofold clause: (1) it is a safe fire because it is on the stage, and because the play always extinguishes the fire, and (2) when there is fire, it is always at one's neighbor's. . . . [But] these neighbors, among whom there is the fire on the stage, are also, as luck would have it, in the theater hall. The humble, who behold the great in the hall respectfully, laugh at the great when the fire on stage affects them [the great], or else they [the humble] find that on the stage which is equally great with which to overcome the crises of their life and their conscience. (*EPP* 556; my translation)

Aesthetic presentation does more than provide a sheltering illusion (the catharsis attributed to Aristotle's and Freud's conceptions of art); it provokes action, presumably revolutionary action by the proletariat to overthrow the bourgeoisie. The aesthetic can serve a critical function as well, exploding the ideological illusion that shields the audience from real danger by promoting a consciousness of the play's fictionality.[9] As at the end of Ken Loach's masterful portrayal of working-class oppression and resistance in the film *Riff-Raff*, the fire that consumes the building site on which the day laborers have been working and that has been started by two of them to avenge the sacking of another worker on the job—that fire is, for some who view the film, the one they themselves might ignite one day to bring down the structure of privilege and exploitation to which they currently submit. This critical function of the aesthetic, which Althusser (following Brecht) emphasizes, is not so far from what de Man proposes is to be found in Kant and Hegel's philosophical reflections on art.

Art as critical reflection on ideology—this late de Manian motif is entirely in the spirit of the passage from Althusser's "Letter on Art" with which this essay began. Explicitly, art's critical reflection is said to produce knowledge, different in kind from scientific knowledge, but knowledge nonetheless. Brecht believed this as well, repeating again and again throughout his career that the purpose of his plays was to induce revolutionary consciousness in the proletariat, with the *Lehrstücke* plainly, but also with less programmatically "didactic" works such as *Mahagonny* and *The Threepenny Opera*.[10] The famous line from the latter, "Erst kommt das Fressen, dann kommt die Moral," imparts a positive spin to Kant's suspicion of the necessarily seductive nature of aesthetic experience in promoting morality. As de Man puts the matter:

> Morality and the aesthetic are both disinterested, but this disinterestedness becomes necessarily polluted in aesthetic representation: the persuasion that, by means of their very disinterestedness, moral and aesthetic judgments are capable of achieving is necessarily linked, in the case of the aesthetic, with positively valorized sensory experiences [Brecht's *Fressen*]. The moral lesson of the aesthetic has to be conveyed by seductive means. (*AI* 84)

But this mistrust of the aesthetic—due in part, one imagines, to that Pietist heritage which made him notoriously among the most ascetic of men (one wonders if Kant ever took pleasure in anything)—is not the last word in Kant.[11]

## SEEING AS THE POETS DO IT

Alongside, and in contradiction to, Kant's critical evaluation of aesthetic pleasure stands his injunction that, in order to experience the true sublimity of the ocean, "we must regard it as poets do [*wie die Dichter es tun*], merely by what the eye reveals [*was der Augenschein zeigt*],—if it is at rest, as a clear mirror of water only bounded by the heavens; if it is stormy, as an abyss threatening to overwhelm everything" (quoted from *AI* 80). De Man terms this seeing "as poets do" "pure aesthetic vision" (*AI* 82), and glosses the concept as follows:

> In this mode of seeing, the eye is its own agent and not the specular echo of the sun. The sea is called a mirror, not because it is supposed to reflect anything, but to stress a flatness devoid of any suggestion of depth. In the same way and to the same extent that this vision is purely material, devoid of any reflexive or intellectual complication, it is also purely formal, devoid of any semantic depth and reducible to the formal mathematization or geometrization of pure optics. The critique of the aesthetic ends up, in Kant, in a formal materialism that runs counter to all values and characteristics associated with aesthetic experience, including the aesthetic experience of the beautiful and of the sublime as described by Kant and Hegel themselves. (*AI* 83)

The materiality of art, seeing "as poets do," is, if you will, anti-aesthetic. Its pure formality evacuates from the work of art any phenomenal content. Kant's understanding of materialism in this passage is, by his own criterion (see the Introduction to the first *Critique*), empty, since it consists of concepts without percepts or intuitions *(Anschauungen)*.[12]

On first inspection, this formal materialism of the aesthetic would seem to have little if anything to do with Althusser's repeated emphasis on aesthetic illusion, or with the "sensory manifestation of the idea" *(das sinnliche Scheinen der Idee)* of Hegel's canonical definition. Art simply cannot do without some degree of phenomenalization, be it only the sparse lines and colors in a Mondrian painting, or the stuttering dialogue in a late Beckett play or story, or the dissonant sounds of atonal music.[13] And so one might speculate that Kant's materialism, as expounded by de Man, is not merely anti-aesthetic, but properly anaesthetic, that is to say, it is nonart.[14]

Althusser himself will hypothesize something similar in his celebration of the late works of the Italian painter Leonardo Cremonini. Here, expounded at some length, is the crux of Althusser's position:

In order to "see" Cremonini, and above all to talk about what he makes visible, we have to abandon the categories of the aesthetics of consumption: the gaze we need is different from that of desire for or disgust with "objects" [Brecht's *Fressen*]. Indeed, his whole strength as a figurative painter lies in the fact that he does not just "paint" "objects" . . . , nor "places" . . . , nor "times" or "moments" . . . Cremonini "paints" the *relations* which bind the objects, places, and times. Cremonini is a *painter of abstraction*. Not an abstract painter, "painting" an absent, pure possibility in a new form and matter, but a painter of the *abstract*, "painting" in a sense we will have to define, real relations (as relations they are necessarily *abstract*) between "men" and their "things," or rather, to give the term its stronger sense, between "things" and *their* "men." (*LP* 230; EPP 574–75)

It is now possible to revise slightly the formulation given earlier concerning the constitutive phenomenalization in works of art. Art cannot do without *materialization*—in Cremonini's case, not only the color and texture of the paint itself, but the forms in which that matter appears in the paintings, what Althusser refers to later on as the "verticals" and "circles" that dominate Cremonini's mature works. But the "matter" of art, in Kant's poetic *Augenschein* and in Cremonini's painting of abstraction, has nothing to do with the phenomenal forms in which it is made to appear—for example, in both Kant and Cremonini, the figure of the mirror. Such forms as the human figures that continue to populate Cremonini's paintings are not ideological, or, better said, to see the figures he paints as representing humanity is to reproduce the ideological illusion par excellence, what Althusser calls "humanism."

The point is made most sharply in Althusser's commentary on Cremonini's deformed faces:

> Strictly speaking, the deformation to which Cremonini subjects his faces is a *determinate* deformation, in that it does not replace one identity with another on the same face, does not give the faces one *particular* "expression" (of the soul, the subject) instead of *another*: it takes *all expression* away from them, and *with it,* the ideological function which that expression ensures in the complicities of the humanist ideology of art. . . . Cremonini's human faces are such that they cannot be *seen,* i.e. identified as bearers of the ideological function of the expression of *subjects.* (*LP* 238–39; *EPP* 582–83)

The similarity to de Man's lapidary summary at the end of "Kant's Materialism" is too striking not to notice:

> The language of the poets therefore in no way partakes of mimesis, reflection, or even perception, in the sense which would allow a link between sense experience and understanding, between perception and apperception. Realism [in Althusser's version, "the humanist ideology of art"] postulates a phenomenalism of experience which is here being denied or ignored. Kant's looking at the world just as one sees it ("wie man ihn sieht") is an absolute, radical formalism that entertains no notion of reference or semiosis. (*AI* 128)

"Pure aesthetic vision," which de Man locates in Kant's exposition of the sublime, fails precisely to connect intuition with concept; it is blind, devoid of sensuous content, mute, equivalent to what Hegel termed *"bloßes Lesen,"* which he associated with the practice of reading silently—a perfectly legitimate practice, but inimical to poetry as art. At the limit, aesthetic materialization has nothing to do with the concept of art as "the sensory manifestation of the idea."[15]

## POLITICS AND HISTORY

That said, it would be incorrect directly to equate de Man's conception of materiality in art with Althusser's. For de Man stops just here, where the most interesting question arises: to wit, what effects are to be achieved by this rigorously antihumanist aesthetic practice? De Man often asserted that the aesthetic and the political are inextricably bound up with each other, but he never, so far as I'm aware, made good on this insight by showing how works of art produce their political effects.[16]

One surmises that this reticence was at least in part due to a certain conception of history, well articulated by Andrzej Warminski. Quoting de Man on the coercive power of tropes over thought, Warminski writes: "The mind is *bound* to do this, not on account of any subjective choice—it is *bound* to do it. It's a linguistic necessity, the ideology built 'into' language . . . it's what is bound to happen. And that's history."[17] History is that which was "bound to happen"; it is governed by structures as invariant and ineluctable as those that command linguistic tropes. Small wonder that de Man would invest so little energy in developing his intuitions concerning the political and ideological effects of art: rigorous examination of the linguistic features of literature would, *ex hypothesi,* disclose the absolute limits imposed on action, limits that can only be ignored by further indulgence in ideological mystification.

For Althusser, certainly, and one should add, for Marx as well (canards about his so-called economic determinism notwithstanding), this strict insistence on historical necessity, on, as it were, the iron laws of the dialectic (to translate de Manian strictures into a familiar idiom), is anything but Marxist. On an Althusserian Marxist account, history is not the record of what "was bound to happen"; it is, rather, a series of contingent possibilities, what the early Althusser termed "over-determined conjunctures."

A single citation, among many that could be adduced in support of this claim, underscores the point with great economy. It comes from a collection of interviews and letters dating from the late 1970s, when Althusser's grasp of the trajectory and the irreducible features of his project was probably surest. To the interviewer's query concerning the possibility of conceiving "another type of history," Althusser responds:

> Yes, the German language presents us with another term: *Geschichte,* which does not designate a history completed *at present,* doubtless determined to a large extent by an already completed past, but only in part, since present, living history *[l'histoire]* is also open to an uncertain, unforeseen future, not yet completed and consequently *aleatory.* Living history only obeys a constant (not a law): the constant of class struggle. Marx did not employ the term "constant" that I borrowed from Lévi-Strauss, but a genial expression: "tendential law," capable of inflecting (not contradicting) *the primary tendential law,* which means that a tendency does not possess the form or figure of a linear law, but that it can bifurcate under the effect of an encounter with another tendency and so forth to infinity. At each intersection, the tendency can take an unforeseeable form, just because it is *aleatory.*[18]

This is the very issue that Althusser tackles head-on at the end of the essay on Cremonini.

### ART AS REVOLUTIONARY WEAPON

According to Althusser, Cremonini's "radical antihumanism" took him down the same road as

> the great revolutionary, theoretical and political thinkers, the great materialist thinkers who understood that the freedom of men is not achieved by the complacency of its ideological *recognition [reconnaissance],* but

by *knowledge [connaissance]* of the laws of their slavery, and that the "realization" of their concrete individuality is achieved by the analysis and mastery of the abstract relations which govern them. (*LP* 240–41; *EPP* 584; translation modified)

Althusser is unyielding (and currently rather unfashionable) on this point, as he had been in the "Letter on Art": art is on the side of knowledge, of science, not on the side of ideology, of which it gives a knowledge, however different in form from that which is given in science. On an Althusserian account, art provides a means by which to discover the true nature of the world, the structure of its social relations, and the possibilities it holds for realizing human emancipation.

If this were the end of the matter, if materialist aesthetic practice were to be limited in its effects to this essentially critical function in relation to ideology, the charge Althusser offhandedly hurls at Brecht—that "there is an aspect of the enlightener in Brecht, the theme of 'theater in a scientific age,' etc." (*EPP* 553)—would double back on Althusser himself (although one should add that there are many worse fates than to be an enlightener). The couplet ideology/knowledge would in principle be immediately and permanently dissolved, for who would continue to subscribe to an ideology having attained a knowledge of it? But, as always, things are not so simple.[19]

The specific relation that works of art establish with ideology is the subject of Althusser's final reflections in the Cremonini essay. If we say that this relation is akin to but distinct from that of the sciences (including politics), it is only to indicate the specificity, the unique material modality of art. Art matters by virtue of the effects it produces, effects manifested precisely *in ideology.* Here, one last time, is Althusser on the relationship between art and ideology:

Every work of art is born of a project both aesthetic and ideological. When it exists as a work of art it produces *as a work of art* (by the type of critique and knowledge it inaugurates with respect to the ideology it makes visible) an *ideological* effect. . . . like every other object, including instruments of production and knowledges, or even the corpus of the sciences, a work of art can become an *element* of the *ideological,* that is to say it can be inserted into the system of relations which constitute the ideological. . . . Perhaps one might even suggest the following proposition, that as the specific function of the work of art is to make *visible (donner à voir),* by establishing a distance from it, the reality of the existing ideology (of any one of its forms), the work of art *cannot fail to exercise* a directly ideological effect, that it therefore maintains far closer relations with ideology than any other *object,* and that it is not possible to think the work of art, in its specifically aesthetic existence, without taking account of this privileged relation with ideology, that is to say without taking account of *its direct and inevitable ideological effect.* (*LP* 241–42; *EPP* 585–86; translation modified)

Scandalously—but with complete consistency—Althusser insists that the ideological (and therefore the political) effectiveness of artworks derives from their aesthetic power, namely, from their production of an "internal distance" in relation to the ideology that they present. The presentation of ideology in art, as it were, estranges ideology from itself, creating the possibility for, not only identification with or interpellation by the ideology presented, but a knowledge of it, a knowledge that the audience can then put to use in transforming the conditions that produced the ideology in the first place. Art's aesthetic power is the source of its pedagogical, scientific function. The key interlocutor, not mentioned by name here, is obviously Brecht.

Consider, for a moment, Brecht's career and posthumous fate. Forced into exile during the Nazi period, his postwar return to the German Democratic Republic saw him attain a transformative power over dramatic practice, in Germany and beyond, that had eluded him during the Weimar period. Not only were his plays performed around the globe, his dramaturgical writings exercised an influence so wide-ranging as to make him, arguably, one of the most significant figures in world literature during the 1950s and 1960s.[20] What one might call "the Brecht-effect" was among the most astonishing developments in postwar culture, not least because the political program he espoused could, during the Cold War, be so easily dismissed with the epithet "Stalinist." Nor has this "Brecht-effect" remained unchanging, frozen in time as the singular model for revolutionary theater. In the post–Cold War era, books like John Fuegi's debunking biography and widespread attempts to "liberate" Brecht from the "burden" of his Marxism are only to be expected.

Yet there remain alternatives, many of them skillfully set forth by Fredric Jameson, whose brief for Brecht's contemporary relevance to Marxist politics is entirely salutary.[21] One that ought to be more fully explored is the very opposite of those aesthetic practices that have conventionally been termed Brechtian and are powerfully associated with Brecht's German disciples such as Heiner Müller, in filmmaking with the French *nouvelle vague* (Godard, Straub) and the German New Wave (Fassbinder in particular), and in British drama with Stoppard and Caryl Churchill, among others. Far from being revolutionary today, in the age of MTV, the Simpsons, and Beavis and Butthead, what was once alienating in Brechtian theater has become a staple of the culture of consumption.[22] In this ideological conjuncture, then, the truly Brechtian project may just be the reinvention of realism, in the theater certainly, but more importantly in film and video, the dominant media of late-capitalist culture. Not Quentin Tarentino or David Lynch, but Ken Loach and Mike Leigh—the latter are the authentic Brechtians of this moment, the ostensible conventionality of their films notwithstanding.[23] But that would be the subject for another paper, one in which the matter of art is more programmatically linked to the project of revolutionary politics. The latter is still very much on the agenda, however distant the horizon of its realization may seem just now.

**NOTES**

This essay is a substantially emended version of a paper delivered at the "Culture and Materiality" conference held at the University of California at Davis April 23–25, 1998. The original included lengthy exegeses of texts by Brecht, Althusser, and Benjamin that are of marginal interest in the present context of Paul de Man's later writings on aesthetics and ideology. To conform better to the occasion, I have omitted this other material and expanded the section that directly addresses de Man's writings.

1. Louis Althusser, "A Letter on Art in Reply to André Daspre," in *Lenin and Philosophy and Other Essays,* trans. Ben Brewster (New York: Monthly Review Press, 1971), 222–23; hereafter, cited parenthetically as *LP*. The French original was first published in *La Nouvelle Critique* 175 (April 1966). I cite from the text as it appears in Louis Althusser, *Écrits philosophiques et politiques,* vol. 2 (Paris: Stock/IMEC, 1995), 561; hereafter, *EPP*. I have occasionally modified the standard English translations of Althusser.

2. Stefano Rosso, "An Interview with Paul de Man," in Paul de Man, *The Resistance to Theory* (Minneapolis: University of Minnesota Press, 1986), 121.

3. Paul de Man, *Aesthetic Ideology,* ed. Andrzej Warminski (Minneapolis: University of Minnesota Press, 1996), 56; hereafter cited parenthetically as *AI*.

4. On Locke's (unsuccessful) attempt to discipline language and subject it to rational principles, to eliminate the abuses to which it is put in discourses of eloquence (namely, rhetoric), see de Man, "The Epistemology of Metaphor," in *AI*, 35–42.

5. Paul de Man, *The Resistance to Theory* (Minneapolis: University of Minnesota Press, 1986), 11; cited by Warminski in his Introduction to *AI*, 8.

6. Louis Althusser, "Ideology and Ideological State Apparatuses (Notes towards an Investigation)," in *LP* 162; in French, "Idéologie et appareils idéologiques

d'État," in *Sur la reproduction* (Paris: Presses Universitaires de France, 1995), 296; hereafter *SR*.

7. The phrase *"en sujets"* is characteristically rendered "as subjects," but it might better be translated "into subjects," namely, into subjectivity. Ideology takes that which is not a subject (individuals) and subjectifies (or subjectivates) them, although it should be said that the ubiquity of ideology makes it impossible to conceive anything like a (nonideological) nonsubject; hence, Althusser's scandalous assertion that "individuals are always-already interpellated by ideology as subjects *[en sujets]*, which necessarily leads us to one last proposition: *individuals are always-already subjects*" (*LP* 176; *SR* 306–7).

8. At least one other commentator on de Man has drawn a similar comparison between the Althusserian concept of ideology and de Man's account of tropes; see Andrzej Warminski's Introduction to *Aesthetic Ideology*, 9–12. Warminski takes up the relationship between de Man's extant texts and *The German Ideology* in his "Ending Up/Taking Back (with Two Postscripts on Paul de Man's Historical Materialism)," in *Critical Encounters: Reference and Responsibility in Deconstructive Writing*, ed. Cathy Caruth and Deborah Esch (New Brunswick, N.J.: Rutgers University Press, 1995), 11–41.

9. Cf. the following: "The point is that the neoclassical trust in the power of imitation to draw sharp and decisive borderlines between reality and imitation . . . depends in the last analysis, on an equally sharp ability to distinguish the work of art from reality. . . . The theoretical problem [of the aesthetic], however, has been displaced [between its original formulation by Schiller and its presentation in Kleist's apologue "Über das Marionettentheater"]: from the specular model of the text as imitation, we have moved on to the question of reading as the necessity to decide between signified and referent, between violence on the stage and violence in the streets" (Paul de Man, "Aesthetic Formalization: Kleist's *Über das Marionettentheater*," in *The Rhetoric of Romanticism* [New York: Columbia University Press, 1984], 280).

10. Cf. de Man: "the political power of the aesthetic, the measure of its impact on reality, necessarily travels by way of its didactic manifestations. The politics of the state are the politics of education" (ibid., 273)—a formulation that Plato would have heartily endorsed.

11. As de Man elsewhere observes: "Thus Kant would have forever ended the play of philosophy, let alone art, if the project of transcendental philosophy had succeeded in determining once and forever the limits of our faculties and of our freedom" (ibid., 283). Notoriously, Kant's project was a failure, the principal evidence for which is the *Critique of Judgment* itself, the text to which de Man turns to disclose this other Kant.

12. In the discussion following her own presentation, Judith Butler contested this formulation, asserting that in this instance materialism for Kant (and presumably for de Man as well) was not a concept at all. That there could be something like a "materiality without materialism" (as Jacques Derrida perspicuously put it in his paper), I would not wish to deny. But to the extent that Kant is attempting in the passage cited to define a representational modality ("seeing as the poets do it") and thereby to make it available to the understanding, what he writes necessarily possesses a conceptual dimension, or else it would not be readable at all. Materiality (that to which Kant refers or that which he posits) may not be conceptual, but a

*theory* (the mode of Kant's referring or positing) of the materiality of art, of seeing "as the poets do it," cannot do without concepts, empty or not. This is the same, elementary, distinction insisted upon by Althusser between the "real-concrete" and the "concrete-in-thought"; see the latter's "On the Materialist Dialectic: On the Unevenness of Origins," in *For Marx,* trans. Ben Brewster (1969; rpt. London: NLB, 1977), 188–89.

13. Even famous limit cases like John Cage's performances of silence require the appearance of the composer/performer on stage sitting motionless for a certain number of minutes before the piano. The silence requires this minimal phenomenalization for the composition to be realized. The point is evident in the passage on the sublime from Kant's third *Critique* cited by de Man, but it is slightly obscured in de Man's translation. The standard English rendering discloses the necessity for even the most rigorously anti-aesthetic practice to exhibit itself in phenomenal form: "we must regard [the sublime], just as we see it *[bloß wie man ihn sieht],* as a distant, all-embracing, vault. Only under such a representation can we ranage that sublimity which a pure aesthetical judgment ascribes to this object" (Immanuel Kant, *Critique of Judgement,* trans. J. H. Bernard [New York: Hafner, 1951], 110; quoted from Rodolphe Gasché, *The Wild Card of Reading: On Paul de Man* [Cambridge: Harvard University Press, 1998], 101).

14. This is the burden of Gasché's exposition of de Man's theory of reading; see especially chapter 3, "Apathetic Formalism," in *The Wild Card of Reading,* 90–113.

15. Gasché discusses de Man's anti-Hegelian, that is, anti-aesthetic, theory of reading in relation to the passage from Hegel's *Aesthetics* on silent reading in ibid., 115–16.

16. One of the anonymous referees who evaluated the present volume for the University of Minnesota Press took my essay to task for "its old-fashioned comparatist strategy," characterized by its "presentation of 'parallels' between the work of de Man and Louis Althusser," and for failing (in contrast to Ernesto Laclau's contribution) "to demonstrate how de Man can help us to read history and politics." The reader also complained that my paper "lack[s a] conclusion" but "'concludes' with a discussion of Brecht that fully 'forgets' de Man." I would have thought that the point of the pages that follow is clear: to contrast Althusser's exploration of the political and ideological effects of artworks and to show how it cashes out de Man's provocative, but practically underdeveloped, assertions. That I have recourse to the example of Brecht to illustrate Althusserian theory is hardly fortuitous. I do not so much "forget" de Man as I suggest that his critique of aesthetics culminates in a gesture toward art's politicality, rather than in any determinate politics of art. My aim is therefore quite different from that ascribed to Laclau's text: it is not "to demonstrate how de Man can help us to read history and politics," but rather, to examine the potential for and the limits of a political practice of art. These are not, in my view, de Manian questions; hence, my turn away from de Man at the end.

17. Warminski, "Ending Up/Taking Back," 34.

18. Louis Althusser, *Sur la philosophie* (Paris: Gallimard, 1994), 45; my translation. On the continuity between the early Althusserian concept of the overdetermined conjuncture and the later program to develop an "aleatory materialism," see Gregory Elliott, "Ghostlier Demarcations: On the Posthumous Edition of Althusser's

Writings," *Radical Philosophy* 90 (July–August 1998): 27–28. That there may be a deeper theoretical affinity between Althusser and de Man connecting the former's "aleatory materialism" with what Gasché identifies as de Man's object of defining the "absolutely singular," an affinity that would involve their respective commitments to nominalism (noted by Fredric Jameson in the case of de Man, and by Warren Montag in the case of Althusser), is a topic requiring detailed examination of the entire corpus of both thinkers. Such a project clearly exceeds the scope of the present occasion, which is devoted to a more restricted inquiry into the relation of aesthetics to ideology, and to the political effects of art.

19. Althusser explicitly rejects the Enlightenment concept of ideology in the ISAs; see *LP* 163–64.

20. The claim is argued more fully by Fredric Jameson in *Brecht and Method* (London and New York: Verso, 1998). See also, inter alia, Michael Patterson, "Brecht's Legacy," in *The Cambridge Companion to Brecht,* ed. Peter Thompson and Glendyr Sacks (Cambridge: Cambridge University Press, 1994), 273–87; and the essays by John Willett (on Brecht's reception in Britain), Bernard Dort (on Brecht in France), Karen Laughlin (on Brecht's assimilation by American feminist playwrights), Renate Möhrmann (on Brecht's influence on women's cinema in West Germany), and Thomas Elsaesser (on Brecht's incorporation by film theory and practice in France, Britain, and Germany), collected in *Re-interpreting Brecht: His Influence on Contemporary Drama and Film,* ed. Pia Kleber and Colin Visser (Cambridge: Cambridge University Press, 1990). A more specialized but highly informative study is George Lellis, *Bertolt Brecht, Cahiers du Cinéma, and Contemporary Film Theory* (Ann Arbor: UMI Research Press, 1982).

21. See Jameson, *Brecht and Method,* especially the two concluding sections, titled "Actuality" and "Historicity."

22. See the concluding pages of Thomas Elsaesser's essay on Brecht and contemporary film, cited in n. 20 above.

23. The Loach-Leigh connection is commonplace in accounts of contemporary British cinema; see, for example, Michael Coveney, *The World according to Mike Leigh* (London: HarperCollins, 1996), 13–14; and the introduction to Leigh's interview with *Cineaste* 20:3 (1994): 10–17. But just as quickly as the connection is asserted, it is disavowed, or heavily qualified (not least by Leigh himself). Despite notable differences in political affiliation, their shared commitment to realism as an aesthetic mode is of the utmost importance, as are each director's methods of preparing cast and narrative for production. Both practice that form which Fredric Jameson argues was Brecht's preferred vehicle for dramatic realization: the workshop or master's class (see *Brecht and Method*).

# Algebra and Allegory: Nonclassical Epistemology, Quantum Theory, and the Work of Paul de Man

Arkady Plotnitsky

The "nonclassical epistemology" of my title refers to the epistemology defined by a particular configuration, to be assembled in this essay, of the concepts of materiality, phenomenality, formalization, and singularity. These concepts would be naturally associated with de Man's work by his readers, as would be the concept of allegory, which is, I shall argue, correlative to the epistemology and the conceptual configuration in question.[1] The appeal to "algebra" is somewhat more esoteric. It is, however, far from out of place, especially in the context of the question of formalization and given the relationships among de Man's work, nonclassical epistemology and quantum theory, which I shall also discuss here.

It would indeed be difficult to circumvent de Man's work in considering these subjects or such figures as Kant, Kleist, and Shelley, to whom a significant portion of this essay will be devoted.[2] In particular, nonclassical epistemology has fundamental connections to aesthetic theory, beginning (at least) with Kant and Schiller, and to the practice of literature and art, such as of Kleist, Shelley, and other Romantic authors, or, as T. J. Clark's "Phenomenality and Materiality in Cézanne" (in this volume) suggests, that of Cézanne. These connections are central to de Man's later works, specifically *Aesthetic Ideology*, where Kant's third *Critique, The Critique of Judgment,* and aesthetics and (the critique of) aesthetic ideology, are given a special place.[3] The history of the particular aesthetic-ideological (mis)reading of the third *Critique* in question in his work is seen by de Man as beginning with and still governed by Schiller's encounter with Kant. By contrast, the work of, especially, Kleist and of some among his Romantic contemporaries appears to mark for de Man the opening of a different aesthetic theory. This opening also leads to a very different type of reading of the third *Critique* (which may be closer to the spirit, or indeed the letter, of the work) by de Man and such authors as Jacques Derrida, Jean-François Lyotard, Jean-Luc Nancy, and several others. This difference is, I argue, defined by the set of, in terms of this essay, nonclassical concepts—in particular, "formalization," "materiality," "phenomenality," and "singularity"—to which I now turn. I begin with formalization and what I call radical or nonclassical formalization.

Paradoxically, or so it may appear, the *radical* character of *radical* formalization, and of its *formal* laws, is defined by the fact that they allow for, and indeed entail, that which is irreducibly unformalizable, irreducibly lawless; that is, whereas the "algebra" of any formalization may be seen as defined by a set of (specified or implicit) laws, here the configuration or ensemble of configurations of elements governed by these laws entails that which cannot be comprehended by these laws or by law in general, and furthermore, that which cannot be conceived by any means that are or even will ever be available to us. Accordingly, the irreducibly lawless in question is not something that is excluded from the domain or system governed by formalization, is not an absolute other of the system, but is instead irreducibly linked to it.[4] This is in part why radical formalization may appear paradoxical, and it does lead to an epistemology that, while technically free of contradiction, is complex and difficult (and, for some, impossible) to accept.

The particular version of radical formalization that I shall now introduce appears to be epistemologically the most radical yet available. But then it may also be the only available (or even possible) model of the configuration of the formalizable and unformalizable just defined. Accordingly, from this point on, by either radical or nonclassical formalization I refer to this version. The complexities and implications of the concept are many and far-reaching. The configuration itself defining it, or constituting the point of departure for it, is, however, simple to formulate: the representation of the "collective" may, in certain circumstances, be subject to formalization and law; that of the "individual" is irreducibly nonformalizable and lawless; and the overall efficacity of both types of effects, formalizable and nonformalizable, is inaccessible by any conceivable means.[5]

This formulation does not merely mean that formalization or law in this case does not apply in certain exceptional situations. Instead, *every individual* entity (element, case, event, and so forth) that belongs to the law-governed ("organized") collectivities in question is in itself not subject to the law involved, or to law in general. More accurately, one should speak of *what is "seen" (is phenomenal) or represented as such an entity or such a collectivity.* The qualification is important to the relationships between "materiality" and "phenomenality" in non-classical epistemology. I shall consider these relationships in detail later. It may, however, be useful to offer a preliminary sketch here, beginning with this qualification.

Although law here does apply only at the level of certain collective, rather than individual, effects, both types of *effects,* lawful and law-less, are *manifest,* materially or phenomenally. Accordingly, when involved, material strata of such effects may, at least, be treated as available to phenomenalization, representation, conceptualization, and so forth, for example, for the purposes of formalization. By contrast, the ultimate *efficacity* of these effects cannot, in principle, be so treated (even though, as will be seen, this efficacity may, at a certain level, be considered as material). In other words, this efficacity is irreducibly inaccessible not only to formalization and law—to "algebra"—but to any representation, phenomenalization, and so forth. Nor, ultimately, can we think of it in terms of any properties or qualities that, while inaccessible, would define it. It is irreducibly inaccessible by any means that are or, conceivably, will ever be available to us; any conception of it is, and may always be, impossible, ultimately even that of the impossibility of conceiving it. As will be seen, it would not be possible to account for the coexistence of both types of effects (collectively lawful and individually lawless) in question otherwise. The presence of both types of effects is logically possible if and only if we cannot conceive of their efficacity at all: the peculiar character of the effects makes one infer the even more peculiar character of the efficacity. It follows that all conceivable terms are provisional, suspect, and ultimately inadequate in describing this efficacity, including *efficacity* or *ultimate,* both quite prominent here. It is worth, however, registering more specifically some of the terms that need to be suspended.

First, although this efficacity manifests itself through the effects of both types, it cannot be thought of in terms of an underlying (hidden) governing wholeness, either indivisible or "atomic," so as to be correlated with manifest (lawless) effects, while subject to an underlying coherent architecture that is not manifest itself. Either type of understanding would (classically) reduce the (nonclassical) "counterposition" of the manifest effects of collective lawfulness, on the one hand, and of individual lawlessness, on the other. This efficacy is neither single in governing all of its effects (individual and collective), nor multiple so as to allow one to assign an unambiguously separate efficacy to each lawless individual effect.

Second, an efficacy of that type cannot be seen in terms of independent properties, relations, or laws, which, while unavailable, would define a certain material entity that would exist in itself and by itself, while, in certain circumstances, giving rise to the (available) effects in question. Instead, it must be seen as reciprocal with and indeed indivisible from its effects: it can never be, in practice and in principle, conceived as isolated, separate from them. Nor, however, can it be seen as fully "continuous" with these effects either. All individuality or, conversely, collectivity in question appears (in either sense) only within the manifest strata of such indivisible configurations. These configurations, however, also contain the inaccessible strata that cannot be isolated and hence cannot *appear,* either as accessible or even as "inaccessible." It is irreducibly inaccessible and yet, indeed as a corollary, equally irreducibly indissociable from that (part of the overall configuration) which is accessible—is subject to phenomenal representation, conception, knowledge, and so forth. One might say that, while the inaccessible in question is indeed *inaccessible* absolutely, it cannot be seen as something that is the *absolutely* inaccessible. It follows that nonclassical epistemology does not imply that nothing exists that, in certain circumstances, gives rise to the effects in question. Instead the point is that this efficacy or the corresponding "materiality" (which also designates something that exists when we are not there to observe it) is inconceivable in any terms that are or perhaps will ever be available to us. Naturally, "existence" or "nonexistence" are among these terms, along with the possibility or impossibility to "conceive" of it, or "possibility" or "impossibility," or "it" and "is," to begin with.

As will be seen, these conditions are the conditions of both quantum epistemology and allegory in de Man. It is true that de Man often associated allegory (or irony) with discontinuity (in earlier work in juxtaposition to the continuity of symbol). We may, however, more properly think of this relation as neither continuous nor discontinuous, or in terms of any conceivable combination of both concepts, or, again, in any given terms, as just outlined. De Man's emphasis on discontinuity of allegory appears strategically to point in this direction, away from the continuity of the symbol or of classical thought in general, for example, aesthetic ideology. Both continuity and discontinuity are retained at the level of "effects," and the effects of discontinuity are indeed more crucial to allegory (or irony).

In the circumstances in question, then, formalization and laws apply only to certain collectivities, but in general not to individual elements composing such collectivities. (I am not saying that they fully describe the latter, since, as follows from the preceding discussion, how the "workings" of the efficacity just considered make lawless individual elements "conspire" to assemble into lawful collectivities is ultimately inconceivable.) Accordingly, the (lawless) individual effects in question can no longer be seen as a part of a whole, so both are comprehended by the same law, or by a correlated set of laws. This possibility defines classical systems and classical formalization, and I use the term *classical* accordingly. A classical formalization may and often must apply within nonclassical formalization. Within classical limits, however, nothing is, *in principle,* lawless, even though, *in practice,* laws may be difficult or, as concerns the ultimate laws, impossible to apply. In the latter case, an underlying lawfulness, however unknown or even unknowable, would be presupposed. By contrast, nonclassical, radical formalization not only figures as lawless the manifest individuality of certain effects involved, but rigorously suspends even the possibility of ascribing any structure, law-governed or not, or properties to the efficacity of all manifest effects, lawful or lawless.

Under these conditions, individuality becomes not only uniqueness but also singularity. Indeed, "singularity" may be defined by this property of *manifest* lawlessness in relation to a given law, or to law in general, perhaps especially when this property arises in a point-like, "singular," fashion—spatial or geometrical; algebraic or analytical (a "singular" point of a function or a "singular" solution of an equation in mathematics); temporal or historical; and so forth. To some degree, one might see the inaccessible efficacity of the singular (or indeed all) effects in question as itself "singular," as Rodolphe Gasché appears to do in his reading of de Man in *The Wild Card of Reading.*[6] Historically, however, the term *singularity* has been associated with the (manifest) point-like configurations or with a relation to the inaccessible, and it is, I would argue, in de Man as well. In addition, the efficacity of such singular events in de Man is indivisible from its effects (in accordance with the analysis just given). Accordingly, it cannot be conceived of as an independent entity severed from them and, hence, as isolated from them either materially or phenomenologically, as the appeal to "singularity" in describing it might suggest. By contrast the singular effects in question can be isolated phenomenologically, although, in view of the same reciprocity, ultimately not materially or efficaciously. Indeed, they are phenomenologically defined by this "isolation" from their (ultimate) history and (both materially and phenomenologically) from each other.[7]

Given the features just outlined, however, nonclassical formalization and nonclassical epistemology are indeed *singularly* radical epistemologically or, as the case may be, antiepistemologically, as well as antiontologically. The view just outlined equally disallows any ultimate ontology and any ultimate epistemology—any possibility of knowing or conceiving how that which is at stake in it is ultimately structured, or is ultimately possible. For example, it would not be possible to predict which information will become available at a later point. Hence, unknowability is not certain either, any more than knowability, except, again, at the ultimate (efficacious) level, where the unknowable becomes irreducible. At this ultimate level, we may adopt Gasché's formulation, "any [ultimate] knowledge, even that of the impossibility of knowledge, is . . . [indeed] strictly prohibited" (*The Wild Card of Reading* 182)—but only at this level, hence I insert "ultimate" here. One would be reluctant to say, especially in the context of de Man's work, that nonclassical epistemology disallows materiality, although at the ultimate level no given concept of matter can apply any more than any other concept. One might say instead that one needs the kind of conceptual architecture here discussed in order to argue for the necessity of a certain form of "materiality," in particular as "materiality" without an ultimate epistemology and an ultimate ontology.[8] De Man specifically associates this radical materiality with both Nietzsche and Derrida (161–62), and earlier Kant and Hegel, although such thinkers as Bataille, Blanchot, and Lacan are pertinent here. De Man also associates this materiality with the "textuality" of Kant's and, by implication, other radical texts. He speaks of "the simultaneous [with idealism] activity, in his [Kant's] text, of a materialism much more radical than what can be conveyed by such terms as 'realism' or 'empiricism'" (*AI* 121). I shall return to de Man's understanding of textuality later.

The qualifier "ultimate," which recurs throughout this essay, is crucial. For it is not that no account or knowledge is possible, which is not an uncommon misunderstanding of nonclassical theories, specifically de Man's or certain interpretations (such as that here considered) of quantum mechanics. On the contrary, rigorous and comprehensive accounts of the situations in question only become possible once the epistemological circumstances in question are themselves taken into account. Specifically, at the level of "effects," classical ontology, epistemology, and phenomenology become possible and necessary. Indeed, these are the effects that make us conclude that their emergence entails something that is ultimately inaccessible to us in that it may not tolerate an attribution of any properties, terms, conceptions, and so forth, including, ultimately, any conception of the ultimate. For, at the very least, the *sum* of these effects is unaccountable for classically, even when they are subject to classical knowledge, as at a certain level they must be, since they would not *appear* to us otherwise. Nonclassical knowledge does not offer us a better knowledge of the irreducibly inaccessible in question in it than classical knowledge does. But it does allow us to infer this inaccessible from its effects and to account for these effects themselves, retaining the irreducibly inaccessible as part of this account.

The overall epistemological situation may, again, appear paradoxical and (ideologically?) unacceptable to some, in the case of quantum physics, Einstein, among them. It is, however, consistently defined and free of any logical contradiction, as Einstein indeed admitted in the case of quantum mechanics in his debate with Bohr. Do such configurations actually exist, or need to be constructed in certain situations? Do we need radical formalization to account for anything, even if it is conceivable and technically free of contradiction? Yes, such configurations do exist, or need to be constructed, both in literature (where they may be more expected as "inventions" of poets) and life (where one may expect them less). They appear to be necessary in facing the "dead nature" as well, at the level of its ultimate constituents, as we understand these constituents now, that is, in terms of quantum physics.

Indeed, in order to make "phenomenality" more rigorously applicable in nonclassical circumstances, we may, following Bohr, define "phenomenon" in terms of the reciprocal or indivisible relationships between the effects in question and their nonclassical efficacity, and, accordingly, recast these relationships in phenomenological terms. A "phenomenon" is a representation of a specific (material or already phenomenal) configuration where such relationships are found.

In quantum mechanics, such configurations are defined by the physical interaction between quantum objects and measuring instruments, while manifesting, in a trace-like manner, the effects of this interaction only in the latter. In contrast with classical physics, the role of measuring instruments is irreducible in quantum physics.[9] The behavior of measuring instruments is described by means of classical physics and in terms of classical epistemology, since classical physics may be treated as epistemologically classical, in particular causal and realist. In these arrangements there "appear" traces (say, on silver bromide photographic plates) of quantum objects, such as elementary particles (or what is so called by convention)—photons, electrons, and so forth. Such traces emerge as the effects of the interaction (itself quantum) between the latter and the measuring instruments. Both the physics of measuring instruments and of the traces in question are available to us, while quantum objects themselves cannot be ascribed physical (or perhaps any) properties, for example, such conventional "quantum" properties as discontinuity, or of being "objects" in any given sense.

The mathematical formalism ("algebra") of quantum mechanics applies to some of these effects, specifically to certain collective effects, found within one type of phenomena, and does not apply to other such effects, specifically certain individual effects, found within the other type of phenomena. Both types of phenomena can never be combined, or be seen as derived from a single efficacious situation, however hidden. Nor can we have both types of effects within a single phenomenon. If we are to "see" each effect of a formalized (lawful) collectivity as lawless, this collectivity has to be (re)phenomenalized so as to be divested of both collectivity and law—either through a single phenomenal collectivity of lawless individual (singular) effects or through a collectivity of singular individual phenomena. In other words, the lawful collectivity and lawless individuality in quantum mechanics, or in any radical formalization, require different phenomenalizations, even when dealing with the "same" set of effects. Accordingly, both the sets of effects and the efficacity of such *phenomena* will be different by virtue of the different material or mental agencies of phenomenalization involved. This is in part why this efficacity can never be seen as an entity isolated from its effects but instead as that which is irreducibly reciprocal with and indivisible from its effects. It may of course be stratified as to the "location" of some of its strata, while retaining the radically inaccessible character of each such stratum.

These circumstances manifest themselves most famously in the appearance of either the ordered or patterned wavelike effects (which pertain only to collectivities of such traces) in some circumstances and the particle-like effects (in general not subject to law in quantum mechanics) in other circumstances. The presence of both types of effects is essential to and defining for quantum physics, even though (and because) it is impossible to ever combine the two types of phenomena together or derive them from a single common configuration. The circumstances of their emergence and hence the phenomena that correspond to them are always mutually exclusive or, in Bohr's terms, complementary. The latter fact is primarily responsible for Bohr's choice of the term *complementarity* for his overall interpretation of quantum mechanics.

"Quantum objects" or, more accurately, that which makes us speak of such entities can be assigned an independent existence as something that may be assumed as existing when we are not there to observe it. That "something," however, cannot be assigned any conceivable independent physical (or other) properties, for example, those defining (classical) particles or waves. Nor can it be isolated from their interaction (itself quantum) with measuring instruments so as to establish their independent impact and hence ascertain their independent properties on the basis of the effects of this interaction. Classical physics fails to describe the sum total of these effects and can be shown to be rigorously incapable of doing so: the possibility of a classical-like description would be in conflict with the experimental data of quantum physics. Quantum theory is able to account for both types of effects and for their complementarity. It does so, however, in a nonrealist and noncausal way. As I said, quantum theory (at least in Bohr's interpretation) does not describe the properties and behavior of quantum objects themselves but only (in a statistical fashion) certain phenomenal effects of their (again, quantum) interaction with measuring instruments. This is why, in contrast to classical physics, in quantum theory this interaction can never be neglected or compensated for, while entailing the irreducibly inaccessible efficacity of the effects constituting the data of quantum physics. "Quantum objects," detected in any given experiment, are part of this efficacity. In general, however, the latter involves other agencies, such as measuring instruments, perhaps in turn ultimately quantum (in view of the ultimate quantum constitution of all material objects).

Bohr's interpretation of quantum mechanics, as just outlined, is, I argue, generalizable to all nonclassical epistemology, and the nonclassical phenomenology it entails, in particular those found in de Man's work. We must, of course, rigorously adhere to the specificity of the workings of the general scheme here presented in different situations, even when we can leave aside technical aspects of modern mathematics and science, including in their connections to each other, such as, in the case of quantum mechanics, making experimentally well-confirmable statistical numerical predictions, or sometimes even exact numerical predictions concerning certain information, say, the position or the momentum of a particle, but never both together. (Hence, from the classical viewpoint, such information is always partial. The laws of quantum mechanics disallow us to assume a wholeness, however unknowable, behind this information, hence making it complete, as complete as any information than can, in principle, be obtained in any experiment performed on quantum objects, or, again, what we infer as such from this information.) In nonscientific nonclassical situations, the nonclassical effects would emerge through such entities as (material) signifying structures of the text (de Man's "materiality of the signifier"); material texture (in either sense), such as that of Cézanne's paintings; the materiality of historical occurrences or events; or certain "mental" configurations of the same joint (classical-nonclassical) type. (At bottom, [material] materiality may be irreducible even in the last case, even though, given the epistemology in question, there is no ultimate bottom line here, and the concept itself of materiality is affected accordingly.) Also, we now deal (or so it appears) with "macroscopic" human subjects (in either sense) rather than the ultimate (microscopic) constituents of matter (seen as material) of quantum physics. The epistemology of quantum mechanics and nonscientific epistemology here considered do, however, (re)converge at certain points, including, from both sides, on the latter point. In particular, they share the supplementary (Derrida) or allegorical (de Man) production of phenomenalization and indeed, as Bohr stressed, idealization from "technomaterial" marks. This term may be applied to such marks with "writing" in Derrida's sense in mind. In quantum mechanics, or already relativity, this application would involve certain parts of the (material) technology of measuring instruments, where the scientific data in question in these theories appear in the form of certain material marks or traces. The situation may be rigorously shown to correspond to Derrida's "economy" of trace, supplement, writing, and so forth.[10]

More generally, in all situations here in question, the key nonclassical features are brought about by the irreducible role of "technology" (in the broad sense of *technē*) in them. From this perspective, we may define as "nonclassical" situations those in which the role of technology is irreducible. The technology of measurement in quantum physics, or of *technē* of "writing" in Derrida's sense, and the *technē* of "linguistic materiality" in de Man's sense (which I shall discuss later), make the situations in question nonclassical. By contrast, in "classical" situations *technē* is, at least in principle, reducible, as, for example, in the case of measurement in classical physics, since measuring instruments play only an auxiliary role there so as to allow us to speak of the independent properties and behavior of classical objects. One can view analogously certain forms of reading or textual processing and production in general, insofar as the role of "writing" may be neglected there. Thus, classical textuality is not only possible but is necessary within certain limits. By definition, we depend on it even in nonclassical situations insofar as (as in the case of measuring instruments in quantum physics) nonclassical effects appear through classical textual processing.

These connections are not coincidental. Although physics played the most decisive role, the ideas of Bohr and other key figures in the history of quantum physics may be traced to nonclassical aspects of the nineteenth-century philosophy, literature and the arts, and then to modernism. Conversely, the relevance of, among other mathematical and scientific fields, quantum mechanics to de Man's work is hardly in doubt. Nor is it surprising in view of the significance of new science for modern intellectual history, even leaving aside that de Man was educated in science and engineering. Relevant elaborations are found throughout de Man's works, if often reconceptualized or allegorized so as to function independently of their scientific frames of reference. "Pascal's Allegory of Persuasion" offers more direct connections to mathematics and science. In particular, de Man's analysis there may be linked both to mathematical formalization and to its role in physics. As will be seen, both subjects are significant for *Aesthetic Ideology* and related work. The connections to physics, from optics to quantum mechanics, could be traced throughout de Man's work. The interplay of optical tropes of "reflection" (admittedly a customary trope in such discussions), "translucence," "transparence," and so forth in de Man's essay "The Rhetoric of Temporality" may be read as metaphorically shuttling between geometrical (linear), wave, and quantum theories of light. "Quantum-mechanical" themes emerge in most of de Man's "optical" tropology and in his epistemological arguments. The connections between both is a more complex question, since nonclassical epistemology does not always govern the architecture of optical tropes, although de Man's essay "Shelley Disfigured" suggests more direct connections of that type. It may, however, be argued that most radical and most significant forms of "blindness" and "insight" in de Man are "quantum-mechanical," even when they relate to the blindness and insight of reading. The latter is not surprising, given the technological and material character of textuality as considered by de Man, and the fact that for de Man epistemology is indissociable from reading. A massive deployment of "optics" is found in "Shelley Disfigured," where it is also especially justified, given Shelley's own deployment of optical theories in *The Triumph of Life* and elsewhere.[11] The essay also contains a number of formulations of a general epistemological, rather than specifically "optical," nature (although in this case they can be brought together) that are parallel and perhaps indebted to quantum epistemology. Thus, de Man writes at the outset, virtually defining his analysis: "The status of all these where's and what's and how's and why's is at stake, as well as the system that links these interrogative pronouns, on the one hand, to questions of definition and of temporal situation and, on the other, to questions of shape and figure."[12] This is strikingly reminiscent of and is epistemologically parallel to Bohr's inaugural definition of complementarity (1927): "The very nature of quantum theory thus forces us to regard the space-time coordination and the claim of causality, the union of which characterizes the classical theories, as complementary but exclusive features of the description, symbolizing the idealization of observation and definition respectively" (*PWNB* 2:54–55).

More interesting at this point, however, is not the influence of modern mathematics and science on de Man's and related work, but the conceptual reciprocity between both domains and the deployment of that work in our approaches to, at least, epistemological, conceptual, and aesthetic aspects of mathematics and science. I shall here consider two such examples—the allegorical character of quantum mechanics, and the relationships between formalization in science and the radical (materialist) formalism that de Man *finds* in the Kantian sublime.

Complementary phenomena are common in and peculiar to quantum physics. Those related to "wave" and "particle" effects and their complementarity are the most famous. Arguably the most significant, however, are those related to the measurement of physical variables, such as position and momentum, or time and energy, correlative to the complementarity of "the space-time coordination and the claim of causality," mentioned earlier. According to Bohr, such variables and the overall quantum-theoretical description can only be applied to quantum objects themselves provisionally or, in his terms, *symbolically*. For, as we have seen, even though we often (by convention) speak of such variables in relation to quantum objects, in actuality we can only measure the corresponding physical quantities (either position or momentum, or time and energy, but never both together) pertaining to the classically described measuring arrangements; that is, we measure classical physical variables pertaining to certain parts of such arrangements, rather than to the quantum objects themselves, but describe the relationships between the mathematical variables corresponding to these physical variables in terms of quantum-mechanical, rather than classical, formalism. Classical physics can only describe each such physical variable in a corresponding experimental arrangement, but never both together, since there is no experimental arrangement that would make it possible. This situation can be numerically represented by Heisenberg's uncertainty relations, which, thus, become mathematical correlatives of this situation.[13] The rigorous impossibility of accounting for this situation in terms of classical physics makes it necessary *(a)* to infer the existence of quantum objects and *(b)* to introduce a different, quantum, theory, including a different mathematical formalism or "algebra," which provides such an account. It does so, however, in a physically and epistemologically nonclassical way.

Now, I would argue that the situation is rigorously allegorical in de Man's sense, thus linking "algebra" and "allegory" within physics itself. The formulation from "Pascal's Allegory of Persuasion" is especially fitting here: "the difficulty of allegory is rather that this emphatic clarity of representation does not stand in the service of something that can be represented" (*AI* 51).[14] Indeed, this clarity may be said to stand in the service of that which cannot be represented by any means. Thus, classical physics can offer us only incomplete and partial—and specifically complementary—allegories of the quantum world. Nothing appears to be able to offer us more. Accordingly, Bohr's "symbolic" means "allegorical" in de Man's sense, for this "symbolism" in fact rigorously prohibits the classical epistemological features of "symbol" (as analyzed by de Man), in particular any possibility of deriving "allegorical" representations from any original or primordial unity. The formalization of collectivities in quantum mechanics does not offer a classical (or classical-physics-like) description of quantum behavior or, again, allow one to claim any primordial unity behind it. It only statistically predicts the emergence of certain collective patterns, but never of individual events or effects. If the mathematical formalism, algebra (no quotation marks are necessary), of quantum theory represents anything at all it represents this nonclassical and (with respect to using conventional concepts of classical physics) allegorical situation.[15] Insofar as one can apply this formalism to quantum objects themselves, either by correlating it in some ways with classical physics and its mathematical formalism or otherwise, it can only be done allegorically.

We can have a further and deeper sense of these connections between quantum mechanics and de Man's work, and the reciprocal theoretical possibilities they offer, by considering the question of the mathematical formalization of physics. Even beyond "Pascal's Allegory of Persuasion" (which would require a separate treatment), the subject of mathematical formalization is significant in Man's work, specifically in his analysis of Kant's sublime. It has, of course, a major significance for Kant's own analysis of the sublime (or of the beautiful) and in his work in general. In de Man's reading it acquires a special prominence not in Kant's treatment of the mathematical sublime, but as Kant's analysis enters the question of what Andrzej Warminski, in "As the Poets Do It: On the Material Sublime," aptly terms "the material sublime." In this case we (must) *"find"* the sublime, if we regard, for example, the ocean, "as poets do, merely by what the appearance to the eye shows [or points] *[was der Augenschein zeigt]."* (I modify de Man's translation [*AI* 80]; a stable, or any, translation may not be possible, only a reading, as Warminski's essay suggests as well.) According to de Man, "Kant's [phenomenal?] architectonic world is not a metamorphosis of a fluid [material?] world into *the solidity of stone,* nor is his *building* a trope or a symbol that substitutes for the actual entities" (*AI* 82; emphasis added). "Flat" and "the third person" as it is, this architectonic world may be seen as a certain configuration of phenomenal "effects" produced by a reciprocal and yet inaccessible efficacity. "The only word that comes to mind," de Man says, "is that of a *material vision*" (*AI* 82).

The nature of this materiality and of the formalism that, de Man argues, accompanies it is complex. Indeed, de Man immediately adds: "but how this materiality is then to be understood in linguistic terms is not, as yet, clearly intelligible." This understanding will bring with it further complications of the concepts of the sublime, materiality, and formalism (or formalization), and a more radical dislocation of aesthetic ideology than those entailed by the material vision, qua *vision*, as here described by Kant and de Man—or at least *as* this vision has been described so far. This vision may entail more radical limits in this respect, which become more apparent through an understanding of its materiality "in linguistic [or/as textual] terms." The analytical and textual pressure put upon Kant's text both by Kant himself and by de Man becomes extraordinary indeed, since we have already come quite far. For, as de Man writes:

> The critique of the aesthetic ends up, in Kant, in a formal *materialism* that runs counter to all values and characteristics associated with aesthetic experience, including the aesthetic experience of the beautiful and of the sublime as described by Kant and Hegel themselves. The tradition of their interpretation, as it appears from near contemporaries such as Schiller on, has seen only this one, figural, and, if you will, "romantic" aspect of their theories of imagination, and has entirely overlooked what we call the material aspect. Neither has it understood the place and the function of *formalization* in this intricate process. (*AI* 83; emphasis added)

It is not altogether clear whether the term *formalization* here refers only to the radical formalism in question at the moment; or whether it is seen more generally so as to encompass other forms of formalization, specifically those analogous to radical formalization; or whether, especially once understood in linguistic terms, the radical formalism of the material vision, qua vision, of the sublime entails something like radical formalization. It is also not altogether clear whether "ends up" refers to this particular moment of Kant's and de Man's analysis or anticipates de Man's final elaborations in the essay. The question, then, is whether this linguistic understanding of the materiality involved is "deconstructive" or even (in Kant's text) "self-deconstructive" in some sense (i.e., whether Kant's text inscribes this understanding against its own grain); or whether this understanding is an actual outcome of Kant's analytical rigor; or whether a yet more complex space of reading is at stake. It would be difficult and perhaps impossible to give a fully determined answer. For one thing, what poets "see" or "do" in finding the (material) sublime, how we understand this materiality in linguistic terms or how poets do so (possibly at the moment of this vision), and the movements of Kant's argument appear to be already irreducibly entangled in Kant's text. Both the material vision in question and its understanding in linguistic terms (and by implication radical formalization) may be brought together by the kind of reading of Kant and de Man offered by Warminski in "As the Poets Do It." According to Warminski's reading, what "poets" in fact *find* in finding the sublime is the radical linguistic materiality that we find in Kleist and, via Kleist, in the end of de Man's essay. Even so, certain differences between the materiality (and phenomenality) of the sublime and those involved in radical formalization may remain, especially as concerns what does and does not appear to the eye. The radically inaccessible in question in radical formalization cannot be "seen" in any conceivable sense. It would also be difficult to disregard the fact that Kant parallels, if not identifies, "[to find the sublime] as the poets do it" and "what the appearance to the eye shows." These complexities do not diminish the radical implications of de Man's analysis, and may be a virtue insofar as it offers new epistemological and aesthetic possibilities, even "insurmountable possibilities."

It appears that, in all circumstances, in order to reach the limits of materiality here at stake we need Kleist's aesthetic formalization, as radical *formalization,* through which de Man develops the linguistic understanding in question, rather than only Kant's radical *formalism,* as it emerges prior to this understanding. In particular, the latter corresponds to and, in a certain sense, is the mathematical formalism of classical physics, specifically, "the mathematization or geometrization of pure optics" (*AI* 83), rather than to the radical *formalization* of quantum physics, as is the aesthetic formalization of Kleist or de Man's linguistic understanding.[16] We recall that de Man closes "Kant's Materialism" by suggesting that Kant's radical formalism (*formalism,* in question at the moment, rather than radical *formalization*) may not ultimately be "formalistic enough" (*AI* 128). He may well have had Kleist's aesthetic formalization in mind, which, along with de Man's essay of Kleist itself, is invoked at the end of "Phenomenality and Materiality in Kant," and something similar is intimated in the end of "Kant's Materialism" (*AI* 89–90; 128).

The question of the mathematization of science, here specifically optics, enters at the point when the (purely) formal character of the (purely) material vision is ascertained. De Man writes:

> The sea [of the material sublime] is called [by Kant] a mirror, not because it is supposed to reflect anything, but to stress a flatness devoid of any suggestion of depth. In the same way and to the same extent that this vision is purely material, devoid of any reflexive or intellectual complication, it is also purely formal, devoid of any semantic depth and reducible to the formal mathematization or geometrization of pure optics. (*AI* 83)

Beyond the more immediate reference to vision—here, moreover, a vision of the sea as "mirror"—the role of optics has, as I said, a special place in de Man's thought, extending to the connections to quantum physics, the ultimate optics, at least for now. The latter, however, allows for no mathematization and particularly geometrization of its ultimate "objects." Instead it entails radical formalization and, with it, both a materiality that is available to phenomenalization and (limited) formalization, and a materiality that is unavailable to any formalization, representation, phenomenalization, and so forth, and hence to any vision. The latter could still be seen as "material," insofar as any conceivable term could apply. It cannot, however, any longer be seen as formal, mathematically or otherwise. It may only form an (irreducibly invisible) part of a formal vision.

By contrast, the mathematization or geometrization of pure classical optics (whether linear or wave optics, or classical particle optics) conforms to the formalization of classical physics. It is an obvious example of what Galileo called and was first to develop as, in his terms, the mathematical (and specifically geometrical) sciences of nature. One might argue that the latter are made possible (I am not saying fully constituted or governed) by a kind of material and formal vision analogous to the one de Man invokes at this juncture of his reading. This vision enables one to treat the properties of material bodies (or of space and time) as experimentally measurable and theoretically mathematizable quantities, which are abstracted from or divested of the other properties that material bodies possess (the procedure sometimes known as the Galilean "reduction").[17] It is crucial, of course, that, although this vision *enables* such a treatment, it is not identical to this (technical) treatment. With this qualification in mind, one might say that the vision of the sublime (or of the beautiful) in Kant is fundamentally mathematical-scientific, for the moment in the sense of classical science—at least short of understanding this vision in linguistic terms.

One might also reverse the point and argue that the formal and specifically mathematical character of the mathematical sciences of nature is fundamentally aesthetic in de Man's radical sense. It is true that most of the disciplinary ("technical") practice of physics, or mathematics, bypasses the experience in question. It cannot be seen as aesthetic in Kant's sense, to begin with, because, to put it in Kant's terms, it involves the concept of understanding. Indeed, one of Kant's deep insights was that understanding can never be purely formal, including any conventionally "formalized," such as mathematical, understanding. The (pure) formalness can only be achieved in aesthetic judgment and perhaps, ultimately, only in the purely material and formal vision of the material sublime. The latter we can only find, as poets (or, at certain points, some physicists and mathematicians) do, by regarding certain objects by "merely [purely geometrically?] what the appearance to the eye [sight] shows," even if it is the mind's eye. If one is a poet like Kleist, Hölderlin, or Shelley, the linguistic understanding of, and now within, this vision can become even more epistemologically radical or nonclassical in the present sense. For the moment, within classical limits, whatever may primarily define the technical practice of mathematics or mathematized science, such as modern physics, they (or perhaps any understanding) would not be possible without this "founding" aesthetic moment or vision. This vision creates the formal "objects" of mathematics, or the mathematized objects of physics, or at a certain level of all theoretical thinking, or even of all understanding, as Kant appears to intimate as well.[18] This "mathematical" or "quasi-mathematical" vision "precedes" (logically rather than ontologically) all mathematical or mathematized physics and even mathematics itself, as we understand them now. Neither would be possible without this "vision," even if the "contemplation" involved may no longer play much, if any, of a role once such objects are put into disciplinary circulation and are subjected to a technical treatment. Although this moment or vision does not occur all the time, it need not have occurred only once either—as a single, absolutely founding moment (a problematic and ultimately untenable conception) of mathematization either in mathematics itself or in the mathematical sciences. It is, I would argue, this aspect or moment (prior to understanding) of "mathematization or geometrization of pure optics," given that de Man sees it as devoid of "any . . . intellectual complication."

It is true that this purely formal and material "vision" in mathematics or specifically geometry (where mathematical objects can be "contemplated" more visually) is not always sublime. It may be with respect to some mathematical, or mathematized, physical "objects," or presumed objects, such as mathematical infinities (now seen in terms of the material rather than mathematical sublime, as Kant defines it). Even when failing the sublime, however, the classical mathematical vision in question is aesthetic, if perhaps not quite a vision of poets, and, specifically, purely formal. Indeed, as de Man observes in the passage in question, the same aspects define "the aesthetic experience of the beautiful" as well. It is, thus, not altogether certain whether de Man, or Kant, associates the vision of poets with any material and formal vision of the type here described, as would appear more immediately, or more strictly the vision of the (material) sublime. The linguistic understanding of this vision brings further complications into this question and into the question of the relationships between this vision and formalization in mathematics and science.

Even short of these complications, however, mathematics and science appear to involve features that make them more aesthetic, and differently aesthetic, than we usually think. The features just discussed are more deeply and radically aesthetic than what is offered to us by usual aesthetic ideologies, the appeal to and reliance on which, by mathematicians and scientists, philosophers, or laypeople we continue to encounter. This appeal is often based on the same ideologizing misreading (it need not entail actual textual encounters) of Kant and others, which, as de Man argues, may indeed be unavoidable. Conversely, the formal materialism in question makes a dislocation of these ideologies possible.

And yet, this materialism or formalism does not go far enough, is not yet "formalistic enough," at least not so far. Both "Kant's Materialism" and, especially, "Phenomenality and Materiality in Kant" take the Kantian sublime further—to the point where a yet more radical stage of reading Kant's text, and of formalization and materiality, is reached. This stage is reached when how "[the] materiality in question is understood in linguistic terms" becomes more "clearly intelligible," whereby the situation acquires the key features of radical formalization in the present sense and, correspondingly, of quantum epistemology.

In particular, the application of the mathematical formalism of quantum mechanics may be seen as *arising* from, or at least as linked to, an extraordinary form of "vision" of the material constitution and, with respect to the viewpoint of classical physics, de-constitution of the quantum-mechanical data. I am now speaking specifically of the vision ("phenomenality") relating to the marks/traces constituting the quantum data, rather than of the theoretical conceptualization of the quantum-mechanical situation as a whole. As the vision of poets in Kant, which helps us to find the sublime, this vision, which helps us to find quantum mechanics, may be seen as material in the same sense. It may, however, no longer be seen as formal, unless in terms of (if one may use such an expression) a radically de-formalized form—that is, if we can, phenomenally, and especially geometrically, "see" anything in this way at all. It may not be humanly possible to do so, even though, in contrast to the ultimate constituents of matter or the ultimate efficacity of the data in question, the elements constituting these data are available to phenomenological apprehension. We do, however, now treat these marks, even their collectivities, purely "formally" (without "form") rather than in any way configuratively. In particular, we divest them of their classical and hence configurable appearance (in either sense), even though they do form configurations, or what can be so seen in certain circumstances—say, wavelike patterns, or a trace of a particle in a cloud chamber. Even within a single phenomenon, where these marks appear, they must be divested of the possibility of being explained in classical terms and hence of their manifest classical configurativity. For example, they should not be seen either as points resulting from classically conceived collisions between "particles" and the screen or as forming a classically conceived wave pattern. Neither "picture" corresponds to what in fact occurs. At this stage, even the radical (Derridean) trace-like character of these marks is suspended, although this character will have to be given to these data in order to explain them in quantum-theoretical terms.

This suspension is necessary, and the vision that results is possible, for the following reasons. As we have seen, the mathematical formalism of quantum mechanics does not formalize or otherwise describe the configurations, individual or collective, of these traces as such, or for that matter any material physical process in the way classical physics would. Instead, it enables statistical (and statistically very precise) predictions concerning certain collective, even if not individual, configurations of material marks in certain circumstances.[19] Insofar as one can interpret the situation and specifically the quantum-mechanical mathematical formalism as applicable to quantum objects themselves or their interactions with measuring instruments in terms of conventional physical (or indeed any) concepts, such an interpretation can only be allegorical in de Man's sense. First, this "allegory" does not at this level describe any physical configuration or process. Second, it does not (in contrast to a symbol, for example) relate the partial (complementary) descriptions involved to, or allow one to presuppose even in principle, any classical wholeness that would reduce their complementary character. Thus, in order for a theoretical formalization and interpretation of quantum physics to take place, these marks, while "visible," have to be divested of any form of mathematical and specifically geometrical representation. Classical physics is largely defined by the possibility of such representation or, more broadly, phenomenalization.[20] In quantum mechanics, neither is possible any longer. This impossibility is reflected in the trace-like or written (in Derrida's sense) character of the marks in question and the allegorical (in de Man's sense) nature of the interpretation of these traces or of the mathematical formalism of quantum mechanics. All such classical representations may be seen (with caution) as forms of (aesthetic) ideology, even when they are divested of everything (tropology, figuration, reflexivity, semantic depth, and so forth) except for mathematical formalization, including of the kind invoked by de Man in the context of the material sublime. At this point mathematization itself (such as that of the Galilean or Newtonian, or indeed Euclidean, program) may be seen as ideological, even if we see it as purely "formal" or purely "aesthetic" and as devoid of technical, or standard ideological, dimensions of the practice of mathematics and science. The efficacious processes themselves will, again, be, in Bohr's terms, far beyond the reach of any pictorial visualization, phenomenalization, representation, conception, and so forth. Now, however, the manifest effects, the visible marks, involved, too, must be seen (in either sense) as divested of any geometrical structure consistent with classical physics. Either individually or collectively, these traces must be seen as allowing for no classical physical description, as would be the case of the "radical *formalism*," at least in the mathematization and geometrization of science, if not of the Kantian sublime itself.

I cannot consider the subject here, but it may be argued that Heisenberg's great paper introducing quantum mechanics appears to reflect the process just described.[21] First, it suspends the application of classical physics to quantum data and the very possibility of configuring these data accordingly. Instead it treats them formally (but, again, without giving them form) as material and phenomenal effects, divorced from all classical configurativity. His introductory elaborations in the paper itself would suggest nearly as much. Heisenberg does not explore the epistemological consequences of the situation, of which he was only vaguely aware at the time. His main concern was to offer a mathematical formalism that would enable theoretical predictions in the situations where all previous attempts had failed. These consequences emerged in the subsequent developments, specifically in yet another great paper by Heisenberg himself, introducing the uncertainty relations, and in Bohr's work.[22] Heisenberg's invention of quantum mechanics, however, appears to have been partly enabled by the deconfigurative phenomenology just discussed.

From this viewpoint, the ultimate "aesthetics" or "poetic vision" of physics is not that of coherence, harmonious wholeness, and other icons of classical aesthetic ideology, although these may apply at other levels of quantum theory. Instead it is the aesthetics of the radical de-coherence, of the formal without form—the quantum aesthetics, if not the quantum sublime, although "the formal without form" would fit the sublime as well. And yet, for all that, the quantum-mechanical for-malism, or radical formalism or formalization elsewhere, may remain only another form of aesthetic ideology projected into the radical and nonformally formal "configuration" (a term henceforth inadequate) of material marks, if any nonaesthetic or nonideological perception of them is possible. I shall return to this topic later. My main point here is that, once divested of all mathematization and, especially, geometriza-tion, such as that of optics, the formalism (mathematical or conceptu-al) of quantum mechanics, for example, of quantum optics, can only conform to radical *formalization*. It does not conform to a radical *for-malism* analogous to the radical formalism of the material sublime, which is parallel to the formalization of classical physics, that is, again, short of "linguistic terms" of understanding it. Linguistically under-stood, it might be seen as subsumed by radical formalization.

Then, reflecting back, the material vision of the sublime would be seen as only appearing (in either sense) to be a classical (and classically architectonic) vision of the mathematization or geometrization of pure optics. In fact, however, as the vision of the sublime qua the sublime, it will have involved radically deconfigurative aspects that are analogous to those found in "contemplating" the data of quantum physics, as just considered. Would this be the vision necessary in order to *find* the sub-lime, as poets do, if not the vision of the sublime itself? The sublime appears to correspond to a vision of that which always escapes archi-tectonics, geometrization, and so forth, while appearing to be available to them. (We recall that, in contrast to the beautiful, this vision cannot be seen as having an object, but rather as making such an object im-possible.) By contrast, in the quantum-mechanical vision the material marks constituting quantum data should be "seen," should be made to be seen, as altogether devoid of any conceivable architectonics, with-out phenomenally suggesting this evacuation of the architectonic. Inso-far, however, as it may not in fact be possible to see anything in that last way, this vision comes closer to the sublime, although it may still be different from what either Kant or de Man had in mind. For, on the other hand, if we apply this more radical deconfiguration or disfigu-ration to the sublime itself, we may enact, as it were, the material desublimation of the sublime. The latter would undermine the already "deconstructive" visions and "ideologies" based on the sublime, which now appear as merely more sophisticated forms of aesthetic ideology. Perhaps once made "more intelligible," "understanding [the materiality of the sublime) in linguistic terms" reveals the un-architectonic un-sublime thus suggested, although, and because, Kleist's and Shelley's disfigurative visions appear to offer its best model.

Although contextualized somewhat differently in relation to the vision of poets ("the way the poets look at the oceans severed from their geographical place on earth"), something of this type is suggested by de Man's remark, via Montaigne. We must, de Man says, consider "our limbs," formally, "in themselves, severed from the organic unity of the body." "We must, in other words, disarticulate, mutilate the body in a way that is much closer to Kleist than to Winckelman," or one might say deprive them of their geometry (*AI* 88). Within the material vision of the sublime thus understood, any, for example, linguistic, formalization of such "parts" is a form of "algebra." Some of its aspects can serve to construct partial and ultimately inadequate allegories (some of them geometrical) of the materiality of the "body" in question, both that of the manifest effects (analogously to those of quantum-mechanical marks) or their efficacities. Indeed, the original "parts" or "limbs" are already such allegories, derived from the classical view, and hence as supplementary as the body itself. Accordingly, a more radical disarticulation, mutilation, disfiguration of the (un)body is at stake, even at the level of manifest effects. Following the overall epistemology here discussed, the efficacity of these effects is, again, inaccessible in any way, no more by means of disarticulation, however radical, than by means of articulation. With respect to this efficacity, the dismemberment and disarticulation in question (at the level of the effects) itself reflects only this inaccessibility. This disarticulating dismemberment of the body will be linked to the linguistic understanding of materiality and specifically to the disarticulation of tropes, as indeed the term (figure? trope?) *disarticulation* suggests.[23]

De Man's reference to Kleist here and in closing "Phenomenality and Materiality in Kleist" is crucial and confirms my overall point. The question, then, would be whether it is any more possible to experience such a vision or even assign it any geometry than to have any vision the (un)configurations of marks constituting the data of quantum mechanics. What would such an experience, say, in a vision of a sea, be? Is it possible? Can it be shown to be rigorously impossible? For, to see something as the poets do, however, may correspond to the situation in question, if we can see "anything" here at all, even beyond the radically inaccessible efficacity of all visible effects involved. The allegorical algebra enabled by this vision or un-vision would be quite enough in itself. We may call such a (nonvisualizable) sublime or unsublime the algebraic or the algebraic-allegorical sublime, as opposed to the geometrical or the geometrical-symbolic sublime. Indeed, the symbol may be argued to always remain geometrical, as is suggested by Coleridge's description of it in terms of translucent geometrical optics—a key starting point of de Man's investigation opened by "The Rhetoric of Temporality" (*BI* 192). This algebraic-allegorical sublime may correspond to the sense Kleist made of Kant's work, from *The Critique of Pure Reason* on. This sense also reflects subtle gradations of proximities and differences, between perhaps ultimately "algebraic" (and "quantum-mechanical") reason and the ultimately "geometrical" judgment of the sublime in Kant, even if in a Kleist-like reading.

Alternatively, the quantum-mechanical "vision" just outlined and the quantum-mechanical formalization overall may indicate the space of differences, infinitesimal and radical (and sometimes simultaneously both), between Kleist's aesthetic, *literary* formalization and Kant's *philosophical* formalization of the vision of the sublime, which self-deconstructs into Kleist's. Either way, here, too, in order to find this more radical formalization, we might want to do what poets do, now also as philosophers. The literary, now defined in accordance with, or indeed as, radical formalization, is part and parcel of this understanding, or reasoning, also in Kant's sense of "reason." The scheme just outlined must, again, be seen as fundamentally correlative to the irreducibility of *technē*—the technology of measuring instruments, the technology of writing, or of reading, or of painting, such as Cézanne's. I would argue that the interaction of materiality and phenomenality, individuality and collectivity, singularity and regularity, in late Cézanne, considered by T. J. Clark in this volume conforms and perhaps for the first time introduces this "quantum-mechanical" vision or un-vision in painting. This may indeed be "the [impossible] truth of painting" for Cézanne, the truth of painting as ultimately algebra, not geometry.[24] This—that is, always working with and through *technē* and the irreducibility of *technē*—is what poets and quantum theorists with a poetic bent do, and how they ultimately find everything, for example, the sublime or quantum mechanics.

I would now like to discuss further features of radical formalization, first, the question of randomness and chance. It is famously invoked at the end of "Shelley Disfigured," where de Man writes: "*The*

*Triumph of Life* warns us that *nothing,* whether deed, word, thought or text, ever happens in relation, positive or negative, to anything that preceded, follows, or exists elsewhere, but only as a random event whose power, like the power of death, is due to the randomness of its occurrence" (*The Rhetoric of Romanticism* 122; emphasis added). This formulation reflects the *nonclassical* concept of chance as correlative to the irreducible lawlessness—singularity—of individual entities, such as random and discontinuous ("quantum") events here invoked. This concept of chance links the thought of earlier figures, such as Kleist and Shelley, to the twentieth-century thinking, mathematical-scientific (specifically in quantum physics) or philosophical, to which de Man's and related nonclassical concepts of chance belong. It is worth, however, recalling the *classical* understanding of chance before defining the *nonclassical* understanding of it.

Classically, chance or, more accurately, the appearance of chance is seen as arising from our insufficient (and perhaps, in practice, unavailable) knowledge of a total configuration of forces and, hence, of understanding a lawful necessity always postulated behind a lawless chance event. If this configuration becomes available, or if it could be made available in principle (it may, again, not ever be available in practice), the chance character of the event would disappear. Chance would reveal itself to be a product of the play of forces that is, in principle, calculable by man, or at least God. In other words, in practice, we have only partially available, incomplete information about chance events, which are nonetheless determined, in principle, by a complete architecture of necessity behind them. This architecture itself may or may not be seen as ever accessible in full, or even partial, measure. The *presupposition* of its existence is, however, essential for and defines the classical view as both causal and realist, for this assumption of the ultimate causal architecture underlying randomness and chance brings classical causality and classical reality together. For example, if we cannot exactly—rather than only in terms of probabilities—predict how the dice will fall, or fully explain why a particular outcome has occurred, it is because the sum total of all the factors responsible is in practice unavailable to us (from a particular movement of a human, or perhaps divine, hand to minute irregularities in the material makeup of the dice themselves). In principle, however, a throw of dice obeys the laws of classical, Newtonian physics (or else chaos theory, which would not, however, change the essence of the point, since chaos theory is classical at bottom). If we knew all such factors, we could predict and explain the outcome exactly by using these laws, which would describe both individual and collective behavior, and (lawfully) correlate them, in accordance with the definition of classical law.

The *nonclassical* understanding of chance, correlative to radical formalization, is fundamentally different. Nonclassical chance is irreducible and irreducibly lawless not only in practice (which may be the case classically as well), but also, and most fundamentally, in principle. There is no knowledge, in practice or in principle, that is or will ever be, or could in principle be, available to us and that would allow us to assume chance to be the product of the imperceptible workings of necessity behind it. Nor, however, can one postulate such a causal/lawful structural necessity as unknowable (to any being, individual or collective, human or even divine), but existing in and by itself outside our engagement with it. This qualification is crucial, since, as just explained, certain forms of the classical understanding of chance allow for or are even defined by the latter assumption. The nonclassical chance is not only unexplainable in practice and in principle, but is also irreducible in practice and in principle. It is *irreducibly* lawless.

We recall that nonclassical formalization or law does not account for individual events (again, understood as phenomenal effects) in the way classical formalization does, thereby also correlating individual and collective configurations they consider. As we have seen, classical formalization is defined by this concept of law. By contrast, it is a law of nonclassical formalization that *individual* events are, generally, not comprehended by its laws or by law in general, certainly not in the way they would be in classical physics. Nonclassical formalization allows for the concept of individuality or discontinuity at the level of the phenomenal effects. Indeed, taken to the limit of the irreducible singularity of the individual, this concept defines nonclassical formalization. At the same time, however, it offers no law that would enable us, in principle (rather than only in practice), to predict with certainty the outcome of individual events or when some of them may occur, or their ultimate nature and emergence (at least only certain, partial aspects of such events). Just about any outcome is possible, anything can happen in any given case, and each case is ultimately unique, singular. In this, the nonclassical world (even that of quantum mechanics) is very much like life, to which—or, one might say with Shelley, to the triumph of which—we must ultimately submit.

This world, however, also contains more order and richer orders than the classical one. Statistical or other (collective) patterns do emerge within it—at the level of phenomenological effects (which is perhaps as much as one can hope for, even classically). Indeed, this emergence of patterns, or that which allows for patterns, is what is truly strange about life, or, again, quantum physics—in view of the irreducible uniqueness of all (rather than only certain) individual events. It also follows that in these circumstances the individual effects involved are in turn reciprocally, if equally enigmatically, affected by this "conspiracy" and, hence, by the collective, even though—this is what is most mysterious and enigmatic—each remains singular and lawless even in these circumstances. Or rather, they would so remain, if one could, in these circumstances, trace them as individual effects. In other words, such lawful collectivities and lawless individualities appear always to be mutually exclusive or, in Bohr's terms, complementary. In the nonclassical world, the irreducibly unknowable coexists with a greater and more multiple knowledge, orders, and so forth. All our accounts, or indeed conceptions, of what gives rise to these orders or these dis-orders or non-orders (they cannot be considered as disorders either) can only be ultimately inadequate allegories, correlative to the formal deformalization of material effects. But then, as de Man argues, this ultimately "algebraic" quality has defined the practice of allegory all along, in part as the practice of reading, reading books or nature, or both, and as each other. In this sense, all allegories may well be the allegories of (epistemologically nonclassical) reading.

And yet, not only possible but very real events—such as, say, those described in Kleist's *Penthesilea* or Shelley's *The Triumph of Life*— leave us no choice, any more than quantum physics leaves physicists a choice here. These events occur and their underlying, or indeed ununderlying, unreality—the lack of any *conceivable* reality underlying them—does not make them any less real, indeed makes them more real, than any (classical) reality we can conceive of. In de Man's terms, any such event manifests (the singularity of) radical material occurrence— "an *occurrence*, which has the materiality of something that actually happens, that actually occurs" ("Kant and Schiller," *AI* 132). I would argue that at stake here is the radical materiality and/as singularity of events, corresponding to nonclassical epistemology. The latter, accordingly, would also disallow one to strictly locate when and where such events actually occur. What actually occurs does occur, but the point or moment itself of this occurrence is indeterminable. It always takes place, in Lucretius's remarkable and remarkably precise phrase, "incerto tempore—incertisque loci" (at an uncertain time and at an uncertain place), and, we may add, at an indeterminate juncture of the efficacious processes of occurrence.[25]

It is, as I have stressed from the outset, crucial that, nonclassically, irreducible lawlessness defines and makes singular all constitutive individual events, including those composing (what is perceived as) ordinary events, rather than only certain absolutely extraordinary events— such as, say, Penthesilea's final encounter with Achilles, the encounter that dismembers his body and Penthesilea's mind and language; Rousseau's encounter with "the shape all light"; or Shelley's dreamlike encounter with Rousseau, in *The Triumph of Life*. Ultimately, every event, specific configuration, or historical trajectory will prove to be unique—irreducibly singular and lawless. Or else each can always be nonclassically reconfigured as composed of certain singular, lawless individual elements, on the one hand, and of certain lawful collectivities on the other; that is, in some situations, lawful individual elements of the classical type may, once refigured nonclassically, always be decomposed into lawless individual constituents. Viewed from this perspective, such elements will no longer be subject to classical law as such but instead will belong to a nonclassical lawful collectivity composed by lawless individual elements. It is worth noting that this decomposition need not be unique, even in quantum physics. From the perspectives centered on lawful collectivities, this lawlessness of the individual may not matter or be perceived at all, since certain patterns, statistical or other, allow us to disregard or make us miss this singularity and lawlessness in the classical, or classical-like fashion. To avoid this, we must, "quantum-mechanically," deconstitute this pattern as classical and complementarily engage both the perspectives—that of lawful collectivities and that of lawless, singular individuality. The classical view, as Blake understood so well, erases particulars as particulars (i.e., ultimate individual constituents of such configurations), either by way of general concepts or by means of ethical, political, and aesthetic practices. Indeed, the present argument as a whole may also be seen as a disfigurative reading or at least an extension of Blake's idea of "minute particulars."

We can now give a more radical and more rigorous meaning to de Man's conclusion in "Shelley Disfigured." "*The Triumph of Life* warns us that, *[ultimately]*, *nothing* [and not only certain things], whether deed, word, thought or text, *ever* [and not only sometimes] happens in relation, positive or negative, to anything that preceded, follows, or exists elsewhere, but only as a random event whose power, like the power of death, is due to the randomness of its occurrence," and hence to the radical, irreducible singularity and discontinuity of this event, and ultimately any individual event or particular historical trajectory. As it makes the allegory irreducible in any representation, phenomenalization, knowledge, and so forth, death, or life-death, becomes a model or, better, allegory, perhaps the allegory, for the structure of *every* event of life. We may indeed define Romanticism in terms of this disassembling magnification or, more accurately (it is, again, not a question of magnifying the small), radicalization of any configuration, classically individual or classically collective, into the irreducibly singular, unique constituents—minute particulars—and the nonclassical reconstitution or reassemblage of such minute particulars (from a necessarily different perspective or set of perspectives) into richly ordered multiplicities. We may, accordingly, also speak of radical organization along with radical lawlessness and singularity. We must, however, keep in mind the very different epistemological status of the nonclassical patterns and laws, the "algebra" and "allegory" of their functioning, as opposed to, one might say, the symbolic "geometries" of classical thought.

This is, then, what such literary texts as Kleist's and Shelley's, or such philosophical texts as Kant's and Hegel's, or Cézanne's paintings, do. They offer us new—efficaciously nonclassical—patterns, orders, or laws, and un-patterning, unordering, and unlawfulness, and new ways in which these relate to each other. Of course, we need to read and understand these texts in great detail in order to study how all this takes place in them. Such texts and such readings also question the philosophical, aesthetic, historical, and other roles and limits of the nonclassical. For, as I said, the latter may ultimately prove to be yet another case of aesthetic (or counteraesthetic) ideology. These complexities are, I think, the main reason why de Man does not close "Shelley Disfigured" with the randomness of death as the final warning of Shelley's poem. Instead he adds the following:

> [The poem] also warns us why and how these events [that is, all events as singularities] *then* have to be reintegrated in a historical and aesthetic system of recuperation that repeats itself regardless of the exposure of its fallacy. This process differs entirely from the recuperative and nihilistic allegories of historicism [or aestheticism]. If it is true and unavoidable that any reading is a monumentalization of sorts, the way in which Rousseau is read and disfigured in *The Triumph of Life* puts Shelley

among the few readers who "guessed whose statue those fragments had composed." Reading as disfiguration, to the very extent that it resists historicism [or aestheticism] turns out to be historically more reliable than the products of historical archeology [or aesthetic ideology]. To monumentalize this observation into a *method* of reading would be to regress from the rigor exhibited by Shelley which is exemplary because it refuses to be generalized into a system. (*The Rhetoric of Romanticism* 122–23; emphasis added)

The last clause must, I think, be read as indicating that Shelley's rigor refuses to be generalized into a system that would not allow for the nongeneralizable. Shelley's poem possesses a great power of generalization and offers us very general aesthetic, historical, and political laws, a whole constitution even. So does Kleist's aesthetic formalization in *Über das Marionettentheater*. In question in both cases, however, are nonclassical organizations of "fragments" and (when possible) the "algebra" and "allegory" of their nonclassical formalization. The latter relates to no underlying pattern ("geometry") of wholeness, and yet (similarly to quantum mechanics) it offers us a better guess as concerns the history or aesthetic (or otherwise cognitive) structure of the configuration in question. In question, again, is only the impossibility of the ultimate knowledge, the knowledge of the ultimate efficacity of the events in question and at bottom of all events. By putting this impossibly into play, however, both a greater richness and a greater reliability of a "guess" become possible as well. But then (which may be the main point of de Man's last sentence) each nonclassical reading may itself remain unique, singular. The lessons of such texts or of their reading or of their grouping together (which apply to de Man's own texts, such as those assembled, in either sense, in *Aesthetic Ideology*) are complicated accordingly. Thus, de Man's essay (via Shelley's poem) and his work in general teach us a lesson of great caution, or indeed issue a stern warning (the word that occurs twice in this passage). The success (or a failure) of any strategy, general (such as methodological) or singular, classical or nonclassical, is never guaranteed, except perhaps that, as the saying goes, "in the long run we are all dead." In other words, ultimately nothing survives, even though in the shorter run (which may be long, even indefinitely long, but is always finite) certain strategies, such as that of Shelley's disfiguration, may be more effective, but even this cannot be certain. These are inevitable consequences, "effects," of the nonclassical efficacity here considered.

In short, the texts in question offer us allegories of nonclassical knowledge, which may also be seen as "reading," and hence the texts in question as "allegories of reading" in this sense as well. By a qualified analogy (considered earlier) with quantum mechanics, such texts may be seen as material signifying "surfaces" in which certain peculiar material effects manifest themselves and make possible certain manifest phenomenological effects. As manifest, these effects may be processed (and the corresponding linguistic clusters read) classically. Some of these effects, however, and, especially, their overall configuration are meaningless, and some of them (certain, to borrow Gasché's phrase, "linguistic atoms") are meaningless otherwise, and remain, or sometimes are *made,* meaningless nonclassically. In a nonclassical reading, all of these effects will be convertible into a nonclassical configuration of singular marks or, again, "linguistic atoms," although in practice this program is difficult to follow through. This is why such texts defy classical reading and resist any reading. This resistance even to reading is ineliminable and defines nonclassical reading or knowledge.[26] Such texts also enact both nonclassical epistemological configurations and their, inevitably allegorical, analytical explorations. They nonclassically and multiallegorically read themselves. Kleist's essay, by its very structure, also enacts the nonclassical grouping of particular texts and is read by de Man as such. It introduces textual particulars/ singularities at all levels, from the "linguistic atoms" of the signifiers to large textual and narrative units, which allegorize each other. In other words, the texts in question allegorize their own reading, which can itself only be allegorical. In the process they offer us allegories of nonclassical reading and, hence, teach us the latter and/as nonclassical knowledge.

De Man, in a nonclassical ensemble of his own *individual* texts, reads these texts as such "allegories of reading," partly classical and partly (and most fundamentally) nonclassical, partly general and partly unique, and so forth. For de Man, nonclassical configurations can only emerge by way of reading, each such reading being, again, unique, rather than in terms of a (independent) conceptual architecture. These readings do contain and enable the latter as well and make it nonclassical. De Man opens his reading of Kleist with a quotation from Schiller:

> I know of no better image of a beautiful society than a well executed English dance, composed of many complicated figures and turns. A

spectator located on the balcony observes an infinite variety of criss-crossing motions which keep decisively but arbitrarily changing directions without ever colliding with each other. Everything has been arranged in such a manner that each dancer has already vacated his position by the time the other arrives. Everything fits so skillfully, yet so spontaneously, that everyone seems to be following his own lead, without ever getting in anyone's way. Such a dance is the perfect *symbol* of one's own individually asserted freedom as well as of one's respect for freedom of the other. (Friedrich Schiller, *Aesthetic Education* 300; *The Rhetoric of Romanticism* 263; emphasis added)[27]

This is, in present terms, a classical and classically "geometrical" description, or at least a description that allows for a classical reading. As such it can be, and is by de Man, contrasted to Kleist's nonclassical "algebraic" allegories (which may also be juxtaposed to Schiller's "symbol" here), which disallow classical readings. Schiller's passage and his related elaborations are considered by de Man both in terms of the aesthetic formalization they offer and as Schiller's points apply to the formal structure of Schiller's text itself. The same strategy will be applied to Kleist's *Über das Marionettentheater,* with an exposure of the nonclassical character of the text and of its self-reading as an outcome. After a complex analysis, de Man arrives at a dance that is very different from the "strictly ballroom" dance of Schiller:

We have traveled some way from the original Schiller quotation to the mechanical dance, which is also a dance of death and mutilation. The violence which existed as a latent background in the story of the ephebe and of the bear now moves into full sight. One must already have felt some resistance to the unproblematic reintegration of the puppet's limbs and articulations, suspended in dead passivity, into the continuity of the dance: "all its members (are) what they should be, dead, mere pendula, and they follow the law of pure gravity." (*The Rhetoric of Romanticism* 288)

The invocation of Newton's law of gravity, the paradigmatic classical physical law, is of much interest and significance in the context of the present essay and in general. Both the question of the classical laws of physics and, hence, the formalization of nature, and how classical such formalization can in fact be are at stake. I cannot pursue these subjects here. I shall, however, return to the question of "falling," physically the defining phenomenon of gravity. In Einstein's general relativity, his theory of gravitation, the fall is merely an aspect of the geometry of a space curved by gravitation. The analysis of this space, however, involves a very complex "algebra" (of the so-called tensor calculus) and the technology of rulers and clocks, which would open yet another chapter in the history of the book of nature, the role of allegory in physics, and the reading of de Man.[28] De Man continues:

> The passage is all the harder to assimilate since it has been preceded by the briskly told story of an English technician able to build such perfect mechanical legs that a mutilated man will be able to dance with them in Schiller-like perfection. "The circle of his motion may be restricted, but as for those available to them, he accomplishes them with an ease, elegance and gracefulness which fills any thinking mind with amazement." One is reminded of the protests of the eyeless philosopher Saunderson in Diderot's *Lettre sur les aveugles* when, to the deistic optimism of the Reverend Holmes, disciple of Newton, Leibniz and Clark, he opposes the sheer monstrosity of his own being, made all the more intolerable by the mathematical perfection of his highly formalized intellect: "Look at me well, Mr. Holmes, I have no eyes. . . . The order (of the universe) is not so perfect that it does not allow, from time to time, for the production of monsters." The dancing invalid of Kleist's story is one more victim in a long series of mutilated bodies that attend on the progress of enlightened self-knowledge, a series that includes Wordsworth's mute country-dwellers and blind city-beggars. The point is not that the dance fails and that Schiller's idyllic description of a graceful but confined freedom is aberrant. Aesthetic education by no means fails; it succeeds all too well, to the point of hiding the violence that makes it possible. (*The Rhetoric of Romanticism* 288–89)

At stake, then, is the possibility of formalization, aesthetic or other, under the condition of the radical, lawless, singularity and deformity—monstrosity—that is quite manifest, materially and phenomenally. Both singularity and law—formalization—and their relationships and conflicts take a very radical form, parallel to the radical disfigurations of Shelley's *The Triumph of Life*. There is also a revealing textual parallel. Here de Man invokes "a long series of mutilated bodies that attend on the progress of enlightened self-knowledge." The essay on Shelley asks about our (according to the present analysis un-Romantic) aesthetic, historical, and other formalization of Romanticism: "For what we have done with the dead Shelley, and with all other dead bodies that appear in Romantic literature—one thinks, among many others, of the 'dead man' that ' 'mid that beauteous scene / Of trees, and hills and waters, bold upright / Rose with his ghastly face . . .' in Wordsworth's *Prelude* (V. 470–72)—is simply to bury them, to bury them in their own texts made into epitaphs and monumental graves" (*The Rhetoric of Romanticism* 121). Thus, the Empedoclean algebra-allegory of the dismemberment of the body, (re)thought or (re)allegorized in "quantum-mechanical" terms, now applies within very broad limits. It can be further correlated with the quantum-mechanical allegories involved in the optics of Shelley's poem: the wave and particle imagery there; the manifest quantum-like discontinuity of events and textual atoms; the divestiture of marks and traces from all architectonics so as also to reveal their inaccessible (material efficacity); the radical material aesthetics; the collapse of realism and causality; the "algebraic" and "allegorical" nature of whatever patterns or forms of order are left to us; and so forth. In other words, the nonclassical features of quantum physics and Shelley's poetic epistemology can be assembled and brought together in reciprocal allegories.[29] De Man's reading does not do this but is in part made possible by these reciprocities, as considered earlier in relation to quantum physics and its nonclassical formalization.

De Man explores the "algebra" of "the mutilated body" at some length in his late essays. The deepest and most significant instance may well be his analysis, considered earlier, of the Kantian architectonics in the third *Critique*. Accordingly, I shall only offer a few supplementary points. In a parallel gesture to his Kleist essay (cited by de Man), de Man invokes Diderot's *Lettre sur les sourds and les muets* in considering the allegorization of the faculties of reason and imagination in terms of both the anthropomorphized dramatic conflict and the sacrificially mutilated body. The invocation has Dionysian overtones and an invocation of the figures of Antigone and Iphigenia (*AI* 86–87). Then, he proceeds, via Kleist and Kant's first *Critique,* to a reading of Kant's architectonics and its self-de-architectonization in the Empedoclean terms of a mutilated body. The conclusion offers extraordinary elaborations on the allegorical algebra of Kant's text. De Man writes: "to the dismemberment of the body *corresponds* a dismemberment of language, as meaning-producing tropes are replaced by the fragmentation of sentences and propositions into discrete words, or the fragmentation of words into syllables or finally letters" (*AI* 89; emphasis added).

One thus encounters the workings of radical materiality, or/as singularity, both in the world and in the text. It would, however, be a mistake to see both as merely (if at all) mirroring or mapping each other, as de Man's usage of *corresponds* here might suggest, but should not. (It is difficult to be certain given the complexities of the concept and the very signifier of "correspondence" in de Man.)[30] Instead, insofar as one wants to or can approach the world by way of a text (or a text by way of reading), the dismemberment or "decoherence" of language—the divergence, ultimately irreducible and uncontrollable, of the meaning of figures, tropes, signifiers, and so forth, indeed of whatever carries meaning in a given text—manifests the irreducible inaccessibility of the world or life through peculiar configurations of material and phenomenological effects. Accordingly, analogously to quantum-mechanical epistemology, the dismembered, decohered language or representation (i.e., the configuration of the corresponding phenomenal effects) does not map or otherwise represent them any more than "coherent" language and representations do, or reading represents a text. However, decoherent representations or allegories appear to be better suited to relate, via the algebra of allegory, to the world and life, or to read the kind of texts in question here. One might say that the radical (material) singularity of individual events of life and the radical inaccessibility of their efficacity find their proper expression or allegory in this circumstance of the dismemberment or decoherence of language and tropes.

Aesthetic formalization as radical formalization and the overall epistemological machinery in question also become, in an antithetical parallel with Schiller's classical text, enacted in Kleist's essay, at the level of figures or tropes. On the one hand, there is a certain "collective" semantic field within which these figures and tropes function and which—that is, a more or less shared meaning or more or less coherent set of meanings—they obey. On the other hand, once rigorously considered individually, or, again, in a certain ultimate decomposition, these figures and tropes can no longer be fully subsumed by such a meaning or a coherent configuration of meanings. Or, in the terms introduced earlier, they begin to decohere. Accordingly, one speaks of (an enactment of) a decoherence of figures and tropes, or of all language, in a nonclassical text, such as Kleist's, or Shelley's, or Kant's, if in the latter case, to some degree, against other forces, conceptual and tropological, of Kant's text.[31] This decoherence or dissemination (in Derrida's correlative sense) defines the functioning of virtually all figures and tropes in these texts. They give the materiality of the signifiers, "linguistic atoms," a formal aesthetic structure or un-structure we encounter in the case of quantum mechanical marks, as considered earlier. Or rather, the materiality of the signifier in de Man's sense is this un-structure, which then requires a very different "algebra" of formalization. De Man writes:

> [W]hen, by the end of the tale, the word *Fall* has been overdetermined in a manner that stretches it from the theological to the dead pendulum of the puppet's limbs to the grammatical declension of nouns and pronouns (what we call, in English, the grammatical *case*), then any composite word that includes *Fall (Beifall, Sündenfall, Rückfall* (#46) or *Einfall)* acquires a disjunctive plurality of meaning.
>
>    C's story of the puppets, for instance, is said to be more than a random improvisation: "die Äusserung schien mir durch die Art, wie er sie vorbrachte, mehr als ein blosser *Einfall.*" As we know from another narrative text of Kleist *["Über die allmähliche Verfertigung der Gedanken beim Reden"],* the memorable tropes that have most success *(Beifall)* occur as mere random improvisation *(Einfall)* at the moment when the author has completely relinquished any control over his meaning and has relapsed *(Zurückfall)* into the extreme *formalization* [emphasis added], the mechanical predictability of grammatical declension *(Fälle).*
>
>    But *Fälle*, of course, also means in German "trap," the trap which is the ultimate textual model of this and of all texts, the trap of an aesthetic education which inevitably confuses dismemberment of language by the power of the letter with the gracefulness of dance. This dance, regardless of whether it occurs as mirror, as imitation, as history, as the fencing match of interpretation, or in the anamorphic transformations of tropes, is the ultimate trap, as unavoidable as it is deadly. (*The Rhetoric of Romanticism* 289–90)

In introducing "the dismemberment of the body" toward the end of "Phenomenality and Materiality in Kant," de Man speaks of the word *Glieder* in Kant as "meaning members in all the senses of the word, as well as, in the compound *Gliedermann*, the puppet of Kleist's Marionettentheater" (*AI* 88). In the same paragraph de Man adds a playful reference to Montaigne's "cheerful" invocation of "Monsieur ma partie," further extending the multilingual decoherence—or again, coherence-decoherence—of tropes by dismembering all members involved in their constitution. "Fall" is a decisive figure and concept in Kleist, including in defining any stability, formal—linguistic or mathematical—or physical, for example, monumental. It is equally decisive for Shelley or Keats (whom de Man discusses in this context in "The Resistance to Theory"), or de Man, who brings all three together, although, interestingly, he does not consider "fall" (or, again, dance), as he could, in Shelley, in the way he does in Kleist or Keats. It would not be possible to consider here the relevant physics, for example, the way gravity bends even light itself (which would bring all three figures and texts together in yet another way). These connections must be relevant to de Man's reading, even if only because from Newton to Einstein and beyond they changed our sense of fall or (they are perhaps ultimately the same) the world. Kleist once said of the arch, another great figural model or allegory: "the arch stands because all the stones want to plunge at the same time," and, I would add, with the preceding analysis in mind, each following its own trajectory. We know, of course, that a random, lawless event, such as an earthquake in Chile, can bring the arch down in any event. What Kleist tells us here, however, is that even the standing arch is a kind of dance in a gravitational field. We all know or assume, naively, that, in dancing, a fall is the least graceful event, or the least graceful—and the least formalizable—form of dance. It is more difficult to realize, as Kleist did looking at dancing marionettes, that dance is perhaps only a graceful form of falling (always commanded by many a gravitational field of our life, or death) and that grace itself is, in each case, a very singular, and very difficult, combination of fall and dance, just as is the grace of Kleist's or Shelley's writing—their dancing pens, without ever falling, except as a form of dance, albeit on thin ice. As Nietzsche tells us, however: "Thin ice is paradise for those who skate with expertise."

**NOTES**

1. The use of the term *concept* requires caution here, especially in applying it to Paul de Man's work. In particular, it may not be possible to "abstract" these concepts from the thought and text of figures involved or indeed to make them "abstract"—free of particularities or even singularities, or, in de Man, (the practice of) reading. Although Jacques Derrida's "assemblages" ("neither terms nor concepts"), such as, most famously, différance, or "concepts" as defined by Gilles Deleuze and Félix Guattari in *What Is Philosophy?*, trans. Hugh Tomlinson and Graham Burchell (New York: Columbia University Press, 1993), offer better models, de Man's practice remains unique in this respect. Andrzej Warminski, "'As the Poets Do It': On the Material Sublime," and J. Hillis Miller, "De Man as Allergen" (both in this volume), and Rodolphe Gasché's *The Wild Card of Reading: On Paul de Man* (Cambridge: Harvard University Press, 1998), offer further guidance.

2. I will not be able to discuss in sufficient detail the secondary literature on de Man and other key authors to be considered here, for example (to give a very incomplete list), by such scholars as Jacques Derrida, Werner Hamacher, Rodolphe Gasché, Carol Jacobs, Peggy Kamuf, J. Hillis Miller, and Andrzej Warminski. By

the time one comes to other figures the list of pertinent commentaries becomes practically interminable, although Jacques Derrida's, Jean-François Lyotard's, and Jean-Luc Nancy's work on Kant is especially significant here, and especially difficult to put aside. I also bypass two related topics—Derrida's analysis of "law," "event," and "singularity," including in his writings on de Man (and commentaries on these topics in Derrida by, among others, Richard Beardsworth, Rodolphe Gasché, and Samuel Weber), and Gilles Deleuze's approach to these subjects (quite different from both that of de Man and that of Derrida). I am also grateful to Jacques Derrida, Rodolphe Gasché, Samuel Weber, and the editors of this volume for helpful discussions.

3. Paul de Man, *Aesthetic Ideology,* ed. Andrzej Warminski (Minneapolis: University of Minnesota Press, 1996), 119–20; hereafter *AI*.

4. The epistemology becomes classical once such exclusion takes place. This point is crucial to Derrida's reading of Kant in "Economimesis" (*Diacritics* 11:3 ([1981]: 3–25).

5. An analogous argument would apply to other pairs of that type, such as the general and the particular, which similarly figure in de Man's work.

6. For Gasché's view of de Man's epistemology, see, especially, *The Wild Card Of Reading* (108–13, 181–83), and of formalism in de Man, the chapter "Apathetic Formalism" (91–113).

7. This point indicates that the rhetoric of allegory in de Man is indeed the rhetoric of temporality. I cannot consider the question of temporality here, although it is crucial in de Man and significant in quantum theory.

8. I am not sure to what degree one can speak of "materiality without matter" in de Man, as Derrida suggests in his "The Typewriter Ribbon: Limited Ink (2)" (in this volume). Some aspects of de Manian "materialism" may be conducive to such a view. However, the material visions of *Aesthetic Ideology,* including that of "the material sublime," as considered by Warminski's in "As the Poets Do It," appear to suggest that a certain economy (inscription) of matter, analogous to the general economy (also in Bataille's sense) of Derrida's *différance* (*Positions,* trans. Alan Bass [Chicago: University of Chicago Press, 1980], 64), is at stake in de Man's work, insofar as this economy relates to the ultimately inaccessible here in question, which makes "matter" yet another ultimately inadequate term and concept, perhaps having less strategic force than "materiality."

9. Bohr appears to apply the term *phenomena* to the material configurations in question themselves rather than to their representation or phenomenalization. His thinking on the subject is, however, quite subtle and is closer to the present understanding, certainly in terms of the epistemology at stake. I have considered this point and Bohr's quantum epistemology overall in a number of previous articles and books, to which I refer here and throughout this discussion, most pertinently, "Techno-Atoms: The Ultimate Constituents of Matter and the Technological Constitution of Phenomena in Quantum Physics," *Tekhnema: Journal of Philosophy and Technology* 5 (1999), and *Complementarity: Anti-epistemology after Bohr and Derrida* (Durham, N.C.: Duke University Press, 1994). For Bohr's own presentation of these ideas, see his essays in *The Philosophical Writings of Niels Bohr,* 3 vols. (Woodbridge, Conn.: Ox Bow Press, 1987), hereafter referred to as *PWNB*.

10. On this point I refer again to *Complementarity* and "Complementarity,

Idealization, and the Limits of Classical Conceptions of Reality," in *Mathematics, Science, and Postclassical Theory,* ed. Barbara H. Smith and Arkady Plotnitsky (Durham, N.C.: Duke University Press, 1997). The connections with relativity emerge in view of the following key aspect of Einstein's theory (whose connections to quantum epistemology were especially significant for Bohr). Rather than being given independently of our instruments of observation, such as rulers and clocks, and, then, represented by means of these instruments, as Newtonian physics assumes, space and time become "products" or effects of instruments. In other words they are products of the technology of observation (and, in more complex ways, of our theories) and indeed represent or embody experimental and theoretical practices.

11. I have considered this subject in "All Shapes of Light: The Quantum Mechanical Shelley," in *Shelley: Poet and Legislator of the World,* ed. Stuart Curran and Betty Bennett (Baltimore: Johns Hopkins University Press, 1995).

12. Paul de Man, "Shelley Disfigured," in *The Rhetoric of Romanticism* (New York: Columbia University Press, 1984), 94.

13. Most immediately, the latter express strict quantitative limits (defined by Planck's constant, $h$) upon any exact simultaneous measurement of both such complementary variables. In Bohr's interpretation, however, the uncertainty relations manifest the impossibility not only of simultaneous measurement but the simultaneous determination or unambiguous definition of both such variables at any point. Once again, not even a single such variable can ever be unambiguously ascribed to quantum objects themselves.

14. This statement cannot be seen as strictly defining allegory, which, as de Man says on the same occasion, is difficult to do (*AI* 51). If, however, there could be one (or any) such definition, the formulation just cited appears to come as close to it as possible. The feature itself indeed appears to characterize the practice of allegory, at least from Dante on. Galileo's project of the mathematical sciences of nature can be seen from this allegorical viewpoint, and connected to Dante, along these lines. (I refer the reader to an article by David Reed and the present author, "Discourse, Mathematics, Demonstration and Science in Galileo's *Discourses concerning Two New Sciences,*" forthcoming in *Configurations.*)

15. The details of quantum-mechanical formalism and of the specific form of algebra (that of the so-called operators in infinite-dimensional Hilbert spaces) are not essential here.

16. Cf. de Man's use of "linguistic terms" in "The Rhetoric of Temporality," in *Blindness and Insight: Essays in the Rhetoric of Contemporary Criticism* (Minneapolis: University of Minnesota Press, 1983), 203; hereafter *BI*.

17. The question of the particular architectonic involved in each case is complex, even though a certain geometrical architectonic is suggested by a kind of (pure) geometrical figure (rather than equation) defining Galileo's or Newton's science. Newton felt obliged to recast his mechanics in (Euclidean) terms of geometry rather than those of calculus in preparing *Principia.*

18. Immanuel Kant, *Critique of Judgement,* trans. J. H. Bernard (New York: Hafner, 1951), 24.

19. As will be seen, the nature of quantum probability is in turn nonclassical, and is not defined, as in classical physics, by, in practice, insufficient information

concerning the systems that, in principle, behave classically. As I have indicated, while quantum theory (at least in Bohr's interpretation) fully conforms to non-classical epistemology, it has its specificity. Accordingly, further qualifications concerning it may be necessary, which, however, would remain consistent with my overall argument here. In particular, in certain idealized cases, some among experimentally measurable quantities and, hence, some *aspects* of individual observable "events" involved can be predicted exactly, that is, with the probability equal to unity, by using the dynamical laws of quantum mechanics, such as Schrödinger's equation. Hence, the prediction of such quantities may be seen as comprehended by these laws. Such predictions, however, would not allow us to define the outcome as an "event" (say, in the way we could in classical physics) even in idealized cases and hence to make overall individual events themselves subject to law. In this sense the conditions of radical formalization would still rigorously apply even in these cases. (I also leave aside for the moment that such predictions can only concern effects of the interaction between quantum objects and measuring instruments, and can never apply to "events" of the quantum world itself.) In general, however, in quantum physics there are always "events" that cannot be comprehended by law even with respect to their partial aspects—in principle, rather than only in practice, which is possible in classical physics as well. Nor, in contrast to classical physics, can we ever be certain concerning the conditions under which an idealization of the type just described would apply, even though we, again, can estimate probabilities when it applies. This is part of the irreducibly statistical character of quantum theory, rather than (as classical statistical physics) its being statistical by virtue of the structural complexity of the systems involved and, hence, our lack of sufficient information concerning them. Quantum theory predicts only correlations between events (and does so exceptionally well), but tells us at best only half a story concerning the correlata themselves. This is of course epistemologically extraordinary, but should not be surprising by this point. As I have indicated, in the field of quantum physics, anything can always happen and nothing is ever fully guaranteed, which, as will be seen, is also the principle of de Man's epistemology.

20. Whether this representation in fact corresponds to any "physical reality" is yet another question, which I shall suspend, since the negative answer would only make the present argument stronger.

21. Werner Heisenberg, "Über quantentheoretische Umdeutung kinematischer und mechanischer Beziehungen," Z. *Phys.* 33 (1925): 879–93.

22. Werner Heisenberg, "The Physical Content of Quantum Kinematics and Mechanics," *Quantum Theory and Measurement,* ed. John A. Wheeler and Wojciech H. Zurek (Princeton, N.J.: Princeton University Press, 1983), 62–84. Heisenberg's German title, significantly, says "anschaulichen" ("actually representable") rather than "physical."

23. It is worth qualifying that my subject here is the relationships between this linguistic understanding and quantum-mechanical epistemology rather than the role of language in quantum mechanics—a related and important (especially in Bohr) but separate subject.

24. One can consider from this perspective Derrida's analysis of Cézanne in *The Truth of Painting,* trans. Geoff Bennington and Ian McLeod (Chicago: University of Chicago Press, 1987).

25. I am indebted to Carlo Rovelli's article "'Incerto Tempore, Incertisque Loci': Can We Compute the Exact Time at Which a Quantum Measurement Happens?" *Foundations of Physics* 28:7 (1998): 1031–43.

26. This is consistent with de Man's argument in "The Resistance to Theory," in *The Resistance to Theory* (Minneapolis: University of Minnesota Press, 1986).

27. Friedrich Schiller, *On the Aesthetic Education of Man, in a Series of Letters,* ed. and trans. Elizabeth M. Wilkinson and L. A. Willoughby (Oxford: Clarendon, 1967), 300; translation modified by de Man.

28. I am also referring to de Man's reading of Keats's *The Fall of Hyperion* in ibid., 16–18. Cf. Cathy Caruth, "The Claim of Reference," in *Critical Encounters: Reference and Responsibility in Deconstructive Writing,* ed. Cathy Caruth and Deborah Esch (New Brunswick, N.J.: Rutgers University Press, 1995).

29. I have addressed this subject in "All Shapes of Light."

30. Cf. Warminski's analysis of de Man's reading of Baudelaire's "Correspondances" in "As the Poets Do It" in this volume. It would also be instructive to follow de Man's earlier approach to "correspondences" of that type in "The Rhetoric of Temporality."

31. Cf. also de Man's analysis of Nietzsche and Rousseau in *Allegories of Reading: Figural Language in Rousseau, Nietzsche, Rilke, and Proust* (New Haven: Yale University Press, 1979), 103–11, 135–60, and "The Epistemology of Metaphor" (in *AI* 34–50).

## II. Deadly Apollo: "Phenomenality," Agency, the Sensorium

# Phenomenality and Materiality in Cézanne


T. J. Clark

*To the memory of Robert Boardingham*


La nature, j'ai voulu la copier, je n'arrivais pas.
**—Cézanne to Maurice Denis, 1906**

The word *materialist* as applied to painting need not mean anything very deep. Painting has always prided itself on being, next to sculpture, the most object-oriented of the arts. A brushy surface is supposed to put the viewer directly in touch with things. Color comes out of a tube into the eye. Most pictures seem happy with their gold frames. Even those painters (like Ingres or Mondrian) who wished to defeat the medium's dumb objectivity took it for granted that the quality was basic and stubborn, and could only very gradually be turned against itself. The gradualness—the slow cunning with surface and framing—is a large part of what makes Ingres's or Mondrian's idealism interesting.

Cézanne is a special case. The words *materialism* or even *positivism* come up in connection with him—they came up from the beginning—but usually shadowed by a sense that his art exemplifies, perhaps even worsens, the slipperiness of both terms. In particular, the question implied by Paul de Man's pairing and contrasting of the concepts "phenomenality" and "materiality" is one writers on Cézanne have posed repeatedly, and never been able to answer to anybody's satisfaction. Is the word *materialist* called for in Cézanne's case because the wedges and commas of color that go to build his pictures are so patiently aligned, "by an infinite variety of devices or turns, . . . with the phenomenality, as knowledge (meaning) or sensory experience, of the signified toward which [they are] directed"?[1] Or do the marks end up proposing another account of matter and sign altogether, in which the

93

grounding of painting practice in the stuff of the world—the world of sensations and experiences—gives way to something darker? Something "suspect and volatile,"[2] maybe fundamentally blind.

I think of a phrase de Man uses to describe what he sees as the key moment (the key impasse) in Kant's analytic of the sublime: "Kant's looking at the world just as one sees it ('wie man ihn sieht')" turns out to open onto a form of "absolute, radical formalism that entertains no notion of reference or semiosis."[3] Is there such a moment in Cézanne? Or compare de Man's verdict on Saussure—on the episode of Saussure's turning back, in something like horror, from his suspicion that Latin poetry was structured around a hidden and arbitrary play of proper names. Scattered anagrams and permutations seemed embedded in the texts he studied, and might turn out to be their main propellants. What was horrible about that suspicion, according to de Man, was the way it called into question Saussure's root assumption as a scientist: that poetic diction, like any other, possessed a "phonic, sensory and phenomenal ground." If it did not, what threatened was a general "undoing of the phenomenality of language, which always entails (since the phenomenal and the noumenal are binary poles within the same system) the undoing of cognition and its replacement by the uncontrollable power of the letter as inscription."[4] Is this a power—for "letter" in the last sentence we would have to substitute something like "brushmark"—Cézanne's painting acknowledges?

Probably yes. Many writers on Cézanne have thought so. The more difficult question is where such an acknowledgment then leaves the version of materialism we started with: that is, Cézanne's dogged attention to sensory fact. Surely the one version does not simply cancel the other. On the contrary, it seems to be a characteristic of Cézanne's best work that in it the two possible vectors of materialism coexist. They intermesh. They stand in peculiar relation to each other, doubting and qualifying each other's truth, but in the end not ironizing or dispersing it. I would say they reinforce it. They *exemplify* the other's account of matter—by showing it at the point it encounters paradox, and begins to follow a contrary logic. This is what gives Cézanne's painting its depth.

I am not suggesting that Cézanne's treatment of these issues—issues of matter and reference, essentially—is much like de Man's in tone. Cézanne can be grave and pungent, but not acerbic. Readers of de Man will have recognized the words *suspect* and *uncontrollable* in the phrases I quoted from him, and known they are typical. *Unreliable* is another favorite. It is true that the terms in de Man are tinged with schoolmaster-ly disappointment. Reference had promised well in the lower forms, but turned out to be a bit of a performer. Cézanne is not severe in this sort of way. He is not inconsolable. Even the admission of defeat in the epi-graph at the beginning of this essay should be read, I am sure, in a flat tone of voice. It is a scientist's verdict. "Il n'y a que la preuve à faire de ce qu'on pense qui présente de sérieux obstacles. Je continue donc mes études" (It is only proving what one thinks that presents real difficulties. So I continue my studies.)[5] This is much more indefatigable—much more late-nineteenth-century—than anything I can imagine de Man coming out with.

Let me start with the picture *Mont Sainte-Victoire Seen from Château Noir*, now in the Edsel and Eleanor Ford House museum (figure 1). The painting was probably done not long before Cézanne died—maybe as late as 1904. Most of the things I shall say about it are true only if lighting conditions are good. In most reproductions the picture's blues are too glossy, or else too grayed and sullen. But given steady north day-light (here I am guessing), or under a reasonably sympathetic mixture of tungsten and neon (which is how the picture was shown to me),[6] color and texture, and color and stroke size, work on each other to aereate—almost levitate—the whole thing. The blues are translucent, floating into and over the answering parallelograms of green. The mountain looks crystalline, made of a substance not quite opaque, not quite diaphanous; natural, obviously, but having many of the charac-teristics—the crumpled look, the piecemeal unevenness—of an object put together by hand.

Color is crucial to this effect, and deeply perplexing. There is a bal-ance of grayed (though often semitransparent) blues, strong greens, pinks, light opaque ochers. The stroke is a choppy, unlovely, inch-to-two-inch rhythm of wedges, hooks, and scrubbed squares. "D'une forme au travail rebelle." It looks almost as if Cézanne was deliberate-ly avoiding the smaller-scale dabs and curlicues of his classic pictures of Mont Sainte-Victoire—the ones in the Courtauld and Phillips collec-tions, for example (figure 2), or the Baltimore Museum quarryface with the mountain looming above (figure 3)—and trying for a hard-edgedness and angularity of touch, carried over from certain aspects of his watercolors. Carried over but also broadened, flattened—I should say, brutalized.

Greens flood the foreground. The farther away from the picture one stands, the more the greens come into their own—because there the middle range of blues can be seen to rest and feed on them, drawing up patch after patch of the wind-blown, slightly unstable color into its steel mesh. A lot of the greens were put on late, over the blues and grays, as if recoiling from their implacability.

Over the left peak of the mountain sits a green "cloud," with even a half-hidden scratching of red in the middle of it. What the cloud does, visually, is pull the mountain back closer to the picture surface. If you screen it out, the green foreground and midground loom too large and close, and the final escarpment goes deep into distance. The cloud lightens the mountain, and does not allow the dark left slope to predominate. Part of the reason most reproductions overdo the picture's sobriety is that they do not give the green cloud its due. In the flesh it is hard to keep your eyes off it.

Yet the color overall is inhuman: the reproductions do not get it completely wrong. It is not the color of rock or foliage, nor a blending of the two. It is crystalline, as I said—not resistant to light, not reflective or refractive. Light seems to go part way through the blues and greens, or get inertly trapped underneath them. The resulting texture is inorganic. The color is at an infinite remove from appetite, foodstuff, or flesh.

This only goes to make the bodily suggestions built into the landscape's midground all the more telling once they present themselves. And surely they do before long. The main edges and declivities of the landscape lend themselves irresistibly to physiognomic reading-in. There are limbs, buttocks, thighs, maybe breasts, a mons veneris with dark pubic hair. A languid body enjoying the sun, prone and glistening, under a plumped-up patterned coverlet. A body of cut glass or faceted flint. An aged face, eyes screwed up against the dazzle.

Richard Wollheim has pointed out that often in Cézanne access to a landscape is partly halted, or at least slowed down, by an empty strip in the foreground, echoing and strengthening the picture's bottom edge.[7] A good example would be the lower four inches or so of *Sea at L'Estaque* (figure 4), which look like the top of a wall, or the ground plane of a terrace on which we are supposed to be standing. Wollheim characteristically wants us to understand this stopping place as an invitation to moderate our eager appropriation of the world beyond: to build a measure of distance and inaccessibility into our dealings with it, and therefore psychological poise: in the end to know it more deeply. Maybe so. But of course the point in making the comparison here (and something of a Wollheim kind could be said of the Phillips and Baltimore versions of the mountain, with their incomplete foreground trees) is to have the *lack* of barrier or entry plane in the Ford picture register as the great fact—the loss of bearings or limits—I think it is. The segment of blue holding the picture's bottom left corner strikes me as the vestige or parody of a structure Cézanne has deliberately denied himself. No poise or slowness here. We go straight to the middle ground; that is, straight to the impossible object—the nonhuman, physiognomically teeming surface "over there where the mountain is," not remote but not nearby. Somewhere a viewer cannot quite place. The painting is naive (but also humane and understanding) about our wish to have that middle distance be *our* world, invested with "the uncontrollable power of the letter." Everything is metaphor in it. Mountains are excuses for bodies. But equally, the picture is certain that it can put a stop to fantasy (to the Unconscious's endless reading-in and gobbling up and multiplication of part-objects) by the singularity of its color and texture. They will make the mountain a mountain again—put it at a determinate distance. Make it an object that in its whole structure and materiality, as opposed to mere accidents of surface, has nothing to do with us and our script.

This is quintessential Cézanne, I think: no doubt harder and fiercer than usual, but with a ferocity and hardness that are always waiting in the wings of the graver, more elaborate structures, ready to transfigure them. (The trees in front of the Baltimore quarryface, for instance, do not ultimately put up much of a fight against the attractions of the wall beyond them: in terms of touch and substance, they are sucked into the general firestorm of yellows.) We are treated in the Ford picture to the spectacle of two kinds of understanding of the material world confronting each other nakedly, with no other mediation than the painter's will. "Les sensations faisant le fond de mon affaire, je crois être impénétrable"[8] (Since what I am doing is grounded in sensations, I believe myself impenetrable). Nietzsche is supposed to have said that art in the late nineteenth century was "the last metaphysical activity within European nihilism."[9] Kurt Badt, who quotes the phrase, wants us to believe it was Cézanne's paintings, particularly ones like that in the Ford House, that Nietzsche had in mind.

What makes the Ford picture a touchstone for me is the way its vision of nature is both the most openly, naively physiognomic that Cézanne ever did, and at the same time the most remote and indifferent to human wishes. The least habitable, the most anthropomorphized. The most like a body, the least like an organism. Dreamlike and machinelike. The two contrary qualities depend on each other, I think: there could not have been such a free flow of desire and analogy if it had not taken place in such an artificial, unplaceable medium: if the landscape body had not also been folded cardboard or hammered foil.

Hence the wedges and right angles and jostling quadrilaterals. Even to call them "handling" is to miss Cézanne's point, I believe: they seem to issue from a pattern book, or a slightly clumsy program or mechanism. No doubt at a distance they are taken up into the rustling, ascending turbulence of the mountainside, and are roughly translatable into rocks and trees; but even as they do this, they never stop marking that ascension as a contrivance, assembled from disparate parts. A landscape is not an organism, they say: the way our mind and eyesight put together the pieces of a mineral and vegetable world and make a scene of them, is not, or need not be, analogous to the way a particular organism's parts are arranged and counterpoised—even if (and this too the painting is full of) landscape painting usually thrives on the idea that it is.

I do not mean to suggest, finally, that the painting's nonhuman texture and color are ominous, or even uncanny. Those qualities would be a comfort, interpretatively speaking: they would put the mountain back into a familiar dialectic of remoteness and sublimity. But that is not where Cézanne has placed it. The nonsublime (but also nonintimate) character of his landscapes is what makes them truly unsettling. Color in the Ford picture has too much lightness and definiteness for it to usher in the notion of infinity. The object-world is uninhabited as opposed to infinite: no more nor less elusive to the mind than the great carpet in the studio, folded ready for its still-life fruit. The colors are not even cold, ultimately. They are warmed just enough by the pinks and ochers. Nonhuman is not the same as hostile and refusing. The mountain may be a machine, but not one of metal or synthetics. Crystalline does not mean *dead*.

The farther I go in describing the two vectors of Cézanne's dealing with the material world, the less sure I am about how they align with one side or the other of de Man's phenomenality/materiality distinction. For a start, the mountain has a nonhuman, mechanical aspect; but that character seems to me the key to its being established by the picture as a separate fact—a phenomenon—existing at an infinite remove from our wish to make metaphors of its features (our attempts to give the mountain a "face"). And where, in any case, are we supposed to place this basic, unstoppable anthropomorphism, in terms of de Man's scheme? To the extent that it converts what it touches into bodies and body parts—and what else does it do? what else do we mean by metaphor?—it is a force that insists on the world's being all one substance, one space chock-full of "experience." That is why the world out there is representable at all. But the Ford picture is a wonderful demonstration of what de Man had most urgently to say about this proceeding: that the moment at which a text or depiction reaches out most irresistibly to a thing seen or experienced is also the moment at which it mobilizes the accidents and duplicities of markmaking most flagrantly, most outlandishly—all in the service of pointing through them, and somehow with them, to another body that is their guarantor. No wonder we can never be sure where materiality ends and phenomenality begins. Each thrives interminably on the other's images and procedures. An account of matter will never be rigorous enough, or vivid enough, to seal itself against the other's metaphorical world.

Right-thinking people (readers of Bourdieu and Jenny Holzer) have lately been taught to hold the category "aesthetic" in suspicion. It has an elitist flavor. It is supposed to usher in a world of universals, at the opposite end of the spectrum from concepts we need if our aim is to grasp the work of art's particularity—concepts like "history," "ideology," and "production." (De Man could be clever and funny about the confidence implied here that "aesthetics" and "history" are notions that have nothing much to do with each other.) I understand what caused the right-thinking suspicions in the first place, and in terms of sheer class gut feelings I still largely share them. The word *Bloomsbury* is my least favorite in the language. But as an approach to the problem of the aesthetic dimension, or impulse, in human affairs, I do not think high-minded disapproval gets us very far. In particular, not very far with pictures.

I need, therefore, to say briefly what is meant by the word *aesthetic* when I use it, and why I think I have to. Let me distinguish between the aesthetic impulse and the aesthetic illusion. The former is simply the urge people feel to make the form of their statements and descriptions embody, fully and adequately, the truth claims, or content, or meaning, of the statements and descriptions in question. This impulse seems to me ineradicable, and ordinary. In every production of a sentence (including even the stodgy ones I am producing now) formal elements of various kinds—intonation, assonance and dissonance, syntactical symmetries or redundancies, rhythm, timbre, pacing—play against the constative or performative sense, enforcing it, staging it, ironizing it, and so on. This is a priori. It has to do with the inherence of thinking and communicating in actual, peculiar stuff, and with that stuff providing irresistible opportunities for persuasion. Form is a great persuader, we think.

In this sense, then, the aesthetic is part of the stuff of life. We should give up feeling it belongs to André Malraux. All the same, I want to keep a place for some suspicion of the category, partly because I think Cézanne (like de Man) may have shared it. There is such a thing as aesthetic illusion. By that I mean the belief, or working assumption, that the aim of the aesthetic impulse can be fulfilled, at least locally, once and for all: that there are moments when form embodies truth in a way unassailable to further challenges, and independent of the mere "positionality" of speakers, describers, and receivers. Philosophy has had many names for this moment, and often staked a great deal (maybe everything) on its existence. "The sensuous [or sensory] appearance of the Idea," was Hegel's formulation. The moment of passage, in other words—of stable or stabilizable relation—between Idea and world, or thinking and sensory appearance. The moment of unity or totality, of a felt adequacy between a statement's form and content: an adequacy which in the end is not dependent on the mere mechanics or materials of the formal process, because the aesthetic moment *is* that at which "form" reveals itself to be the clothing of an intuition (a true ingathering) of the world's order—its manifoldness, its belonging together in difference.

This brings me back to phenomenality, and the key idea in de Man's discussion of it: the "phenomenality of the sign." The phrase does no more than slightly dramatize a deeply held, and commonsensical, assumption about the nature of signs and their power: the belief that signs or statements are part of a world we know through the senses—a world that is always already "experienced," made up of perceptions, intuitions, acts of consciousness—onto which the sign opens, or to which it belongs, or from which it derives its ultimate substance, its actuality as audible and visual stuff. This language—this vocabulary of matter and sense—was threaded through my summary of the aesthetic case. Of course it was. For built into our very idea of the aesthetic moment is the notion of the aesthetic rescuing us from abstraction, or from mere material production of persuasions, and putting the sign back in mind of its "world." The aesthetic is that moment (this is the claim) at which the materiality of the sign is grasped again, and grandly played with, but precisely *as* "phenomenal substance," as part of a world of stuffs and perceptions. It is this tourniquet of the world's substance and the sign's substance, or better still, of the texture and structure of sentences, say, or metaphors, or passages of paint, and the texture and structure of experience—it is this twisting together and analogizing of procedures and intuitions that the aesthetic brings up to the surface of signifying, and lets us do again.

What would it be like for art *not* to do this, or at least to try to? Not like Cézanne, by the looks of it; and maybe not like any artwork we would count as such. Nonetheless, in practice the very twisting and grasping can lead artworks, on occasion, to come to suspect—and to voice or envisage the suspicion—that maybe what they are doing is not analogizing or "realizing" at all. This suspicion is not *anti*aesthetic. But it is a kind of horror, and elation, at what the work of form might be about. I sense that horror and elation in Cézanne.

No doubt the only way I can make the sense seem less bald and ominous is by showing what I mean by it in relation to particular sequences of brushmarks. But before I do that, let me state again what questions seem to me worth asking of pictures with the category "aesthetic" in mind. From the cluster of problems touched on, I take two. First, the notion of the aesthetic as a moment of adequacy of form to content, in which form is revealed as the necessary clothing of an intuition. And second (another way of putting the same point, essentially), the notion of the aesthetic as a moment or dimension of representation in which the phenomenality of the sign is retrieved. The aesthetic—I quote de Man directly in his discussion of Kant's *Critique of Judgment*— "is always based on an adequacy of the mind to its physical object, based on what is referred to . . . as the concrete representation of ideas— *Darstellung der Ideen*."[10] The relation of form to content, in other words, is rooted in a relation of mind to world. The one relation analogizes the other. And the world, as I have been saying, is unthinkable save as a texture and structure of phenomena, of sensate "experiences."

These givens, to repeat, are built deep into the category "aesthetic" as it comes down to us. And of course Cézanne's achievement has been taken as an object lesson of them. "In a picture like 'L'Estaque'"—this is Roger Fry in 1910, discussing a painting now in the Philadelphia Museum of Art (figure 5)—"it is difficult to know whether one admires more the imaginative grasp which has built so clearly for the answering mind the splendid structure of the bay, or the intellectualised sensual power which has given to the shimmering atmosphere so definite a value."[11] I retain from this sentence the phrases "built so clearly for the answering mind" and "intellectualised sensual power." They seem to me the aesthetic in a nutshell; and no doubt Fry meant us to catch the echo of Hegel above all in the latter.

The assumption of adequacy and totality, then, and the assumption of sensuousness, of "imaginative grasp": I am saying the concept "aesthetic" is built around these terms. Now, in the case of Cézanne the first assumption has always been challengeable. Obviously there is a side to Cézanne's art that lends itself to a discourse of unfinish, disparity, and inadequacy of sorts. His pictures are "exactes parfois jusqu'au désarroi"—this is a critic writing as early as 1892.[12] The point is that excitement or bewilderment at Cézanne's disequilibrium (which is another word that crops up in the early responses) has coexisted entirely peacefully with the structure of assumptions about the aesthetic I have outlined so far, and with our taking Cézanne to exemplify them. Disarray and inadequation either function as a kind of brilliant descant to totality in the pictures—"the splendid structure of the bay" and so forth—or they are taken as the form totality assumes in this (modern) instance. Modern experience just is this evenness and disequilibrium in high tension. It looks as though the notion of the aesthetic in Cézanne is only going to be open to radical reworking if the second assumption is put in doubt. That is, if we start from the (obviously uncongenial) supposition that the individual brushmarks in Cézanne do *not* analogize or open onto "sensations" or "phenomena": that they posit a lack or failure of any such opening or analogy; and that they do so precisely in their material individuality as marks—their atomized facticity, their separateness.

I know these are counterintuitive suggestions. ("Counterintuitive" about sums it up.) And I do not want to revel in their disagreeableness. They are disagreeable, and on the face of it preposterous, because they seem to go against the qualities that critics and philosophers have always valued in Cézanne—what looks like vividness and openness to the least incident of seeing. Of course vividness and openness are the right terms. But I want to ask: Out of what circuit of intentions and assumptions, and intentions and assumptions defeated in practice, or altered beyond recognition (including the painter's)—out of what circuit does the vividness come? I am not suggesting, again to state the obvious, that Cézanne's project did not exist under the auspices of nineteenth-century positivism. Of course it did. He was a phenomenal-

Figure 1. Paul Cézanne (French, 1839–1906), *Mont Sainte-Victoire Seen from Château Noir*, circa 1900-1904. Oil on canvas, 65 cm x 81 cm. Copyright Edsel and Eleanor Ford House, Grosse Pointe Shores, Michigan; reprinted by permission.

Figure 2. *Mont Sainte-Victoire with Large Pine,* circa 1886–87. Courtesy of The Phillips Collection, Washington, D.C.

Figure 3. *Mont Sainte-Victoire Seen from Bibémus Quarry,* circa 1897. Courtesy of Baltimore Museum of Art: The Cone Collection, formed by Dr. Claribel Cone and Miss Etta Cone of Baltimore, Maryland.

Figure 4. *Sea at L'Estaque*, circa 1878–83. Courtesy of Musée Picasso, Paris, France.

Figure 5. *Bay at L'Estaque*, circa 1878–83. Courtesy of Philadelphia Museum of Art, the Mr. and Mrs. Carroll S. Tyson Jr. Collection.

Figure 6. *Trees and Houses*, circa 1885. Musée de l'Orangerie, Paris, France. Courtesy of Erich Lessing/Art Resource, New York.

Figure 7. *The Village of Gardanne*, 1885–86. Courtesy of The Brooklyn Museum, Ella C. Woodward and A. T. White Memorial Funds.

Figure 8. *A Pyramid of Skulls*, circa 1898–1900. Private collection.
Courtesy of Erich Lessing/Art Resource, New York.

Figure 9. *Boy with a Skull*, circa 1896–98. Oil on canvas, 51-¼ inches x 38-¼ inches. Barnes Foundation Inv. No. 929, Gallery XIII. Courtesy of Barnes Foundation.

Figure 10. *Woman in Blue*, circa 1900–1906. Courtesy of Hermitage Museum, Saint Petersburg, Russia.

ist through and through—made for Merleau-Ponty to hero-worship. But the question is: What did "existing under the auspices" actually give rise to in his case? A doubting, anxious not-quite-confirmation of that phenomenalism, or its doing to death in particular passages of paint? (Maybe, in the *Large Bathers*, in pictures as a whole?)

I shall ask these questions mainly of *Trees and Houses* (figure 6), a painting in the Walter-Guillaume collection in the Orangerie, done probably in the late 1880s. But before I do, let me head off a possible answer to them. I do not think the one given by Clement Greenberg, interesting as it is, gets us very far.[13] In the painting Cézanne did over the last two decades or so of his life, it is simply not the case, in my experience, that the logic of marks can be plausibly rehearsed in terms of a positivist phenomenalism somehow instinctively adjusted to the "facts" of the picture's, or picture making's, physical limitations. The materialism of Cézanne's markmaking, I want to argue, acknowledges no such phenomenal constraints: it is not surreptitiously or naively structured around *another* phenomenalism, of "flatness," "rectangularity," and so forth. Maybe there is a brief period in Cézanne's career, for three or four years around 1880, when Greenberg's descriptions work. For a while the paintings are put together largely out of nearly identical, same-size-and-direction mosaic dabs. But even here the invocation of "flatness" and "rectangularity" has a willed, self-consuming edge to it. It is hyperbolic and mechanical: more like a parody of simpleminded materialism than an attempt to pursue it. And once the mosaic stroke is abandoned (as it is), it reappears (as it constantly does here and there) always as false certainty—a hopeless, sporadic afterlife of positivism, lost in the imaginary world from which it struggles to get free.

There is some of this in *Trees and Houses*. Part of the lower front wall of the houses, as well as the space between them, is done in upright bricks of light brown and mauve, as if to imply a dusting of undergrowth. The same stroke is tilted to left and right of vertical and repeated in the midground fields, or along the path that cuts through them, and at place after place in the trees—sometimes believably as moss or foliage, sometimes as free-floating notation. I would not deny that these kinds of marks (art historians call them "the constructive stroke") contribute to the painting's overall evenness and delicacy; nor that evenness of attention is the picture's most touching quality. But the regular brushmarks are always on the verge—and sometimes over it—of not "applying" to anything in particular. And they coexist with other sorts of painterly activity, which make their placid atomism look not so much tentative as willfully flimsy.

Look at the tall central house, for example, the one with the red roof. Look in particular at the marks of the brush that are meant to put together, into a single sequence on the flat, the line of the house's red eaves, the faint shadow the eaves cast, and the gentle curve of a branch half-concealing them, seemingly in a plane parallel to the housefront but much nearer to us. Then, focusing on the right-hand side of this already small area, look at the triangle of sunlit wall between the eaves and the branch, and a second branch, maybe sprouting from the other, which seems as though it must be twisting toward us and down, crossing in front of the branch it sprouts from. We have only just started. In the angle of the two branches there is an area of deep blue; it consists, when we look closer, of two broad smears of gray-blue and off-white paint, the first overlapping the thicker branch and the second apparently painted over a line of blue-violet just above it—the line we are invited to take as the twisting branch beginning. The off-white, as I say, seems to override the twisting branch; but the branch fights back. There is a final thin trace of paint—purplish, more cursive and transparent—painted in turn on top of the shadow line. And then on the underside of the thicker branch there is another kind of paintmark, pale orange-brown picked up from the top of the roof and applied more lightly and dryly, putting the thick branch in silhouette. And an oilier brown on the shuttered window just to the right, which half invades the blue-purple of the branch that hides its top edge. And all of this—trying now to move back from the local adjustments and see what they do to the wider pattern of branches and shutters and plaster and tile—all this ferocious involution of markmaking in and around the intersecting branches is constantly altering their relation to the open, more insubstantial, floating "flats" of the other two windows to the left, and the lighter, more discontinuous brown of the branch bisecting the house below. And so on.

I choose to focus on this area of *Trees and Houses* partly because it seized my attention in the Orangerie, and once seen was endlessly absorbing. And also because it strikes me as typical of many other such organizing incidents in Cézanne's work—places where foreground and background come into active, difficult touch, or where a flat screen of forms, drawn across the picture surface almost like a veil, is punctuated by lines or planes that lead back or forward, sometimes violently, into depth. These are the pictures' seams, as it were, and have to be tightly stitched; whereas a lot of the pictures' broader visual material—the approximations of grass and undergrowth here, or the possible signs of foliage—can be left flapping comparatively loose (the looseness also being part of Cézanne's proposal). Edges are difficult. Foreground and background are potentially crutches for the mind, which painting should put in question. There are plenty of paintings—*The Village of Gardanne* in Brooklyn (figure 7) is one—in which the spatial seams of the subject have been left mostly empty, as if the painter had deferred them to a time of totalization that never arrived.

The question I promised to ask of the *Trees and Houses* sequence is what pattern of intention drove it on, and how the balance within it shifted between a wild analogizing of paint and vision (paint and world) and an intimation, in the brushmarks themselves, of their coming to obey a different logic—not a logic of analogy at all. I am not looking for an iconoclastic answer to the question, in which we discover that Fry and Greenberg and Merleau-Ponty got Cézanne all wrong. On the contrary, I want to go with them as far as possible. "Cézanne," said Roger Fry,

> inheriting from the Impressionists the general notion of accepting the purely visual patchwork of appearance, concentrated his imagination so intensely upon certain oppositions of tone and color that he became able to build up and, as it were, re-create form from within; and at the same time that he re-created form he re-created it clothed with color, light, and atmosphere all at once. It is this astonishing synthetic power that amazes me in his work.[14]

I think what we are looking at is a fair example of such concentration and synthesis. And partly—partly—it answers to Fry's line of thought.

Take the violent forward movement of the smaller branch. I interpret the to-and-fro of paintmarks around this movement—the evidence of fine-tuning and improvisation going on right up to the last minute, and maybe in a sense never having been brought to a stop—as Cézanne's trying to see if a play of direction, and one the eye seems not to be able to lay hold of completely, could be made as much part of an uninterrupted paint surface as the plain face of the house next door. I guess Fry's "purely visual patchwork" is helpful here. Putting aspects of the world into the same surface is, for Cézanne, putting them into the eye. But that does not grasp the kind of effort going into the twisted branch. Its being in the eye *is*, as I understand Cézanne's metaphysic, its being over there in space, being "outside" not "inside," taking place at a distance, staying separate and self-sufficient. This is the Cézanne effect. The world has to be pictured as possessed by the eye, indeed "totalized" by it; but always on the basis of exploding or garbled or utterly intractable data—data that speak to the impossibility of synthesis even as they seem to provide the sensuous material for it.

Now I shall make my iconoclastic move; because in the end I wonder whether these *are* the terms in which the sequence of marks we have been looking at makes sense. Do the marks follow, or go on following, a logic of visual sensation? Are *synthesis* and *re-creation* the right words for the force that drives them? Or is the logic they come to pursue generated out of a different set of opportunities and constraints, which sounds in the telling a bit less exalted? Let us call them "formal tactics" as opposed, say, to "imaginative grasp"; material accidents as opposed to phenomenal complexity; ironic, automatic facility, not "intellectualised sensual power." Fanatic display and technical imperiousness, not Fry's "supreme spontaneity, as though he had almost made himself the passive, half-conscious instrument of some directing power."[15] In the realm of the aesthetic, spontaneity is always presented as a ventriloquism of the world, a giving over of will to intuition. But why? Why should the will not be in unflinching charge—a will that is ultimately happy to settle for a world made up of separate and incommensurable realms, each one of sheer procedure? Are not the marks we have been concentrating on procedural with a vengeance? Are not they more like a Nietzsche aphorism than a paragraph of Proust? Fierce, declarative, and self-canceling, not edging toward the truth of consciousness step by qualified step.

These are rhetorical questions, I know. And as usual the answer to them is yes and no. Let me give the answer first in general terms, and then see how it applies to the sequence of brushmarks.

Cézanne's is the most radical project of nineteenth-century positivism. It stakes everything on the possibility of re-creating the structure of experience out of that experience's units. I am sure Fry was right in this basic hypothesis. But the very radicality of the project delivers it: because this painting stakes everything on the notion of the unitary, the immediate, the bare minimum of sensation, the momentary-and-material "ping"; because it goes on and on searching for ways to insist that here, in this dab, is the elementary particle out of which seeing is made; because it fetishizes the singular, it discovers the singular as exactly *not* the form of "experience." It shows us a way of world-making in which the very idea of a "world"—the very idea of totality, or synthesis, or Fry's three-times-repeated word *power*—is not drawn from some prior texture of unit-sensations "out there," and therefore (potentially) "in here." It follows that notions as seemingly basic as foreground and background may no longer apply. (Look back at the sequence of brushmarks in *Trees and Houses* and see if they do.) Maybe not even "inside" and "outside." Nor "experience" and "representation." Nor "now" and "then."

Of course, what we get of this other way of world-making in Cézanne is no more than a glimpse. But "glimpse" in Cézanne exactly does not mean that the other possibility appears momentarily, or just round the edges of things. The glimpse is everywhere (in Cézanne's last two decades). The nonidentity of mark and marked is foundational. I call it a glimpse only because nonidentity of this sort cannot be thematized: it cannot once and for all replace the phenomenalism it shadows. It *shadows* that phenomenalism; it disperses and thins it out; it reveals the logic of the singular and re-creative to have nothing to do with the subject of sensation. If the reader then wants to know what phrase I would put in place of "subject of sensation"—and any one phrase is bound to be overstressed, or overneat—the one I would opt for is "object of the exercise." The logic of the singular and constructive in Cézanne has nothing to do with the subject of sensation but everything to do with the object of the exercise. That formulation will do, as long as we do not allow "object" and "exercise" to collapse back into the familiar modernist version of phenomenalism—the sensuous reality being rediscovered "here," on the surface, where the picture is made. There is no "here" in painting. Picturing is not a physical matter—least of all in Cézanne, in the nine or ten (typical) marks we have been looking at. The exercise called picturing is a deep, notional, physically irretrievable dimension—a dimension of social practice. And the object of the exercise in Cézanne is the object posited by that strange line of thought we call eighteenth- and nineteenth-century materialism—by that project pushed and stressed (as it very often was) to its utopian limits. The world of objects reached after in Cézanne, and laid before us in all its manifoldness, overtness, and pungency, could hardly signal its counterfactual status more clearly. It is a horizon of meaning, an alternative to experience, a contentment with nonidentity. Nobody is saying, least of all me, that such contentment could be lived in more than fitfully.

The thing to recognize about the sequence of brushmarks, then, is that there is no one point within it at which the phenomenal is displaced by the material or "formal." The displacement is there and not there from the start—in the very first mark of the sequence, supposing the terms *first* and *sequence* could ever be stabilized, which they cannot. *There* and *not there* all the way through: from (not-)first to (not-)last. This is the Cézanne effect. Always, at every point, there appears to be reference to the nth degree, fierce and immediate, punctual, acute: but always the reference is haunted by the fact of its precisely being (only) to the nth degree: that is, a touch or a point or a patch in a merely numerical, repetitive, indeed "formal" sequence, of degrees to the nth quantity, with *this* one only *implying* the nth—meaning the final, infinite place in the series, the nonnumerical, nonrepetitive, unpredictable moment at which reference is secured. This is the anxiety, and also the utopian horizon, that drives the fanatic process forward. The next mark might (somehow) not be a mere sign in a sequence but a true figure of things seen—a figure that cancels the marks preceding, or raises them to a different power.

Interminability and hesitation in Cézanne are thus not rooted in an epistemology of addition—though of course some such naive positivism is operative, at the level of ideological framing and self-understanding—but in an (equally naive) Hegelian prevarication, a waiting and hoping for the moment when the addition of units turns quantity into quality. What goes on in practice is not so much addition as erasure: that is what the logic of the nine or ten brushmarks suggests. Or maybe "erasure" is overstressed. Call it "interference," then: a radical (at times a positively melodramatic) interference of each unit with those it is put next to: the hope being, I think, that erasure and interference might save the mere sequence from itself, and make its unities into a world. Cézanne is looking for a mark that would not be a further "one" in a series but a kind of "zero," with the power to replace the dab after dab of addition by connectedness and unity—by a truly magical multiplier effect. There is no such mark, of course. Effects like this are beyond painting's grasp. But the fact that they are is precisely what generates vividness in the sequence of marks that concerns us. The sequence is required to show that no feat of painterly energy, no moment of "supreme spontaneity," no demonstration of "intellectualised sensual power," can ever perform the aesthetic conjuring trick. Vividness, then, is the vividness of defeat. The vividness of procedure. *Even this,* says the painting, cannot secure the phenomenality of the sign. You see why the "even this" had to be so monstrously good.

Therefore, consistency of touch and color, the guarantor of phenomenality in Cézanne, is always in his painting the other face of disequilibrium or overload, or dispersal of energy. Evenness in his work has a forced, or counterfactual, quality. It is a device, not a condition. Put a Cézanne next to a Corot and that is immediately clear.

Writers about Cézanne have often felt called on to answer this question: What, do we think, was going on in the painter's mind during the famous endless minutes he sometimes spent between brushstrokes—the minutes Vollard and others recall so ruefully? Any answer is going to be figurative. I imagine him looking around, as it were, for a rule to follow for the next mark, and hesitating because he wished not to recognize that no such rule existed. He did not want to know that any next mark he might make would be accurate and inaccurate at once; and accurate above all by reason of what he would do to it—the force he would apply to it more than the sight of it in relation to whatever it was of. Marks respond to each other as rhymes, or beats. But it was exactly this being always inside a metric or a rhyme scheme that Cézanne would not accept.

Look at the way any sequence of marks, even one that strikes out for the detail of optical experience as unflinchingly as that in *Trees and Houses,* is overtaken by a logic of contrivance, not perception. Look at the way something so basic and constitutive of painting as "calling on the accidents of process"—which no one in their right mind (certainly not Cézanne) objects to—sets off an unstoppable automatism whereby accidents become what the process is directed to as well as by. And the words we need to describe the process are contingency, performance, and will, not necessity, imagination, and "half-conscious instrumentality." There is a sentence of Roger Fry's that seems to me to sum these things up. I admire it greatly, and find myself disagreeing with it more or less phrase by phrase. "[Cézanne's] composition," he says, "at first sight looks accidental, as though he had sat down before any odd corner of nature and portrayed it; and yet the longer one looks the more satisfactory are the correspondences one discovers, the more certainly felt, beneath its subtlety, is the architectural plan; the more absolute, in spite of their astounding novelty, do we find the color harmonies."[16] Felt certainty, absoluteness, architecture, satisfactory correspondence: whatever the noise on the aesthetic message, says Fry, the message comes over finally loud and clear. The Cézanne I am proposing is one where none of these terms of value applies, and the list of implied contingent negatives—I am precisely not going to name them, I want them to go on unappeasedly haunting Fry's positives—is what gives this painting its strength.

I said I did not want to end with an iconoclastic answer to the Cézanne problem, but inevitably my rhetoric has drifted that way. *Forced* and *automatism* are hard words. I should try to amend their tone. I realize that in putting "accident, performance, and will" in place of "necessity, imagination, and openness" I look to be preaching a heartless creed. But what if I settled for the words "practice, exercise, and object" rather than "spontaneity, experience, and subject"? At least then the ethical balance becomes less clear. We know what violence has been done in the name of the latter triad's brand of organicism. In any case, ultimately I refuse to go along with the notion that an aesthetic of performance and will is, by its nature, less humane and empathetic than one of totality and phenomenon. I do not think it need lead us in Nietzsche's direction. Part of Cézanne's importance to me is that in him it does not.

What other direction, then? Answering this question without falling into bathos involves me saying what I think Cézanne's art is "about"— beyond the trying and failing to stay true to the facts of vision, which is certainly a main part of it. I flinch from doing this, or doing so more explicitly than in my description of the Ford *Mont Sainte-Victoire*, because of course the proposals about the world and our knowledge of it—and I am sure Cézanne's art contains such proposals—are deeply embedded in technique. That is part of the pictures' argument. "Tracking shots are a question of ethics." Yet if I do not at least sketch an answer, I shall have colluded in what seems to me the dreariest remainder of the early-twentieth-century myth of Cézanne: the myth of his paintings' ineffability. Because a picture is not a proposition does not mean that it cannot be translated into one or more. *Technical* and *ineffable* are not cognates.

Let me put side by side the Baltimore *Mont Sainte-Victoire Seen from Bibémus Quarry* (figure 3) and the painting, probably done around the same time, now called *A Pyramid of Skulls* (figure 8). I realize the pairing is tendentious, and that *A Pyramid of Skulls* is exceptional in Cézanne work; equally, when I suggest that we read the one (more typical) painting in light of the other, I am not meaning to elicit some daft detection of a hidden iconography. The two central rocks in the quarry are not disguised skulls, and Mont Sainte-Victoire is neither a skull nor a pyramid. Yet I do want to say that the view from Bibémus is at one level a view from the tomb; the skulls intend, by the simple act of pyramiding, to give form to death and therefore survive it. (The pyramid is the first and last form of the aesthetic illusion.)

You see my problem. Because the embedded propositions in Cézanne are so simple and primordial, and so entirely dependent on the ironic feats of matter—of paint—which breathe life and death back into them, putting them into words is exactly betraying "what they have to say" about material existence; and about where the recognition of the human world as one of accident, device, persuasion, and will might actually lead us. Not necessarily, it seems, into a realm of deep nihilism or contingent power. But certainly into some kind of graveyard or charnelhouse.

> I died for Beauty—but was scarce
> Adjusted in the Tomb
> When One who died for Truth, was lain
> In an adjoining Room—
>
> He questioned softly "Why I failed"?
> "For Beauty", I replied—
> "And I—for Truth—Themself are One—
> We Brethren, are", He said—
>
> And so, as Kinsmen, met a Night—
> We talked between the Rooms—
> Until the Moss had reached our lips—
> And covered up—our names—

We should not need Cézanne's picture *Boy with a Skull* (figure 9) to know that death is this painter's ultimate subject. Any of the later portraits would convince us of that. In all of them costume and posture are rigid, and ineffectual, against the surrounding pressure of the void. Nature, in the landscapes, is Emily Dickinson's Moss. It goes on "deathless progressing to no death," "forever decaying and never to be decayed." Its presence in the folds of *Boy with a Skull*'s stiff tapestry, or on the tablecloth of *Woman in Blue* (figure 10), is no doubt quietly accurate about its normal place and function in Cézanne's bourgeois world. Most people are in no danger of dying for Beauty. Out there, on the other hand, is the mountain above the quarry. Nature reaching our lips. Whether its deathly animation is consoling or enraging is something, I believe, Cézanne's pictures never stop trying to decide.

**NOTES**

This essay owes much to conversations with Fred Orton and Kathryn Tuma. For Orton's de Manian reading of Cézanne and allegory, see Fred Orton, "(Painting) Out of Time," *parallax,* no. 3 (September 1996): 99–112. For Tuma's account of Cézanne and positivism (much more complex and historically responsible than the one gestured toward here), see Kathryn Tuma, "Cézanne, Lucretius and the Late Nineteenth-Century Crisis in Science," Ph.D. dissertation, University of California, Berkeley, 2000.

1. Paul de Man, "Hegel on the Sublime," in *Aesthetic Ideology* (Minneapolis: University of Minnesota Press, 1996), 111.

2. Paul de Man, "The Resistance to Theory," in *The Resistance to Theory* (Minneapolis: University of Minnesota Press, 1986), 10.

3. Paul de Man, "Kant's Materialism," in *Aesthetic Ideology,* 128.

4. Paul de Man, "Hypogram and Inscription," in *Resistance to Theory,* 37.

5. Paul Cézanne to Émile Bernard, September 21, 1906, in Paul Cézanne, *Correspondance* (Paris: Grasset, 1978), 326.

6. My thanks to Maureen Devine and Josephine Shea, head and assistant curators of the Edsel and Eleanor Ford House, for their patience and helpfulness during my visit there.

7. Richard Wollheim, "Cézanne and the Object," paper presented at a conference, "Cézanne and the Aesthetic," National Gallery, London, 1996.

8. Paul Cézanne to his son, October 15, 1906, in Cézanne, *Correspondance,* 332.

9. Quoted in Kurt Badt, *The Art of Cézanne,* trans. Sheila Ogilvie (London: Faber and Faber, 1965), 181.

10. Paul de Man, "Phenomenality and Materiality in Kant," in *Aesthetic Ideology,* 88.

11. Roger Fry, "Art. The Post-Impressionists.—II," *Nation,* December 3, 1910, 402.

12. Georges Lecomte, "L'Impressionisme," *Revue de l'Évolution Sociale* (May 1892): 217. Compare the following sentence, on Cézanne's paintings: "Au temps héroïques du naturalisme, on se plut à exalter l'équilibre incertain de quelques-unes d'entre elles, leur bizarrerie fortuite, comme si l'art pouvait s'accommoder de disproportion et de déséquilibre." Lecomte, at this point anarchist and Symbolist in his sympathies, is presumably relaying the terms of his friend Pissarro's enthusiasm for Cézanne in the 1870s.

13. See for instance, Clement Greenberg, "Cézanne and the Unity of Modern Art," in *Clement Greenberg: The Collected Essays and Criticism,* ed. John O'Brian (Chicago and London: University of Chicago Press, 1986–93), 3:82–91. The following sentences (88) sum up the argument: "No wonder he complained to the day of his death of his inability to 'realize.' The aesthetic effect toward which his means urged was not that which his mind had conceived out of the desire for the organized maximum of an illusion of solidity and depth. Every brushstroke that followed a fictive plane into fictive depth harked back by reason of its abiding, unequivocal

character as a mark made by a brush, to the physical fact of the medium; the shape and placing of that mark recalled the shape and position of the flat rectangle that was the original canvas, now covered with pigments that came from pots and tubes. Cézanne made no bones about the tangibility of the medium: there it was in all its grossness of matter."

14. Fry, "The Post-Impressionists.—II," 402.

15. Ibid.

16. Ibid.

# Political Thrillers: Hitchcock, de Man, and Secret Agency in the "Aesthetic State"

Tom Cohen

The picture opens with a scene at St. Moritz, in Switzerland, because that's where I spent my honeymoon with my wife. From our window I could see the skating rink. And it occurred to me that we might start the picture by showing an ice-skater tracing numbers—eight—six—zero—two—on the rink. An espionage code, of course. But I dropped the idea.
    **—Hitchcock to Truffaut**

(Teresa Wright) remembered, too, the endless series of word games and puns Hitchcock used to keep his cast and crew entertained.
    **—Spoto, *The Dark Side of Genius***

We must bear in mind that, fundamentally, there's no such thing as color; in fact, there's no such thing as face, because until the light hits it, it is nonexistent.
    **—Hitchcock to Truffaut**

There is a road that goes from this notion of *Schein* to the notion of materiality.
    **—de Man, "Kant and Schiller"**

Why the perpetual motif of writing beneath surfaces in Hitchcock—as a tracing visible, perhaps, by certain spy agencies alone, of letters, carved in the ice? In *The 39 Steps,* the secret formula is all letters and numbers; we are barely into *Shadow of a Doubt* when the motifs of telegrams and telepathy interface with a little girl's automaton-like, compulsive reading; Hitchcock, in his first overt cameo in a "talkie" *(Blackmail)* is interrupted reading on a train—that is, interrupted within a stasis within the accelerated semiosis of a cinemallographic shuttle.[1]

If these examples among numerous others indicate, point to something else (and such pointing is the blackmailer Tracey's last, accusatory, yet cutoff gesture—as it will be that still of the Hitchcock opus, the last image of *Family Plot*), they point to an alternate scene of writing that has nothing to do with "pictures of people talking," and everything to do with an attempt to indict, displace, and politically subvert the consumerist logic of mimesis to which the history of film—and for that matter, "film theory"—has been linked.[2] Interestingly, this puts Hitchcock in contact at once with a Benjaminian practice, since the latter's argument that film begins with a divestiture of "aura" is to say that it takes place as the abolition of much of what film theory has striven to restore—logics of identification, primarily, but also Oedipal maps, and the relapse of cultural studies into mimetic codes. This essay will attempt to ask where a rethinking of the trope of "materiality" through the late, and in many ways still unread, work of de Man strikes a strange accord not only with this other Hitchcock—a Hitchcock for whom the mnemonics of *inscription* has a political import that is irreducible—but with a transformation in the very terms of the culture's hermeneutic program: what is called materiality, to be sure, but also the aesthetic, the political, "light," memory, and so on. Hitchcock's work is traversed with secret agents, yet the term itself, as in the film with John Gielgud and Peter Lorre so named, seems for him to question an irreducibly *material* question: that is, in a medium dependent on the projected repetition of old prints and mnemonic inscription—like film or, perhaps, ideology—what kind of reflexive agency can in effect reach into its own prerecordings to intervene in or alter history, which is at once to say the past and virtual futures?

Careful readers of Hitchcock's *Secret Agent*—pointedly evoked in the telescope shot of Mount Rushmore in *North by Northwest*—are not surprised that the turning point of the film is when Gielgud and Lorre end up at a Chocolate Factory in a multilingual Switzerland. The two ineffective and bumbling actants are tracking a "secret agent" tellingly named *Mar*vin (Robert Young), tellingly since Hitchcock's ceaseless recurrence to the syllable *Mar-* in proper names draws attention to an interrogation of *marking* that pervades this work. On the success of this disclosure of identity and reflexive chase, the film's narrative MacGuffin pretends, the outcome of the first world war will hang, which is to say, the fate of Britain, the "world," and so on. In fact, Marvin will have to be stopped on a train headed for Constantinople— that is, a trope for Hitchcock of a certain cognitive realization echoed elsewhere in names such as Conway, or Constance, or Conrad, or Victor Constantine *(Family Plot)*. What is interesting is not that it is the American "college boy"—irritating, mock-flirtatious, and overlooked—who is the deadly agent, but that the Chocolate Factory is itself so misleading. Deafening and machinal, gigantic in its "expressionistic" troping of Lang's *Metropolis,* the conveyor belts that turn out the "chocolate" also purvey letters, notes in code and transliterated script sent out to all the other spies. The deafening machinal Chocolate Factory with its white-coated mutlilingual Swiss attendants and ridiculous gigantic churning wheels is termed the "Spies' Post Office." The deafening roar is not new to the film: it suggests the reduction of all languages to sheer sound, a kind of Benjaminian *reine Sprache,* suggested in the first murder in Langenthal Kirche (Fritz Lang, language), where again a deafening single organ note and then a giant bell obliterate speech and leave us with the close-up shot of an almost deaf ear being shouted into by the linguistically incoherently and obscurely (non)ethnic and many-named General (Lorre).

The chocolate in which spy messages are transposed—like the networks of puns and repetitions sent out across all of Hitchcock's films, binding them in transformative systems of revision and commentary—is not just something sweet and tasty, like the bonbon of film entertainment itself. We know from related "political thrillers" like the first *Man Who Knew Too Much,* that this semiotic and migratory black hole is also allied to an eclipsed sun (the skeet-shoot, the fake Temple of Sun Worshipers which parodies a movie house and is the assassin Abbott's front [again, Lorre]), to excrement,[3] to little black dogs, and again, in *Secret Agent,* to obliterating sound, feet, letters, and so on. The "secret agency" pointed at in the title, in short, is a kind of mnemonic trace, neither living nor dead, void of semantic content yet that on which all switchboard relays or translation or even visibility (reading) seems to rest. As political thrillers go, the job of Gielgud and Lorre seems inverted: Britain will thrive, the course of the world or *world war* will be maintained, official history of a sort will seem secure, if Marvin is kept from Constantinople, if the mnemonic network of marking on which cinema and "life" depend is not disclosed, does not alter the material premises of cognition. "Britain," again, names not the good guys for the early Hitchcock, but a certain hermeneutic state of relapse or effacement with elaborate policial networks, much as Marvin in this scenario might well count for the "knowledge" of a critic such as de Man (or, clearly, Hitchcock). What is momentarily disclosed is the dependency of all programmatized perception on mnemonic pre-recordings, like the record player resting on a toilet in Gielgud's hotel room against the backdrop of which Lorre throws a famous tantrum. And this state has long arms. With Gielgud unable to "act" (in any sense) and Lorre unable to stop acting or acting up (in every sense), and with Marvin speeding on his train (that is, cinema) to Constantinople, it is left for the British spymaster back in London to order an air strike of the train altogether—to brutally intervene in any narrative development and simply command the latter's total derailment by extra-cinematic means. Not surprisingly within this system of specular doubles on which aesthetic politics here resides—yet on which, in turn, the "world" depends—this is done by a letter, by "old man R," as the master agent is alone named (that is, like the "R" of *Rebecca,* insignia of a reclaiming *re*petition that Marvin would break with). The victory of Britain is nothing more or less than the pretended victory of an aesthetic state over a knowledge of technicity identifiable with Hitchcock's posthuman project.

Thus, when Hitchcock repeats certain names and syllabic or even letteral patterns across his films, they appear to link up in active networks or mnemonic constellations—not "thematic" motifs so much as trace-chains confirming alternative modes of sense and perception (which is to say, other techniques of reading) at utter variance with the mimeticism of the film commodity. Such repetitions isolate specific signifiers—individual letters or letteral clusters, sounds (often drawn attention to with the phrase "sounds like" inserted into dialogue), visual "puns," and citations—which may operate like monadic and nomadic switchboards whose proliferation continues to alter the afterlife not only of the film texts themselves (their cumulative interpretive literature, their reception), but the literary or cultural mnemonics that they have become embedded in.[4] This operation, in ways a virtual sabotage for Hitchcock of interiorist and oculist ideology (which is to say mimeticism *tout court*), has the added effect of supplanting, exteriorizing, transposing the very memory reserve that this oeuvre would have been framed by or staged within. Memory, temporality, will have been or come to be altered. This may be the materialistic and technical crossing that many "political" plots in Hitchcock's "thrillers" covertly point to, circle, and defer. Such a focus finds an unexpected parallel with the "late" essays of de Man as well, where there is a heightened focus on the problems of memory, materiality, and intervention. Of course, in making this connection, an obvious link would be Benjamin, whose treatment of cinema parallels his own revision of allegory, on which de Man draws—and which, in fact, de Man may be seen as a penultimate technician or engineer of on the *microtextual, micromnemonic* level. I will suggest that the problem probed by the "late" de Man as a certain *passage, shift,* or *direction* which this project involves—an encounter with a formal aporia as the premise for such a "direction"—is at work in Hitchcock's cinematic project as well, and is purveyed as a political task (and task of translation), one represented by the "villain's" attempted crossing of political borders with a transformative and explosive secret that has the potential to alter the world (say, Mr. Memory—a transparent figure of a certain cinematic project— in *The 39 Steps,* or the micro-film in *North by Northwest*). We will ask, in the process, what sort of politics is practiced here, why this entails an altered definition of the "aesthetic" itself, and why the statist enemy will be identified not with this or that political ideology (fascist, democratic, capitalist) but with an entire regime of cognition, interpretation, and experience governed by what de Man calls, more generally, the "aesthetic state." Such questions frame, of course, the delayed publication of *Aesthetic Ideology*,[5] as well as the event or nonevent posed by its (impossible) reinsertion in today's alien critical registers.

Cinema, for Benjamin, is not a machine of mimetic reproduction so much as technical analogue of mnemonic orders that project and, implicitly, intervene in or alter the perceptual *sensorium* (which is always already hermeneutically programmed and constituted): a virtual mnemotechnic. In "The Work of Art" essay, Benjamin links cinema to a technology associated with an alteration in the entire history and field of perception ("the mode of human sense perception changes with humanity's entire mode of existence" [222], "the entire spectrum of optical, and now also acoustical, perception" [235]): this "constitutes the shock effect of the film. . . . By means of its technical structure, the film has taken the physical shock effect out of the wrappers in which Dadaism had, as it were, kept it inside the moral shock effect" (238). Later again, we hear of "film with its shock effect" (240). Like "allegory," whose covert logic so-called *cinema* parallels in Benjamin, what is called cinema takes a traditional figure associated popularly with a logic of mimesis. It appears as one model in which the projection of inscriptions appears openly phenomenalized by way of a spectral prejection—one dependent on a naturalized technicity of light that countersigns and regenerates metaphoric premises of cognition (the Greek *eidos*). It, cinema, rewrites the dependency of consciousness on the mechanics of memorization, marking "light" itself as a secondary, and not originary, effect. This material problematic informs the plotting of Hitchcock's work from *The Lodger* and *The 39 Steps* through *Spellbound, The Birds, Marnie,* and so on, and it is no surprise that *Family Plot* opens by likening this cinema to a faux séance (for which the medium-ghost will be named "Henry"); that is, precisely that hypnopoetic invocation of the putative dead by a putative "present" not for (mere) entertainment or even *sham* business (both are marked), but to redetermine the past as well as recast the future (Julia Rainbird's lost family progeny and heir, however disastrously). Foremost among these forms of subscripts and *secret* or unread agencies are bands of names and markers that assert the priority and materiality of a pre-letteral function, the prosthesis of the visible itself. Such include, in Hitchcock's oeuvre: the "bar-series" of slashes or syncopated spacing (the best example being the parallel lines of *Spellbound*), the chain of names with the syllable *Mar-* for marring and marking in it (Marnie, Marion, Mark, Martin, Marvin, Margo, and so on).[6] In Hitchcock's so-called political thrillers, what is generally conceived as "home," such as England in the early films, is always also being plotted against by an allegorical stand-in for Hitchcock's work or style. The assassin or saboteur, such as Verloc in *Sabotage* (who runs a movie theater, the Bijou), always also represents a failed project—let us call it, with the punning "con-" series in mind, or the title, *The Man Who Knew Too Much,* an epistemological critique of tropes—which is politically aimed at England, at the economy of the home, the hermeneutic state, and so on. We will call that the "aesthetic *state*"—a de Manian moniker we will return to—for now only noting the political and global historical role given to these plots (in which, before this device was wholly taken over as a device and trivialized, a world-altering event hangs in the balance, such as the start of a "world" war, or the change of a war's outcome).

It is in fact the "villains" who are assaulting this state in the espionage films and they, not the "heroes," who represent the world-altering potential of Hitchcock's *cinemallographic* project—the ability to alter perception, reading, time, the "human." In the terms of the narratives, such projects will always appear defeated by the "aesthetic state," England and its players or detectives. Mr. Memory (so clearly a mnemotechnic allied to cinema, like the "microfilm" in *North by Northwest*) will not quite cross the border in *The 39 Steps,* nor Marvin arrive at Constantinople, and so on. Yet in giving Hitchcock such an itinerary, one presupposes a system of formalized signature-effects that, some-how, allows us to connect Hitchcock not only with what is meant by "allegory" in Benjamin but with what seems to have been implied by the material, the prefigural, the inscriptive in de Man. To suggest that this conjunction might profanely illuminate what links cinema with al-legory—"materialistic historiography" and the very prospect of *historial intervention* in Benjamin through a kind of sabotaging mnemo-technics—is to recall, in a way, that much of "film theory" has con-trived to reinstall what Benjamin saw cinema as (elaborately) terminat-ing or foreclosing; that is, what Benjamin calls *aura,* implying not only tropes of personification, *mimesis,* and identification, but implicitly much that had been attempted by a fetishizing use of "gaze" itself.

If much of "film theory" returns us to humanizing and subjectiviz-ing tropes, under the cover of psychoanalytic codes, it regresses to a pre-Benjaminian—which is to say, in his terms, precinematic—topos.[7] This accords in general with that "relapse" or "regression" that de Man finds in the Schillerian effacement and reinscription of the Kantian event viewed as "a materialism much more radical than what can be conveyed by such terms as 'realism' or 'empiricism'" (*AI* 121). Such appropriating interpretation—more or less systemic—is constitutive in de Man's sense not only of the institutions of "liberal education" but of the aesthetic state. This ghost state without temporal or geographi-cal borders, technically nonexistent, is linked to the institutional grids of mimeticism and historicism, yet it also creates and reconfirms the "human" as a closed interpretive system: such a spectral "state," though it does not exist (like a drug cartel), nonetheless determines referential codes, programs nervous systems and sensoria, enforces hermeneutical programs, and services archival politics that it itself has no means to read or determine. The "aesthetic state" appears struc-tured like Hamlet's Denmark, since its ideological machinery—variant forms of referentialism, pragmatism, empiricism, realism, historicism—contradicts and is designed to efface a materiality of inscription the facticity of which generates antithetically each linguistic evasion. What would be effaced is the programming, the mnemotechnics, so as to af-firm a putative immediacy of the perceived, of facticity, and so on—yet just this mnemotechnic order is what would have to be assaulted, or al-tered, if the prerecordings of historicism, agency, or for that matter the sensorium were to be ex-posed or suspended.

This gives Hitchcock's kaleidoscriptic system of reading—where the site of machinal memory, imprinting, and projection is allied to language—an affiliation to Benjamin's problematic of revolutionary action, to the inadequate metaphoric category (again) of "shock" (the bomb on the bus, say, of *Sabotage*), of which de Man is perhaps unrecognizedly the most patient mnemotechnician. In the latter's sense, the traditional category of the "aesthetic"—marginal, secondary, Schillerian "play"—is here constructed to neutralize the field of inscription, of the event: "as a logical conclusion of that, the concept in Schiller of an aesthetic state . . . would be the political institution resulting from such a conception" (*AI* 150). De Man will link the "humanism" of Schiller (which stands in for the general hermeneutic regression, or relapse, from the material event, from inscription) to that *aesthetic education* which still defines "liberal education" today, the university surely, and the "aesthetic state." The too-familiar scandal, of course, is that what thinks itself liberal, by playing to a hermeneutic evasion (and regression from) the material and nonhuman historical event, the order of inscription that bars a closed model of interiority, perception, semantics, or the "human" as such, constitutes itself as a coercive and exclusionary domain. Pretending to be originary, it represents a relapse (as Schiller to Kant); it values transparency and communication, and the pretense of "liberal humanism," while enforcing a statist system of exclusions and foreclosures deemed the nonhuman:

> That is how the human is defined also. The human is defined as a certain principle of closure which is no longer accessible to rational critical analysis. . . . To say that the human is a principle of closure, and that the ultimate word, the last word, belongs to man, to the human, is to assume a continuity between language and man, is to assume a control of man over language, which in all kinds of ways is exceedingly problematic. (*AI* 151)

The "aesthetic state"—and recall here the root of the term in the Greek *aisthanumai,* for perception, where the senses are programmed—exiles the "aesthetic" as mere play, neutralizing dialectical forces, occluding the site of inscription or materiality: "Play means, first of all, *Spielraum,* the play, the space that you need in order to prevent the dialectical encounter from taking place" (*AI* 151). It reminds us that the "materiality" of the terrestrial, today, is approaching numerous historical bottlenecks or aporias on the outcome of which the relatively short trajectory of the "human" may be determined. Dismantling the "aesthetic state" perhaps extends beyond the MacGuffinesque logics attributed to "capital" today, where much Marxian language is still rooted in the ontological-referential epistemologies that the "aesthetic state" ordains. Accordingly, perhaps the most irreducible agent in Hitchcock's signature-systems, the *bar-series,* a corrolary to what Benjamin calls *"reine Sprache"* or de Man aesthetic formalization, appears a tool of disinscription, transforming *allegory* itself, disrupting every mimetic logic and the sensoria as such, deregulating temporality, however ghostly and officially nonexistent. In the manner of Benjamin's *The Arcades Project,* in which the word *Konvolut* names a type of folio, the anamorphic unfolding of sample or minimal texts, one may interrogate de Man's relation to Benjamin around the problematic of "cinema," then proceed to where this interfaces with Hitchcock's aesthetico-political or epistemo-political marking system. Each suspends historial trace-chains. As in Benjamin's *Theses,* the "enemy" linked even to fascism is an epistemo-critical regime of reference, of archivization: mimeticism or mimetic historicism. In addition, a reconfiguration of anteriority, of inscription—which is also to say the human, perception, and the material—appears linked to the prospect of a certain *passage,* on which alternative pasts and futures hinge. When de Man speaks of an "irreversible" direction or passage to a theorization that depends on no individual—"there is a road that goes from this notion of *Schein* to the notion of materiality" (*AI* 152), "there is a single-directed movement" (*AI* 133), *"pass* from that conception of language to *another* conception of language" (*AI* 132), "the *passage* from trope . . . to the performative" (*AI* 132)—I will suggest that he has a particular direction in mind, what Hitchcock calls "north by northwest."

I

There is a persistent interaction with, and frank attempt to cast off, Benjamin in the "late" de Man—often covert, as when the term *aura* recurs, or in direct evocations of Baudelaire and the logics of a self-destroying concept of allegory, but also in the plain address of Benjamin's "translation" essay in the only piece devoted to this precursor.[8] The entanglement reverts to the site where a certain invocation of materiality is conceived as mnemonic trace, from which in turn the phenomenalization of the sign configured as the "aesthetic" (perception or the sensorium) appears forgetfully generated. De Man dismisses the tropological gestures of his nonprecursor, precipitating an inversion: whereas it is Benjamin who will be generally perceived as tropologically open to history (while, in fact, warring with its mimetic-political premise incessantly), it is de Man who practically engages the problem of disinscription, exploring the mnemotechnic use of "materialistic" that Benjamin relies on more and more. De Man insinuates a spectral passage that attends this precession of aura, personification, or trope—it is a passage not from one intellectual system to another, but from a closed system of transformative if endless substitution allied to trope (eliciting Heidegger's identification of metaphor with metaphysics), toward a(n) (a)materiality inferred to be protogrammatic, allo-"human," mnemotechnic. What Derrida calls a "materiality without matter," it cannot be mapped referentially. There is "the entire transformational system of tropes" (*AI* 114) that sustains representation or mimetic ideologies, and there (already) is a "movement" that tries to locate itself in different indices—an interruption of "movement" as though by itself, like Hitchcock interrupted reading on a train—as if from trope to inscription, from representation to what precedes apostrophe or prosopopeia (and we will return to the problematic of *face* in Hitchcock), or in Hegel "from the aesthetic theory of the sublime to the political world of the law" (*AI* 115). It is the putative movement in or through the structure of an aporia, yet this prospect de Man appears not only to wager but to call "irreversible."[9] In Benjamin, the misleading figure of *reine Sprache*, "pure language" that is the sheer formalization of all (a)material elements generating linguistic memory, transformation, or effect, will emerge as a site by which an act of (literal) translation precipitates transvaluation.

Why is Hitchcock's cinematic project connected, then, not only to (frustrated) scenes of border crossing—like the end of *North by Northwest*—but to epistemo-political subversion?

Eduardo Cadava, when commenting on the collusion in Benjamin of the snapshot with Benjamin's trope of shock (or mnemonic intervention), reminds us of a "convergence of photography and history, a convergence Benjamin often locates within the historiographical event," as well as of a "secret rapport between photography and philosophy."[10] It is in examining the purportedly sublime fiat lux in the Old Testament in Hegel's example that de Man questions what "light" itself functions as: "'Light' names the necessary phenomenality of any positing *(setzen)*" (*AI* 113). Like the *eidos* ("The idea appears only as a written inscription" [110]), "light" conjures a phenomenality that is the displaced effect of signification ("the phenomenalization of the sign" [111]). Light, the aftereffect of a pulsion of shadows that demarcate, like measure or the bar-series, is stripped of its paternal and solar promise. It is the effect of a certain *technē*. *Light,* already, differently, undoes the mimetic ideology—politically compromised through and through—which is built upon the ideology of "light" as its epistemological and metaphorical premise.[11] At times in Hitchcock this appears as overt parody of the solar itself, which too is preceded by this parallel bar effect: the assassin Abbott in the first *Man Who Knew Too Much* takes as his front the false Temple of Sun Worshipers—at which the paying audience, so to speak, worships—or the shot in *To Catch a Thief* of "mother" putting out a cigarette in a sunny-side-up egg.[12] "Light," in the domain of what pre-cedes the premise of perception or face, *like a series of bars or aural intervals,* already implies a project of translation before and outside aura, the human, that is itself proto-linguistic, an effect of *reine Sprache* before vision or any eye itself.[13] This dispossession of "light"—which appears nonoriginary and itself a kind of marking effect—undoes, in its path, not only that logic which centralizes human cognition in an imaginary and naturalized *sight* but the metaphoric thread against which the promise of (the) "Enlightenment" rests. Again, this time on Kant, de Man speaks of a movement from representation to something else, "a passage . . . a shift from a tropological to a different mode of language" (89), from "the phenomenality of the aesthetic . . . to the pure materiality of *Augenschein,* of aesthetic vision" (88). This site, at which Benjamin too locates the possibility of epistemo-political intervention, is a *translational* site attendant from the first in Hitchcock's project. It is not incidental that all those scenes in the early spy thrillers occur in an Alpine setting, in the European Babel where English, French, Italian, and German conflict and overlap as sheer sound (as in the *Secret Agent* scene in the Langenthal church), mutingly regressing to marks and inscriptions. How does the fact, however, that Hitchcock knows this—*knows too much,* in fact—alter the politics of his text?

## II

If de Man burrows into a technical zone of mnemonic intervention—of inscription and disinscription—which Benjamin metaphorizes under the rubric of Marxian and "theological" tropes, it is at a price. Of course, Benjamin all but drops the word *allegory* following the *Trauerspiel.* For him, it is obvious, the term cannot undergo the translation it names and performs intact, cannot bear and contract the fundamental *alteration* in the signifying structure of anteriority, in the mnemonic sensorium, that it contrives to name under a literary-

historical figure that, traditionally, like cinema, was supposed to up-
hold the precise mimetic or representational system under assault. In
Benjamin's sense, allegory presumes a reflexive operation upon itself
within a linguistico-epistemological structure. In Hitchcock, this formalization and reflexive marking refines itself into the effects of a
*signature-system in general,* whose most economic and nonhuman
avatar is the bar-series. Here is how Rothman first identified this marking, talking about a shot in *The Lodger*:

> The view is through the bars of the bannister, and the frame is dominat-
> ed by the bars in the foreground. I call this pattern of parallel vertical
> lines Hitchcock's / / / / sign. It recurs at significant junctures in every one
> of his films. At one level, the / / / / serves as Hitchcock's signature: it is
> his mark on the frame, akin to his ritual cameo appearances. At another
> level, it signifies the confinement of the camera's subject; we might say
> that it stands for the barrier of the screen itself.[14]

As a performative, this bizarre series appears like the knocking beneath the table at a séance, or like (a)rhythm, measure *(metron)* as
such, at one moment morphing into a precession of "light," seriality
(as in the Avenger's murders in *The Lodger*), spacing, (a)materiality, at
another citing repetition or sequential narration. Virus-like, it roams
textual surfaces, and may even appear ciphered by letteral names like
*Lil,* or turn up in words ("ill"), proper names (Judy *Bar*ton, *Bar*low
Creek), and so on. What de Man posits in "The Rhetoric of Temporality" as an impacting of sign on sign in dedefining "allegory" is described, in Benjamin, as a *negating* power of this operation at the very
site of (dis)inscription. It partakes of a reflexive shift that Benjamin
calls, in the translation essay, "to turn the symbolizing into the symbolized." As Benjamin elaborates it in the *Trauerspiel*: "(Allegory)
means precisely the *non-existence* of what it (re)presents [Und zwar
bedeutet es genau das Nichtsein dessen, was es vorstellt]."[15] This leads
to what is finally called "materialistic historiography." Something
emerges here which de Man calls inevitable and irreversible: "then
certain linguistic elements will remain which the concept of trope cannot reach, and which then can be, for example—though there are
other possibilities—performative. That process . . . is irreversible. That
goes in that direction and you cannot get back from the one to the one
before."[16]

Nonetheless, he allows his attraction to the theoreme of "modernism" to interfere with the unpacking of allegory, which he sees as

a reflexive and still referential function, supplanting for an abstract content an account of the work's own mode of production. He stops short of the implied "negation" that Benjamin names as the essence of allegory.[17] We have to restore to Benjaminian allegory the interventionist agency of "shock," in which that site of production can itself be re-ordered, altered, anteriority reengineered, out of which future "presents" stand to be otherwise (re)produced. Allegory, where or if it exists, would already be dangerous as "an other conception of language," in its performativity, in which not only sensoria but temporality is engaged otherwise—like a silent warplane formula that Mr. Memory would pass out of the "aesthetic state," sheer exteriority, unreadable letters and numbers.

If de Man will be dependent on a term, similarly to *materiality,* whose power to reinscribe itself in a flat literary-historical tradition he perhaps underestimates (allegory), he compels it to self-destruct, to turn its negative power on itself beyond the point where Benjamin abandons it or changes horses. The subject of allegory, it turns out, will be called a depersonalized grammar. It disinvests successive subjects, voids personification, precedes prosopopeia. At times, this will itself be viewed as a (mock epochal) shift in the installation of a (mock new) signifying order, that is, as the debris of a certain historial event: "Language as symbol is replaced by a new linguistic model, closer to that of the sign and of trope, yet distinct from both in a way that allows for a concatenation of semiotic and tropological features" (*AI* 116). The banality of this sublime implies the destruction of all models of interiority, including the very trope of the sublime: "The spatial metaphor of exteriority *(Aüßerlichkeit)* is not adequate to describe the knowledge that follows from the experience of the sublime. The sublime, it turns out, is self-destroying in a manner without precedent" (116). In a characterization that has general application, it is said of Hegel that "[a]llegory functions . . . like the defective cornerstone of the entire system" (104). Moreover, it first absorbs the very site of personification (or aura) and interiority:

> Allegory . . . is primarily a personification. . . . But this I, which is the subject of allegory, is oddly constructed. Since it has to be devoid of any individuality or human specificity, it has to be as general as can be, so much so that it can be called a "grammatical subject." Allegories are allegories of the most distinctively linguistic (as opposed to phenomenal) of categories, namely, grammar. (104)

As emerges in the essay on Pascal, de Man's invocation of allegory at the price of its inapplicability performs a double gesture—at once defining its pragmatic or material operation outside of any mere utility (which is renounced): "To say then, as we are actually saying, that allegory (as sequential narration) is the trope of irony (as the one is the trope of zero) is to say something that is true enough but not intelligible, which also implies that it cannot be put to work as a device of textual analysis" (61). No *use* then?

This problem takes on a different political import within an early British film of Hitchcock in which a persistent war on an installed mimetic regime or "aesthetic state" (then called "England") is mobilized as a "political thriller"—*Sabotage*. Here the target of Verloc's sabotage is at one point called the "center of the world" (in London, Picadilly). His front as a spy, however, is running a film house: cinema, in its prefigural logic, is the locus of this politicized assault on the sensorium, light, memory, the animal (we will see), and "Britain." Where "allegory" appears in Benjamin not a mimetic genre but rather a *technē* of historial intervention, the term photo-*graphesis* suggests a graphics precedent to the eye, or "light" itself. This is the site where film is marked, banally enough, as an endlessly reprojected imprint by an artificial light. One might speak of an *allographics* or *cinemallographics* that posits, echoed as the MacGuffin of the plot, the debris of an engineered interaction in which anteriority is exposed as prosthetic and stands to be transformed (one point of *Vertigo*). Hitchcock's politics is not one of antithetical sides, between us and them, Britain and its (often unnamed) threats, America and its enemies, the "home" and its imaginary others *(Shadow of a Doubt, Psycho)*. Hitchcock's politics—and the great wars, hot and cold, run throughout his films—does not partake of the specular or fratricidal system of the enemy other, it is not left or right as such, it is already pre– and post–Cold War, regardless. *Saboteur* shows American industrialists as Nazis, the would-be propaganda short *L'Aventure Malgache* displays French racism and colonialism on Madagascar as parallel to the German. "Fascism" appears itself located not in a historical-political movement but in an epistemo-critical model and programming, Benjamin's "historicism," foundation of the "aesthetic state," the accord between liberal humanism and that mimetic ideology which "film" had been forgetfully made as if to itself police (the photograph as reproduction).[18]

The exteriority of inscription that de Man associates with the mnemonic trace plays a particularly grammatical role in Hitchcock. The "bar-series" that Rothman identified at once pursues and is pursued as the riddle and faux cause of a general amnesia in *Spellbound*—in relation to which the exemplary subject, Gregory Peck here, appears a *cipher* or identityless zero or null figure. This complex at once marks and precedes (or even disowns) the pretext of (fratricidal) murder. The "spell" that would as if be broken by this pursuit, or that fails to be broken, is simultaneously that of a general hermeneutic regime (here, Green Manors, or "psychoanalysis" ostensibly), and inversely *spelling* itself, which demands sequence and grammar—which the "bar-series" virtually precedes as a marking from which all visibility proceeds (and sound, when that series is converted into sequential knocking). What de Man calls *exteriority* is irreducible in Hitchcock (and sometimes remarked in mocking "exit" signs). Among other things, a machinal logic of inscription bars any return to interiority, subjectivity, aura—knowing that the hermeneutic impulses of the audience will, in a pre-scripted "relapse," precisely seek to impose such humanizing, closed systems on the text. As a marking motif that constructs, precedes, and suspends visibility, light, or even sequence, the bar-series appears affiliated with all agency, any intervention or disinscription—that is, the premises of semiosis or "perception." Without any mimetic function, it nonetheless guarantees the *possibility* of disinscription and reinscription—like the trope of *reine Sprache,* which seems aurally evoked (and woven into the plot) in the "Babel" scenes where simultaneous spoken languages appear as sheer desemanticized sound in the first *Man Who Knew Too Much, The Lady Vanishes,* or *Secret Agent.* It is not accidental that, in *The Lodger,* face has so much difficulty coming into being. The "Avenger's" face is swathed, and when it struggles to emerge it has no individual focus, occurring first in relation to the relays of information, and more specifically to *typography,* the giant news presses and on the box face on the back of a news truck, or else it appears multiple, faces morphing into one another, linked to the telecommunications of the wireless. This allographematic effect which subtends all imagery is also capable of dissolving any mimetic pretense into the play of lines, alternation, shadow, and from its fiat non-lux Hitchcock's cinemallography derives its usurpative (non)authority (and nonauteuriality). It mutes and assumes as banal and instantaneous everything Benjamin would dramatize as "shock." The *cinemallographic effect* also registers a(n) (a)materiality precedent to any anthropomorphisms—as in the slashing movements of "mother's" knife. In de Man's terms, the bar-series stands not only as the remnant of a marker that precedes "light" and constitutes a devastation in advance of any aura—like the opening blackout of *Sabotage*. It is prehistorial. In the rendition of Mr. Memory in *The 39 Steps* as a music hall performer evocative of the muse Mnemosyne, Hitchcock not only allies his cinemallographics to the earliest "epical" tradition of poetics, but exposes the latter as itself forgetfully premised on the sort of mechanical inscriptions it is openly theorizing—the secret memorized formula that would be smuggled across the borders, there threatening to be turned against the state, cites in advance the micro-*film* of *North by Northwest*.

Interestingly, when Jameson attempts to retheorize "allegory" with the Benjaminian legacy in mind, his example is Hitchcock ("Spatial Systems in *North by Northwest*"). And it is specifically when he returns to the bar-series effect he puzzled over inconclusively when earlier reviewing Rothman's book.[19] Attempting to reclaim Benjamin's evisceration of the *auratic*, Jameson openly aims at "doing away with consciousness, 'character', and the anthropomorphic."[20] It would, that is, empty out the mimetic "contents" of auteurist interpretation *tout court*:

> But [the pine wood scene] is not the only feature of the empty-field sequence which 'rhymes' with scenes and spaces elsewhere in the film. We must also note the peculiar inscriptions, here, which streak both versions of the empty surface of space—the expanse of the sky fully as much as the expanse of the empty land below. Both are furrowed with a set of parallel lines that is not without some distant affinity with the 'trauma' of *Spellbound*: the fateful ski tracks in the snow, reproduced by Gregory Peck's fork upon the white linen of the dining-table. The plane leaves its ephemeral traces on the sky fully as much as the empty fields retain the serrated grooves of tractor and plow. (64)

Something here precedes and dispossesses even what might be called the materiality of earth itself with what amounts to a marking system, even as it precedes face, or the giant faces of Mount Rushmore. Here—but what "here" or America is at stake, what political borders or state?—an allographical trajectory bars any strategy of interiorization:

> Here, far more abstractly, we confront the same grid of parallel lines, systematically carved into the rock surface like a strange Mayan pattern. Again, what is confirmed by this pattern, and scored into the space of the scene, is the primacy of surface itself: the earth as a surface upon which

the ant-like characters move and agitate, the sky as surface from which intermittently a mobile and deadly technological mechanism dips; and here finally the upending of the surface into the vertical monument, prodigious *bas-relief* which has no inside and cannot be penetrated. (64)

Jameson uses this bar-series to blast one's way out of the auratic and auteurial tradition—which has largely defined film theory and Hitchcock commentary. Yet this precedes not only face itself, it appears, but *earth*. If, for Benjamin, *cinema* can simulate that machine of inscription out of which the sensorium appears projected, Jameson would exceed the "modernist" conception of allegory as an "autoreflexive" model that merely accounts for its own conditions of historical production (or consumption), which is to say, one that is still mimetically defined. Yet here the most mimetic of media—departing from the photograph—seems undone by a marked writing that precedes figuration, and the referential ideology of the state. Hitchcock's "political" thriller, again, has a decidedly epistemo-aesthetic determination. It is set against the "aesthetic state" as a doomed version of the prerecordings— what the myriad black-flecks of birds attack in hitting the schoolhouse, place of imprinting, just as the children form a zombie chorus reciting memorized lines.[21] Moreover, to address this passage or translation effectively—which does not so much move from the "human" to some other, since the human, as a closed system or phantasm, as something put in place and enforced as a kind of hermeneutic *relapse,* never was the case—one must be poised between the two positions, in transit, "equally poised" but irreversibly: "So it is not a return to the notion of trope and to the notion of cognition; it is equally balanced between both, and equally poised between both, and as such is not a reversal, it's a relapse. And a relapse in that sense is not the same" (133). We might say that the site of the relapse is the mimetic image of the narrative, every logic of knowingly solicited identification or gestural commodity, the MacGuffin, while the *other* interrupts that constructed narrative like the Waltzing Couples descending into *Shadow of a Doubt*—the order of mechanical memory, inscription, (a)materiality, projection evinced in the formalized dance of markers and choreographed signature-effects, parabases and letteral or preletteral repetitions, a machinal *prostheses of the visible that is itself marked, "allegorized" in every narrative MacGuffin.* In the opening of *The 39 Steps,* another precursor text to this, the neon letters spell out M-U-S-I on the way to "Music Hall." Here letters are seen as points of phenomenalization, or neon light, en route to the theorization of "memory" as a machinal Mnemonsyne whose secret "formula" will finally be disclosed to us as unintelligible letters and numbers—as if to say, as the marking system that precedes all visibility on Hitchcock's screen. This, much as, in the credits to *Vertigo*, the Möbius-like graphics pre-inhabit the eye, seems implanted from the (speaking) lips as the shot tracks up the blonde's face, and a *woman*'s eye at that—in preemptive contradiction of everything stored in a mock archive of the "male gaze" alone.[22]

## III

Hitchcock tells Truffaut: "We must bear in mind that, fundamentally, there's no such thing as color; in fact, there's no such thing as face, because until the light hits it, it is nonexistent." Does this (a)*materiality*, which precedes light and face, leave *earth* intact? In *Sabotage* Hitchcock links Verloc's fantasy of a time bomb exploding in Picadilly (the "center of the world")—a bomb later, again, associated with film canisters, and the film title, *Bartholomew the Strangler*—to a tank of premammalian fish at the zoo that, we hear a passerby note, includes females that can change their gender. The viral import of a nonhuman semiosis that seems registered by the haunted bar-series, this sheer (a)materiality, recalls Benjamin *Thesis XVIII*, where "the history of organic life on earth" is invoked to situate "the paltry fifty millennia of homo sapiens" as "something like two seconds at the close of a twenty-four-hour day," civilized mankind "one fifth of the last second of the last hour." Like the steak knife turned on Verloc, which makes of him meat too, or the Disney animation in that film of bird-humans (*Who Killed Cock Robin?*), this invocation of "natural" time displaces the "human"—which de Man identifies as in fact nonexistent: "there is, in a very radical sense, no such thing as the human."[23] The core myth of the aesthetic state determines the nonhuman as material or economic reserve, as slave, as means of consumption. This state perhaps does not exist but is entirely coercive in its effects, and linguistic controls (the professor in *North by Northwest* won't identify his agency as CIA or FBI except to reference letteration: "We're all in the same alphabet soup"). It keeps secrets, moreover, such as that about the nonexistence of the "human." What can be assumed, perhaps, is that the idea of *agency* itself, indeed, of secret agency (as with the spies post office in the film *Secret Agent*), is linked by Hitchcock to this "alphabet soup" of letteral and preletteral markers, of numbers and signature-effects that dispossess any recuperative metaphorics of the visual, the "gaze," and so on: the agency sought acts, performs if it does, in the domain of the prefigural, as an altering of hieroglyphics, monumental faces.

Hitchcock's Cold War America never names its *other* as the Soviet Union, the unnamed place across a border at the end(s) of the Earth where Van Damm would go with his *micro*-film (that is, Hitchcock's cinemallographic project). So ironized is the setup that it is difficult indeed to see Van Damm as some sort of courier, a Moses figure by default marking the "passage" de Man theorizes.[24] This "America," which presents (and precedes) the patriarchal faces of its presidents in Egyptian fashion on Mount Rushmore, is also linked to the mnemonic and referential programming heard, first, in Thornhill's advertising jingles. It is, also, a linguistic state. So how can a "materiality" that is intangible and prephenomenal, such as what de Man places at the point where anteriority and material markers cross, be of any political import—even if it proposes itself as alone "preparatory" to an intervention in memory or programming itself?[25] The "circularity" that Hitchcock uses to void representation exceeds that of the double chase—the "villain" chasing those (police, villains) who are already hunting him in what is an invocation and evisceration of the "hunting" motif as a trope for the hermeneutic program's ability to place in memory what "it" would then as if discover there. This double chase or voiding circularity, which echoes in the "O" of Roger O. Thornhill, is hyperbolically rendered in *To Catch a Thief* (where Grant-Robie, "the cat" as ex-thief and simulacrum, is made to pursue, that is, copy, the copycat who is already copying his [then original?] signature style, and so on), yet marked in the very trope of *advertising*—that manipulative use of language that anticipates a calculated response based on a fabricated referent, self, become fictional addressee. When Grant-Thornhill discovers that Kaplan is a signifier generated by a disinhabited hotel room (virtually "Grant's" own at the Plaza) together with clothes and messages, the "human" is itself exposed as choreographed by the effect of specific social rituals that have no referent (or necessary embodiment). In *North by Northwest,* the shift to the performative, or "event," must, as always, go by way of or exceed the *mise en abîme* of performance or "acting like" (a favorite signal-phrase across Hitchcock), the thing one is supposed to represent (male or female, police, "actor," exec, "Cary Grant," and so on).

So what passage can be said to (have) occur(red)? First, "language" is (already) morphed into "another conception of language," perception is altered since it incorporates the theorization of its linguistic and pro-grammatic nature. The *mnemotechnicity* that de Man circulates within assumes that what is anthropomorphized as "nature," and certainly the network of organic variants and life-forms, remains semio-aesthetic effects.[26] "Human" assumptions about language's mimetic and referential service—that it always pretends to fixed or transparent referents in the regulation of mnemonic imprints—appear remarkably stunted or primitive when compared to the semiotic systems of other organisms: that is, if we regard as virtual reading models the alloplastic mutations, chemical wars, predatory and cross-species camouflage, shape-shifting, instantaneous adoptions of colors or simulated organs, the changing of sex of some (fish) species, electromagnetic telepathies, and so forth of some rain-forest or coral creatures—modes of what might be called a *proactive mimesis without model or copy,* a simultaneous reading and morphing forward in accord with external environments *without reference back to the idealization* of a fixed meaning or "property." We may suggest, in a sense, that "materialistic historiography"—which de Man seems to present the most literal techniques for engaging, well beyond Benjamin—drifts toward a model we might project onto non-human life-forms (including "us"), as *zoographematic* systems, sheer technicities.[27]

In *Blackmail,* the trace—or the blackmailer, *Tracey*—operates like a perpetual witness in the form of a prehistorial reminder. Emerging first from the shadows in association with never-explained notes left in the mailroom of the artist Crewe, the final chase by Scotland Yard pursues this figure into the British Museum, around historical artifacts and the hieroglyphic origins of (pictorial-cinemallographic) writing. So pursued through the universal reading room of the museum, past all historial artifacts in the Egyptian wing—including the giant Nefertiti—he will crash, index finger extended in a muted gesture of accusation and paraverbal pointing (or *indication*).[28] At the end, Trac(e)y—the name is spelled both ways, alternately, in the silent and the "talkie" print—is muted in falling through the dome of the same *universal reading room,* after virtually running through and hence preceding what may be called monumental history (preceding, even, the Egyptians). In *North by Northwest,* where Mount Rushmore cites *Blackmail*'s giant head of Nefertiti, we learn that the trace is not particularly terrestrial, that the (a)*materiality* of the bar-series precedes that of "earth," invariably, disowns the conceit of earth as ground, as material or as maternal order. In Hitchcock, this dispossessing nonorigin is often called "mother" (for Derrida, it is perhaps called *khora*). De Man will draw attention to where, as in Wordsworth, supposed "nature poet," the sky falls away (falls up) from the *Earth* ("the sky suddenly separates from the Earth and is no longer, in Wordsworth's terms, a sky of earth, we lose all feeling of stability and start to fall, so to speak, skyward, away from gravity"). Gravity grounds the centrality of an Earth, and its annulment rewrites the Earth as unearthly, *antigrav,* as the effect of an alloterrestrial trace. Hitchcockian vertigo sometimes names this site of a fall without ground, like the trick track shot in *Vertigo* that goes up and down at once, or in *To Catch a Thief*'s seeming loss of gravity, everything rising to roof or mountaintops or being lifted in a moment of sheer *formalization,* as it is called in the last film (when Cary Grant, at the beginning, asks to change into something "more formal," a promise realized only in the closing costume gala). Indeed, the animated bird-humans on the Disney screen in *Sabotage* expose a precedence of this trace to animation, animation conceived as *zoographematics,* "earth" de-anthropomorphized, the "human" fashioned otherwise than as a blind and embattled hermeneutic closing off of its other(s) to conceal its own nonexistence as such. That a technicity inhabits the black-flecked birds in *The Birds* is underlined in the "final" scenes, where a machinal hum attends their gathering.

*Sabotage* marks for us how a signature that precedes figuration involves a subversive politics dependent on the recalibration of the "aesthetic" (and material) itself. *Sabotage* departs from Conrad's *Secret Agent.* Coming right after *Secret Agent* and unable to use that title, it nonetheless returns more darkly and unrelievedly to the question that title posed. Here, of course, the saboteur Verloc operates out of a movie house—affiliating the last syllable of Ver*loc* with Hitch*cock.* Yet his opening act of sabotage at and before the beginning of the film, coincident almost with its titles, is the putting out of a lightbulb, of all "light," the electricity or "juice" of London, the *generator.* Aside from the fact that it interrupts or curtails the show, emptying that same movie theater into the street, it places another reflexive rupture within its narrative opening. It (the film itself) casually marks a caesura that inhabits and precedes (this) film. Marking Hitchcock's dilemma, the Londoners do not get it, but respond only with laughter (though a kind of explosively unhoused Homeric laughter will return, later, when Mrs. V watches the Disney bird cartoon following the death of Stevie by the ill-timed bomb Verloc gave him to transport). The laughing Londoners emerge from the Underground, moreover, which is a trope not only of cinema but of the afterlife of semiotic consciousness they are already unknowing effects of ("the illusion of a life that is an after-life," says de Man). This *caesura* or blasting—the premise to any "sabo-tage" within the mnemonic order governing meaning, temporalization, relays, hence of any intervention as reinscription—is first marked in the dictionary definition of the word *sabotage* that opens the credit se-quence, thereby calling definition and words into question. It marks the rupture of the word by its aural parts: "*Sa-botage, sa-bo-tarj*. Wilful destruction of buildings or machinery with the object of alarming a group of persons or inspiring public uneasiness. *Sa-bre (-er), n. & v.t.* Cavalry sword with a curved blade (the s., military . . .)" By breaking the word, phonetically, into sound, cutting it as with another (s)word, and offering an official (dictionary) definition of sabotage—what oc-curs in the theater, and as the emptying out of identificatory or meta-phoric viewing—the text, also "before" its opening, links the facticity of the letter and sound to a *blackout* from which the scene, or film it-self, will appear reflexively reconstituted, *r*ebegun, or as if proceeding in the parenthesis this affords. The doubling in the word *sabotage*—a term marked by Hitchcock, reissued in the later *Saboteur*—not only inflects the French *sabot,* or shoe, picking up on the material figure of legs or feet or steps marked and associated with f(r)act(u)al mnemonics in *The 39 Steps*.[29] It again casts a black light on the problem of "alle-gorization without allegory" as such—how such a term, the film's po-litically subversive title (later associating a time bomb with film canis-ters), is not contained by the "official" or state definition, ruptured by the facticity of the letter, doubled. Thus the first reflexive or modernist notion of allegory, noted earlier in association with Jameson, that of reflecting on the text's own scene of production (or consumption), the movie house, Verloc's Bijou, is first marked then cut off as a front by Verloc's own secret and ineffectual "act" (as his handler complains, the citizens only laugh in the dark, as they had turned Hitchcock's defacing productions into mere entertainment), and it is supplanted by the sec-ond episode—that of, and as, the "film" itself, allegory as a destroying and world-altering, time and memory–altering material prospect—involving the failed attempt to bomb Picadilly Square ("the center of the world").[30]

This problematic is echoed in the text's second "definition" of a word, that in the Detective Ted's tautological double-talk concerning the legal responsibility for the blackout: "As laid down in the Act of William IV, where an act is *defined* as an activity actuated by actual ac-tion." We will note, here, two factors that frame this—recalling that the disruption of the generator (or generation) involves, too, that of a "juice" that animates not only movement, (the) cinema, but any switchboard or relay system. First, Hitchcock names the problem of "allegory," of the other allegory that stands to the official one as the spectral or nonetheless letteral double of the dictionary definition of *sabotage* itself. The detective seeking out Verloc will be named Spenser, Ted or Edmund Spenser perhaps, the hoary agent of traditional allegory trying to track down his politically subversive and modernist spin-off or double. He is first met in disguise, as a fruit seller next to the Bijou, keeping the Bijou (and cinema) under surveillance, and yet intervenes on behalf of Mrs. Verloc ("Mrs. *V*") in the opening, only to lie, to banter, to prevaricate about the "law" and about the definition of an "act." And about what this piece of film, badly timed yet explosive, does or does not *perform*. That "act" (a word at stake in all its senses in the concealed title, *Secret Agent,* used, preemptively, in Hitchcock's preceding film) involves not only the definition of responsibility—should Mrs. V, as she's called, give the patrons back their money?—but of any intercession, of the effect of the sabotage (of mere light). Which is also to say, of a certain passage from fiction into fact, say, or, in de Man's words, the "passage from the aesthetic theory of the sublime to the political world of the law" (*AI* 115). (Elsewhere we might ask why, in Hitchcock, such a sublime is written always and only as an allo-human and material instance, preletteral, mnemonic, banal, the mere "facts" memorized by Mr. Memory or, putatively, recorded by the camera in mock-mimetic ritual.) Detective (T)Ed(mund) Spenser, set to apprehend and stop the sabotaging Verloc, is dragged out of literary history itself, the purest representative of classical "allegory," of what purports to be the mimetic model, aiming, essentially, to restrain or undo the deviant form not of a mere modernist reflexive model (the movie house, recall, is closed down at once, emptied of patrons) but of that other "allegory," that scene of generally (non)apocalyptic *translation* without specific ideology (Verloc is essentially mercenary, or in it for pay). (Indeed, like Spenser, one thinks of Inspector Le Pic in *To Catch a Thief*—should we hear the name as *le pic*[ture], that is, as a mimetic figure hunting down the premimetic trace and simulacrum figure of "the cat.")[31] The translation is not only that from Conrad to the screen, or from aesthetic play to devastation and historial intervention—it involves another, material figure that disrupts the very model of inscription or (mimetic) reference as such. Thus the tool of Verloc, the *time bomb* that the idiot boy Stevie will carry (and which goes off on a bus, precisely a stationary figure of transport), is associated not only with birds singing (having been passed to Verloc by the professor, the bird-man nonetheless named Chatman—or cat-man—in a general bestiary that pervades the text, including its visit to the zoo and aquarium), but with film. It is carried, again, with two film canisters, whose twisted remnants are discovered after the blast, tipping off Detective Spenser, who saw Stevie carrying them through the Lord Mayor's Day parade toward Picadilly.[32] The film's title, noted repeatedly as popular, is *Bartholomew the Strangler*—that is, a name containing the bar figure or series as the material, mnemonic, or semiotic premise of the *time bomb,* of Hitchcockian writing or cinema, of what alone is or could be explosive, prefigural, like the exploding dictionary word. But if the text already performs the sabotaging of "light" that recurs to ruptured letteration and defaced quests for new definitions, it suspends in advance of itself the reflexive model of allegory (mode of production, movie house) and places it under surveillance of an archaic icon of policing mimeticism (Spenser). Spenser is at once the "law" and an open dissimulator rehearsing a profoundly misapplied Oedipal script (his compromised and coercively empty and even blackmailing courtship of too-letteral *Mrs. V).* The bar insignia that marks the cinematic time bomb, an alteration of "time" under the Benjaminian model of "cinema" and its "shock," operates erratically. It claims the life of its unwitting carrier on a bus (site of transit), the idiot brother Stevie, here a third or neuter figure within the already fictional family (he is not the Verlocs' progeny but Mrs. V's brother).[33]

The bar-series appears the marker of irreducible (a)materiality, itself prefigural and a sort of *reine Sprache* surrogate. It dismantles any logic of signature applied to Hitchcock's case—the very logic of the *cameo* appearance, for instance, rather than securing an auteurial presence, dissolves all linear and mimetic logic by folding the external frame into diverse postal relays, in the process establishing virtual relay networks between all other signed texts (the Spies' Post Office), fragmenting the Hitchcockian body (the famous profile, the girth, the pouting lower lip) into textual markers that generate deposed Hitchcock-doubles across the texts much as the "body" itself appears from the first abstractly dismembered as feet, hands, teeth, and so on take on agency of their own (*The 39 Steps* is hardly unique in this). This "bar-series" is associated with a *time* bomb and a film canister in *Sabotage* for a purpose. It not only deregulates the premise of conventionally mapped time. Inspector Talbott, following the final bomb that decimates the entire Bijou, sacrificing the very pretense of "movies," can't remember whether Mrs. V's remark came *before or after* the professor's auto-explosion itself. It deregulates sequence as well as pictorial or mimetic fictions. The sabotage that semiotically annotates the inaugural blackout (or *caesura*) is rewritten in Benjamin through tropes of blasting, "shock," and historial disinscription. This (a)correspondence between the bar-series and allohuman time is pointedly related to the problematic of the animal in *Sabotage*—evidenced in the proliferation of birds (the bomb is kept beneath a birdcage) and fish as well as figures of eating and consumption (eating is also allied to the consumption displayed by the filmgoers blocked, at first, from the Bijou). When Verloc is killed by Mrs. V's steak knife—or steps into it, is as if reflexively suicided—he is also marked as meat, a stripping of personification and the human in a film long complained of as without aura.[34] If Hitchcock's (non)"act" of sabotage aims at a *passage* from trope to performative, from mimesis to inscription in a Benjaminian fashion, and this because—as the blackout performs—the very *technē* of cinema casts it at and before the (recurrent) simulation of the sensorium itself, the aesthetic politics of this intervention, which casts the policial hermeneutics of mimetic-humanism with its techniques of identification and personification, depends, as in Benjamin and de Man, on a nonhuman history.

The explosive "bar-series" registers where the semiotic shock of this site reverberates, in *Sabotage,* across zootropic and zoographic zones—as when, in the Aquarium in the London Zoo, Verloc envisions the tank as a screen on which the buildings of Picadilly melt away. The mock-apocalyptic *Abbauen* of this scene,[35] however, enlists a throwback to premammalian "life," a transitional reflection less dependent on a prehuman fantasy than a dislocation of the trope of *life* itself that the *zoo* marks—the afterlife of the screen, of consciousness, of any effect dependent on the bar-series against which mimetic ideologies emerge. One consequence of this is the denaturalization and dislocation of *gender* itself—italicized in the quips by a strolling couple about the fish that, after birthing millions of young, changes sexes, or the singing Mae West *bird* (a female female impersonator) of the cartoon sequence (where *"animation"* in general is conceived of as a material or semio-aesthetic effect). Thus one of the mystifications of Ted Spenser, which destructively drives the narrative, is his mindless pursuit and imposition of an Oedipal fantasy that misreads the Verlocs' sexless family arrangement—a simulacrum family based on the care of the idiot brother Stevie, which suspends the premise of natural generation.[36]

## IV

Much depends here on how we read the passage on *the passage*, on translation as occurrence, on passing *over*, on "that direction (which) you cannot get back from," irreversible—which direction Hitchcock names "north by northwest."[37] It is a technically *nonexistent* and hence ghostly direction citing Hamlet's undecidable projection of a certain *madness* (that he is mad but "north-northwest").[38] For in that film text much depends on how we read travel, movement, or traffic, not to mention the material effort to *transport* what we only hear is a roll of microfilm whose "secrets" are never discussed, one concealed in a primitive-modernist art fetish that—with whatever information it purveys—is to be moved across the *border*, across all borders generally and one above the stone heads of the Earth, the limit of anthropomorphism. The scene takes us to the edge of what is clearly viewed as an abyss beneath Mount *Rush*more, a site of acceleration (Rapid City) converted into verticality and vertiginousness at the failed prosopopeia of an unearthly Earth.[39]

One agency of "passage" appears recurrently marked by Hitchcock's use of the circular insignia associated with an aporia of (eternal) recurrence. The letter "O," a ring, a wheel or zero—such ciphers attached to diverse markers void the premise of identity (like Peck's amnesia in *Spellbound*), as do the *back-spinning* wheel that opens *Blackmail,* the smoke rings of Uncle Charlie, the names Johnny-"O" Ferguson, or Roger "O." Thornhill of whom, famously, the "O" in the anagram "ROT" (as in *Hamlet*'s phrase "something is rotten") stands, we hear, for nothing. They are not symbols (signifying, for instance, that Cary Grant as advertising executive is a "nobody") but performatively wager an already active transvaluation of time, direction, memory, and circularity all too familiar as a banal technical dilemma associated with the film spool's repetition. Since it will often be tied to a name, or a chain of names, we might link it with how de Man presents the logic of the zero. The back-turning circle can imply, in advance of any narrative as such, reaching into the prestructure of memory or anteriority as well as closing out a received circuit of repetitions (which the film spool banally incarnates). It suggests in a faux Nietzschean register[40] some of what is at stake in the border crossings—that is, in the temporal, political, hermeneutic shifts, crossings in the definition of the eye, of mnemonics, of repetition, of the human and nonhuman, a logic of sheer exteriority. The implied logic intersects with de Man's reading of number in Pascal:

> The notion of language as sign is dependent on, and derived from, a different notion in which language functions as rudderless signification and transforms what it denominates into the linguistic equivalence of the arithmetical zero. . . . There can be no *one* without zero, but the zero always appears in the guise of a *one*, of a (some)thing. The name is the trope of the zero. The zero is always *called* a one, when the zero is actually nameless, "innommable." (*AI* 59)

What is elsewhere in Hitchcock denoted as a "ring"—and what, in the silent film of that title, seems already identified with explosive material signifiers or even sound, with a circular armband called a "bangle"— affirms the rupture of a traditional back loop. Such might be termed the *shift* from mimetic model (Thornhill as advertising executive) to a proactive mimesis without model or copy (Thornhill assuming and inventing himself as "Kaplan"), a break with historicist archivism that precedes, too, the anthropormorphism of Earth. The passage as if from trope to performative. For to a degree this is what "north by northwest" indicates: a direction that is also a nondirection, beginning in sheer traffic, citing Hamlet, and geared hopelessly toward its own deferred "event." Grant or Thornhill begins as an advertising executive whose use of language is sheer mimetic manipulation, presented as hopelessly clichéd jingles in *dictation* to his amanuensis, Maggie (that is, virtually, "*M*argaret"—another *mar*-name). The film's first exchange involves the elevator man's saying that he and the wife "aren't talking." This barring of communication involves, already, the installation of a faux loop not only in the transparent messages Thornhill dictates but in the advertising jingle he tells Maggie to place on his own desk as an auto-mnemonic ("Think thin"), thus dictating a memory device to return to him from another's hand. No wonder Roger wants to contact "mother"—we are only one film from *Psycho*—not by phone but in writing, even if by telegraph, at her *bridge* game. And trying to do so in the Oak Room at the Plaza[41] gets him abducted as that other linguistic fiction, or zero, George Kaplan, who nonetheless already names the giant heads *(Cap-)* of Earth *(Geo),* permeating which are the barred lines Jameson rightly notes. "Think thin," which repeats the syllable "in," yields the "drink" (and "ink") of Van Damm's *library,* the book room where Roger, as if on behalf of Hitchcock's cinema, is forced to drain the bourbon like liquefied books or print (the bottles located in the library shelving, as mother later quips). The *direction* that takes over the film's course beyond the crop-duster scene's attack by that prosthetic or mechanical sun mimes Roger's adoption of the fictional identity, now aping invention forward—which brings him to the abyss below the presidents' heads. "Here," non-place, at an Earth not only stripped of origin, stripped of personification, *preceded* by the bar-lines itself, an unearthly Earth. The specular opponents of the mimetic states, America and its nameless Cold War "other," are vaporized before the overriding mimetic politics of the Earth that the very cinematography evokes and participates in. Here a crossing of borders with (and as) the micro-film, of the aesthetic logic of the micro-film in the pre-Columbian fetish artwork (that is, all *artwork*), is both projected and barred, interrupted, stopped by the professor's agents, *by the "aesthetic state."* The micro-film accords with the logic of shock, of "materialistic historiography"—like the canisters of *Bartholomew the Strangler* associated with the bomb on the bus—with an aesthetic materiality that entails "another conception of language." Like de Man's project, it marks an "irreversible" movement, a positive "nihilism" preparatory to the possibility of an "event." It entails the precession of metaphor, the deregulation of an interpretive and temporal program, the exposure of mimetic machines, the precession of mute stone "faces," the aesthetic materiality of the micro-film, the fall and the abyss of linguistic specularity—the "passage," in short, from one model of language (tropological, metaphorical, advertising media) to another ("material," performative, exceeding "mother" and earth). It projects a failed transformation of reading at the presidential site where reference and identificatory processes, mnemonic management and the nonhuman appear legislated. Its "irreversibility" is registered in the excess it maintains over all ocularist, auteurist, Oedipal, retro-Cartesian, mimetic, or identificatory "models." This bar-series occupies what de Man perhaps calls the subject position of *grammar* in all allegory. As measure or rhythm, as what dispossesses and engenders "light" or perception, as the slashing knife of "mother" or the pretense of a serial narrative, as the signature of inscription's precedence to all description, the *bar-series* is the irreducible prosthesis of the visible, the guarantor (and betrayer) of exteriority—what can always dissolve the mimetic and metaphoric and auratic readings it nonetheless compels.

## V

Well "before" the silent film *The Ring,* Hitchcock solicits a problematic of the circle, of circularity and circuitry, that pervades still the comic
nil-point of Roger "O." Thornhill, "Johnny-O" Ferguson, and so on.
If this ringlet or circle performatively invokes a mnemonic destructura-
tion with a decidedly Zarathustran resonance, it signals a disruption at
once of mimetic and temporal ideology. Like an inscription that precipitates both phenomenalization and ideology, it turns back on and
counters the logic of generation on behalf of another gamble or risked
crossing. In *North by Northwest*—Hitchcock's name for what de Man
calls an "irreversible" direction (and Benjamin, perhaps, a "one-way
street")—this movement precedes face or prosopopeia (the visages of
Mount Rushmore and the sheer traffic of tropes). It also precedes and
evacuates a failed personification of Earth, echoed in the fictional
name George Kaplan, one that opens upon a marking system represented by the striation or bars that Jameson remarks; that is, what is
not yet semaphoric, a "materiality without matter," neither capable of
pathos nor narration nor metaphor nor the pretense of light.

It is not that one sees de Man as a Van Damm type strictly—a double
agent, smooth and faintly accented, into *"import-export"* (the diaphanous working of a membrane, or border, as we hear of Van Damm)—
but that, like *Hamlet,* a certain theorization of performance and *act*
seems hyperbolically at stake in the text, one related to a fall that
inhabits this direction, which itself ends up on the top of Mount
Rushmore—a kind of acceleration-arrestation (like *Rapid City*), atop
the prosopopeia of the Earth in the giant stone faces that Thornhill (Cary
Grant) slips across. We might seem, with Van Damm, arrested before
such borders are crossed with a micro-film, a material rewriting of the
aesthetic that also represents the film we would then be viewing—
it implies a sheer formalism in the absence of any other, any faux
interiority. The halted passage out of the "aesthetic state" (America,
Denmark) is or would-be Mosaic in structure—devolving into a mechanical stutter, like Moses', pointing to what the text itself cannot entirely pass to (or already has), an otherness that is not that of an other
political fiction, an other history, or an other human. The hypnopoetic
logic of Hitchcock's practice of reinscription, evoked in the first *Man
Who Knew Too Much* with Uncle Clyde's momentary hypnosis by a
black ball (or sun), recurs in the opening of *Family Plot* as a faux séance
of sorts (crystal ball evoking a spool, the medium Blanche's mock evo-

cation of "Henry," her H-named helper, and so on)—on which, none-theless, both the dispositions of diverse "family" pasts and futures appear to depend. Irony, as de Man uses it, does not suspend this game but is the predicate of its having consequence at all, and not merely repeating, or being reinscribed in, the mnemonic system of the "aesthetic state." In *Frenzy*'s opening, by contrast, the female corpse floating in the river bearing the necktie, the serial destruction of women—and turning their bodies into admired corpses—is linked to the pollution and destruction of an Earth, as well as to the poetry (Wordsworth is being read) whose aesthetic pretexts are intricately complicitous with that evisceration. Hitchcock's assumption of the order of inscription—the movement, in de Man, from trope to performative, from metaphoric displacement or figuration to what precedes it—occurs, however, with a deregulation of statist temporality and mappings as well. The circle spins back upon itself, like the agent Louis Bernard's reaching for the knife in his back of pure anteriority in the second *Man Who Knew Too Much*, and finds the originary memory a prosthesis or implant, as does the entire Madeleine episode in *Vertigo*. What is vertiginous, what loses ground or earth, is the disclosure that what is being repeated, or sought to return to, like "mother," was not even there the first time—resolves itself into a bar-series, a series of knocking sounds (those, in *Marnie*, on a window), into which inscriptions themselves appear dissolved. The blackmailer Tracey falling through monumental history at the British Museum, however, plummets from the glass dome into the universal reading room—what Hitchcock is "interrupted" doing in his cameo on a train in the Underground. When the anterior ground of inscription is shaken or altered, the "direction" can no longer be mapped as before and after, up or down. The circle or ring figure, in short, like Roger's trajectory, mimes a shift from a mimesis of model and copy (the machine regulating time and reference for the "aesthetic state") to a proactive mimesis without model or copy. This replicates the logical intervention of Benjaminian allegory or "materialistic historiography"—which is predicated on a rupture of and with historicism and an intervention within the mnemonic site of inscription itself. Whatever is "Mosaic" about this cinemallographics passes through a *zoographematics,* much as it disperses the ocular-centrism of an entire epistemo-political history. When, in the opening music hall scene of *The 39 Steps,* Mr. Memory—the machine-man who, seeming like a camera, only records "facts"—references the Hesiodic muse Mnemosyne, the gesture does not say: modern cinema is the heir of the novel, indeed, of epic poetry, to ennoble the former. It says rather: writing, including the ancient epic sublime, was never anything but dependent on this utterly banal and machinal, indeed (a)material, work of inscription, work of sheer exteriority—and that even the ancient texts were nothing other than this apparatus which, if understood, barred the fantasy of a closed "human" system from before the "beginning." That the entire tradition has been housed in this coerced hermeneutic relapse, in the policial regimes of the aesthetic state.

Perhaps this *zoographematics*—where "life" is the produced effect of movement, of speed *(vif)*, departing from the programs of animation and the alternating bars or knocking of breath or spirit—is notched almost in passing in a typically too quick citation in *To Catch a Thief* (for by now, it is clear, *the Hitchcock shot operates like a network of citations* preceding any pretext of representation). The picture, of course, is all about simulacra in the absence of any "real thing": the jewel thief called "the cat," the *actor* Cary Grant who is a thief of identification and projected emotions if not Being itself, is in pursuit of his own copy, a copycat—but the black cat is already, as thief, a figure of imitation. The original "cat" (an oxymoron) must anticipate, hence imitate, his own imitation in a ruptured circularity or "double chase." In fact, undisclosed at the time, the two are together in a boat sequence early in the film (the "copycat," the "young" French girl Danielle, to whom Grant has given "language" lessons ["nouns," "adjectives"]). The name of the boat flashes before us briefly: *Marquis Mouse*. At once, an allusion to a marquee reflected in the credit sequence Travel Service window, a mouse evoked that contains the two "cats" that should be pursuing it (the container as contained), the allusion to Mickey Mouse citing, in fact, Steamboat Willy—the first animated feature, precursor to animated film *tout court*. Animation is what Robin Woods observes, in passing, may be the closest analogue to Hitchcock's cinema—itself a web of preplanned, entirely artificed markings and rebuses. At the "origin" of film, not representation but animation, troped in the Travel Service window itself, reflecting the other scene of a movie marquee across a street traversed (we can make out) by buses like that in *Sabotage*. The "Travel Service," of course, offers a theoretical commentary on travel, tourism, transport, movement, acceleration, and cinema we need not go into, except to note the final placard in the window that promises transport to a place called "France." It, too, is a cartoon, a Parisian-style sketch and solicitation with writing on it: if you love life, you will love France. Let us ignore again the name of

Grace Kelly's character, Francie, an American girl about whom the figure of "love" will have to be artificed, compelled or trapped out of a resistant "cat" (Grant). We will only note the role that "life" plays, as a word, in this puzzling hypothesis (*if* you love life . . .).

**NOTES**

1. Such "transport" as a precession—yet promise—or metaphoric "travel" is extensively developed as a deceptive trope for the movement heard in cinema in the "Travel Service" window opening *To Catch a Thief*'s credit sequence.

2. In the early British films, this political regime marks itself before the film credits by way of the prominently displayed governmental certificate of censorship. This, as seems never remarked, implicitly extends to the topos of what is called "England" in all of the "political thrillers" of that phase.

3. This association—that of chocolate (the black sun, the film bonbon) with excrement—is made all too plain in the first *Man Who Knew Too Much,* when Lawrence is held in the Temple of the Sun Worshipers by Abbott. The gun-toting cleaning woman, who does not want to be associated with holding the little girl, is made to take off her skirt to reveal black-stockinged legs so she won't leave. In a visual pun easy to miss but impossible to ignore, her handler reaches down to take a chocolate off of a shelf at the very level of her buttocks when bent over, then pops it in his mouth. The routine fits into a series of interrogations of representation, death, "knowing," consumption, fake light, deception of the (film) audience, and so on.

4. Hitchcock has been approached as a figurative problematic with a system of marking, as by Gilles Deleuze: "Hitchcock produces original signs, in accordance with the two types of relations, natural and abstract. In accordance with the natural relation, a term refers back to other terms in a customary series such that each can be 'interpreted' by the others: these are *marks*; but it is always possible for one of these terms to leap outside the web and suddenly appear in conditions which take it out of its series, or set it in contradiction with it, which we will refer to as the *demark*" (*Cinema 1: The Movement-Image,* trans. Hugh Tomlinson and Barbara Habberjam [Minneapolis: University of Minnesota Press, 1986], 203). The latest of these may be Slavoj Žižek's notion of *sinthoms* ("Hitchcock's Sinthoms," in *Everything You Always Wanted to Know about Lacan (But Were Afraid to Ask Hitchcock),* ed. Slavoj Žižek [New York, Verso, 1992], 125–28), in each case only producing a random tropology to avoid theorizing the prefigural logics of the "mark" as such (as Hitchcock italicizes that through his series of "Mar-" names). Hitchcock has become one of the, if not the most "theorized" of film texts—in part in response to something that exceeds the critical models available to "film theory" as that has evolved in conjunction with cultural studies more and more. Even Žižek, who deems Hitchcock a "theoretical phenomenon" (*Everything* 2) generating systems of thinking possible to juxtapose to Hegel and Lacan, blocks the linguistic theorization that is its basis—pleaing, instead, for a movement "beyond 'the wall of language'" that sustains this mimetic ("Cartesian") tradition. The stature "Hitchcock" has risen to as an agent of transformation is remarked indirectly by Godard: "I incorporate Hitchcock into the *Histoire(s) [du cinéma]* because I believe

that at a certain epoch he had absolute control over the world. More so than Hitler, or Napoleon. No one before him was ever in such control over the public. This was the control of poetry. Hitchcock was a poet on a universal scale, unlike Rilke. He was the only *poète maudit* to encounter immense success. What is quite surprising with Hitchcock is that you don't remember the plot of *Notorious,* nor why Janet Leigh goes to the Bates Motel. You remember the pair of glasses, or the windmill— that is what millions and millions of people remember" (Jean-Luc Godard, interview with Jonathan Rosenbaum in "Bande-annonce pour les *Histoire(s) du cinéma de Godard," Trafic* 21 [spring 1997]: 12). In the article in which this quote is cited, George Collins's "Incidence of Instant and Flux on Temporal and Pictorial Objects, Listeners and Spectators" (*Tekhnema* 4: 26-61), Nietzsche is linked to Hitchcock by addressing "Nietzsche's three throws at 'maintaining a sense' for 'God' in light of the will to power." Collins: "Is the age of the spread of the American way of life inscribed on its films throughout the world the same age as Hitchcock's, or a subsequent one, an underlying one? Might Hitchcock only be an epiphenomenon in the process of its ineluctable advance?" (28). Or its deconstruction? This association of Hitchcock with the thinking of technicity before a (Nietzschean) passage anticipates a next reading of his text that would move beyond those programmed by mimetic "relapse" of culturalist hermeneutics, identity politics, neo-Lacanian codes.

5. The trope of the "aesthetic state" is developed in the previously unpublished talk, "Kant and Schiller," in Paul de Man, *Aesthetic Ideology,* ed. Andrzej Warminski (Minneapolis: University of Minnesota Press, 1996), 129–62; hereafter *AI.*

6. A particularly inventive use of this is the name of the assassin-*mark*sman Ramon in the first *Man Who Knew Too Much*: Ramon, which reverses as "No-Mar," also cites Amon Ra, laying down the faux thematic of Egyptic sun worship— that is, the worship of imaginary light, of Schillerian relapse—that he too uses as a front: in the process, a breakdown of the name Ramon also links "repetition" (R[a]) to the proper, to property, to what is mine or *"mon"* (*The 39 Steps'* final show at the Palladium, for instance, being "Crazy Mo*nth*," remarking Hannay's "Montreal" allusion in the music hall scene). I will return to the "bar-series," which William Rothman calls Hitchcock's "signature" and locates in every film.

7. Not only this, but more often than not it is this project that cites Benjamin, inversely, as one of the earliest "mourners" of this "loss of humanity" in today's "society"; the "aura" is mourned—the opposite of Benjamin's point—and this legitimizes numerous attempts to reinstate it. Film "theory" and the cultural studies' reading of film, despite the desires of each, adheres to a model of cinema that Benjamin declared closed with the advent, precisely, of cinema itself.

8. Paul de Man, "'Conclusions': Walter Benjamin's 'The Task of the Translator,'" in *Resistance to Theory* (Minneapolis: University of Minnesota Press, 1986); hereafter *RT.*

9. Indeed, if he is caught in elaborating a nonterm, "allegory," which Benjamin dropped as unable to sustain the burden put on it—that of transforming the historial from within an epistemo-critical network of material and mnemonic traces, within monads, as he termed the sites of intervention—it is part of the gamble.

10. Eduardo Cadava, "Words of Light: Theses on the Photography of History," *Diacritics* 22:3–4 (fall–winter 1992): 86, 87. If I use this "rapport" to read Hitch-

cock, it is not that in shifting from a literary text to the sabotage of the cinemato-graphic pretense to mimesis we are engaging, simply, in a more "political," referen-tial event: the event reflexively theorized within every Hitchcock text (to which titles such as *Secret Agent* semiotically aver and disname) has to do, above all, with the way the aesthetic text transformatively theorizes its material, mnemonic, and allohuman role in the history of otherness for a hypothetical and inscribed "com-munity," as well as how (as with Benjamin) the cinematic apparatus is conceived as analogous to the site of inscription. Hitchcock apprehends the installation of a tex-tual system as working within the technical apparatus of cultural mnemonics in a manner that stands to divest and alter the very domain of face, memory, the visible: the cultural regime of mimetic-humanism, ideology of the "aesthetic state."

11. When *To Catch a Thief* opens with the prefigural and mobile trace of the black cat signifying (Promethean) theft, or the first *Man Who Knew Too Much* with a skeet or marksman's shoot in which a black disk is shot down, a black sun, light is preceded—generated and eclipsed—by the mark. Implying a cinematic logic fre-quently theorized in Hitchcock's invocations of travel and tourism, de Man focuses in commenting on a passage in Locke on the idea of motion and its relation to metaphor: "motion is a passage [Locke says] and passage is a translation; transla-tion, once again, means motion, piles motion upon motion. It is no mere play of words that 'translate' is translated in German as *übersetzen*, which itself trans-lates the Greek *meta phorein* or metaphor" (*AI* 38). Passage, translate, motion, metaphor—the series collapses at the very point, we might say, where "light" does, where *setzen* (as the domain of positing, the event, inscription) itself passes into a hypermode, *über-setzen*, into a mode of passage that cannot be affirmed within its own (representational) system, unless and except by passing outself of a system for which such passage must be projected.

12. This persists, of course, with the "birds" in that film blotting out of the very idea of the solar in a multiplicity of simulacra, of black holes, "(a)material," machi-nal animation; such interfaces with formal logics that emerge, for instance, where de Man in "Phenomenality and Materiality in Kant" notes a coincidence of a con-cept of pure ocular vision with a totally nonsolar logic: "Not being part of trope or figuration, the purely aesthetic vision of the natural world is in no way solar. It is not the sudden discovery of a true world as an unveiling, as the a-letheia of Heidegger's *Lichtung*. It is not a solar world and we are explicitly told that we are not to think of the stars as 'suns moving in circles'" (*AI* 82).

13. De Man: "*reine Sprache*, a pure language, which does not exist except as a permanent disjunction which inhabits all languages as such, including and especial-ly the language one calls one's own" (*RT* 104).

14. William Rothman, *Hitchcock—The Murderous Gaze* (Cambridge: Harvard University Press, 1982), 33.

15. Walter Benjamin, *The Origin of German Tragic Drama*, trans. John Osborne (London: NLB, 1977), 233; *Ursprung des deutschen Trauerspiels* (Frankfurt am Main: Suhrkamp, 1963), 265.

16. De Man, "Kant and Schiller," in *AI* 133.

17. This Benjamin, covertly, appears to derive from too precise a reading of the material dimension of *The Birth of Tragedy*, upon which the *Trauerspiel* seems to be grafted. It is not surprising that de Man's seeming turn from tropological systems

toward an implicit materiality (out of which trans-epochal ideological wars are marked), leads in his late essays to a seemingly ceaseless—if only occasionally marked—*Auseinandersetzung* with Benjamin, a recurrent pretext, moreover, of going "beyond" topoi one associates with the earlier critic, such as aura (or personification), mourning, the reading of Baudelaire, allegory.

18. Benjamin concludes the "Work of Art" essay by addressing the state of humanity during overt war: "Its self-alienation has reached such a degree that it can experience its own destruction as an aesthetic pleasure of the first order. This is the situation of politics which Fascism is rendering aesthetic. Communism responds by politicizing art" (in *Illuminations,* ed. Hannah Arendt, trans. Harry Zohn [New York: Harcourt, Brace & World, 1968], 262–63). What Benjamin calls a "communist" seems to be something like de Man ("communism responds by politicizing art"): this is the entire direction (that word is used) of the "Aesthetic Ideology" papers. What "politicizing art" means suggests locating where the *technē* of signs operates through mnemonic systems to program the sensoria and modes of metaphoric "experience," and where the aesthetic is itself constituted as a ghost category to neutralize or manage this excess.

19. This review was first called "Reading Hitchcock" when it appeared in *October,* and later redubbed "Allegorizing Hitchcock" as a chapter in *Signatures of the Visible*: in each case, for reasons unnoted, retaining a clearly de Manian echo. See Fredric Jameson, "Allegorizing Hitchcock," in *Signatures of the Visible* (New York: Routledge, 1992), 97–127.

20. Fredric Jameson, "Spatial Systems in *North by Northwest,*" in *Everything You Always Wanted to Know about Lacan (But Were Afraid to Ask Hitchcock),* 51.

21. Such memorization, which pretends to internalize, defines a moment of sheer exteriorization which de Man reminds us Hegel terms *auswendig lernen.*

22. An analysis of this inversion might begin with Scottie's final accusation to Judy/Madeleine about what a good "pupil" she had been (technically, of Elstir—a name otherwise evocative of a Proustian motif in which mnemonics and the aesthetic are reprogrammed). The references in *North by Northwest* to *Hamlet* suggest a "rotten" or paralyzed state. Such recalls the paralyzing contradiction between a knowledge of inscription (do not forget!) and the order of phenomenalization that denies, inverts, "relapses" from or Schillerizes their import (Denmark's present court)—Iris Henderson's knowledge, in *The Lady Vanishes,* of Miss Froy, whose presence (like inscription) everyone denies on the train, yet who turns up, in Egyptian fashion, as a mummy (Miss Froy wrapped in bandages). "*Iris*'s" Hamletian counterknowledge is structurally cited as that of the eye (iris) and tropology (color)—the knowledge of "perception" countered by a premimetic anteriority allied to the Egyptian. In *Marnie,* an office mate flirts appallingly: "Have I got a *danish* for you"—that is, an abysmal version of this Hamletian bind, troped as a banality.

23. In fact, like Benjamin's trope of "natural history"—which does not refer to nature of (human) history—the collapse of temporal perspectives operates in parallel to a caesura inhabiting linguistic structures, which de Man might call, simply enough, "death."

24. Interestingly, the crossing or passage that is of course blocked in *The 39 Steps* (Mr. Memory does not get "out" of the country, any more than Van Damm

will) can never "succeed" in the same representational logics. It is associated with Professor Jordan, that is, a site of *Mosaic* crossing as though "out" of the Egypt not of hieroglyphic cinema so much as the always already inverted desert of the aesthetic state and its police. While this is denoted as "England" in the British "thrillers," it is expanded to include the double system of Cold War others by *North by Northwest* (much as, during the world war period, it began to include "both" sides of the conflict, the democratic and the fascist West as specular others in the same systematics). Thus, in the later film Professor Jordan is split into Van Damm and "the professor"—chief of an American spy operation never identified as either CIA or FBI, any more than the enemy other is definitively identified or referenced as the Soviet Union. Many Hitchcockian political "thrillers" track and perform a failed usurpation or transformation that, at the same time, testifies to the latter's having already been the case technically. The specter of an (ana)Mosaic crossing, or passing, which is also to say of *aporia,* is disseminated in Hitchcock by the syllable *port-,* heard both as door or passage and carrier, feet, material steps or signifiers (Portland Place, Constance Porter, Portland [Oregon]): this collusion, which returns us to the prefigural motif of *transport* (and translation), couples the transformation of impasse to passage with a shift from signified to material carrier—what Benjamin calls "to turn the symbolizing into the symbolized" of allegorical and mnemotechnic praxis—from trope to performative: the nonexistent di-rection called "north by northwest." (For an account of how the figure of "Annabella" Smith in *The 39 Steps* triggers an exploration of the Greek motif of the aesthetic and the materiality of steps—led through Hesiod, Mnemosyne, and Mr. Memory— see the last chapter of my *Anti-Mimesis from Plato to Hitchcock* [Cambridge: Cambridge University Press, 1994].)

25. Today, perhaps, there is a distinct relation between how the "human" constructs itself semantically—that is, as a closed system—and the impending devastation of terrestrial systems and reserves we might want to call *material,* a relation between models of reference and models of consumption. It is interesting that the problematic of this "materiality" returns at a time presented with the predicted human-governed impasses in the material environments and interlocking biosystems of Earth, aporia that confront us in daily media simultaneously deferred and neutralized as information. De Man is interested in a kind of criminality, to know something about it, which we might hear in association with what Derrida, in *The Politics of Friendship,* calls "that crime in which . . . the political being of politics, the concept of politics in its most powerful tradition is constituted." See Jacques Derrida, *The Politics of Friendship,* trans. George Collins (New York: Verso, 1997), ix.

26. See Benjamin, *The Origin of German Tragic Drama,* 233; *Ursprung des deutschen Trauerspiels,* 265. In the context of noting that for Benjamin in the "Translation" essay "history is not human . . . it is not natural . . . it is not phenomenal . . . and it is not temporal either, because the structure that animates it is not a temporal structure" [92]), we hear that "we are to understand natural changes from the perspective of history, rather than understand history from the perspective of natural changes" (83). Like the concept of "natural history" in Benjamin, which has nothing to do with "nature" but much to do with a nonhuman

figure of history, any trope of "nature" is to be understood in terms of semiotic effects and systems.

27. Among ecocritics the connection between the evisceration of biosystems and language conventions that program human perception has not gone unremarked—although it is typically mapped, along the phenomenological model, by inversion. That is the case, say, in David Abram's *The Spell of the Sensuous: Perception and Language in a More-Than-Human World* (New York: Pantheon, 1996), which nonetheless mounts its critique from within the very program he would, without knowing it, disrupt: *phenomenology* is presented as the longed-for norm to be returned to, whereas alphabetic representation—the materiality of the letter—marked the historical alienation of the human from nonhuman otherness and the senses. So the work of the prosaic, of the letter in de Man, here intervenes at the heart of the human escapade or parenthesis—it is an acceleration of attention to and use of this site, of allowing it to theorize its (a)materiality at the point where "perception" is phenomenalized or programmed, which ruptures the human semantic and perceptual closure Abram properly assaults. For if "materialistic historiography" departs from a suspension of historicist narrative and turns to where the trace accords with a movement of anteriority that belongs to signification but is not explicitly human, it is not because the letter or mark *resembles* nature. The *materiality of the letter* jams any transparency of the aesthetic state, and in Abram's inverse reading it is the letter, in fact, that stands as a disruptive intervention of the material in the "human" epistemo-political systems—one that also leads to a deregulation of perceptual blinds, organic and empiricist borders, temporalization, and programmatics of reserve, identity, and economy that rely on its occlusion. The eviscerations of terrestrial traces and nonhuman reserves, it seems, may be programmed by models of reference: it is into these systems and programs that de Man, and Hitchcock, differently intervene. The "shift" that de Man tracks posits a technicity that traverses the human and alternative life-forms jointly as effects—where, too, the figure of "life" (like death for de Man) occurs as a linguistic dilemma in a specific sense.

28. This includes an allusion to fingerprints that leads us back through a vertiginous meditation of the precedence of prints (including the alluded to detective film, *Fingerprints,* which *Blackmail* momentarily alludes to itself as within its narrative) and of artificed narrative to all pretense of documentation or fact.

29. The class warfare signaled by the *sabot* is kept in play by Hitchcock and, as in de Man's use of the "slave" trope, linked to the materiality of inscription. Thus, in *To Catch a Thief,* the motif of service, or *"service compris,"* is tied to the lower-class kitchen help, ex-thieves connected to Bertani's restaurant and his new thieving operation (actually, as the denouement italicizes, a film-production unit, as the kitchen too is inflected to be): cinema's space of ironization is associated, as in Benjamin, with class struggle—though less with the idea of "liberation" than exposure, pure exteriorization, to which the semantics of class struggle too falls prey. For a more epistemo-political analysis of this problematic, see chapter 5 of my *Ideology and Inscription: "Cultural Studies" after Benjamin, de Man, and Bakhtin* (Cambridge: University of Cambridge Press, 1998).

30. In his own attempt to appropriate Jameson's trope for what becomes, in practice, a more generally mimetic or regressive hermeneutic (Hitchcock as pro-

grammatic exemplar of a certain interpretation of Lacanian mappings, one hinged on a posthumanist yet still occulist and auteurist trope of the "gaze"), Žižek attempts to summarize: "This modernist notion of allegory is, of course, opposed to the traditional one: within the traditional narrative space, the diegetic content functions as the allegory of some transcendental entity (flesh-and-blood individuals personify transcendent principles: Love, temptation, Betrayal, etc.; they procure external clothing for suprasensible Ideas), whereas in the modern space, the diegetic content is posited and conceived as the allegory of its own process of enunciation. . . . The classical Marxist reproach here would be, of course, that the ultimate function of such an allegorical procedure, by means of which the product reflects its own formal process, is to render invisible its social mediation and thereby neutralize its sociocritical potential—as if, in order to fill out the void of social content, the work turns to its own form. . . . Yet one is tempted to defend here the exact opposite of this line of argument: the strongest 'ideologico-critical' potential of Hitchcock's films is contained precisely in their allegorical nature" (Slavoj Žižek, "'In His Bold Gaze My Ruin Is Writ Large,'" in *Everything,* 218–19).

31. The agency and figure of the black cat—thief, eclipsed sun, what precedes "light"—in the France of *To Catch a Thief* is linked directly, if covertly, to the French poet of cats, Baudelaire, and specifically the text "Correspondances," in readings of which Benjamin's (and de Man's) conception of "allegory" is elaborated. This becomes explicit during the drive to inspect villas with the "real-estate list."

32. To assign *Picadilly* the moniker of "center of the world" is more than a descriptive exploitation, since it depends on the word itself. Like "Inspector Le Pic," the first syllable both tropes a mimetic pretense—picturation—yet ties it to a letter sequence, (d)ill(y), which abrupts and suspends that. Elsewhere in Hitchcock, the syllable *Pi-* will be linked to a destructive sublime ("What causes pips in poultry?" asks the frustrated interlocutor of Mr. Memory opening *The 39 Steps,* that is, a disease that brings down flightless birds), but a numerical inscription, either 1 and 3 or 3 and 1, tied to a muting of the subject, a "death" that precedes human speech or coincides with its auto-dispossession. Thus Pi is incribed as the Pythagorean Pi—3.14—in *The Torn Curtain,* much as the number thirteen haunts the entire Hitchcock opus (and names a lost early title directly, not to mention the auteur's birth date). Hence, "ill" less cites than performs a letteral variant of the bar-series—/ / / as i-l-l—which is verified, among other texts, in *Marnie,* both in the name Lil's troping of the erased pre-Edenic female (Lillith) and in the zombie children's choral: "Mother, mother I am ill, send for the doctor on the hill," and so on, where the word *ill* emerges directly in association with the bar-series—what returns us, as *Marnie* frequently does, to *Spellbound.*

33. He must be dismembered, erased, and sacrificed as a witness to the family's sexless fictitiousness and his own function as excess, as simulacrum. Stevie, in this, recalls the boy who interrupts Hitchcock reading on the train cameo of *Blackmail.*

34. One could say of Hitchcock's *Sabotage*—or its history of reception—what de Man says of a passage in Hegel on the *Gesetz der Äußerlichkeit:* "Completely devoid of aura or *éclat,* it offers nothing to please anyone" (*AI* 116).

35. The term *Abbauen* is applicable particularly given the "construction" site, a digging in the street before the Bijou, a signal that the text conceives itself as a fundamental reworking of the site of transport and of the "earth."

36. This is one reason for Mrs. V's excessive, "mad" Homeric laughter when watching the Disney cartoon after learning of Stevie's erasure: she disowns any mimetic ideology of film.

37. De Man's text reads: "this passage, if it is thus conceived, that is, the passage from trope to performative—and I insist on the necessity of this, so the model is not the performative, the model is the passage from trope to performative—this passage occurs always, and can only occur, by ways of an epistemological critique of trope. The trope, the epistemology of tropes, allows for a critical discourse, a transcendental critical discourse, to emerge, which will push the notion of trope to the extreme, trying to saturate your whole field of language. But then certain linguistic elements will remain which the concept of trope cannot reach, and which then can be, for example—though there are other possibilities—performative. That process . . . is irreversible. That goes in that direction and you cannot get back from the one to the one before" ("Kant and Schiller," *AI* 133).

38. For a fairly unilluminating review of this association with Hamlet, see Stanley Cavell, "North by Northwest," in *A Hitchcock Reader*, ed. Marshall Deutelbaum and Leland Poague (Ames: Iowa State University Press, 1986), 249–64.

39. To address this passage effectively—which is also the movement from a mimetic to an allomorphic order of memory, from advertising jingles as bleak mnemonics to proactive invention—one must be poised between the two, "equally poised," says de Man, if irreversibly: "So it is not a return to the notion of trope and to the notion of cognition; it is equally balanced between both, and equally poised between both, and as such is not a reversal, it's a relapse. And a relapse in that sense is not the same" (*AI* 133). There are now two "relapses." To invoke Hitchcock as an example, the site of the relapse is the mimetic image of the narrative, every logic of knowingly solicited identification, whereas the *other* interrupts that like the Waltzing Couples, without reference, descending into *Shadow of a Doubt*: the order of mechanical memory, inscription, materiality, evinced in the formalized system of markers and signature-effects, parabases and letteral or preletteral repetitions that recall the narrative to the machinal prostheses of the visible marked by such devices as the number of names bearing the syllable *Mar,* the cameos (that effectively collapse any exterior frame into the frame), or the unintelligible bar-series.

40. For instance, we find the same "O" or circularity in the pseudonym Cary Grant adopts in *To Catch a Thief,* that of "Conrad Burns," the lumberman or logger/lodger from Oregon—the "Con" of cognition linked to such circularity (Rad), in a cutting of trees, or the natural image (the referent become carrier of sense), in a scorching mode, an erasure of and at the "origin" (Oregon) of the referent.

41. The "Oak Room" is another such trope, binding the "O" figure to an inhabitation of the preeminent natural emblem, the tree—a figure familiar not only through other repetitions such as that of Uncle Charles Oakley in *Shadow of a Doubt,* but the rings within the cut giant redwood of *Vertigo*: supposed to interface natural and human history or time, their invocation of the vertigo-swirl violently places a graphematic anamorphosis within and before the pretense of the "natural" altogether. A similar dispossession of any logic of generation or origination occurs, relentlessly, about the figure of "mother." The logic of preinhabitation by the material other is established, of course, in *The Lodger.*

# Resistance in Theory

Laurence A. Rickels

If it is true that the concept of *resistance to analysis* cannot unify itself, for non-accidental or noncontingent reasons, then the concept of analysis and of psycho-analytic analysis, the very concept of *psychoanalysis* will have known the same fate. Being determined, if one can say that, only in adversity and in relation to what resists it, psychoanalysis will never gather itself into the unity of a concept or a task. If there is not *one* resistance, there is not "*la* psychanalyse"—whether one understands it here as a system of theoretical norms or as a charter of in-stitutional practices.

—Jacques Derrida, *Resistances of Psychoanalysis,* 20

Permit me an ellipsis here since I do not have much more time or space. Transference and prosopopeia, like the experience of the undecidable, seem to make a responsibility impossible. It is for that very reason that they require it and perhaps subtract it from the calculable program: they give it a chance. Or, inversely: responsibility, if there is any, requires the experience of the undecid-able as well as that irreducibility of the other, some of whose names are trans-ference, prosopopeia, allegory.

—Jacques Derrida,
"Like the Sound of the Sea Deep within a Shell: Paul de Man's War," 151

Is it possible to explore a resistance in theory to or in terms of the transferential setting of theorization, from formulation and reformula-tion, for example, to delivery and reappropriation? Yes. The setting shifts to and fits the displaced occasion of the transference dynamic. In the case of Theodor W. Adorno and Walter Benjamin's pooling and schooling of their thoughts, the correspondence would be the place to look for all the staticky aftereffects and side effects of the proposed union in theory (including the forced marriage between Marxism and Freud's science) which add up to a veritable couples theory that cannot be transferred intact and undisclosed to the cognitive-theoretical registers of argument or influence otherwise organizing the reception of the published work. That the reception of the collected works of Adorno and Benjamin doubles as a resistance to acknowledgment of their Freudian formation, repeats or displaces what begins as a resistance in their own theorization, as acted out, for instance, in the closed sessions of their couples dynamic of submission and anticipation.

These displacing effects whereby Benjamin's reception in particular has become divided between that of American deconstruction and another one identified with a certain sociological humanism, both of which share a symptomatic exclusion of Freud's formative influence, and has then undergone (without saying) ultimate displacement from a difference *within* Benjamin's thought to a radical separation between his and Adorno's work, also follow from a certain resistance in Paul de Man's theorization. In de Man's essay "The Resistance to Theory," which belongs to a subgenre of his work in which we catch him in the act of what he proclaimed as his main calling, the didactic act, we are given a definition of teaching in theory that adjusts the contrast to a relationship in therapy:

> Teaching is not primarily an intersubjective relationship between people but a cognitive process in which self and other are only tangentially and contiguously involved. The only teaching worthy of the name is scholarly, not personal; analogies between teaching and various aspects of show business or guidance counseling are more often than not excuses for having abdicated the task. (4)

Is it possible that de Man assumes here that "self and other" relations are primarily intersubjective, rather than, as in the transference dynamic, intrapsychic? Would transference, or for that matter resistance, even begin to take place in a relationship that can only be taken interpersonally? De Man offers up therapeutic correctness as the straw man—and, behind the scenes, invites psychoanalysis to pull the long straw. But then de Man rightly addresses the measure of the "depth of resistance" as the "recurrent strategy of any anxiety to defuse what it considers threatening by magnification or minimization" (5). Then he assigns the "psychological" model to those approaches that "were unable to reach beyond observations that could be paraphrased or translated in terms of common knowledge" (9). This psychological model, however, at the same time marks the spot de Man is in with this essay, which was commissioned and then rejected by the MLA. But even in its no longer submitted or submissive form, all "traces" of the "original assignment" could not be removed, and they in turn "account for the awkwardness" (still evident in the final product) "of trying to be more retrospective and more general than one can legitimately hope to be" (3).

De Man's foreclosure or, if one prefers, bracketing out of psychoanalysis is legend. But that legend became legible in another sense with his resistance address. There are indeed moments in the essay where all you would need to do is replace the subject of de Man's sentences with "psychoanalysis" and an extraordinary compatibility suddenly seems to emerge, but from another place, deep down between the lines. For example:

> It is therefore not surprising that contemporary literary theory came into being from outside philosophy and sometimes in conscious rebellion against the weight of its tradition. Literary theory may now well have become a legitimate concern of philosophy but it cannot be assimilated to it, either factually or theoretically. It contains a necessarily pragmatic moment that certainly weakens it as theory but that adds a subversive element of unpredictability and makes it something of a wild card in the serious game of the theoretical disciplines. (8)

Resistance to theory as, in the accumulating turns of de Man's essay, theory's resistance to language, as resistance to reading, as resistance to itself, as its own resistance, sparks recognition of the other closed system that also must at the same time contain itself in an openly pragmatic moment in which theory is seemingly taught a lessening with regard to its limits. Psychoanalytic discourse is pragmatic or (as I would prefer to say) materialist to this extent that it accumulates its body of reformulation in the space of tension between its own self-reference and the emergency contacts it must nevertheless make with what lies outside. The constitutive push and pull in psychoanalytic theory thus lies between the "closure" of the system within which it moves to complete itself and that same system's inability to generate all its terms out of itself. Intrapsychically reconfigured, resistance in theory to the transferential setting, to the in-session materiality of analytic discourse, refers to the "allegorical" tension between the transference materials and the shorthand, in-group idiom, or jargon of the theory.

This, then, is the discursive force field of psychoanalysis, which I am calling allegorical in Walter Benjamin's sense. It means that, after Freud, we are always in session and at the same time beside ourselves, in the big between of this tension span.

The change I have introduced into the title of de Man's "Resistance to Theory" registers the difference that is already there in de Man's posthumous publications, for example. There is an undeniable in-session dynamic discernible in the transcriptions of taped deliveries of de Man's spontaneous readings or teachings. Among these post-humous reconstructions and publications, "Kant and Schiller" in *Aesthetic Ideology* invites, already by the transferential force of the "and," closer analysis. The breakdowns or scratches in the groove of this record must be read in terms of a double setting of resistance at once to the transferential setting and to the technologization along for the transmission of the session. It is in the genealogy of tape technology, with which "Kant and Schiller" comes to us complete, that we discover another resistance in theory which is psychohistorical in context and metapsychological in fact: still today, for the time being, and for some time to come, every tradition, transmission, and transference coming down to us passes through a Nazi past while at the same time containing saving reference to Freud. Unlike critics who would pass judgment on the modernist institutions and inventions appropriated by National Socialism (including psychoanalysis itself) as collaborationist or, at best, as open invitationals to every application imaginable, I prefer to consider these convergences, which are still coming down to us, as "uncanny," in other words, not as limited to the social studies of cause and effect or influence. In this very rereading or rewriting, another possibility for psychoanalytic criticism is offered than the one informing a topic of "resistance to theory." The resistance that tapes together de Man's and Benjamin's receptions is not different in kind or diagnosis from what a certain psychoanalytic record has to show for all its troublemaking. Since one return deserves another, I will close by interpreting the transcribed taped words from Lacan's sponsorship of Freud for their resistance to the transferential setting of the son.

### FIRST CONTACT

The 1997 movie *Contact* looked forward to a future of communication with other worlds that gets lost in the static of the recording. It's a future taken out deep inside the recent past, which is always also, as Adorno wrote to Benjamin in 1936, the most repressed and therefore most primal, catastrophic past. Every recent past will still be the most repressed—just consider the wrenching turnaround through blackout and nostalgia that makes the decade that came right before come back, surprise attack. But our prehistory of or as catastrophe still refers to what was crossing Adorno and Benjamin's correspondence, the Second Coming of World War. The genealogy of media has us irreversibly stuck in this scratch in the record, deep in the groove of modernism, on the record of psychoanalysis.

Arroway, the movie's protagonist, makes audio contact with an alien species that has been staying in touch ever since receiving our first message, transmitted in 1936, when Nazi Germany put on the television show of live coverage for the Berlin Olympics. Encoded in the line-by-line, connect-the-dots breakdown of the retransmitted video image of Hitler opening the games are instructions for building a rocket that will take one of us to a first encounter with the alien species. Arroway, who takes the trip, has always been looking for the long distant, the dead or undead, within the outer reaches of long distance. As a child she makes radio contact with ever more distant points on the map and wonders if one day she will contact Saturn or, she adds in passing, maybe even her dead mother. Her father answers that mother's too far gone. Then *he* goes. He dies of a heart attack, the way to go that always gives the evil I to a survivor's death wishes. We aren't told how she is raised between age ten, when she has two down, and her coming of age as a scientist. A grandparent or, as the actress's name echoes it, a foster parent must have taken over, replacing the particular static that's always given in the Oedipal relation with a kind of transparency, the doubling going down, according to Ernest Jones, within the trans-parent relations between grandparents and grandchildren. During this holding-pattern period of her development, Arroway is free, static free, to enter her science fantasy and retrieve losses that all fell down inside the complex. When she goes the longest distance ever gone before, the alien presence openly simulates a West Coast beach on which Arroway can be reunited with her father, because it just knew that this sensurround veiling their direct contact would be easier on her. It is the ultimate and ultimately fantastic gift of the trans-parent.

When Arroway returns to Earth, or to consciousness, all her tapes are filled with static and noise. The transparental encounter has left behind only static on the record of evidence of the senses. Two conspiracy theories take over—Roswell-style—where Arroway's consciousness left off for just the moment the tape of the launching recorded. But the tapes she brings back record static for the full eighteen hours she claims to have been away, way away. Neither tape seems admissible as truth. But we must work with what we have, with what is brought to the session. Arroway brings back from contact with dead or dad a record of static, white noise, the sound between radio stations, the snow between TV channels. In the analytic setting this counts down as a show of resistance. In the other words or worlds of parapsychology, it's the happy medium out of which contact with voices and images of the departed can be made.

In Karl Abraham's essay "Should Patients Write Down Their Dreams?" psychoanalysis took note of new voice-recording technologies as the latest pressure point or push button of resistance. Freud had already addressed the written recording of dreams as bound to the in-session dynamics of transference and resistance. Even or especially the most perfect transcription is vacuum-packed: the dreamer's associations typically vanish, an evacuation that announces the resistance, which if anything is thus better placed to block analytic contact. Abraham could confirm Freud's reservations. One of his patients was so tormented by her repeated forgetting of the content of her serial dreaming each time just at the moment she was about to tell Abraham all about it that she suggested the writing cure. But Abraham told her the repress release pressure packed inside a repeating dream would in time break through to consciousness. But she wasn't good about being patient, I mean a patient. She thought she had at least at last interrupted the series of her forgetting when, waking up once more from such a dream, she wrote herself a memo before dropping back to sleep. But then she overslept, was late for her session next morning, and had to hand the slip to Abraham without having had the time to read it first. The message: "Write down the dream despite agreement" (34).[1]

Another one of Abraham's patients, a gadget lover who makes use of a recording device, a dictaphone, to get his dreams down, first forgets that it wasn't working properly to begin with. A staticky, unclear record was the result. Once the dictaphone has been repaired, he tries it again. But this time even the clearly audible reproduction was so confusing that the patient just couldn't put it all together again as something he could relate or relate to. Only now can the patient begin the work of re-pairing his analytic relationship by remembering in association, in session, in the transference.

The original fit between Freud's exploration of transference and countertransference phenomena and the analogical hookup he initiated with such technologies of projection and identification as printing, photography, and film was left behind, in fits and starts, by technologies of as-liveness. New transference phenomena, such as projective identification, were therefore on the rise, same time, same station as the ascent of tape technologies during World War II. Freud's placeholder for this new field of differentiation or diversification was, back then, in the early 1930s, telepathy, a beyond of the transference into and for which Freud saw the telephone already plugging away.

There's the in-session materiality of analysis, from the top of the mourning to the working on the transference and all that it puts in the way. But where analysis keeps the short hand on theory it's the work of analogy that organizes a parallel universal of concepts. This work of analogy was left, up in the dead air between Freud and us, up to the autobiography of media. And Freud's analogical record, especially when it went endopsychic, was technologized on one track and haunted on the other (or same) track. Freud first greeted the figures of the transferential relationship as revenants, spooks. In 1959, Friedrich Jürgenson, originally Russian, by then living in Sweden, discovered the Voice Phenomenon. In the same year that saw the realization of videotape recording and videotape editing, the innovation that made possible live or as-live performances before studio audiences, Jürgenson turned on the playback of his tape recorder to listen to the birds he thought he had recorded by leaving the device running outside for a time. "Suddenly the voice of his dead mother addressed him. He heard her saying: 'Friedel, my little Friedel, can you hear me?' That was all" (Stemman 92).[2] Konstantin Raudive, also displaced by the events of World War II, from Latvia to Sweden, followed the news of Jürgenson's discovery all the way to the source.[3] Like Jürgenson, he, too, heard the voice of his own deceased mother, who called him by his boyhood name: "'Kostulit, this is your mother'" (Kubis and Macy 106). Peter Bander, yet another person displaced by the war, was converted to belief in Raudive's mediumship when he heard his first electronic voice: you guessed it, it was his long-distant mother speaking to her little boy in German. Then he had just two questions, one for each dead parent:

> "I will give father ten seconds, and mother twenty seconds to answer my questioning because my mother would anyhow talk more."—I then addressed myself to my father and said: "Father can you help me?" (in English). I waited ten seconds and then I said: "Mother, you know what I have to do, am I right in doing it?" I waited twenty five seconds and

then switched the recorder off. . . . On playback, watching the revolution counter on the tape recorder, I heard within a fraction of the first revolution a man's voice. After only three playbacks, the contents were quite clear to me. The language used was a dialect in which my father used to speak to his intimate friends (and although neither my mother nor I ever spoke it ourselves, we understood it): "Jung, wenn ich doch nur kuennt", (meaning: "Boy, if only I could"). The interesting word is "Jung". This was indeed the way my father used to address me when he was alive. Then came the turn of my mother's answer; again within a fraction of a second after asking my question the answer had manifested itself. "Und trotzdem sagst Du nein."—A literal translation would mean "And you still say no."—However, seen in context and knowing my mother's way of speaking, I prefer to translate it: "Whatever I say, you still will do the opposite." . . . The first electronic voice I ever heard, purporting to be my mother, and the two sentences above, are the only examples I can quote of a personal communication received. (Bander 35)

Bander closes the account with his swearing of an oath of sorts that he never again attempted to make contact with a particular person. He knew his mother's way of speaking and, preferring to translate, ended the direct connection.[4]

The interesting word is *Jung*. Beginning in 1959 Carl Gustav Jung's counsel was regularly offered on the air of the Voice Phenomenon. "His voice appears to manifest itself frequently during Raudive's recordings. Furthermore, what the voice purports to be saying makes sense" (Bander 25). As early as 1946, Jung began working on the UFO phenomenon, a phenomenon in Jung's case of unidentification. In one of his flying-saucer articles, Jung translates Freud's notion of the superego into the terms of his notion of a collective unconscious. Via another collectivity, Jung acquitted himself in 1946 for his season of open collaboration with the Nazi German institution of Aryan psychotherapy through his postwar doctrine of collective guilt. Back in the 1930s, when he agreed to put on a show of legitimacy for the Nazi German eclecticization and totalization of the psychotherapies (including psychoanalysis) by letting them make him into their international leader, Jung's only concern was that he would thus be getting back in contact after all with Freud's science. One has to give him credit for making everything in his life and work after his psychotic break with Freud, no matter how archetypical he thought it was, or whatever, only legible or decodable, point by point, in the terms of negative transference.

Jung's flying-saucer connection hits air pockets of isolated reference to the air war, the miracle rockets, and the foo fighters (which Allied pilots spotted before their eyes giving outer-space assist to the other side). But it's really all about the postwar conditions of life in the 1950s. "These rumours, or the possible physical existence of such objects, seem to me so significant that I feel myself compelled, as once before when events of fateful consequence were brewing for Europe, to sound a note of warning. I know that, just as before, my voice is much too weak to reach the ear of the multitude" (Jung, *Flying Saucers* 5). A footnote inserted right after "as once before" makes the connection with his 1936 essay "Wotan," which he thus rewrites within the underworld as his warning shout. Back in 1936 it sure looked, by all accounts, pro-Nazi in an upbeat.[5]

After noting that Jung was reaching the ears of Raudive's set with special clarity, Bander concludes that all the voices Raudive received "were attributable to persons who had died no longer than twenty or thirty years ago; also, when first manifesting themselves, they show definite characteristics of anxiety and eagerness" (25). Raudive established that, no accident, spirits need white noise, vibrations, or carrier sounds to communicate. Without their former vocal organs, spirits must modulate existing static into voice patterns strong enough to be captured on tape. Raudive collected and studied thousands of voices on tape, on which he based his definitive treatise on the Voice Phenomenon.[6]

Raudive had one competitor to diss, the discoverer of the unconscious, because he was one to know one who could only translate paranormal discoveries back inside the terms or limits of the psyche. "The hypothesis of the unconscious can be confronted by that of an 'anti-world,' which is based on the theory of relativity" (9). As Einstein proved, everything is relatives, dead or alive.

What soon came to be known as the Raudive voices were often agrammatical communications given invariably in several languages at once.[7] Gordon Turner, a well-known spiritual healer, although or because he was turned on to the authenticity of the Voice Phenomenon, worried about the dangers involved in contacting entities who, given the limited range of the tape-recording medium, must inhabit the lowest regions of the next world.[8] According to Turner, the Raudive voices were on the same wavelength as the messages Himmler had received: "There is a direct link between fascism, black magic and contact with impersonating earthbound entities who deliberately delude and pervert others. . . . If the . . . voices are stemming from a paranormal source, then I would regard some of the references to Hitler as significant and dangerous" (in Bander 84).[9] But Raudive also summoned Churchill, who is perhaps the most frequently contacted ghost on all the talk shows of the Voice Phenomenon.[10] World War II was—or is it still?—on the air.[11]

In the beginning, ghosts were seen but not heard when photography proved to be the first medium that could record on its own contacts with the otherworld. The projection of the modern rocket was reserved for the purpose of transporting the camera to new vantage points, not only in the service of military surveillance, but also, at the same time, as afterthought or even as main focus, for making first visual contact with outer space. Robert H. Goddard, the Father of American Rocketry, the sole pioneer whose focus was only on space photography, had his POV on target by the time airplanes rose to the occasion of reconnaissance. But Goddard didn't live to see his photo op. "He died August 10, 1945. A year later, a captured German V-2 (A-4) rocket with a standard De Vry 35 mm motion picture camera was launched from White Sands, New Mexico, reached a peak altitude of 65 miles . . . , and successfully made a continuous record of its ascent through the Earth's atmosphere to the threshold of outer space" (Winter 98).

Motion-picture technology had by the late 1940s completely crossed over to sound following intensive industry development inspired by the samples of German magnetic tape brought back to the United States after the war. Established in principle at the turn of the century, Third Reich scientists discovered for the recording the tape medium with just the right chemistry to lead the way to our playback, record, fast forward, or rewind functions (*A History of Technology* 1315). Developed originally for the purpose of war reporting along battle lines where no record had gone before, the tape recorder was right away used to censor any between-the-lines attempts by captive Allied agents to signal warnings mixed in with their Morse messages, which the Nazi captors had filled with false leads. Every Morse message composed by the captive authors was copied, analyzed, and, if necessary, manipulated before being put on the air. The era of simulation thus opened wide.[12] The words from the sponsor were invited to join right in and set their spell: "The first widespread application [of magnetic tape recording] occurred during World War II when speeches by Hitler and other prominent Nazi leaders were broadcast at times and places calculated to confuse Allied intelligence" (*The Encyclopedia Americana* 282).

Tapes of liveness are the medium of the split second, the splitting and postponement of the broadcast for the little time it takes to censor, manipulate, simulate. But the splitting image of the moment thus gives or takes all the time in the world.

In 1947, in Roswell, the hometown of Goddard's camera-rocket and outer-space research, the UFO phenomenon took off with a crash. Jung would hear a synchronicity; but, to stick to the moment, the V-2 rocket backfire of the primal Roswell sightings is completely in sync with the takeoff of Jung's investment in objects of unidentification. The alien forms that were witnessed or denied were humanoid in appearance but reduced in strength and scale, in every part but the head, as though by starvation. The visual contact first established in 1947, which keeps reentering the controversy over destroyed evidence, unprovability, only your imagination, and so on, seems to occupy interchangeable places with a certain reception, again, of World War II, that went to outer space and back, in the form of believe-it-or-not visitations by aliens who have the appearance of the victims we both do and do not recognize.[13]

The year 1983 saw the successful first run of the American Association of Electronic Voice Phenomena, which had "received an international publicity boost with the announcement by George Meek, a retired engineer, that he and a medium, William O'Neil, an electronics expert, had built a device called Spiricom that could communicate with the Other Side" (Kubis and Macy 107). Spiricom, which thus offered two-way conversations with the dead, opened up "the new field of ITC, or Instrumental Transcommunication—the use of electronic systems to undertake meaningful communication across dimensions. Thus, George Meek and Bill O'Neil are usually regarded as the fathers of ITC, just as the Wright Brothers are regarded as the fathers of modern flight" (Kubis and Macy 113).[14] Sure enough, soon enough contact could be made with Timestream, the telecommunications corporation on the other side. "Amazingly, Friedrich Jürgenson and Dr. Konstantin Raudive, the great pioneers of EVP, . . . have died and are now coming across on television, computer, radio, telephone and fax. . . . Today, Konstantin Raudive and Friedrich Jürgenson add a new dimension to their roles as paranormal experimenters. From their perspective on the astral plane, they have become philosophic mentors as well" (Kubis and Macy 114–15). But what gets realized here in the exchange, somewhere between parapsychology and philosophy, is the circumvention of the uncanny first contact with what the recording showed.

Already in 1920 Edison was convinced that there just had to be a radio frequency between the long and the short of the waves which, once he contained it and gave it an on/off gadget switch, would put through the direct connection to the world of the dead. Marconi claimed to have come up with a gadget through which he could travel back in time and record great historical events. He was hoping to get the words spoken by Christ on the cross just for the record. But it all changes once we let the recording speak for itself. Telephone and telegraph alone, without the recording or taping connections, were never enough. Edison thought he heard voices, like overhearing people speaking in the next room, when he played back a recording of a telegraphic transmission. Thus he was inspired to invent the answering machine, in which telephone and telegraph would find the completion of their system.[15] Only the recording can speak for itself, and thus for contact with the dead other, while remaining at the same time inadmissible as evidence of the senses.

## ON RECORD

The recorded voice, the uncanniest double of all, according to Adorno, because it always comes life-size, was the inspiration for Mina Harker's internal assemblage of Bram Stoker's *Dracula*. She transfers Dr. Seward's audio recording of his journal, which she has just listened to and which she concludes is just too unbearable for another's ears, to typewritten record. All the information gathered in the group service of defeating vampirism makes the transfer, subsequently, to Mina's one record, which she types up in triplicate. At the end of all that typing, all that's left of the group effort that defeated the vampire count, the novel itself, is nothing but a "mass of typewriting," a mass or communion that neither proves nor disproves undeath. But by World War II, tape technology had introduced both the uncannily perfect recording and the undecidability of its truth or simulation. But this vacancy and overfullness of tapes, their inadmissibility as evidence and their self-evidence, at the same time invited contact with the Voice Phenomenon, by all accounts the widest-ranging communication with the dead to date. When it comes to simulation, we're fast on the intake. Freud originally gave transference phenomena a matching accessory, the transference neurosis, an artificial illness that gets generated within the analytic relationship as a more tolerable simulation of the disturbance that's out there, bigger than life. Just like an inoculation, the transference neurosis bestows the great health by proxy or antibody in the course of its miniature illness and cure. Those shocks or shots of inoculation against trauma that Walter Benjamin addressed, in Freud's company, are always simulated conditions that, just like transference neuroses, take on an existence of their own in relation to what's out there, bigger than the two of us, and to what's in session, the big between. When everything out there can enter the session, the analytic relationship, as transference, the outside traumatic contacts have been dated, miniaturized, simulated, given the gadget click of the analyst's last words: "It's time."

Paul de Man's 1983 as-live performance "Kant and Schiller" introduces class analysis, I mean the analysis of in-class transference, into the writing of his reading. With the sole exception of this lecture, which we have on tape, de Man was not at all interested in the easy reading of mass culture or of its owner's manual, psychoanalysis. This station break, forever marked and dated with remarkably forgettable language, has at the same time absorbed the posthumous shock that Benjamin, still in Freud's company, attributed as aftereffect to all recording following from the click of a gadget connection. It wasn't so necessary for de Man to write the reading in this case, he reassures us, because he's "dealing with a much easier text" (129). What would be improv nightmare over the corpus of Kant is no problem when it's Schiller time. "I'll have some change in pace today, because this time I have not written out a lecture. . . . So what I'll be doing will be . . . more in the nature of a class than a lecture" (129).

The helping "and" reaches across Kant and Schiller, detailed textual analysis and speaking out in class. But the class situation is not an even-anded coupling. There are also secret sharers in the "and" that's dealt us here. Their address lies in the turning around of the *Trieb*, the pivotal point of de Man's yoking about Kant *and* Schiller. The other two are, one, Freud—at the first mention of Schiller's *Triebe*, de Man gives us credit for his aside, "*Triebe*, a word that you know from Freud" (137)—and, two, the gadget that has it all on tape:

> The tropological system in Kant . . . is . . . a purely linguistic structure which was shown to function as such, whereas in Schiller it is the *use* made of tropes, of chiasmus as the *teleology*, as the aim of an ideological desire, namely, the desire to overcome terror—it is in such a way that tropology is made to serve a *Trieb*, to serve as device. . . . It acquires therefore an empirical and a pragmatic content . . . at the very moment that it asserts its separation from all reality. (147)[16]

But the overcoming of terror through the playback or reversal of a device isn't de Man's point, it's ours. When de Man gives his topic for the lecture, namely, the "problem of the question of reversibility, of the reversibility in the type of models which I have been developing on the basis of texts" (132), what seems to get raised at the same time is the question of our misunderstanding. De Man must insist, in contradistinction to us, on an irreversibility in relations between the performative and the constative. Even if reinscription or recuperation in cognitive terms takes place, what we have then is a relapse, which, "however, is not the same as a reversal" (133). In the middle of all this setting up and putting down, de Man breaks for a "question which is closer to our concern here." This is where he directly addresses in-session dynamics. But then the discourse starts breaking up, the connection goes bad, static takes over, we're disconnected, *and* he's back:

> because it seems to be, as so often is the case, that . . . Since I have now had questions from you and since I've felt some resistances . . . You are so kind at the beginning and so hospitable and so benevolent that I have the feeling that . . . But I know this is not the case and there's always an interesting episode in a series of lectures like that, I know that from experience. One doesn't necessarily begin in as idyllic a mood as things were here. But it doesn't take you too long before you feel that you're getting under people's skin, and that there is a certain reaction which is bound to occur, certain questions that are bound to be asked, which is the interesting moment, where certain issues are bound to come up. (131–32)

De Man's transcribed or reinscribed performance puts us in frame for a slightly loopy but still self-contained feedback mechanism or machine for writing. The theme of our regression meets this frame like its match and maker: it's time to talk about the psychology of terror. The psychology of terror becomes the thematic interpretation of the regressive reception going down between Kant and Schiller, and between de Man and his audience. Schiller's drives, which, remember, can we talk, we freely associate with Freud, double as the drive to know, represent, or even change nature and as the drive to leave things unaltered by change or preserve oneself ultimately against death. Schiller thus introduces a "notion of physical danger, of a threatening physical Nature, in an empirical sense" (139). The danger zone in Kant belongs to "the shock of surprise, of *Verwunderung*, which we experience when confronted with something of extreme magnitude" (139). It's a shock of recognition that there's a failure of representation within the overall structure of the imagination. But Kant does not tell us about self-preservation, about "how to protect ourselves, so to speak, psychologically, from danger" (139). In contrast, Schiller, just like the rest of us, is directly concerned with the how-to of self-help:

> How am I going to fight off terror, how am I going to resist terror?—by means of a psychological device, which emphasizes reason and the ability to maintain reason in the face of terror. That's a way to live through terror, even if you're physically annihilated by it. Curiously, this emphasis on the practical, this emphasis on the psychological, on the empirical, leads to a greater stress on the abstract powers. (141)

Schiller and the audience make a "correct psychological observation," which, de Man advises, is still just not philosophical enough. "You know that from your own experience if you have ever been in immediate danger. There is a kind of exhilaration of the mind—if you are given the time—at watching yourself being in that state of danger" (142). But de Man's admission of his own experience of dissociation or splitting is so close to Schiller's turn to ultimate safety in the face of terror, which de Man dismisses right in the typeface of what he said we knew by our own experience. What we net from Schiller's safety-zoning prescriptions is the ultimate safety net, called "moral safety." When all else fails in the face of physically overwhelming danger, you learn to consider the sensory part of your being, that part that can be endangered, as something exterior, dissociated, like a natural object, to which your moral self is completely indifferent.

Schiller argues for terror's imaginative remove from the danger as but its representation. But for all that it remains just as vivid, to the point of turning on our sense of self-preservation, and thus, Schiller concludes, "it produces something analogous to what the real experience would produce" (143). What just doesn't interest de Man is that this production of something analogous is for the medical doctor Schiller just a dosage away from an inoculation, which thus becomes a differentiating part of the argument or procedure. By metonymy and absence, our Freud and a Freudian Benjamin join Schiller at this point of injection. The Benjamin de Man just couldn't shake—for example, among all those trends in criticism he piled up hysterically in his first footnote to "Rhetoric of Temporality"—reads allegory as though it were, looking back to the first works, Benjamin's only pre-Freudian works, the allegory of language origins. This represents a telepathically precise elision of the Freudian Benjamin. But even *The Origin of the German Mourning Pageant* can also be read as looking forward, in close association with Freud's study of Daniel Paul Schreber's *Memoirs,* for example, to the work on technocultures that will follow out the trauma organization of fields of representation and repetition.

According to Schiller's inside view, without the administration of analogies horror must take us to a place of unprotectedness, the place of origins. According to Freud, repetition is (just in case) the happening event of the psyche's attempt to get back posttrauma into the transferential context of anxiety. In Benjamin's reading, shocks are the inoculative shots that give it to the media consumers, but in metabolizable doses of the trauma or horror.

The therapeutic and theoretical rapport with technologization is not imposed from without but, like the work on the transference, interprets or interrupts what's already happening. What's on the tapes of media technology at the same time jumps the cut of intervention to anticipate and confirm the psychoanalytic or allegorical theory and therapy of shock, terror, horror. In the year of the discovery of the Voice Phenomenon, Alfred Hitchcock exhibited in *Psycho* the ultimate scene of horror, the *Schauer* scene, to which countless slasher and splatter films have been shock-treating us ever since. This serial following or understanding of Hitchcock's film never completely reverses the traumatic intersection, in Hitchcock's murder scene, of three unseens: the murderer's stabbing, the cut of film editing, and the cutting edge of our death wishes. Robert Bloch, the author of the novel *Psycho,* followed up the filmic reception of the *Schauer* scene with his own book sequel, *Psycho II.* This time around, the legacy of horror is transmitted through Norman Bates's psychiatrist, who does the psycho's mass murdering for him. Although Hitchcock's *Psycho* had left it all up to psychiatry, which was thus up there, untouchable, to put the aberration of the trans- to rest, the slasher sequels, to this day, resituate their remakes of the *Schauer* scene in a transferential setting that cannot contain the transgression, violence, identification cutting across it. *The Cabinet of Dr. Caligari, The Legacy of Dr. Mabuse,* and *Spellbound* introduced the horror plot of transference transgression. But there is no other plot of horror and terror. *Psycho* interrupted or extended it, and thus doubled the impact of a scene of horror we've been doubling and containing ever since. The transference transgression was directed with and against us. But that also means that our reception of *Psycho* keeps on going, going, along Benjamin's lines, as successful containment and dating of our first traumatic contact with murder, with the mass of murder that the media sensurround in every sense contains. "Most everyone has a *Psycho* story," Janet Leigh reassures us: "People remember where they saw it first, with whom they saw it, their reactions at the time, and the effect the film had on them afterward" (131).

But in *Psycho,* the problem of the trans-, the across we all must bear, which the closing psychiatric diagnosis has all locked up, is at the same time stored or realized in the taped zone of simulation. Paul Jasmin, hired to provide Mrs. Bates's voice, was amazed by the final audio portion, in which he had a hard time recognizing his share:

> In postproduction, . . . [Hitchcock] spliced and blended a mixture of [the voices] so that who's speaking literally changes from word to word and sentence to sentence. He did that to confuse the audience. I recognize my voice before Tony carries Mother down the stairs. But the very last speech, the monologue, is all done by a woman—Virginia, with probably a little of Jeanette spliced in. (In Leigh 81, 83)

Coming to the *Psycho* project and projection from his new TV series, Hitchcock constructed the clash of the two media, one old, one new, over a scene of unseen incessant cutting and then, over what's heard inside the audiotape, the splicing together of different taped voices that gives the psycho's voice or voices a range across identities, generations, and genders. Everything can be made to cross over on tape. And on tape it all jumps the cut of editing, the cut that Hitchcock dreaded so much when not in his hands that he took the hand in marriage of Britain's leading film editor.

At the close of World War II Hitchcock was offered the evidence of Nazi extermination as film assignment. He skipped that ready-made and made *Rope* instead, a film about the life-or-death stakes of misreading notions of superhumanity. The film, which the director welcomed then as his most exciting project to date, was "shot without cuts" (Gottlieb 284). "Until *Rope* came along, I had been unable to give full rein to my notion that a camera could photograph one complete reel at a time, gobbling up 11 pages of dialogue on each shot, devouring action like a giant steam shovel" (275). In 1948 Hitchcock's camera swallowed it all whole, the hole in one. The haunting rebound upon intake was released with the cuts Hitchcock made in 1960, sight unseen but all on tape, right down the receiving line into our psyches.

### REWOUNDING

Lacan delivered his primal mirror-stage address that year in Marienbad, that year of the Berlin Olympics, on his way to attend the games and witness what he hails as "the spirit of the times." In his text *Television,* Lacan came full circuit. When he locks in his interest in the discursive event of TV, he shoots right up to the first moon landing. But it's just the tip of realizations of the science fantasy that landed from those first stirrings of Nazi German rockets, and which were transmitted back to Earth, live, via the medium before which Nazi Germans had first stood at total attention.

As documented in the essay "The Direction of the Treatment and the Principles of Its Power," Lacan went to Berlin in 1936 against the mocked protests of Ernst Kris, whose interpretation of a transference Lacan dismisses in the essay as on one fault line with Kris's refusal to go to the Nazi TV show. Kris's patient is a professor who lives in mortal dread of being a plagiarist. Yes, there is something missing in Kris's interpretation and intervention that both the patient and Lacan point out or act out. But Lacan in turn misses the reference to improper burial openly lying there between the lines of a disembodied plagiarism.

The mirror stage gives us the preprogram on which prospects for the "phantom, the double, the automaton" are already given, and given without all that static of projection of an identifiable, and because identifiable, material, loss. In *Four Fundamental Concepts,* Lacan admits the loss of Freud's moment or field as constitutive of the transferences brought on by the in-session presence of the analyst, who is, in the first place, witness to this loss ("Presence of the Analyst" 483). We're always inside this transferential frame with all our relations since Freud to Freud. But it's a dead loss, Lacan continues, the source of "a certain deepening of obscurantism, very characteristic of man in our times of supposed information" (483). Lacan thus stresses the noncontact, a "function of missing" that "lies at the center of analytic repetition" (484). "The transference is the means by which the communication of the unconscious is interrupted, by which the unconscious closes up again" (486). The transference closes "shutters" that the analyst must open up. Transference thus also, between the lines and languages, renews the Freudian analogy with photography. The unconscious, however, is all on tape: "The unconscious is the sum of the effects of speech on a subject" (483).

The essay in which Lacan recounts his rejection of a certain Krissy understanding of transference and acting out comes across in the long stretch as almost a topography of psychoanalytic history in the twenties and thirties and then, looking back, in the fifties, in the decade it takes to skip the Nazi era of psychoanalysis and follow instead the American upbeat of adaptation through that old eclectic mix of psychodynamic therapies with or within U.S. psychiatry. But the consolidation of ego assets externalized as American is only the late arrival (and victorious rival) of that more primal and less consciously deliberated-upon era of Nazi German accommodations for a greater psychoanalytic setting that was changed, back then already, to the channel of improved efficiency, functioning, healing, bonding.

Thus, when Lacan takes on the American streamlining of analysis in this essay he straddles the almost two-decade span of his own united states of amnesia between the basic conception, research, or first airing of his findings in the thirties and, in the fifties, the final work of revision and publication. In other words, for the fifties, Lacan sets up all the pinhead goals of American neo-analysis—autonomous ego, happiness, security, team spirit—for one strike (231). But underneath the tall order of these charges there reemerges, not without psychohistorical connection to the era Lacan always leaves out, long-distant references in theory to melancholia. It's always in the course of duking it out with the dupes of analysis that he trips up and over the melancholic consequences of the other's takes on analytic theory.

Object relations is top of a line that slides immediately into implied or excluded zones of material loss. The pattern and patter of American psychology or self-help for success holds on to the related, objectional attempt to balance as "economic" activity the opposition between life and death drives (243). On "the other side of the coin" is the focus on what precisely "eludes the transference, namely, the axis taken from the object relation." While granting the focus on this relation a noble origin in the work of Karl Abraham (and thus—just take a look—in a melancholic collection of parting objects), Lacan attributes to this legacy (with Melanie Klein at the front of this line) the workings of such an imaginary. The "notion of intersubjective introjection," for example, merely reflects the establishment that produced it inside the dual relationship (246). The tensions that attracted the object-relationists in the first place, like the span of attention awarded this force field in the same place, come down to a security drive that Lacan diagnoses within Anglo-American analysis.

It has nothing to do with any counter-transference on the part of this or that individual; it is a question of the consequences of the dual relation, if the therapist does not overcome it, and how can he overcome it if he sees it as the ideal of his action? . . . But that one should confuse the physical necessity, the patient's presence at the appointment, with the analytic relation, is a mistake that will mislead the novice for a long time to come. (235)

This security drive covers the analyst with its blanket order whenever he treats the transference as the object or objective of consolidation and then, once interpretation can be made, as the model to which all else can be reduced. Thus all systems are going for the "working through" that grants the analyst open season to do whatever it takes to strengthen the patient's ego.

In a review of transference theories, in particular with regard to their revaluation by object relations analysts, Nathan Leites, another individual radically displaced by the events of World War II, points to the proliferation of disguised transferences that have reversed the original reception of transference work: originally it was the past that was back via transference onto the analyst. But since the 1940s, we tend to see experiences with extra-analytic figures, including figures from the past, as displacements of and defenses against what's being experienced in the relationship to the analyst in session. This reflects the growing admissions of narcissism into analytic theory taken down largely via the analysts who followed Melanie Klein right into the session where anything at all refers to the analyst. Leites notes the paradox that by now direct contact with original objects, rather than via the transference, occurs only when there is death, loss, and bereavement in the patient's life. Leites comments: "what used to be the normal power of the analytic situation has now become the privilege of catastrophe (even that extremity, as we have seen earlier, may not suffice to break through the wall which the analyst interposes)" (451).[17]

The technical difficulties Lacan had with official psychoanalysis in the 1950s concerned the analytic frame, and the interpretation of the transference that is given when "it's time." But session time for Lacan was always tape time, voice activated. Catherine Clément comments: "Through lengthy investigation Lacan had come to the conclusion that the length of each session should be adjusted according to what the patient was saying: some long, some short, in any case no predetermined fixed length" (110). Lacan insisted instead that the adjustment of the length of the session should become one of the techniques of psychoanalysis. In the final analysis, remember, it will all be on tape. Lacan's seminars were also consigned to recording. Clément was there: "there were tape recorders and the room bristled with wires. . . . A stenographer recorded the lectures on a stenographic machine as Lacan spoke" (12–13). To be in control of the time, in session or in seminar, is the prerogative of the one who identifies with the tape recorder. Andy Warhol was raised as his dead sister and wanted to be a machine. He left his memoirs on the call-activated tapes of the other's answering machine.

It is over an audio device that Lacan comes closest to acknowledging an identifiable because-identified-with loss. He takes issue with an analyst from the United Kingdom who confronted her patient when he came to session in a state of stupor with his fear that his recent successful radio broadcast on a topic that greatly interested her had aroused her jealousy. "The rest of the account shows that it took a year for the subject to recover from this shock-interpretation, which hadn't failed to have some effect, since he had instantly recovered his spirits" (Lacan, *Freud's Papers on Technique* 31). She makes her duo interpretation even though she knows that he went ahead with the broadcast only a few days after his mother's death. Lacan turns to "the psychology of mourning" to imagine what was going through when the patient went ahead and went through with his scheduled broadcast. While the invisible receiver, the mother, is being addressed by the equally invisible speaker, her son, the missing mother at the same time gets lost in the crowd of invisible listeners.

> It may be said that, in the imagination of the speaker, it isn't necessarily addressed to those who listen to it, but equally to everyone, the living and the dead. The subject there enters into a relationship of conflict—he might regret that his mother was not able to be a witness to his triumph, but perhaps, at the same time, in the speech which he gave, to his invisible listeners, there was something that was intended for her. (31)

What masses of spirits are summoned to admit the unlocatable receiver of her son's live broadcast! But when we flick the switch from radio to tape recording, what's also lost in the crowd is who the invisible speaker is and who the invisible receiver.

**NOTES**

1. Abraham: "The patient had written down, not the dream, but only her intention of doing so. . . . About a week after this unsuccessful attempt she was able to relate the dream, which had recurred several more times. Its content derived from a powerful transference. The patient dreamed that I was approaching her, and the dream ended every time by her waking in fright. After other transference symptoms had made a detailed analysis of this incident necessary, the reason for concealing the dream had disappeared. I should like to mention briefly the motives which lead patients to attach such importance to an immediate writing-down of their dreams. It is in many cases a transference-phenomenon. The patient who brings to the analytical hour notes of a dream unconsciously desires to show the physician that the dream particularly relates to him. In some cases a dream set down in writing and handed to the analyst is in effect a gift to him" (34–35).

2. "For 14 years Jürgenson let it be thought that the startling voice of his mother on the bird-call recording was an unexpected event. He now admits that he had been experimenting for several months before with the aim of receiving 'something' on electro-magnetic tape" (Stemman 94).

3. Under the subsection titled "First Contacts" in *Breakthrough,* Raudive summarizes their relationship: "Towards the end of 1964 a book appeared in Stockholm under the title *Rösterna frän Rymden (Voices from Space).* The author's name was Friedrich Jürgenson.

"All my life I have been preoccupied with parapsychological problems, especially with those concerning death and life after death. These problems play a part in all my books and particularly in *Der Chaosmensch und seine Überwindung (Chaosman and His Conquest).* . . . After the war I lived in Sweden and I am closely connected with those interested in parapsychological research in that country. Jürgenson's name struck me as that of an outsider.

"Reading Jürgenson's book carefully several times gave me a very definite impression of the author as a highly sensitive and susceptible man. Many of his ideas seemed to me to have been formed by a vivid imagination; the kind that could conjure up pictures in an empty room or voices out of the stillness. Later in his book, however, he came to develop a fascinating theme: he maintained that with the help of tape-recorder, microphone and radio he was able to hear voices on tape which he called 'voices from space'; that these voices did not belong to any other 'physical' world, but to a world in contrast to ours, a spiritual world; *that the voices were those of the dead.* Jürgenson gives a detailed account of this in a book called *Sprechfunk mit Verstorbenen (Radio-Link with the Dead),* 1967. He heard not only the voices of near relatives or friends, but also those of historical personages of the recent past, such as Hitler, Göring, Felix Kersten, the Yoga-author Boris Sacharow, the controversial Chessman etc. . . .

"I felt an immediate sympathy towards Friedrich Jürgenson: all that he told me had a ring of sincerity and deep emotional involvement. . . .

"Renewed contact with Jürgenson and deeper insight into his personality and his life's history confirmed my view that this man was utterly sincere; that he was completely immersed in the mystery of this phenomenon and firmly convinced that he was dealing with a world beyond—a world into which we merge after death and where we continue our activities in a transcendental existence. Faith and intuition can never harm a cause; for my part, I endeavoured to understand the phenomenon in its factual sense" (13–15).

4. In one of the books he was moved to write to popularize Raudive's research, Bander wonders "whether it will be possible in the near future to 'dial M for Mother'" (63). But even if Bander doesn't, we can put on Freudian ears and hear the murder with which mother gets associated.

5. Jung's resistance targets psychoanalysis and media technology. In his analysis of an actress's UFO dream—the dream thus "comes from California, the classic Saucer country, so to speak"—Jung overlooks the endopsychic perceptiveness of the dreamer, and symptomatically confuses auto-analytic breakthrough with psychotic breakdown. In the dream the UFO, which the dreamer first takes to be real, is identified as a trick: "'I looked up behind me and saw someone with a movie projector.'" Jung informs us right away, before commencing commentary, that the "dreamer, a young film actress, was undergoing psychological treatment for a marked dissociation of personality with all the accompanying symptoms." The commentary, a comment on Jung's disappointment in the actress, is the only one in Jung's collection that does not take the UFO into any account: "The dream insists on the projection character of the UFO. . . . It is not easy to see why the dream brings in the UFO at all, only to dispose of it in this disappointing way. . . . Any insight into the nature of the UFO phenomenon is not to be expected from this dream" (*Flying Saucers* 66–69).

6. Raudive's study, *Breakthrough,* appeared first in 1968 in German under the title *Unhörbares wird hörbar* (The inaudible becomes audible). "The publication of the book caused a near riot in parapsychology. The basic attitude was reactionary. Several parapsychologists argued that Raudive was merely picking up radio interference. Others denied that 'taped voices' could even exist and complained that Raudive was projecting his own ideas as to what the random sound on the tapes meant. These arguments are hackneyed and easily refuted. While it must be admitted that the voices are often unintelligible, very often they will call Raudive's name quite clearly. When I listened to examples of Raudive's tapes, in a few instances very clear voices were heard, even overlapping with his. It is inconceivable that radio pickups could consistently call Raudive's name or that radio pickups would consistently be picked up on Raudive's tapes, not only in Germany but in England as well" (Rogo 80).

7. Raudive explains: "The sentence construction obeys rules that differ radically from those of ordinary speech, and although the voices seem to speak the same way we do, the anatomy of their speech apparatus must be different from our own" (in Kubis and Macy 106).

8. "Turner pointed out that the communicators, with whom Raudive claimed to have established contact, included Hitler, and there was a strong 'neo-Fascist undertone' to some of the voices" ("Our Next Program" 71).

9. Raudive's mother communicated to her son from the beyond, in three languages at once, that she loved the Jews: "'Mona, ljubi judi'" (*Breakthrough* 36).

10. But as Turner observed of Raudive's recording of Churchill's voice from the beyond, which aired on British television at the time the Voice Phenomenon had everyone's attention: "This is obviously one of Churchill's less important speeches which he saved to broadcast from the other side" (in "Our Next Program" 71).

11. Henry Mandel, for example, who doesn't invite any Nazis to his talk-show masses, does tune in, same time, same station, Churchill's ghost: "I wish to remind you in your experiences that, although on a lesser scale than what I underrwent in the last Life Experience—reminding you also that I was the being upon whom many decisions depended, and I underwent grueling responsibilities during the days of the late holocaust of World War Two—I must tell you that your experiences are the same, although on a lesser scale. . . . The 'V' for Victory . . . let it be yours now and evermore. There is no reason to ever accept any intimation of defeat" (156).

12. The Allies had taken note of German broadcasts during the war, which had a clarity of sound and a staying power that beat all records. The mystery was solved in 1944 with the Allied liberation of Radio Luxemburg: a new magnetic tape recorder of unheard-of capacities was waiting for the booty call. As Friedrich Kittler tells the story, the media loop between record and radio had been one-way all the way. Developed in the 1940s for the purpose of war reporting along battle lines where no record had gone before, the magnetic tape recorder, through motorization and mobilization, released broadcasting from its record stores. The acoustic chamber of warfare could now be played back (Kittler 162–73). In his *Infoculture: The Smithsonian Book of Information Age Inventions*, Steven Lubar gives more evidence for the first use of magnetic tape recording: "During the war the Germans improved the tape recorder enormously and put it to use in radio stations, recording and rebroadcasting propaganda. (Hitler insisted that all radio programs be recorded so that nothing unauthorized could be broadcast.)" (183). But the credit he gives the enemy is overextended: he thus begins his history of television with the German precursor Nipkow (243), whose alleged role as father of TV was a Nazi plant. Edward Kellogg confirms the scoop on tape: "Development of magnetic coatings on paper or other base materials was undertaken by the AEG [Allgemeine elektrische Gesellschaft] in Germany about 1928, but up to the outbreak of war nothing of outstanding quality had appeared. At the close of the war the American occupying forces brought back samples of a new German magnetic tape and equipment. The magnetic material was a finely divided iron oxide, mixed with and coated on a thin Cellulose base. . . . In cleanness of reproduction, low ground noise and volume range the German system set a new high standard" (215).

13. Hence the overlaps between alien abduction and the child-abuse charge, which as charge is made ultimately against the father of psychoanalysis. Whether as fiction implanted by the analyst or therapist, or as the scene of a crime that analysis with its interest in fantasy and transference helps cover up, repressed memories literalize, split off, and project onto analysis the memory of a repression.The white snow of TV sets now signals the last recollection before hypnosis-induced blackout covers another abduction episode. A repressed memory is always in the first place a memory of a repression that can or cannot come up in session. Whenever it is a question of "The Law of Psychic Phenomena," subsections surface on "Psychotherapeutics." It is therefore not entirely now-ive that Californian psychotherapist Edith Fiore decided to specialize in overcoming resistances to remembering the repressed memories of alien abduction, close encounters of the fourth kind. She first made a name for herself in the supermarket checkout headlines when she published her first specialization, treatment of patients suffering from phantom possession *(The Unquiet Dead)*. In her second book, *Encounters,*

Fiore declares her split reception of the truth of her patient's repressed memories: "I am a therapist, so my primary goal in doing regressions to close encounters is to help the patient overcome symptoms, problems, and difficulties. Recently, I've taken on the additional role of a UFO investigator, in which collecting data (exposing the event) is the primary objective. Often in doing an investigation, I decided to ask questions that may actually have led the person in the suspected direction in order to facilitate our work. If a strict researcher had been peering over my shoulder, he would have frowned and shaken his head, because he would have been after proof of the validity of the contact, whereas my goal may have changed to quickly relieving anxiety that had surfaced" (5).

14. "EVP [Electronic Voice Phenomena] voices typically speak in short, cryptic and sometimes grammatically poor phrases. They speak in a variety of languages, regardless of the languages known to the listeners" (Guiley 107). "Voices also report that they communicate through one of many 'central transmitting agencies' on the Other Side" (107).

15. It was always first in the recording, rather than in the direct telephone connection, for example, that we made audio contact with the dead. Parapsychology is as scientific or science-fictive as the space program: mediums possessed and ventriloquized at a séance or the ghostly caller at the other end of the line just don't cut it.

16. According to Freud in *Civilization and Its Discontents* (second paragraph of section 6), Schiller was the inspiration or placeholder for Freud's *Trieblehre*.

17. Hans Loewald, for example, still finds application for Freud's 1914 theoretical elaboration of transference and transference neurosis in the treatment of character neurotics (a population that, since the end of both world wars, has been on the rise). "If we do not cling to the word 'symptoms,' but include the wider areas of character and of ego pathology, this still stands today as the procedure at which we aim. In this sense transference neurosis is not so much an entity to be found in the patient, but an operational concept. We may regard it as denoting the retransformation of a psychic illness which originated in pathogenic interactions with the important persons in the child's environment, into an interactional process with a new person, the analyst, in which the pathological infantile interactions and their intrapsychic consequences may become transparent and accessible to change by virtue of the analyst's objectivity and of the emergence of novel interaction-possibilities" (429).

**REFERENCES**

Abraham, Karl. "Should Patients Write Down Their Dreams?" In *Clinical Papers and Essays on Psychoanalysis,* ed. Hilda Abraham, trans. Hilda Abraham and D. R. Ellison. Vol. 1. New York: Basic Books, 1955 [1913]. 33–35.

Bander, Peter. *Voices from the Tapes: Recordings from the Other World.* New York: Drake Publishers, 1973.

Benjamin, Walter. "Über einige Motive bei Baudelaire." In *Gesammelte Schriften,* ed. Roy Tiedemann and Hermann Schweppenhäuser. Vols. 1 and 2. Frankfurt am Main: Suhrkamp, 1980.

Clément, Catherine. *The Lives and Legends of Jacques Lacan.* Trans. Arthur Goldhammer. New York: Columbia University Press, 1983 [1981].

de Man, Paul. "Kant and Schiller." In *Aesthetic Ideology,* ed. Andrzej Warminski. Minneapolis: University of Minnesota Press, 1996. 129–62.

———. "The Resistance to Theory." In *The Resistance to Theory.* Minneapolis: University of Minnesota Press, 1986. 3–20.

Derrida, Jacques. "Like the Sound of the Sea Deep within a Shell: Paul de Man's War." Trans. Peggy Kamuf. In *Responses: On Paul de Man's Wartime Journalism,* ed. Werner Hamacher, Neil Hertz, and Thomas Keenan. Lincoln and London: University of Nebraska Press, 1989. 127–64.

———. *Resistances of Psychoanalysis.* Trans. Peggy Kamuf, Pascale-Anne Brault, and Michael Naas. Stanford, Calif.: Stanford University Press, 1998 [1996].

*The Encyclopedia Americana.* Vol. 26. Danbury, Conn.: Grolier, 1999.

Fiore, Edith. *Encounters: A Psychologist Reveals Case Studies of Abductions by Extraterrestrials.* New York: Ballantine Books, 1990.

———. *The Unquiet Dead.* New York: Ballantine Books, 1988.

Freud, Sigmund. *The Standard Edition of the Complete Psychological Works of Sigmund Freud.* Vol. 21. Ed. and trans. James Strachey. London: The Hogarth Press, 1961 [1930].

Gottlieb, Sidney, ed. *Hitchcock on Hitchcock: Selected Writings and Interviews.* Berkeley, Los Angeles, and London: University of California Press, 1997.

Guiley, Rosemary Ellen. *The Encyclopedia of Ghosts and Spirits.* New York: Facts on File, 1992.

*A History of Technology.* Ed. Trevor I. Williams. Vol. 7, *The Twentieth Century c. 1900 to c. 1950.* Part II. Oxford: Clarendon Press, 1978.

Jung, Carl Gustav. "After the Catastrophe." In *Civilization in Transition,* trans. R. F. C. Hull. New York: Pantheon, 1964 [1945]. 194–217.

———. *Flying Saucers: A Modern Myth of Things Seen in the Skies.* Trans. R. F. C. Hull. Princeton, N.J.: Princeton University Press, 1978.

———. "Wotan." In *Civilization in Transition,* trans. R. F. C. Hull. New York: Pantheon, 1964 [1936]. 179–93.

Edward Kellog. "History of Sound Motion Pictures." In *A Technological History of Motion Pictures and Television,* ed. Raymond Fielding. Berkeley and Los Angeles: University of California Press, 1967. 174–220.

Kittler, Friedrich. *Grammophon Film Typewriter.* Berlin: Brinkmann & Bose, 1986.

Kubis, Pat, and Mark Macy. *Conversations beyond the Light: With Departed Friends and Colleagues by Electronic Means.* Boulder, Colo.: Griffin Publishing in conjunction with Continuing Life Research, 1995.

Lacan, Jacques. "The Direction of the Treatment and the Principles of Its Power." In *Écrits: A Selection,* trans. Alan Sheridan. New York and London: W. W. Norton, 1977). 226–80.

———. *Freud's Papers on Technique 1953–1954.* Book 1, *The Seminar of Jacques Lacan.* Ed. Jacques-Alain Miller, trans. John Forrester. New York and London: W. W. Norton, 1988 [1975].

Lacan, Jacques. "The Mirror Stage as Formative of the Function of the I as Revealed in Psychoanalytic Experience." In *Écrits: A Selection,* trans. Alan Sheridan. New York and London: W. W. Norton, 1977. 1–7.

———. "Presence of the Analyst." In *Essential Papers on Transference,* ed. Aaron H. Esman. New York and London: New York University Press, 1990. 480–91.

———. *Television: A Challenge to the Psychoanalytic Establishment.* Ed. Joan Copjec. Trans. Denis Hollier, Rosalind Krauss, and Annette Michelson. New York: W. W. Norton, 1990 [1973].

Leigh, Janet (with Christorper Nickens). *Psycho: Behind the Scenes of the Classic Thriller.* New York: Harmony Books, 1995.

Leites, Nathan. "Transference Interpretations Only?" In *Essential Papers on Transference,* ed. Aaron H. Esman. New York and London: New York University Press, 1990. 434–54.

Loewald, Hans W. "The Transference Neurosis: Comments on the Concept and the Phenomenon." In *Essential Papers on Transference,* ed. Aaron H. Esman. New York and London: New York University Press, 1990. 423–33.

Lubar, Steven. *Infoculture. The Smithsonian Book of Information Age Inventions.* Boston and New York: Houghton Mifflin, 1993.

Mandel, Henry A. *Banners of Light.* New York: Vantage Press, 1973.

"Our Next Program Comes to You from the Other World." In *Out of This World: The Illustrated Library of the Bizarre and Extraordinary.* New York: Columbia House, 1976. 69–74.

Raudive, Konstantin. *Breakthrough: Electronic Communication with the Dead May Be Possible.* New York: Zebra Books, 1971.

Rogo, D. Scott. *An Experience of Phantoms.* New York: Taplinger Publishing Company, 1974.

Stemman, Roy. *The Supernatural: Spirits and Spirit Worlds.* London: Aldus Books, 1975.

Winter, Frank H. "Camera Rockets and Space Photography Concepts before World War II." In *History of Rocketry and Astronautics.* AAS History Series, vol. 8, AAS, San Diego (1989): 73–102.

# III. Re-Marking "de Man"

# Paul de Man as Allergen

J. Hillis Miller

## WHY READING DE MAN MAKES YOU SNEEZE

It is easy to see why the institution of literary study in the United States, or, in a different way, in Europe, including journalistic reviewing in both regions, is antipathetical to de Man and needs to suppress him in order to get on with its business. De Man's work is a violent allergen that provokes fits of coughing, sneezing, and burning eyes, perhaps even worse symptoms, unless it can be neutralized or expelled. "Allergen": a substance that causes an allergy. The word *allergy*, oddly enough, comes from the German *Allergie*, meaning "altered reaction," a Teutonic formation from the Greek *allo*, other, plus *ergon*, work. The "gen" in *allergen* means generating or causing. De Man's work as allergen is something alien, other, that works to bring about a reaction of resistance to that otherness. The best antihistamine might be to forget his essays altogether and get on with the reproduction of some form or other of aesthetic ideology. The trouble is that once you have read de Man seriously it is difficult to do that without a vague uneasy feeling that you are laying traps for yourself and others, or, to put it more simply, as de Man himself put it in the first paragraphs of "The Resistance to Theory," promulgating something false, perhaps dangerously false.

In a remark near the beginning of the "Kant and Schiller" essay, which, it should be remembered, is the transcription of an oral performance, Paul de Man observes that though his Cornell audience has been "so kind at the beginning and so hospitable and so benevolent," nevertheless, in this case as in others in his experience, "it doesn't take you too long before you feel that you're getting under people's skin, and that there is a certain reaction which is bound to occur, certain questions that are bound to be asked, which is the interesting moment, when certain issues are bound to come up."[1] My figure of de Man as allergen is a slight transposition of this figure. An allergen causes an allergic reaction. It gets under your skin or into your nose, and "there is a certain reaction which is bound to occur." You sneeze or break out in a rash. The figure is only a figure. It compares what happens to some people in reading de Man to what happens in a certain material reaction to a foreign substance by a living organic body. The figure is not innocent, however. In comparing something seemingly "abstract," intentional, linguistic, or "spiritual," reading, to something material, automatic, autonomic, and involuntary, something "bound to happen," that is, an allergic reaction, the question of the relation of language to "materiality" is raised. Does any substantial connection justify the figure? This is one of the central questions in de Man's conception of a "material event." How can a linguistic act, such as the formulations reached by Kant's philosophic rigor, intervene in the "material" world and bring about what de Man calls "the materiality of actual history"?[2] How can writing or reading be a material event? How can speech be an act? As I shall show, de Man's transformation of the usual meaning of "materiality" (the transformation is itself a speech act) goes by way of a new conception of the relation of language to that reconceived materiality.

Almost any page of de Man's work, but especially the beginnings and endings of essays, contains rejections of well-established received ideas about literary study. These rejections can best be characterized as ironically and joyfully insolent or even contemptuous, as well as dismayingly rigorous and plausible.[3] Salient examples are the first two pages of "The Resistance to Theory" and the last three pages of "Shelley Disfigured."[4] De Man's essays have the structure he identifies in "The Concept of Irony" as "the traditional opposition between *eiron* and *alazon,* as they appear in Greek or Hellenic comedy, the smart guy and the dumb guy" (*AI* 165). De Man is of course the *eiron,* the smart guy, and all the previous experts on whatever topic or text he is discussing are the *alazons,* the dumb guys.[5] The received ideas he attacks, often fundamental assumptions of our profession, are characteristically called aberrant, deluded, or simply false. The reader can only hope or assume that "This does not, cannot, mean me! Surely I would not make such stupid mistakes." De Man forestalls that defensive move, however, when he asserts, for example, in the "Kant and Schiller" essay in *Aesthetic Ideology,* that everyone, including himself, however ironically, in a collective "we," is still bewitched by aesthetic ideology:

> Before you either contest this [what he has been saying about Schiller's distortion of Kant], or before you not contest but agree with it and hold it against Schiller, or think that it is something we are now far beyond and that we would never in our enlightened days do—you would never make this naive confusion between the practical and the pragmatic on the one hand and the philosophical Kantian enterprise on the other— before you decide that, don't decide too soon that you are beyond Schiller in any sense. I don't think any of us can lay this claim. Whatever writing we do, whatever way we have of talking about art, whatever way we have of teaching, whatever justification we give ourselves for teaching, whatever the standards are and the values by means of which we teach, they are more than ever and profoundly Schillerian. They come from Schiller, and not from Kant. (*AI* 142)

De Man goes on to make a warning that certainly applies to what has happened in his own case, in spite of the fact that he was protected by being a Sterling Professor at Yale, which is about as much security as you can get:

> And if you ever try to do something in the other direction [in the direction of Kant, that is, rather than Schiller] and you touch on it you'll see what will happen to you. Better be very sure, wherever you are, that your tenure is very well established, and that the institution for which you work has a very well-established reputation. Then you can take some risks without really taking many risks" (*AI* 142).

I have said that de Man's work is threatening to "us all" because almost any page contains cheerfully taunting rejections, explicit or implicit, of "our" most basic ideological assumptions, the ones "we" most need to get on with our work, the ones the university most needs to get on with its work. His counterintuitive concept (it is not really a concept) of materiality is an example of this.

## DE MAN'S MATERIALISM

The " 's" in this subhead is a double genitive, both objective and subjective. It names both de Man's theory of materiality and the way his own writings may show materiality at work or may be examples of materiality at work. De Man's materiality is one of the most difficult and obscure parts of his work.

De Man's use of the terms *materiality* and *materialism* poses several special problems, resistances to comprehension. First, one or the other word is most often introduced only briefly and elliptically. If the reader does not keep a sharp eye out for it, it appears in a given essay for an instant, for the blink of an eye, like a meteor, and then vanishes. Moreover, in these passages de Man seems to be saying exceedingly strange things, such as the assertion that materiality is not "phenomenal." Second, unlike "performative" and "irony" (terms not on everyone's lips and concepts that clearly need some explaining), we tend to think we already know what materiality is. It is the property possessed by these hard objects right in front of me now, impassive, impassible, resistant, not dependent on my perception for their continued existence, like that stone Samuel Johnson kicked to refute Berkeley's idealism: "I refute him thus [kicking the stone]." Third, the term *materialism* is extremely difficult to extricate from its associations with modern empirical science or with vulgar understandings of Marxism. Is not Marxism to be defined as "dialectical materialism"? De Man is supposed to be in one way or another a linguistic formalist, someone who believed, as all so-called deconstructionists are supposed to believe, that it is "all language," though the reader might remember that de Man began his higher education as a science, mathematics, and engineering student at the École Polytechnique of the University of Brussels (1936). His professional interest in language came later. Nevertheless, for de Man to call himself a materialist, or for us to call him one, seems as absurd and counterintuitive as for de Man to call Kant and Hegel materialists or to find crucial materialist moments in their work, since everybody knows (without necessarily having read them) that they are "idealists." Equally absurd would be to think one might find any kinship between de Man's thinking and Marxism, though the truth is that a deep kinship exists between de Man's work and Marx's thought in *The German Ideology,* as Andrzej Warminski has been demonstrating in his seminars. To show this it is necessary actually to go back and read Marx, as well as de Man, no easy tasks.

The term *materiality* or its cognates appears at crucial moments in de Man's work as early as a citation from Proust in "Reading (Proust)" in *Allegories of Reading.* What Proust calls the "symbols," in Giotto's *Allegory of the Virtues and Vices* at the Arena in Padua, meaning representations like the Charity that looks like a kitchen maid, are "something real, actually experienced or materially handled."[6] That this passage was important to de Man is indicated by the way he cites it again at a crucial moment on the symbol in Hegel just at the end of one of his late essays, "Sign and Symbol in Hegel's *Aesthetics.*" This time de Man translates the phrases himself somewhat differently from the Moncrieff translation, and he cites the French original: "the symbol represented as real, as actually inflicted or materially handled [. . . *(le symbole représenté) comme réel, comme effectivement subi ou matériellement manié]*" (*AI* 103). The terms *material, materiality,* and the like then appear with increasing frequency in de Man's later work. It is as though de Man had discovered in such words a way to "call" more accurately something he wanted performatively to name, perhaps even to invoke, that is, to "call forth": "The only word that comes to mind is that of a *material* vision . . ." ("Phenomenality and Materiality in Kant," in *AI* 82). What Michael Riffatere misses or evades in Hugo's "Écrit sur la vitre d'une fenêtre flamande" is just what the title indicates or names, namely, what de Man calls "the materiality of an inscription" (*RT* 51). A climactic passage in Shelley's *The Triumph of Life* is said to stress "the literal and material aspects of language" (*RR* 113). "Anthropomorphism and Trope in the Lyric" ends, in a phrase I have already cited, with an appeal to "the materiality of actual history" (*RR* 262). A cascade of such terms punctuates the essays in *Aesthetic Ideology,* not only in "Phenomenality and Materiality in Kant" and in "Kant's Materialism," where "a materialism that Kant's posterity has not yet begun to face up to" (*AI* 89) is the focus of the argument, but also in "Sign and Symbol in Hegel's *Aesthetics,*" where we read that "The idea, in other words, makes its sensory appearance, in Hegel, as the material inscription of names" and also in the way Hegel's "theory of the sign manifests itself materially" (*AI* 102, 103), and in "Kant and Schiller," where we read of the irreversible progression "from states of cognition, to something which is no longer a cognition but which is to some extent an *occurrence,* which has the materiality of something that actually happens, that actually occurs" and of "the materiality of the inscribed signifier in Kant" (*AI* 132, 134).

The reader will have seen that the term *materiality* and its cognates occur in three related, ultimately more or less identical, registers in de Man: the materiality of history, the materiality of inscription, and the materiality of what the eye sees prior to perception and cognition. In all three of these registers, as I shall try to show, materiality is associated with notions of performative power and with what seems materiality's opposite, formalism. In all three modes of materialism, the ultimate paradox, allergenic idea, or unintelligibility is the claim or insinuation that materiality is not phenomenal, not open to the senses. Just what in the world could that mean?

The phrase "materiality of history" seems the easiest to understand and accept as commonsensical. Of course history is material. It means what really happened, especially as a result of human intervention (though we speak, for example, of the history of the mollusks, or of geological history). History is wars, battles, the building of the pyramids, the invention of the steam engine, migrations of peoples, legislative decisions, diplomatic negotiations, the clearing of forests, global warming, that sort of thing. De Man's materiality of history, however, is not quite like that. For him the materiality of history, properly speaking, is the result of acts of power that are punctual and momentary, since they are atemporal, noncognitive and noncognizable performative utterances. History is caused by language or other signs that make something materially happen, and such happenings do not happen all that often. The most radical, and allergenic, counterintuitive, scandalous formulation of this is in "Kant and Schiller." There de Man asserts that Kant's *Critique of Judgment* was an irreversible historical event brought about by the shift from cognitive to efficaciously performative discourse in Kant's own words, whereas Schiller's ideological misreading of Kant and its long progeny in the nineteenth and twentieth centuries were nonevents, certainly not irreversible material events. In "Phenomenality and Materiality in Kant" de Man speaks of the crucial shift to a "formal materialism" in Kant's *Critique of Judgment* as "a shift from trope to performance" that is "a deep, perhaps fatal, break or discontinuity" (*AI* 83, 89, 79). This is the place, as he puts it in "Kant and Schiller," at which Kant "found himself by the rigor of his own discourse [the project of aesthetics as articulation of pure reason and practical reason or ethics] to break down under the power of his own critical epistemological discourse" (*AI* 134). This was an event, strictly speaking an irreversible historical event, "to some extent an *occurrence*, which has the materiality of something that actually happens, that actually occurs. And there, the thought of material occurrence, something that occurs materially, that leaves a trace on the world, that does something to the world as such—that notion of occurrence is not opposed in any sense to the notion of writing" (*AI* 132). Since the event of Kant's materialism is punctual and instantaneous, it is in a curious sense not within time, though it has a permanent and irreversible effect on what we usually (mistakenly) think of as the temporality of history:

history is not thought of as a progression or a regression, but is thought of as an event, as an occurrence. There is history from the moment that words such as 'power' and 'battle' and so on emerge on the scene. At that moment things *happen*, there is *occurrence*, there is *event*. History is therefore not a temporal notion, it has nothing to do with temporality [there's allergenic assertion for you!], but it is the emergence of a language of power out of a language of cognition. (*AI* 133)

I do not think de Man meant that the words *power* and *battle* are in themselves always historical events in the sense de Man is defining such events, but that he means the uses of such words in effective performative utterances are historical events. As opposed to the moment of Kant's self-undoing materialism in the third *Critique*, Schiller's recuperation of Kant within aesthetic ideology and its long progeny, the procedures of which are identified in the main body of "Kant and Schiller," did not happen, were not historical events:

> One could say, for example, that in the reception of Kant, in the way Kant has been read, since the third *Critique*—and that was an occurrence, something happened there, something occurred [de Man's stuttering iterations here mime the punctualities of historical events; the reader will remember that this is the transcript of an oral presentation that was not written down as such]—that in the whole reception of Kant from then until now, nothing has happened, only regression, nothing has happened at all. Which is another way of saying there is no history . . . that reception is not historical. . . . The event, the occurrence, is resisted by reinscribing it in the cognition of tropes, and that is itself a tropological, cognitive, and not a historical move. (*AI* 134)[7]

These sternly recalcitrant statements may be more understandable and perhaps even more acceptable if we remember that Althusser, and de Man in his own way, following Marx, define ideology as having no history, as being outside history, as having no purchase on history, since ideology is precisely an illusory misunderstanding of the "real conditions of existence," as Althusser put it in "Ideology and Ideological State Apparatuses,"[8] or, as de Man puts this in "The Resistance to Theory": "What we call ideology is precisely the confusion of linguistic with natural reality, of reference with phenomenalism" (*RT* 11).[9] The reception of Kant by Schiller and his followers, including you and me as inheritors of aesthetic ideology, is ideological, therefore not historical.

We are (I am) now in a position to answer the puzzling assertions de Man makes in "The Concept of Irony." "Irony," he says, "also very clearly has a performative function. Irony consoles and it promises and it excuses" (AI 165). What could de Man mean by saying that irony is performatively efficacious, that it promises, consoles, or excuses? If we take seriously de Man's claim later in the essay that irony is a permanent parabasis that radically suspends meaning by the incursion of chaos, madness, and stupidity (Friedrich Schlegel's terms) into language, then it would seem radically counterintuitive to say that irony has a successful performative function. A statement at the end of the essay is equally baffling: "Irony and history seem to be curiously linked to one another" (AI 184). If irony is permanent parabasis it would seem to have little to do with history, but to be rather the withdrawal from effective historical action. The analogy between the noncognitive aspect of irony and the noncognitive aspect of performative utterances gives the clue. Irony is perhaps the most radical example of the rupture between cognitive and performative discourses. Insofar as an utterance is performative, it is unknowable. Irony suspends cognition. It is just because irony is error, madness, and stupidity that it can be performatively felicitous. Promises, excuses, consolations can be performed by irony, or can be especially done by ironic utterance, just because irony is the radical suspension of cognition. Another way to put this is to say that even the most solemn performative utterances are contaminated by being possibly ironic. Jacques Derrida includes irony along with literature among the parasitical presences that are possibly incorporated within any performative as a result of its intrinsic iterability.

What I have just said will also indicate the surprising and "curious" connection of irony with history. Since the materiality of history as event is generated by acts of linguistic power, that is, performative speech acts, though by no means necessarily intentional ones, irony as a form of such power or as an ingredient of any such act of power, against all our instinctive assumptions, can be said not only to promise, console, and excuse, but also to generate the events that make up the materiality of history. Just as, for Derrida, the possibility of felicitous speech acts depends on the possibility that they may be "literature," so for de Man the efficacy of performative utterances, including those that generate history, depends on the possibility that they may be ironical. They may be. You cannot tell for sure.

If speech acts generating history are, strangely enough, one form of materiality or are the place where language touches materiality, leaves a mark on it, materially handles it, the materiality of what the eye sees appears more obvious but turns out to be more difficult to grasp. Of course, we say, what the eye sees is material. That received opinion or doxa turns out, however, once again not to be quite what de Man means. What he does mean is the central argument of the two essays on Kant, "Phenomenality and Materiality in Kant" and "Kant's Materialism." For received opinion, what we take for granted, phenomenality and materiality are the same thing or are two aspects of the same thing. Because something is material it is phenomenal, open to the senses. For de Man, following Kant, phenomenality and materiality are not conjoined but opposed. How can this be? De Man sees in Kant's theory of the dynamic sublime two radically contradictory notions. On the one hand, the sublime is the moment when the imagination triumphs over fear and puts all the elements of the sublime scene together, articulates them in a grand aesthetic synthesis, as tropes articulate, or as the body's limbs are articulated: "The imagination overcomes suffering, becomes apathetic, and sheds the pain of natural shock. It reconciles pleasure with pain and in so doing it articulates, as mediator, the movement of the affects with the legal, codified, formalized, and stable order of reason" (*AI* 86). In so doing, the imagination of the sublime or the sublime itself accomplishes the goal of the third *Critique,* which was to find a "bridge" between the first and second *Critiques,* between pure reason and the practical reason of moral obligation and choice. On the other hand, Kant's analysis of the dynamic sublime contains a moment that radically disrupts, interrupts, and suspends this happy articulation. Kant reaches this moment through the very rigor of his critical thinking. He proposes that the paradigmatic example of the dynamic sublime is when the overarching vault of the sky and the outstretched mirror of the sea are seen just as the eye sees them, or as the poets see them, without thought for their meaning. Seeing them as meaningful would occur, for example, when we view the sea as a reservoir of edible fish, or the sky as a producer of life-giving rain. De Man quotes section 28 of Kant's *The Critique of Judgment:* "we must regard it [the starry heaven], just as we see it *[wie man ihn sieht],* as a distant, all-embracing vault *[ein weites Gewölbe].* . . . To find the ocean nevertheless sublime we must regard it as poets do *[wie die Dichter es tun],* merely by what the eye reveals *[was der Augeschein zeigt]"* (*AI* 80). De Man goes on to argue that this way of seeing is radically nonphenomenal. It does not involve the mind that in its activity of perception would make sense of what is seen. It just sees what it sees, in an activity of the eye operating by itself, enclosed in itself, wholly detached, disarticulated, from thinking and interpreting: "No mind is involved in the Kantian vision of ocean and heaven. . . . That is how things are to the eye, in the redundancy of their appearance to the eye and not to the mind, as in the redundant word *Augenschein*, . . . in which the eye, tautologically, is named twice, as eye itself and as what appears to the eye" (*AI* 82). De Man's name for this way of seeing is "material vision": "The only word that comes to mind is that of a *material* vision" (*AI* 82), which is another way of saying, in a paradigmatic performative speech act, "I call this '*material* vision.'" The word *material* then appears in a cascade of phrases in the subsequent pages: "the vision is purely material"; "what we call the material aspect"; "a materialism that, in the tradition of the reception of the third *Critique*, is seldom or never perceived"; "If the architectonic then appears, very near the end of the analytics of the aesthetic, at the conclusion of the section on the sublime, as the material disarticulation not only of nature but of the body [traditional examples of the beautiful or the sublime], then this moment marks the undoing of the aesthetic as a valid category. The critical power of a transcendental philosophy undoes the very project of such a philosophy leaving us, certainly not with an ideology—for transcendental and ideological (metaphysical) principles are part of the same system—but with a materialism that Kant's posterity has not yet begun to face up to" (*AI* 83, 88, 89).

How could we "face up to" something that we can see but not face up to in the sense of clearly confronting it and making it intelligible to ourselves? The idea of a way of seeing that is performed by the eye alone, wholly dissociated from the mind, is, strictly speaking, unintelligible, since any sense we give to this *Augenschein* is an illicit, ideological imposition: "To the extent that any mind, that any judgment, intervenes, it is in error" (*AI* 82). That is what I mean by saying that de Man's materiality is nonphenomenal, since phenomenality always involves, instantly, making sense or trying to make sense of what we see. This "material vision" would be pure seeing prior to any seeing as the sort of understanding that we name when we say, "I see it all now." It would be a pre-seeing seeing, that is, something unthinkable, unknowable, unintelligible, a tautological eye eyeing: "Realism postulates a phenomenalism of experience which is here being denied or ignored. Kant's looking at the world just as one sees it ('wie man ihn sieht') is an absolute, radical formalism that entertains no notion of reference or semiosis" (*AI* 128).

The idea of a materiality that would not be phenomenal does not make sense. Nevertheless, that is just what de Man affirms, most overtly and in so many words at the end of the essay on Riffaterre, "Hypogram and Inscription." There he speaks of "the materiality (as distinct from the phenomenality) that is thus revealed [when we remember that Hugo's poem was supposed to have been written on a window pane], the unseen 'cristal' whose existence thus becomes a certain *there* and a certain *then* which can become a *here* and a *now* in the reading 'now' taking place" (*RT* 51). The paradox is that the window glass, figure here for the materiality of inscription, is not what the eye sees but what the eye sees through. In the Kant essays, as in "Hypogram and Inscription," the rigor of de Man's own critical thinking brings him repeatedly, by different routes, across the border of the intelligible and into the realm of the allergenic, in this case the recognition of a materialism in Kant that has seldom or never been recognized in the whole distinguished tradition of Kant scholarship and so is anathema to it, just as de Man's reading of somewhat similar material moments in Hegel was anathema to the distinguished Hegel specialist Raymond Geuss.[10]

The final version of materiality in de Man is the "prosaic materiality of the letter" (*AI* 90). Just what does de Man mean by that? No one doubts that writing (and speaking too) have a material base, marks on paper or modulated waves in the air. This materiality is the benign base of the meaning, permanence, and transmissibility of language. No problem. De Man of course does not mean anything so in agreement with common sense and received opinion. When de Man calls Kant's sublime *Augenschein* of sky and sea a "*material* vision" he goes on to raise a further question that is not answered until the end of the essay: "how this materiality is then to be understood in linguistic terms is not, as yet, clearly intelligible" (*AI* 82). The answer is the materiality of the letter, but just what does that mean? The essay ends with an explanation that if not clearly intelligible, at least indicates why these "linguistic terms" must be unintelligible. The reader is given intelligence of unintelligibility, new news of the unknowable.

The prosaic materiality of the letter, linguistic "equivalent" of a materialism of vision, has two main features. One is a disarticulation of language equaling the disarticulations of nature and the human body de Man has found in Kant's dynamic sublime: "To the dismemberment of the body corresponds a dismemberment of language, as meaning-producing tropes are replaced by the fragmentation of sentences and propositions into discrete words, or the fragmentation of words into syllables or finally letters" (*AI* 89). Strictly speaking, as linguists, not to speak of language philosophers like Wittgenstein, have shown, words do not have meaning by themselves. They have meaning only when they are used, incorporated into sentences. To detach them from their sentences and leave them hanging there in the air or on the page, surrounded by blank paper, is the first stage in a progressive disarticulation of meaning that goes then to syllables and finally to letters. It is extremely difficult to see words, syllables, or letters, for example on a printed page, in this way, just as it is extremely hard to see as the eye sees. One has to be a poet, as Kant says, to do it. The mind instantly interprets what the eye sees, "perceives it," and gives meaning to it, just as the mind projects meaning into those mute letters on the page. It is almost impossible to see letters as just the material marks they are. Even words in a language we do not know are seen as language and not as sheer materiality. We tend to see random marks on a rock as possibly writing in an unknown language.

The other feature of the materiality of the letter stressed by de Man makes that materiality more likely to be glimpsed, in the wink of the eye, before the mind starts "reading." This is repetition of words and word parts that calls attention to the absurd and unmotivated echoes among them at the level of syllable and letter: puns, rhymes, alliterations, assonances, and so on, that is, precisely those linguistic features poets especially use, "the play of the letter and of the syllable, the way of saying . . . as opposed to what is being said" (*AI* 89). The "persuasiveness" of the passage in Kant about the recovery of the imagination's tranquillity through material vision depends, de Man says, "on the proximity between the German words for surprise and admiration, *Verwunderung* and *Bewunderung*" (*AI* 89). The reader, de Man continues, is led to assent to the incompatibility or aporia between the imagination's failure and its success by "a constant, and finally bewildering alternation of the two terms, *Angemessen(heit)* and *Unangemessen(heit)*, to the point where one can no longer tell them apart" (*AI* 90). One additional example of this in de Man's essays is the cascade of words in *"fall"* that he finds in a passage by Kleist: *Fall, Beifall, Sündenfall, Rückfall, Einfall, Zurückfall, Fälle*: "As we know from another narrative text of Kleist ["On the Gradual Formation of Thoughts while Speaking"], the memorable tropes that have the most success *(Beifall)* occur as mere random improvisation *(Einfall)* at the moment when the author has completely relinquished control over his meaning and has relapsed *(Zurückfall)* into the extreme formalization, the mechanical predictability of grammatical declensions *(Fälle)"* (*RR* 290). By the time the reader gets to the end of this the root *"fall"* is fast becoming a mere surd, a sound emptied of meaning: *"fall, fall, fall, fall."* The reader will see that "formalism" of "formalization" names for de Man not the beautiful aesthetic formalization of the artwork, but a principle of mechanical senselessness in language that he associates with the arbitrariness of grammar, of declensions, *Fälle.* De Man goes on to make a pun of his own. Since *Falle* also means trap in German, he can say that everyone falls into "the trap of an aesthetic education which inevitably confuses dismemberment of language by the power of the letter with the gracefulness of a dance." That trap, however, is not a benign aestheticizing of the random formalizations of language in grammar and paronomasia such as poets are known to play with. It is a mortal danger, a *pericolo de morte,* according to the last words of the last essay in *The Rhetoric of Romanticism,* "the ultimate trap, as unavoidable as it is deadly" (*RR* 290). The reader will note that this aspect of the materiality of the letter tends to disappear in translation. It depends on the unique idiom, idiolect, or even "idiocy," in the etymological sense, of a certain language. Ultimately, this repetition of words and bits of words empties language of meaning and makes it mere unintelligible sound, as when the poet Tennyson, as a child, used to repeat his own name over and over, "Alfred, Alfred, Alfred," until it ceased to mean anything at all and he melted into a kind of oceanic trance. Try it with your own name, as I do here with mine: "Hillis, Hillis, Hillis, Hillis."

De Man's formulation of this in one notable place is more prosaic. As he shows, Hegel's theory of memory as *Gedächtnis,* in opposition to *Erinnerung,* is that it memorizes by emptying words of meaning and repeating them by rote, as pure arbitrary signs that might be in a foreign language or in no language at all:

> "It is well known," says Hegel, "that one knows a text by heart [or by rote] only when one no longer associates any meaning with the words; in reciting what one thus knows by heart one necessarily drops all accentuation." [I suppose Hegel means that one repeats the words mindlessly, like a schoolchild or a robot—*JHM*.] . . . The idea, in other words, makes its sensory appearance, in Hegel, as the material inscription of names. (*AI* 101–2)

Speaking in "Hegel on the Sublime" of Hegel's "Gesetz der Äußerlichkeit (law of exteriority)," de Man says, "Like a stutter, or a broken record,

it makes what it keeps repeating worthless and meaningless" (*AI* 116).
This had already been exemplified in a truly vertiginous couple of
paragraphs in "Sign and Symbol in Hegel's *Aesthetics*." There de Man
takes two at first innocent-enough-looking, but in fact "quite astonishing," sentences in Hegel's *Encyclopedia*: "Since language states only
what is general, I cannot say what is only my opinion [*so kann ich
nicht sagen was ich nur meine*]," and "When I say 'I,' I *mean* myself as
*this* I to the exclusion of all others; but what I say, I, is precisely anyone; any I, as that which excludes all others from itself [*ebenso, wenn
ich sage: 'Ich,'* meine *ich mich* als *diesen alle anderen Ausschließenden;
aber was ich·sage, Ich, ist eben jeder*]" (*AI* 97, 98). The sentences
themselves are bad enough in English, though worse in German (e.g.,
wenn Ich sage, Ich, *meine* ich mich"), but by the time de Man gets
through with these sentences the reader is dizzied by the repetitions,
like Tennyson repeating his own first name, or as if he had been caught
in a revolving door.[11] Through this dizziness the reader reaches in the
emptying out of meaning a glimpse of the materiality of the letter. In
commenting on the first sentence de Man plays with *mein* and *meinen*
as *mine* and *mean* and generates a sentence in which the cascade of
"sinces," and sinces within sinces, produces its own stuttering repetition, like a broken record:

> "Ich kann nicht sagen was ich (nur) meine" then means "I cannot say
> what I make mine" or, since to think is to make mine, "I cannot say
> what I think," and, since to think is fully contained in and defined by
> the I, since Hegel's *ego cogito* defines itself as mere *ego*, what the sen-
> tence actually says is "I cannot say I"—a disturbing proposition in
> Hegel's own terms since the very possibility of thought depends on the
> possibility of saying "I." (*AI* 98)

The other sentence, with its repetitions of *ich* and *ich* in *mich,* is already
"astonishing" enough itself, as de Man says, in the sense of numbing
the mind, turning it to stone (to play on a false etymology; the word
really means, etymologically, "to strike with thunder"). The sentence
shows the impossibility not only of the deictics "here," "now," "this,"
as when I say, "This sentence which I am here and now writing on my
computer at 8:51 A.M. on November 4, 1997," or, in Hegel's example,
this piece of paper on which I am now writing, but also of the deictic
use of "I" to point to me myself alone as a unique I. These words are
"shifters," placeholders. Instantly, as soon as they are uttered, the
words assume the utmost generality and can be shifted to any I, any

here, now, and this.[12] However hard you try, you cannot say this I here and now or this keyboard, processor, and computer screen at this moment that are prostheses of my body and by means of which I think. "I cannot say I." "Aber was ich sage, Ich, ist eben jeder (but what I say, I, is precisely anyone)." De Man takes the otherness of *"jeder"* not to refer to another I, "the mirror image of the I," but to name *"n'importe qui* or even *n'importe quoi"* (*AI* 98); that is, anybody at all or even anything at all, just as the name Marion, in de Man's reading of the "purloined ribbon" episode in Rousseau's *Julie*, is ultimately just a random sound, not even a proper name: "Rousseau was making whatever noise happened to come into his head; he was saying nothing at all, least of all someone's name" (*AR* 292).

As de Man says of Rousseau's excuse in *Julie* for what he had done to Marion, "When everything fails, one can always plead insanity" (*AR* 289). A certain madness, the madness of words, the reader can see, often infects de Man's own language. He mimes in what he says the materiality of the letter he is naming. At this point his own work becomes a performative utterance working to lead the reader to the edge of unintelligibility, this time by the route of the materiality of the letter, and once more in a way that is counterintuitive, since it is another materiality that is nonphenomenal, unable to be seen, like the "cristal invisible" of that Flemish windowpane on which Hugo's poem was scratched.

The back cover of de Man's *Aesthetic Ideology* speaks of the "ironic good humor that is unique to him." I find de Man's irony, especially when it expresses itself in wordplay, much more threatening than this phrase implies, and so have many of de Man's readers or listeners. Such passages as I have been discussing, where the madness of words has crossed over into de Man's own language, are places that readers or auditors have found especially allergenic, that they have especially resisted. The audience of de Man's "Semiology and Rhetoric," for example, when the essay was presented as a sort of inaugural lecture after de Man took up his professorship at Yale, was more than a little scandalized or even offended by the elaborate pun de Man develops based on the Archie Bunker television show. This pun depends on the difference between lacing your shoes over or under. ("What's the difference?" asks Archie Bunker.) This leads to the punch line of calling Jacques Derrida an "archie Debunker" (*AR* 10). The audience did not find that wholly appropriate for such a solemn occasion. The complex double talk that de Man, in an exuberant reading, finds in Proust's phrase "torrent d'activité" (*AR* 64) has seemed to some readers just going too far. Raymond Geuss especially resisted what de Man says about *"mein"* and *"meinen"* in Hegel. De Man's "Reply to Raymond Geuss" patiently laces over and under, that is, explains what he meant and why he is right and Geuss wrong, guilty of "misplaced timidity" (*AI* 190), an unwillingness to face up to what is truly wild in Hegel's text.

The resistance to de Man, what I have called an allergic reaction to his writings, is not a resistance to theory in the etymological sense of the word *theory*, a resistance to a generalizable "clear-seeing," but rather a resistance to what in his work precisely cannot be seen clearly, the penumbra of the unknowable, the unintelligible, the nonphenomenal that is everywhere in his work. This is perhaps most threateningly present not in the radical incompatibility of the cognitive and performative dimensions of language, and not even in what Friedrich Schlegel called the madness and stupidity reached by irony as permanent parabasis, nor even in Kant's materiality of vision, but in the prosaic materiality of the letter. The latter is present at every moment, though for the most part it is invisible, suppressed, covered over, in all those words that surround us all the time and that generate the reassuring ideologies in terms of which we live our lives. What is most threatening, most allergenic, most truly frightening about de Man's writings, is the way they force their readers to confront a darkness of unknowability that is not just out there somewhere, beyond the circle of light cast by the desk's reading lamp. That would be bad enough, but this darkness has woven itself into the light of reason itself and into the "instrument" by which it expresses itself, language. "No degree of knowledge can ever stop this madness, for it is the madness of words" (*RR* 122).

## PAUL DE MAN'S AUTHORITY

Another double genitive there: the authority Paul de Man exerts and the authority in whose name he speaks. This essay began by identifying what is insolent or outrageous about de Man's writings, namely, his calm, laconic assertions that all the basic assumptions of literary studies as a discipline, along with all the greatest authorities in that discipline, are often just plain wrong. Where does de Man get his authority to say such things? In the light of my investigation of his materialism I propose now in conclusion three braided answers to the question of what justifies de Man to say what he says. All these may be inferred from de Man's own writing.

First, he might be imagined as replying that what he says, allergenic as it is, is not his own willful desire to cause trouble, but something that just happens, through reading. De Man's work is all reading of some text or other, primarily canonical texts that are among the most revered and cherished in our tradition. Therefore all these outrageous statements are not de Man speaking, but him speaking in indirect discourse for what his authors say. It is Shelley, not de Man, who says that nothing is connected to anything else. Hegel or Kleist, not de Man, who repeats the same words or syllables until they become senseless. It is not I, Paul de Man, speaking, but I speaking in the name of, with the authority, of my authors. As Chaucer says, "My auctor wol I folwen if I konne."[13] In the "Reply to Raymond Geuss," de Man says,

> The move from the theory of the sign to the theory of the subject has nothing to do with my being overconcerned with the Romantic tradition, or narcissistic, or ("c'est la même chose") too influenced by the French. It has, in fact, nothing to do with me at all but corresponds to an inexorable and altogether Hegelian move of the text. (AI 189)

Or, second appeal to authority, what I, Paul de Man, say happens through the rigor of critical reading. This rigor is something that produces the generalizations of theory, something that is wholly rational, logical, transmissible, the product of rigorous thinking that might have been done by anyone with de Man's intelligence and learning. Theory grows out of reading and is authorized by it, though it is in a different register and even though theory and reading, as "The Resistance to Theory" shows, are not symmetrical. Although "the resistance to theory is in fact a resistance to reading," nevertheless "rhetorical readings, like the other kinds, still avoid and resist the reading they advocate. Nothing can overcome the resistance to theory since theory *is* itself this resistance" (RT 15, 19). In the "Reply to Raymond Geuss," de Man asserts that the commentator should accept the "canonical reading" up to the point where something is encountered in the text that makes it impossible to go on accepting the canonical interpretation. De Man's formulations are couched in the language of ethical obligation and inevitability: "should," "could," and "necessity." The necessity arises from the reader's encounter with the text. What happens in reading happens, and it imposes implacable obligations on the reader that exceed the presuppositions both of the canonical reading and of "theory":

> The commentator should persist as long as possible in the canonical reading and should begin to swerve away from it only when he encounters

difficulties which the methodological and substantial assertions of the system are no longer able to master. Whether or not such a point has been reached should be left open as part of an ongoing critical investigation. But it would be naive to believe that such an investigation could be avoided, even for the best of reasons. The necessity to revise the canon arises from resistances encountered in the text itself (extensively conceived) and not from preconceptions imported from elsewhere. (*AI* 186)

Third source of de Man's authority, deepest and most serious: the scandalous, counterintuitive things de Man says come into language through the encounter, at the limits of the most exigent theoretical rigor and obedient close reading, of the unintelligible. De Man takes the rational to the edge of irrationality, or identifies the unintelligible as that which has always already infected the pursuit of rational knowledge: "after Nietzsche (and, indeed, after any 'text'), we can no longer hope ever 'to know' in peace" (*AR* 126). Wherever de Man starts, whatever texts he reads, whatever vocabulary he uses leads ultimately beyond itself to its limits at the border of a dark unintelligibility, what Friedrich Schlegel called "der Schein des Verkehrten und Verrückten oder des Einfältigen und Dummen" ("the appearance of error and madness, or simplemindedness and stupidity").[14] Three names de Man gives this unintelligibility are performative language, irony, and materiality. Kant may be taken as the paradigmatic model here. Kant's rigor of critical thinking led him to what undid his enterprise of architectonic articulation, disarticulated it. The same thing can be said of de Man's writing, except that de Man's writing is throughout a long meditation on what happens when thinking encounters that momentary event when the unintelligible, error, madness, stupidity, undoes the rational enterprise of critical thinking, or turns out to have been undoing it all along.

De Man speaks in the name of, on the grounds of, these three quite incompatible but nevertheless inextricably intertwined justifications for the allergens that he generates in words. This authority is, however, no authority in the ordinary sense. It is an authority without authority, or the authority that undoes all grounds for speaking with authority. How can one speak intelligibly on the grounds of the unintelligible? At the limit, and indeed all along the way, de Man's writings are allergenic because they pass on to the reader an allergen, an otherness, with which they have been infected and that is quite other to the calm, implacable, rational, maddeningly difficult to refute,[15] rigor of de Man's argumentation. Or rather, the latter turns out to be the same as the former, reason to be other to itself.

## NOTES

1. Paul de Man, *Aesthetic Ideology,* ed. Andrzej Warminski (Minneapolis: University of Minnesota Press, 1996), 131–32; hereafter *AI.*

2. Paul de Man, *The Rhetoric of Romanticism* (New York: Columbia University Press, 1984), 262; hereafter *RR.*

3. I use the word *joyfully* as an allusion to Nietzsche's "joyful wisdom" or "fröhliche Wissenschaft." Anyone who fails to see the exuberant or even comic joy in de Man's writings, anyone who sees him as a "gloomy existentialist," as one commentator calls him, simply lacks an ear. The ironic comedy sometimes surfaces openly, as when he says, apropos of Kant's assertion that the Dutch are all phlegmatic, "interested only in money and totally devoid of any feeling for beauty or sublimity whatsoever": "I have never felt more grateful for the hundred or so kilometers that separate Antwerp [de Man's home city] from Rotterdam" (*AI* 124–25). Another example is what he says as part of an assertion that the self-undoing of Kant's critical enterprise through "the rigor of his own discourse" was not felt as a subjective, affective shudder: "I don't think that Kant, when he wrote about the heavens and the sea there, that he was shuddering in mind. Any literalism there would not be called for. It is terrifying in a way which we don't know. What do we know about the nightmares of Immanuel Kant? I'm sure they were . . . very interesting . . . Königsberg there in the winter—I shudder to think (*AI* 134). This joy is no doubt one of the things that is held against de Man, as Derrida's exuberant hijinks—in format, for example—are held against him. Both make ironic jokes about deadly serious matters. There is no room for comedy or for joy either in philosophy and theory. They are solemn matters for which you should, if you are a man, always wear a shirt and tie.

4. Paul de Man, *The Resistance to Theory* (Minneapolis: University of Minnesota Press, 1986), 3–4; hereafter *RT;* and *RR* 121–23.

5. De Man goes on to recognize that the final twist of irony in Greek or Hellenic comedy is that the smart guy is "always being set up by the person he thinks of as being the dumb guy, the *alazon.* In this case the *alazon* (and I recognize that this makes me the real *alazon* of this discourse) is American criticism of irony, and the smart guy is going to be German criticism of irony, which I of course understand" (*AI* 165). This seems to be a rare example of an overt admission by de Man that he is bound to be caught in the traps he sets for others, that what is sauce for the goose is sauce for the gander. In the rest of "The Concept of Irony," however, de Man allows precious little in the way of smart-guy attributes either to American criticism of irony, exemplified by Wayne Booth, presented as a dumb guy through and through, or to German and Danish criticism of irony either, with the exception of Friedrich Schlegel. Hegel, Kierkegaard, Benjamin, Szondi, and so on, are all as dumb as Booth, though in different ways. In the vibrating irony of the passage I have quoted from de Man, it is ironic for de Man to claim that he represents American criticism of irony, though of course he is not German either. In any case, for him to say he is "the real *alazon* of this discourse" is at the same time to say that

he is the real *eiron,* since the *alazon* always turns out to be the disguised *eiron,* the smartest smart guy, or the only smart guy around.

6. Paul de Man, *Allegories of Reading* (New Haven: Yale University Press, 1979), 78; hereafter *AR.*

7. The anonymous reader of this essay for the University of Minnesota Press strongly resisted this account of de Man's concept of historical events in their materiality. "Miller's idea of history, moreover," the reader said, "is of little merit and has, as far as I can tell, very little to do with de Man." This is a good example of what I mean by an allergic reaction. My own idea of history is not expressed anywhere here, only de Man's, although in the sentence beginning "History is wars, battles . . ." I am miming ironically what history is conventionally assumed to be. Can the reader have taken my irony straight? After a careful rereading of my essay, I claim that the citations from de Man I make support what I say about de Man's concept of history. It is de Man's concept, not mine, that scandalizes the reader, makes him (or her) sneeze and cough. I have, however, altered one phrase that apparently misled the reader into thinking I understand de Man to be saying that history is caused by "intentional" uses of language and that might therefore mislead you, dear reader. As any careful reader of de Man knows, his theory of the performative "use" of language (as opposed to its mention) is detached from any conscious intention in the user. Language works performatively, on its own, most often against the intentions or knowledge of the speaker or writer. As he says, in the conclusion to "Promises *(Social Contract),*" "The error is not within the reader; language itself dissociates the cognition from the act. *Die Sprache verspricht (sich)*" *(AR* 277), which means "Language promises" and also "Language makes a slip of the tongue." I have thought it worthwhile to refer directly to the comments of the Minnesota reader in order to try to forestall similar errors on the part of readers of the published essay.

8. Louis Althusser, "Ideology and Ideological State Apparatuses (Notes towards an Investigation," in *Lenin and Philosophy and Other Essays,* trans. Ben Brewster (New York: Monthly Review Press, 1972), 162. See page 159, where Althusser says, "ideology has no history," and goes on to remark: "As we know, this formulation appears in so many words in a passage from *The German Ideology.*"

9. In an equally important, though much less well known, definition of ideologies near the beginning of "Phenomenality and Materiality in Kant" de Man asserted that ideologies are on the side of what Kant called "metaphysics," that is, in Kant's use of the term, precritical empirical knowledge of the world. Only critical analysis of ideologies will keep ideologies from becoming mere illusion and critical philosophy from becoming idealism cut off from the empirical world *(AI* 72). The anonymous reader for the University of Minnesota Press sternly challenged my understanding in this footnote of Kant's use of the term *metaphysics.* This is another allergic reaction, one that demonstrates just the point I am making about de Man. Surely Kant cannot have meant something so strange as this by "metaphysics"! At the risk of making this footnote tediously long for those who have read Kant and de Man's commentary on Kant, here is the relevant passage from Kant, followed by de Man's comment on it. I think my reader is mystified through having accepted received opinion about what Kant must be saying because everyone knows that is what he says. That received opinion is, precisely, a species of "ideology," even of

"aesthetic ideology." Kant says: "A transcendental principle is one through which we represent *a priori* the universal condition under which alone things can become Objects of our cognition generally. A principle, on the other hand, is called metaphysical [Dagegen heißt ein Prinzip metaphysisch], where it represents *a priori* the condition under which alone Objects whose concept has to be given empirically [empirisch], may become further determined [bestimmet] *a priori*. Thus the principle of the cognition of bodies [der Erkenntnis der Körper] as substances, and as changeable substances, is transcendental where the statement is that their change must have a cause [Ursache]: but it is metaphysical where it asserts that their change must have an *external* cause [eine *äußere* Ursache]. For in the first case bodies need only be thought through ontological predicates (pure concepts of understanding [reine Verstandesbegriffe]), e.g. as substance, to enable the proposition to be cognized *a priori*; whereas, in the second case, the empirical concept of a body (as a movable thing in space) must be introduced to support the proposition [diesem Satze zum Grunde gelegt werden muß], although, once this is done, it may be seen [eingesehen] quite *a priori* that the latter predicate (movement only by means of an external cause) applies to body" (Immanuel Kant, *Kritik der Urteilskraft*, ed. Wilhelm Wieschedel [Frankfurt am Main: Suhrkamp, 1979], 90; *The Critique of Judgement*, trans. James Creed Meredith [Oxford: Oxford University Press, 1982], 20–21). De Man comments, in "Phenomenality and Materiality in Kant": "The condition of existence of bodies is called substance; to state that substance is the cause of the motion of bodies (as Kant does in the passage quoted) is to examine critically the possibility of their existence. Metaphysical principles, on the other hand, take the existence of their object for granted as empirical fact. They contain knowledge of the world, but this knowledge is precritical. Transcendental principles contain no knowledge of the world or anything else, except for the knowledge that metaphysical principles that take them for their object are themselves in need of critical analysis, since they take for granted an objectivity that, for the transcendental principles, is not a priori available. Thus the objects of transcendental principles are always critical *judgments* that take metaphysical knowledge for their target. Transcendental philosophy is always the critical philosophy of metaphysics" (*AI* 71). De Man goes on to associate ideology with metaphysics as Kant defines it. The passage is an important gloss on de Man's definition, or, more properly, "calling," of ideology in "The Resistance to Theory," just cited. In the sentences that follow just after the ones already quoted from "Phenomenality and Materiality in Kant" de Man associates ideology with Kantian "metaphysics" and argues for an intricate interdependence of critical thought on ideology and of ideology, if it is to other than "mere error," on critical thought. If metaphysics or ideology needs critical thought, critical thought also needs ideology, as its link to epistemological questions. The link is "causal." The "passage" is a good example of that almost imperceptible crossing, in de Man's formulations, of the border between rigorous reading of passages in the author being discussed and statements that are de Man's own, authorized by his own rigor of thought, as it extrapolates from what the author in question says: "Ideologies, to the extent that they necessarily contain empirical moments and are directed toward what lies outside the realm of pure concepts, are on the side of metaphysics rather than critical philosophy. The conditions and modalities of their occurrence are determined by critical analyses to which they have no access. The object of these analyses, on the other hand, can only be ideologies. Ideological and critical thought are interdependent and any attempt to separate them collapses ideology into mere error and critical thought into idealism. The possibility of maintaining the causal link between them is the controlling principle of rigorous philosophical discourse: philosophies that succumb to ideology lose their epistemological sense, whereas philosophies that try to by-pass or repress ideology lose all critical thrust and risk being repossessed by what they foreclose" (AI 72). The only responsible way to challenge de Man's reading of Kant would be to go back to Kant for oneself and read him with scrupulous care, trying not to be misled by ideological presuppositions about what Kant must be saying. This is extremely difficult, not just because Kant is difficult, but because those ideological presuppositions are so powerful and are unconscious to boot, as Althusser says, that is, a taken for granted assumption that something really linguistic is phenomenal.

10. See de Man's "Reply to Raymond Geuss" (AI 185–92), first published in Critical Inquiry 10:2 (December 1983), a rejoinder to Geuss's "A Response to Paul de Man," in the same issue of Critical Inquiry.

11. Speaking in "Autobiography as De-Facement," of what Gérard Genette says about the undecidable alternation between fiction and autobiography in Proust's Recherche, de Man says: "As anyone who has ever been caught in a revolving door or on a revolving wheel can testify, it is certainly most uncomfortable, and all the more so in this case since this whirligig is capable of infinite acceleration and is, in fact, not successive but simultaneous" (RR 70).

12. Jacques Derrida approaches this problematic from another direction in his second essay on Levinas, "En ce moment même dans cet ouvrage me voici," in Psyché: Inventions de l'autre (Paris: Galilée, 1987), 159–202.

13. Geoffrey Chaucer, Troilus and Cressida, 2:49.

14. Friedrich Schlegel, Kritische Schriften (Munich: Carl Hanser, 1964), 501–2.

15. I do not mean that it is impossible to disagree with what de Man says or to challenge his positions, as I have done elsewhere (by way of calling attention to the way de Man cannot expunge one trope, prosopopoeia, from his own language, though he rejects prosopopoeia as a false projection), or as I am doing here in stressing what is "unintelligible" in what de Man says, or as Jacques Derrida does with exemplary care and delicacy in his essay in this volume apropos of de Man's sense of the relation of Rousseau's Confessions to literary history. I mean that challenging de Man persuasively and responsibly is not all that easy, and that de Man will most often have foreseen and effectively forestalled the objections that it occurs to a skeptical or antagonistic reader to make.

# Anthropomorphism in Lyric and Law

Barbara Johnson

*Anthropomorphism. n.* Attribution of human motivation, characteristics, or behavior to inanimate objects, animals, or natural phenomena.
**—American Heritage Dictionary**

Through a singular ambiguity, through a kind of transposition or intellectual quid
pro quo, you will feel yourself evaporating, and you will attribute to your . . .
tobacco, the strange ability to *smoke you.*
**—Baudelaire, *Artificial Paradises***

Recent discussions of the relations between law and literature have
tended to focus on prose—novels, short stories, autobiographies, even
plays—rather than on lyric poetry.[1] Literature has been seen as a locus
of plots and situations that parallel legal cases or problems, either to
shed light on complexities not always acknowledged by the ordinary
practice of legal discourse, or to shed light on cultural crises and de-
bates that historically underlie and inform literary texts. But, in a
sense, this focus on prose is surprising, since lyric poetry has at least
historically been the more law-abiding or rule-bound of the genres.
Indeed, the sonnet form has been compared to a prison (Wordsworth),[2]
or at least to a bound woman (Keats),[3] and Baudelaire's portraits of
lyric depression *(Spleen)*[4] are often written as if from behind bars.
What are the relations between the laws of genre and the laws of the
state?[5] The present essay might be seen as asking this question through
the juxtaposition, as it happens, between two sonnets and a prisoners'
association.

More profoundly, though, lyric and law might be seen as two very different ways of instating what a "person" is. There appears to be the greatest possible discrepancy between a lyric "person" (emotive, subjective, individual) and a legal "person" (rational, rights-bearing, institutional). In this essay I will be trying to show, through the question of anthropomorphism, how these two "persons" can illuminate each other.

My argument develops out of the juxtaposition of two texts: Paul de Man's essay "Anthropomorphism and Trope in the Lyric,"[6] in which I try to understand why for de Man the question of anthropomorphism is at the heart of the lyric, and the text of a Supreme Court opinion from 1993, *Rowland v. California Men's Colony, Unit II Men's Advisory Council.*[7] This case has not become a household name like *Roe v. Wade* or *Brown v. Board of Education,* and probably with good reason. What is at stake in it appears trivial—at bottom, it is about an association of prisoners suing for the right to have free cigarette privileges restored. But the Supreme Court's task is not to decide whether the prisoners have the right to smoke (an increasingly contested right, in fact, in the United States). The case has come before the court to resolve the question of whether the prisoners' council can be counted as a juridical "person" under the law. What is at stake, then, in both the legal and the lyric texts is the question, What is a person?

I

I will begin by discussing the article by Paul de Man, which is one of the most difficult, even outrageous, of his essays. Both hyperbolic and elliptical, it makes a number of very strong claims about literary history, lyric pedagogy, and the materiality of "historical modes of language power" (262). Toward the end of his text, de Man somewhat unexpectedly reveals that the essay originated in an invitation to speak on the nature of lyric. But it begins with some general remarks about the relation between epistemology and rhetoric (which can stand as a common contemporary way of framing the relations between law and literature). The transition between the question of the lyric and the question of epistemology and rhetoric is made through the Keatsian chiasmus, "Beauty is truth, truth beauty,"[8] which de Man quotes on his way to Nietzsche's short and "better known than understood" (239) essay "On Truth and Lie in an Extra-Moral Sense."[9] "What is truth?" Nietzsche asks in that essay's most oft-quoted moment: "a mobile army of metaphors, metonymies, and anthropomorphisms." Thus it would seem that Nietzsche has answered, "Truth is trope, trope truth" or "epistemology is rhetoric, rhetoric epistemology." But de Man wants to show in what ways Nietzsche is *not* saying simply this. First, the list of tropes is, he says, "odd." Although metaphor and metonymy are the names of tropes that designate a pure structure of relation (metaphor is a relation of similarity between two entities; metonymy is a relation of contiguity), de Man claims that anthropomorphism, while structured similarly, is not a trope. It is not the name of a pure rhetorical structure, but the name of a comparison one of whose terms is treated as a given (as epistemologically resolved). To use an anthropomorphism is to treat as *known* what the properties of the human are.

> "Anthropomorphism" is not just a trope but an identification on the level of substance. It takes one entity for another and thus implies the constitution of specific entities prior to their confusion, the *taking* of something for something else that can then be assumed to be *given.* Anthropomorphism freezes the infinite chain of tropological transformations and propositions into one single assertion or essence which, as such, excludes all others. It is no longer a proposition but a proper name. (241)

Why does he call this a proper name? Shouldn't the essence that is taken as given be a concept? If "man" is what is assumed as a given, why call it a proper name? (This question is particularly vexed when the theorist's proper name is "de Man.") The answer, I think, is that "man" as concept would imply the possibility of a proposition. "Man" would be subject to definition, and thus transformation or trope. But proper names are not subjects of definition: they are what they are. If "man" is taken as a given, then, it can only be because it is out of the loop of qualification. It is presupposed, not defined.

Yet the examples of proper names de Man gives are surprising: Narcissus and Daphne. Nietzsche's triumvirate of metaphor, metonymy, and anthropomorphism then functions like the plot of an Ovidian metamorphosis: from a mythological world in which man and nature appear to be in metaphorical and metonymic harmony, there occurs a crisis wherein, by a process of seamless transformation, a break nevertheless occurs in the system of correspondences, leaving a residue that escapes and remains: the proper name. De Man's discussion of Baudelaire's sonnets will in fact be haunted by Ovidian presences: Echo is lurking behind every mention of Narcissus, while one of the recurring cruxes is whether there is a human substance in a tree. It is perhaps not an accident that the figures that occupy the margins of de Man's discussion are female. If de Man's enduring question is whether linguistic structures and epistemological claims can be presumed to be compatible, the question of gender cannot be located exclusively either in language (where the gender of pronouns, and often of nouns, is inherent in each language) or in the world. By extension, the present discussion of the nature of "man" cannot fail to be haunted by the question of gender.

The term *anthropomorphism* in Nietzsche's list thus indicates that a *given* is being forced into what otherwise would function as a pure structure of relation. In addition, Nietzsche calls truth an *army* of tropes, thus introducing more explicitly the notion of power, force, or violence. This is not a notion that can fit into the oppositions between epistemology and rhetoric, but rather disrupts the system. In the text of the Supreme Court decision that I will discuss in a moment, such a disruption is introduced when the opposition on which the case is based, the opposition between natural person and artificial entity, opens out onto the question of policy. There, too, it is a question of truth and power, of the separation of the constative—what does the law say? from the performative—what does it do?

The bulk of de Man's essay is devoted to a reading of two sonnets by Baudelaire: "Correspondances" and "Obsession," which I here reproduce.[10]

### Correspondances

La Nature est un temple où de vivants piliers
Laissent parfois sortir de confuses paroles;
L'homme y passe à travers des forêts de symboles
Qui l'observent avec des regards familiers.

Comme de longs échos qui de loin se confondent
Dans une ténébreuse et profonde unité,
Vaste comme la nuit et comme la clarté,
Les parfums, les couleurs et les sons se répondent.

Il est des parfums frais comme des chairs d'enfants,
Doux comme les hautbois, verts comme les prairies,
—Et d'autres, corrompus, riches et triomphants,

Ayant l'expansion des choses infinies,
Comme l'ambre, le musc, le benjoin et l'encens,
Qui chantent les transports de l'esprit et des sens.

**[Correspondences**

Nature is a temple, where the living pillars
Sometimes utter indistinguishable words;
Man passes through these forests of symbols
Which regard him with familiar looks.

Like long echoes that blend in the distance
Into a unity obscure and profound,
Vast as the night and as the light,
The perfumes, colors, and sounds correspond.

There are some perfumes fresh as a baby's skin,
Mellow as oboes, verdant as prairies,
—And others, corrupt, rich, and triumphant,

With all the expansiveness of infinite things,
Like ambergris, musk, benjamin, incense,
That sing the transports of spirit and sense.]

**Obsession**

Grands bois, vous m'effrayez comme des cathédrales;
Vous hurlez comme l'orgue; et dans nos cœurs maudits,
Chambres d'éternel deuil où vibrent de vieux râles,
Répondent les échos de vos *De profundis.*

Je te hais, Océan! tes bonds et tes tumultes,
Mon esprit les retrouve en lui; ce rire amer
De l'homme vaincu, plein de sanglots et d'insultes,
Je l'entends dans le rire énorme de la mer.

Comme tu me plairais, ô nuit! sans ces étoiles
Dont la lumière parle un langage connu!
Car je cherche le vide, et le noir, et le nu!

Mais les ténèbres sont elles-mêmes des toiles
Où vivent, jaillissant de mon œil par milliers,
Des êtres disparus aux regards familiers.

**[Obsession**

You terrify me, forests, like cathedrals;
You roar like organs; and in our cursed hearts,
Chambers of mourning that quiver with our dying,
Your *De profundis* echoes in response.

How I hate you, Ocean! your tumultuous tide
Is flowing in my spirit; this bitter laughter
Of vanquished man, strangled with sobs and insults,
I hear it in the heaving laughter of the sea.

O night, how I would love you without stars,
Whose light can only speak the words I know!
For I seek the void, and the black, and the bare!

But the shadows are themselves a screen
That gathers from my eyes the ones I've lost,
A thousand living things with their familiar looks.]

Both poems end up raising "man" as a question—"Correspondances" looks upon "man" as if from a great distance, as if from the outside; "Obsession" says "I," but then identifies with "vanquished man" whose laugh is echoed in the sea.

"Correspondances" is probably the most canonical of Baudelaire's poems in that it has justified the largest number of general statements about Baudelaire's place in literary history. The possibility of literary history ends up, in some ways, being the real topic of de Man's essay. De Man will claim that the use of this sonnet to anchor the history of "the symbolist movement" is based on a reading that ignores a crucial element in the poem, an element that, if taken seriously, will not allow for the edifice of literary history to be built upon it.

"Correspondances" sets up a series of analogies between nature, man, symbols, and metaphysical unity, and among manifestations of the different physical senses, all through the word *"comme"* ("like"). A traditional reading of the poem would say that the lateral analogies among the senses (perfumes fresh as a baby's skin, mellow as oboes, green as prairies) are signs that there exists an analogy between man and nature, and man and the spiritual realm.

De Man focuses on this analogy-making word, *"comme,"* and notes an anomaly in the final instance. Whereas the first uses of *"comme"* in the poem equate different things into likeness, the last one just introduces a list of examples—there are perfumes that are rich and corrupt, like musk, ambergris, and frankincense. This is thus a tautology—there are perfumes like . . . perfumes. De Man calls this a stutter. He writes, "Comme then means as much as 'such as, for example'" (249). "Ce Comme n'est pas un comme comme les autres" (249), writes de Man in a sudden access of French. His sentence performs the stutter he attributes to the enumeration of the perfumes. Listing examples would seem to be quite different from proposing analogies. If the burden of the analogies in "Correspondances" is to convince us that the metaphorical similarities among the senses point to a higher spiritual unity, then sheer enumeration would disrupt that claim.

There is another, more debatable, suggestion in de Man's reading that attempts to disrupt the anthropomorphism of the forest of symbols. De Man suggests that the trees are a mere metaphor for a city crowd in the first stanza. If the living pillars with their familiar glances are metaphorically a city crowd, then the anthropomorphism of nature is lost. Man is surrounded by tree-like men, not man-like trees. It is not "man" whose attributes are taken on by all of nature, but merely a crowd of men being compared to trees and pillars. De Man notes that everyone resists this reading—as do I—but the intensity with which it is rejected does make visible the seduction of the system that puts nature, god, and man into a perfect unity through the symbol, which is what has made the poem so important for literary history. Similarly, if the last *"comme"* is sheer enumeration rather than similarity, the transports in the last line of the poem would not get us into a transcendent realm, but would be like getting stuck on the French transportation system (which, as de Man points out, uses the word *"correspondance"* for changes of station within the system). All these tropes would not carry us away into the spiritual realm, but would be an infinite series of substitutions. The echoes would remain echoes and not merge into a profound unity.

If "Correspondances" is said to place man in the center of a universe that reflects him in harmony with all of nature, the poem "Obsession" places all of nature and the universe inside the psychology of man. Even the senses are projections. "Obsession" is the reading of "Correspondances" as hallucination. While "Correspondances" is entirely declarative, "Obsession" is almost entirely vocative. (Interestingly, de Man does not comment on another anomaly in the meaning of the word *"comme"*—the *"comme"* in "Obsession" that means "How!"—which is surprising, since it enacts precisely what he calls "the tropological transformation of analogy into apostrophe" [261].) Nature is addressed as a structure haunted by the subject's obsessions. Everywhere he looks, his own thoughts look back. For psychoanalytically inclined readers, and indeed for de Man himself in an earlier essay,[11] "Obsession" demystifies "Correspondances." There is no profound unity in the world, but only, as Lacan would say, paranoid knowledge.[12]

But de Man sees the psychological gloss as another mystification, another anthropomorphism—the very anthropomorphic mystification that it is the duty of lyric, and of lyric pedagogy, to promote. "The lyric is not a genre, but one name among several to designate the defensive motion of understanding" (261). De Man concludes provocatively: "The resulting couple or pair of texts indeed becomes a model for the uneasy combination of funereal monumentality with paranoid fear that characterizes the hermeneutics and the pedagogy of lyric poetry" (259). What comes to be at stake, then, is lyric poetry itself as a poetry of the subject. By juxtaposing lyric and law in this essay, I am implicitly asking whether there is a relation between the "first person" (the grammatical "I") and the "constitutional person" (the subject of rights).

"Only a subject can understand a meaning," claims Lacan. "Conversely, every phenomenon of meaning implies a subject."[13] What de Man seems to be arguing for here is the existence of a residue of language or rhetoric that exists neither inside nor outside the "phenomenon of meaning." Does lyric poetry try to give a psychological gloss to disruptions that are purely grammatical? Are the periodizations in literary history such as Parnassian and Romantic merely names for rhetorical structures that are not historical? For de Man, "Obsession" loses the radical disruption of "Correspondances" by making enumeration into a symptom, which is more reassuring than endless repetition. It is as though de Man were saying that "Obsession," despite or rather because it is so psychologically bleak, falls back within the pleasure principle—that is, the psychological, the human—whereas "Correspondances," which seems so sunny, contains a disruption that goes beyond the pleasure principle. When de Man says that we can get "Obsession" from "Correspondances" but not the other way around, this is a way of repeating Freud's experience of the disruption of the pleasure principle in *Beyond the Pleasure Principle,* a study in which Freud grappled with the very limits of psychoanalysis. Freud noticed that there were experiences or facts that seemed to contradict his notion of the primacy of the pleasure principle in human life (negative pleasures, the repetition compulsion, the death instinct). As Derrida has shown, Freud kept bringing the beyond back within explainability, and the beyond of Freud's theory kept popping up elsewhere.[14] He could, in effect, get the pleasure principle to explain its beyond, but not anticipate it. The beyond of the pleasure principle could only exist as a disruption.

De Man makes the surprising claim that "Correspondances" is *not* a lyric, but contains the entire possibility of lyric: "'Obsession,' a text of recollection and elegiac mourning, *adds* remembrance to the flat surface of time in 'Correspondances'—produces at once a hermeneutic, fallacious, lyrical reading of the unintelligible" (262). The act of making intelligible, whether in the lyric or in the terminology of literary history, is for de Man at the end of the essay always an act of "resistance and nostalgia, at the furthest remove from the materiality of actual history." This would mean that "actual history" is what escapes and resists intelligibility. Here is how de Man ends the essay:

> If mourning is called a "chambre d'éternel deuil où vibrent de vieux râles," then this pathos of terror states in fact the desired consciousness of eternity and of temporal harmony as voice and as song. True "mourning" is less deluded. The most *it* can do is to allow for non-comprehension and enumerate non-anthropomorphic, non-elegiac, non-celebratory, non-lyrical, non-poetic, that is to say, prosaic, or, better, *historical* modes of language power. (262)

Earlier in the essay, de Man had said of Nietzsche's general analysis of truth that "truth is always at the very least dialectical, the negative knowledge of error" (242). In another essay, de Man speaks of "literature as the place where this negative knowledge about the reliability of linguistic utterance is made available."[15] Negativity, then, is not an assertion of the negative, but a nonpositivity within the possibility of assertion. This final sentence is clearly a version of stating negative knowledge. But it is also a personification. "True 'mourning'" is said to be "less deluded." Stressing the word *it* as the agent, he writes, "the most *it* can do is to allow for non-comprehension." "True mourning" becomes the subject of this negative knowledge. The subjectivizations performed by lyric upon the unintelligible are here rejected, but by a personification of mourning. Is mourning—or rather, "true 'mourning'"—human or inhuman? Or is it what makes it impossible to close the gap between "man" and rhetoric? In other words, does this type of personification presuppose knowledge of human essence, or does it merely confer a kind of rhetorical agency? Is it anthropomorphic? Is there a difference between personification and anthropomorphism? Is the text stating its knowledge as if it were a human, or is it just performing the inescapability of the structures it is casting off? Has de Man's conclusion really eliminated anthropomorphism and reduced it to the trope of personification, or is anthropomorphism inescapable in the notion of mourning? Is this what lyric poetry—so often structured around the relation between loss and rhetoric—must decide? Or finesse? The least we can say is that de Man has given the last word in his own text to a personification.

## II

> That which henceforth is to be "truth" is now fixed; that is to say, a uniformly valid and binding designation of things is invented and the legislature of language also gives the first laws of truth: since here, for the first time, originates the contrast between truth and falsity. The liar uses the valid designations, the words, in order to make the unreal appear as real, e.g., he says, "I am rich," whereas the right designation of his state would be "poor."
> **—Nietzsche, "Truth and Falsity in an Ultramoral Sense"**

The case of *Rowland v. California Men's Colony, Unit II Men's Advisory Council* is based on a provision in the United States legal code permitting a "person" to appear in court *in forma pauperis*. The relevant legislation reads in part:

> Any court of the United States may authorize the commencement, prosecution or defense of any suit, action, or proceeding, civil or criminal, or appeal therein, without prepayment of fees and costs or security therefor, by a person who makes affidavit that he is unable to pay such costs or give security therefor.[16]

In other words, a "person" may go to court without prepayment of fees if the "person" can demonstrate indigence. The question to be decided by the court is whether this provision applies to artificial persons such as corporations or councils, or whether it is meant to apply only to individuals. In the case that led to *Rowland v. California Men's Colony, Unit II Men's Advisory Council,* a council of prisoners in California has tried to bring suit against the correctional officers of the prison for the restoration of the practice of providing free cigarettes for indigent prisoners, which was discontinued. They try to sue *in forma pauperis* on the grounds that the warden forbids the council to hold funds of its own. The court finds that they have not sufficiently proven indigence. They are allowed to appeal *in forma pauperis* in order to enable the court to decide whether the council, as an artificial legal person, is entitled to sue *in forma pauperis*. The appeals court decides that they are so entitled, but this conflicts with another court ruling in another case. The Supreme Court therefore gets to decide whether the provisions for proceeding *in forma pauperis* should apply only to natural persons, or also to legal persons such as associations and councils. The case is therefore about what a person is, and how you can tell the difference between a natural person and an artificial person.

Justice Souter's majority opinion begins with something that in many ways resembles de Man's stutter of infinite enumeration. In order to find out what the legal meaning of "person" is, Souter turns to what is called the "Dictionary Act." The Dictionary Act gives instructions about how to read acts of Congress. It states:

> In determining the meaning of any Act of Congress, unless the context indicates otherwise, the word "person" includes corporations, companies, associations, firms, partnerships, societies, and joint stock companies, as well as individuals. (1 United States Code 1)

Thus, the word *person* does include artificial entities unless the context indicates otherwise. Now the court asks, but what does "context" mean? It turns to *Webster's New International Dictionary,* where it notes that it means "the part or parts of a discourse preceding or following a 'text' or passage or a word, or so intimately associated with it as to throw light on its meaning." The context, then, is the surrounding words of the act. Of course, Webster's does offer a second meaning for the word *context,* "associated surroundings, whether material or mental"—a reference not to the surrounding text but to the broader reality or intentionality—but Souter dismisses this by saying, "we doubt that the broader sense applies here." Why? Because "if Congress had meant to point further afield, as to legislative history, for example, it would have been natural to use a more spacious phrase, like 'evidence of congressional intent,' in place of 'context.'"

The word *natural,* which is precisely at issue here, since we are trying to find out whether the statute applies only to natural persons, is here applied precisely to an artificial person, Congress, which is personified as having natural intentionality. "If Congress had meant . . ." The Court's decision repeatedly relies on this type of personification: it is as though Souter has to treat Congress as an entity with intentions, even natural intentions, in order to say that Congress could not have meant to include artificial entities in its ruling. There is a personification of an artificial entity, Congress, embedded in the very project of interpreting how far the law will allow for artificial entities to be considered persons.

Turning to the Dictionary Act for *person* and to Webster's dictionary for *context,* Souter also notes that he has to define *indicates.* The difficulty of doing so pushes him into a volley of rhetorical flourishes: "A contrary 'indication' may raise a specter short of inanity, and with something less than syllogistic force." "Indicates," it seems, means more than nonsense but less than logical necessity. In other words, the task of reading becomes an infinite regress of glossing terms that are themselves supposed to be determinants of meaning. De Man's linguistic stutter returns here as the repeated effort to throw language outside itself. We could read a text, this implies, if only we were sure of the meaning of the words *context* and *indicate*. But those are precisely the words that raise the question of meaning in its most general form— they cannot be glossed with any finality because they name the process of glossing itself.

Souter's text, in fact, is most anthropomorphic at those points where the infinite regress of language is most threatening. Congress is endowed with "natural" intentionality in order to sweep away the abyss of reference. Souter's dismissal of the prisoners' association as an "amorphous legal creature" is the counterpart to the need to reinforce the anthropomorphizability of the artificial legal creature, Congress.[17]

Souter's opinion proceeds to detail the ways in which he thinks the *in forma pauperis* ruling should only apply to natural persons. If an affidavit alleging poverty is required for a person to proceed *in forma pauperis,* then can an artificial entity plead poverty? Souter again turns to Webster's dictionary to find that poverty is a human condition, to be "wanting in material riches or goods; lacking in the comforts of life; needy." Souter also refers to a previous ruling, which holds that poverty involves being unable to provide for the "necessities of life." It is as though only natural persons can have "life," and that life is defined as the capacity to lack necessities and comforts. "Artificial entities may be insolvent," writes Souter, "but they are not well spoken of as 'poor.'" An artificial entity cannot lack the necessities and comforts of life. Only life can lack. The experience of lack differentiates natural persons from artificial persons. To lack is to be human. In a sense, we have returned to de Man's question about mourning. Is lack human, or just a structure? Whatever the case, the Court holds that associations cannot be considered persons for the purpose of the *in forma pauperis* procedure.

The majority was only five to four, however. In a dissenting opinion, written by Clarence Thomas, it is argued that there is no reason to restrict the broad definition of "person" to natural persons in this case. Thomas quotes the Court's view of "poverty" as an exclusively "human condition," and comments:

I am not so sure. "Poverty" may well be a human condition in its "primary sense," but I doubt that using the word in connection with an artificial entity departs in any significant way from settled principles of English usage. . . . Congress itself has used the word "poor" to describe entities other than natural persons, referring in at least two provisions of the United States Code to the world's "Poorest countries"—a term that is used as a synonym for the least developed of the so-called "developing" countries.

Souter has glossed the word *poor* as though speakers of English could only use it literally. Thomas responds by including the figurative use of *poor* as included within normal usage. The boundaries between natural persons and artificial persons cannot be determined by usage, because those boundaries have always already been blurred. In treating Congress as an entity with natural intentions, indeed, Souter has already shown how "natural" the artificial can be.

At another point, Thomas takes issue with Souter's discussion of a case in which an association or corporation *is* considered a person despite strong contextual indicators to the contrary. In the case of *Wilson v. Omaha Indian Tribe*, 442 U.S. 653, 666 (1979), it was decided that "white person" could include corporations because the "larger context" and "purpose" of the law was to protect Indians against non-Indian squatters, and would be frustrated if a "white person" could simply incorporate in order to escape the provision of the law. Souter admits that "because a wholly legal creature has no color, and belongs to no race, the use of the adjective 'white' to describe a 'person' is one of the strongest contextual indicators imaginable that 'person' covers only individuals." Justice Thomas argues that if the Court "was correct in holding that the statutory term 'white person' includes a corporation (because the 'context' does not 'indicate otherwise')—the conclusion that an association is a 'person' for *in forma pauperis* purposes is inescapable." Perhaps another inescapable conclusion is that despite its apparent reference to the physical body, the phrase "white person" is the name, not of a natural, but of a corporate person.

Justice Thomas refutes the reasons Souter has given for finding that artificial entities are excluded from the *in forma pauperis* provision, noting that there may be sound policy reasons for wanting to exclude them, but that the law as written cannot be construed to have done so. The Court's job, he writes, is not to make policy but to interpret a statute. "Congress has created a rule of statutory construction (an association is a 'person') and an exception to that rule (an association is not a 'person' if the 'context indicates otherwise'), but the Court has permitted the exception to devour the rule [a nice personification]" (treating the rule as if artificial entities were excluded rather than included unless the context indicates otherwise). "Whatever 'unless the context indicates otherwise' means," writes Thomas, "it cannot mean 'unless there are sound policy reasons for concluding otherwise.'"

Permitting artificial entities to proceed *in forma pauperis* may be unwise, and it may be an inefficient use of the government's limited resources, but I see nothing in the text of the *in forma pauperis* statute indicating that Congress has chosen to exclude such entities from the benefits of that law.

Thus, Thomas's two conservative instincts are at war with each other: he would like the government not to spend its money, but he would also like to stick to the letter of the law.

The question of what counts as a juridical person has, in fact, been modified over time in the legal code. It was in 1871 (significantly, perhaps, at the beginning of the end of post–Civil War Reconstruction) that the so-called Dictionary Act was first passed by Congress, in which the word *Person* "may extend and be applied to bodies politic and corporate." More recently, the question of fetal personhood has been debated, not only in the *Roe v. Wade* decision, where it was decided that a fetus was not a legal person, but also in *Weaks v. Mounter,* 88 Nev. 118, where it was decided that a fetus *was* a person who could sue for intrauterine injuries, but only after birth. Recently, the question of granting patents for forms of life such as oil-slick-eating bacteria or genetically altered mice has raised the question of whether a hybrid between humans and close animal relatives can be patented. And also, of course, the question of the ethics and legality of cloning humans has been raised. The law has reached another crisis about the definition of "person." In an article on constitutional personhood, Michael Rivard writes:

> Current law allows patents for genetically-engineered animals but not for human beings. Humans are not patentable subject matter because patents are property rights, and the Thirteenth Amendment forbids any grant of property rights in a human being. Nevertheless, this exclusion for humans will prove impossible to maintain: within ten to thirty years, or perhaps sooner, advances in genetic engineering technology should allow scientists to intermingle the genetic material of humans and ani-

mals to produce human-animal hybrids. . . . It may soon be possible to patent—and to enslave—human-animal hybrids who think and feel like humans, but who lack constitutional protection under the Thirteenth Amendment.[18]

The Thirteenth Amendment is the amendment that abolishes slavery. The constitutional protection against slavery operates as a constraint on the patent office, but it does so in a paradoxical way. The fear of re-instituting something like slavery, or property in humans, is a reaction to, but also a sign of, what must be an ongoing research goal to come as close as possible to creating the ownable, enslavable human.[19]

Constitutional personhood has in fact often been defined in proximity to slavery. The contradiction between equal rights and chattel slavery led from the beginning to verbal gymnastics, even in the drafting of the Constitution itself. By not using the word *slavery* in the Constitution, and by revising the text of the original fugitive slave clause to refer to the legality of slavery only on the level of the states rather than of the federal government, the framers built a double intentionality into the very foundation of their law. Douglas Fehrenbacher, studying the egregious understanding of original intent later employed by the Supreme Court in the case of *Dred Scott v. Sanford,* writes of the Constitution: "It is as though the framers were half-consciously trying to frame two constitutions, one for their own time and the other for the ages, with slavery viewed bifocally—that is, plainly visible at their feet, but disappearing when they lifted their eyes."[20] A written text of law can thus contain a double intention, the trace of a compromise between differing opinions. No wonder interpreting the law's intention is so complicated. That intention can always already be multiple. The distinction Justice Thomas made between interpreting the law and making policy cannot hold if the law's ambiguity allows for the possibility that the policy it governs will change.

III

The "inhuman" is not some kind of mystery, or some kind of secret; the in-human is: linguistic structures, the play of linguistic tensions, linguistic events that occur, possibilities which are inherent in language—independently of any intent or any drive or any wish or any desire we might have. . . . If one speaks of the inhuman, the fundamental non-human character of language, one also speaks of the fundamental non-definition of the human as such.

   **—Paul de Man, "Benjamin's 'The Task of the Translator'"**

Only smoking distinguishes humans from the rest of the animals.
—**Anonymous (quoted in Richard Klein, *Cigarettes Are Sublime*)**

The case of *Rowland v. California Men's Colony, Unit II Men's Advisory Council* was ostensibly about whether a council of inmates could sue prison officials *in forma pauperis* to get their cigarettes back. The details of the case seemed irrelevant to the question of whether an artificial person has the right to sue *in forma pauperis*. Yet perhaps some of those details deserve note. Is it relevant that the suit to decide this question is brought by a council of inmates? The phenomenon of the inmate civil suit has grown to the point where the case law may very well be transformed by it. In a 1995 study of inmate suits in California, it was reported that "For the last fourteen years at least, the federal courts have faced a growing caseload and workload challenge posed by inmate cases. . . . By 1992, these filings numbered nearly 30,000, and constituted 13% of the courts' total civil case filings nationwide."[21] The majority of these suits are filed *in forma pauperis*.[22] The Supreme Court's decision may well have been affected by what Clarence Thomas calls "policy decisions."

If prisoners are affecting the nature of civil proceedings, they are also, at least figuratively, affecting theoretical discussions about the nature of rational choice and the evolution of cooperation. The celebrated "Prisoner's Dilemma" has been central to questions of self-interest and social goods since it was introduced by Albert Tucker in 1950. Max Black has even entitled his discussion of the issues raised "The 'Prisoner's Dilemma' and the Limits of Rationality."[23] Why is it that the theoretical study of rational choice has recourse to "man" conceived as a prisoner? Does this have anything to do with the poets' tendency to see the sonnet form as a prison?

And is it by chance that *Rowland v. California Men's Colony, Unit II Men's Advisory Council* is about cigarettes? On the one hand, it seems paradoxical that the council has to demonstrate its indigence in order to pursue its suit against the prison directors for depriving the prisoners of access to cigarettes, which in prisons function as a form of currency. On the other hand, it seems fitting that the personhood of the association is the counterpart to the humanity of the inmates, which, as common wisdom (quoted above, second epigraph) would have it, is demonstrated by the act of smoking. The prisoners would thus, in a very attenuated way, be suing for their humanity. As Richard Klein has wittily shown, smoking serves no function other than to enact a structure of desire—of human desire for self-transcendence, for repetition, for bodily experience corresponding to something other than the "necessities of life" required for existence alone: in short, desire for the sublime.[24] Far from being what defines natural personhood, then, need for the "necessities of life" alone is precisely what *cannot* define the human.

In the article cited earlier, Rivard declares that "corporations would be presumed constitutional *non*persons," especially for liberty-related rights, unless the corporation could rebut its nonperson status by showing specific natural persons "who would be affected if the corporation were denied these rights."[25] This is the opposite of the Dictionary Act, which considers a corporation a person "unless the context indicates otherwise." Rivard's article is arguing for the rights of new biological species who can pass the "self-awareness test" (which, in a surpisingly Lacanian move derived from Michael Dennett, he defines as wanting to be different from what one is), and he claims that corporations, by their nature, do not pass this test.

But the question of the nature of corporations as persons has never been a simple one, as Rivard admits. In an article titled "The Personification of the Business Corporation in American Law" (*University of Chicago Law Review* 54 [fall 1987]: 1441), Gregory A. Marks outlines in detail the history of corporate personhood. The relation between corporations and the natural persons who compose them has grown more complicated over time, but in most discussions of the matter, it is the "natural" person that functions as the known quantity, and the "artificial" who is either just an "aggregate" of natural persons, or a fiction created by the state, or a mere metaphor, or actually resembles (is *like*, to return to the Baudelairean word) a natural person in that it has a "will" of its own. Such a corporate will is a form of agency separate from that of the natural corporators, who exist behind the "veil" of the corporation. Much of Marks's article concerns the exact rhetorical valence of this personification:

> American law has always recognized that people's activities could be formally organized and that the resulting organizations could be dealt with as units. Personification, however, is important because it became far more than a quaint device making it possible for the law to deal with organized business entities. In American legal and economic history, personification has been vital because it (1) implies a single and unitary source of control over the collective property of the corporation's members,

(2) defines, encourages, and legitimates the corporation as an autonomous, creative, self-directed economic being, and (3) captures rights, ultimately even constitutional rights, for corporations thereby giving corporate property unprecedented protection from the state. (1443)

Marks takes seriously the role of language in the evolving history of the corporation. Philosophers and legislators have gone to great lengths to minimize the rhetorical damage, to eliminate personification as far as possible, but he asserts that it is not just a figure of speech to speak of a corporation's "mind," or even its "life." "Practical experience, not just anthropomorphism, fixed the corporate mind in the management hierarchy" (1475). The corporation resembled a human being in its capacity to "take resolves in the midst of conflicting motives," to "will change." Yet the analogy is not perfect. The corporation, for example, unlike its corporators, is potentially immortal. The effect of personification appears to derive its rhetorical force from the ways in which the corporation *resembles* a natural person, yet the corporation's immortality in no way diminishes its personification. When Marks says that it is "not just anthropomorphism" that underpins the agency of the corporation, he still implies that we can know what anthropomorphism is. But his final sentence stands this presupposition on its head. Far from claiming that a corporation's characteristics are derived from a knowable human essence, Marks suggests that what have been claimed to be the essential characteristics of man (especially "economic man") have in fact been borrowed from the nature of the corporation:

> Personification with its roots in historic theological disputes and modern business necessity, had proved to be a potent symbol to legitimate the autonomous business corporation and its management. Private property rights had been transferred to associations, associations had themselves become politically legitimate, and the combination had helped foster modern political economy. The corporation, once the derivative tool of the state, had become its rival, and the successes of the autonomous corporate management turned the basis for belief in an individualist conception of property on its head. The protests of modern legists notwithstanding, the business corporation had become the quintessential economic man. (1482–83)

Theories of rationality, naturalness, and the "good," presumed to be grounded in the nature of "man," may in reality be taking their notions of human essence not from "natural man" but from business corporations.

Ambivalence about personification, especially the personification of abstractions, has in fact permeated not only legal but also literary history. Nervousness about the agency of the personified corporation echoes the nervousness Enlightenment writers felt about the personifications dreamed up by the poets. As Steven Knapp puts it in his book *Personification and the Sublime*:

> Allegorical personification—the endowing of metaphors with the agency of literal persons—was only the most obvious and extravagant instance of what Enlightenment writers perceived, with a mixture of admiration and uneasiness, as the unique ability of poetic genius to give the force of literal reality to figurative "inventions." More important than the incongruous presence of such agents was their contagious effect on the ostensibly literal agents with which they interacted.[26]

The uncanniness of the personification, then, was derived from its way of putting in question what the "natural" or the "literal" might be.

We have finally come back to the question of whether there is a difference between anthropomorphism and personification, which arose at the end of the discussion of the essay by Paul de Man. It can now be seen that everything hangs on this question. Not only does anthropomorphism depend on the givenness of the essence of the human and personification does not, but the mingling of personifications on the same footing as "real" agents threatens to make the lack of certainty about what humanness is come to consciousness. Perhaps the loss of unconsciousness about the lack of humanness is what de Man was calling "true 'mourning.'" Perhaps the "fallacious lyrical reading of the unintelligible" was exactly what legislators count on lyric poetry to provide: the assumption that the human *has been* or *can be* defined so that it can then be presupposed without the question of its definition's being raised as a question—legal or otherwise. Thus the poets would truly be, as Shelley claimed, the "unacknowledged legislators of the world," not because they covertly determine policy, but because it is somehow necessary and useful that there *be* a powerful, presupposable, unacknowledgment. But the very rhetorical sleight of hand that would instate such an unacknowledgment is indistinguishable from the rhetorical structure that would empty it. Lyric and law are two of the most powerful discourses that exist along the fault line of this question.

## NOTES

1. I am thinking of Richard Posner's *Law and Literature* (Cambridge: Harvard University Press, 1988), Richard Weisberg's *The Failure of the Word* (New Haven: Yale University Press, 1984), and Peter Brooks, *Troubling Confessions* (Chicago: University of Chicago Press, 2000). But for a legal approach that *does* address poetry, see the interesting discussion of Wallace Stevens by Thomas Grey and Margaret Jane Radin in the *Yale Journal of Law & The Humanities* 2:2 (summer 1990), as well as the more extended treatment of Wallace Stevens in Thomas Grey, *The Wallace Stevens Case: Law and the Practice of Poetry* (Cambridge: Harvard University Press, 1991).

2. William Wordsworth's sonnet, "Nuns Fret Not at Their Convent's Narrow Room," contains the lines, "In truth the prison, into which we doom / Ourselves, no prison is: and hence for me, / In sundry moods, 'twas pastime to be bound / Within the Sonnet's scanty plot of ground" (*Selected Poetry and Prose of Wordsworth* [New York: Signet, 1970], 169).

3. John Keats's sonnet on the sonnet begins, "If by dull rhymes our English must be chained, / And, like Andromeda, the sonnet sweet / Fettered . . ." (*The Selected Poetry of Keats* [New York: Signet, 1966], 264).

4. One of several poems by Baudelaire titled *Spleen* describes a mood produced by or analogized to a rainy day: "Quand la pluie étalant ses immenses trainées / D'une vaste prison imite les barreaux . . ." (Baudelaire, *Œuvres complètes*, vol. 1 [Paris: Pléiade, 1975], 75).

5. For a suggestive discussion of what it means for a text to obey the law of genre, see Jacques Derrida, "The Law of Genre," in *Acts of Literature*, ed. Derek Attridge (New York: Routledge, 1992).

6. Paul de Man, "Anthropomorphism and Trope in the Lyric," in *The Rhetoric of Romanticism* (New York: Columbia University Press, 1984). Page numbers in parentheses refer to this essay.

7. *United States Law Week* 61:25 (January 12, 1993). Page numbers in parentheses refer to this text.

8. This allusion to Keats's "Ode on a Grecian Urn" stands in for the premise of the compatibility of literary aesthetics with linguistic structures, and of linguistic structures with perceptual or intuitive knowledge, that de Man is often at pains to contest. See his remarks on the pedagogical model of the trivium in the titular essay of *The Resistance to Theory* (Minneapolis: University of Minnesota Press, 1986).

9. Friedrich Nietzsche, "Truth and Falsity in an Ultramoral Sense," in *Critical Theory Since Plato*, ed. Hazard Adams (Fort Worth: Harcourt Brace Jovanovich, 1992), 634–39. If the Keats poem stands as the claim that aesthetic and epistemological structures are compatible, Nietzsche's text, for de Man, stands as a parody of that claim.

10. The translations are mine, for the purpose of bringing out those aspects of the poems that are relevant to my discussion.

11. "Allegory and Irony in Baudelaire," in *Romanticism and Contemporary Criticism* (Baltimore: Johns Hopkins University Press, 1993). This essay is part of the Gauss Seminar given by de Man in 1967.

12. Jacques Lacan, "Aggressivity in Psychoanalysis," in *Écrits: A Selection*, trans. Alan Sheridan (New York: W. W. Norton, 1977), 17: "What I have called paranoic

knowledge is shown, therefore, to correspond in its more or less archaic forms to certain critical moments that mark the history of man's mental genesis, each representing a stage in objectifying identification."

13. Ibid., 9.

14. Jacques Derrida, "Freud's Legacy," in *The Postcard,* trans. Alan Bass (Chicago: University of Chicago Press, 1987).

15. De Man, "The Resistance to Theory," 10.

16. United States Code (1994 edition), vol. 15, 438.

17. In a response to the present paper given at the Yale Law School, Shoshana Felman made the brilliant suggestion that Souter would have wanted to rewrite Baudelaire's "Correspondances" as: "Le Congrès est un temple où de vivants piliers laissent parfois sortir de confuses paroles . . ." The neoclassical, Parnassian architecture of official Washington, D.C., and the common metaphorical expression "pillars of the community," add piquancy to this suggestion.

18. Michael D. Rivard, "Toward a General Theory of Constitutional Personhood: A Theory of Constitutional Personhood for Transgenic Humanoid Species," *UCLA Law Review* 39: 5 (June 1992): 1428–29.

19. See A. Leon Higginbotham Jr. and Barbara Kopytoff, "Property First, Humanity Second: The Recognition of the Slave's Human Nature in Virginia Civil Law," *Ohio State Law Journal* 50:3 (June 1989): "The humanity of the slave, requiring that he be treated with the care due other humans and not like other forms of property, became *part* of the owner's property rights" (520).

20. Douglas E. Fehrenbacher, *Slavery, Law, and Politics: The Dred Scott Case in Historical Perspective* (Oxford: Oxford University Press, 1981), 15.

21. Kim Mueller, "Inmates' Civil Rights Cases and the Federal Courts: Insights Derived from a Field Research Project in the Eastern District of California," *Creighton Law Review* 1228 (June 1995): 1258–59. In the Eastern District of California, inmates' civil rights actions constituted nearly 30 percent of the case filings. (California Men's Colony is not in the Eastern District; it is in San Luis Obispo.)

22. Ibid., 1276 and 1281.

23. Max Black, *Perplexities* (Ithaca, N.Y.: Cornell University Press, 1990). See also Robert Axelrod, *The Evolution of Cooperation* (New York: Basic Books, 1984).

24. Richard Klein, *Cigarettes Are Sublime* (Durham, N.C.: Duke University Press, 1993). Klein notes, incidentally, that Baudelaire is one of the first French writers to use the word *cigarette* in print (in his "Salons de 1848," 8).

25. Rivard, "Toward a General Theory of Constitutional Personhood," 1501–2.

26. Steven Knapp, *Personification and the Sublime* (Cambridge: Harvard University Press, 1985), 2.

# IV. The Mnemopolitical Event

# The Politics of Rhetoric

Ernesto Laclau

Why would a political theorist like me, working mainly on the role of hegemonic logics in the structuration of political spaces, be interested in the work of a prominent literary critic such as Paul de Man? I could suggest at least two main reasons. The first is that one of the leitmotifs of Paul de Man's work has been the subversion of the frontiers separating theoretical from literary disciplines, so that those dimensions that had traditionally been conceived as privative of literary or aesthetic language became, for him, actually defining features of language *tout court*. Against all attempts to differentiate between "appearance" and "saying," between a primary text whose message would have been mediated by the materiality of the signs, of the figural, and a language of inquiry governed by reason, de Man had always insisted that any language, whether aesthetic or theoretical, is governed by the materiality of the signifier, by a rhetorical milieu that ultimately dissolves the illusion of any unmediated reference. In this sense a generalized rhetoric—which necessarily includes within itself the performative dimension—transcends all regional boundaries and becomes coterminous with the structuration of social life itself. Conceived at such a broad level of generality, the literariness of the literary text breaks the limits of any specialized discipline and its analysis involves something like the study of the distorting effects that representation exercises over any reference—effects that become, thus, constitutive of any experience.

Moreover, de Man himself was perfectly aware of the political and ideological implications of his approach to texts. In a famous interview with Stefano Rosso that discusses the increasing recurrence in his works of the terms *political* and *ideological,* he answered as follows:

I don't think I ever was away from these problems, they were always uppermost in my mind. I have always maintained that one could approach the problems of ideology and by extension the problems of politics only on the basis of critical-linguistic analysis, which had to be done on its own terms, in the medium of language, and I felt that I could approach those problems only after having achieved a certain control over those questions. It seems pretentious to say so, but it is not the case. I have the feeling I have achieved a certain control over technical problems of language, specifically problems of rhetoric, of the relation between tropes and performatives, of saturation of tropology as a field that in certain forms of language goes beyond that field. . . . I feel now some control of a vocabulary and of a conceptual apparatus that can handle that.[1]

As for the second reason for a political theorist to be interested in de Man's work, it has to do with something related to the political field itself. Gone are the times in which the transparency of social actors, of processes of representation, even of the presumed underlying logics of the social fabric could be accepted unproblematically. On the contrary, each political institution, each category of political analysis shows itself today as the locus of undecidable language games. The overdetermined nature of all political difference or identity opens the space for a generalized tropological movement and thus reveals the fruitfulness of de Man's intellectual project for ideological and political analysis. In my work, this generalized politico-tropological movement has been called "hegemony." I intend in this essay to stress some decisive points in the work of de Man, especially in his late work, where the direction of his thought could be helpful in developing a hegemonic approach to politics.

I

The requirements of "hegemony" as a central category of political analysis are essentially three. First, that something constitutively heterogeneous to the social system or structure has to be present in the latter from the very beginning, preventing it from constituting itself as a closed or representable totality. If such a closure were achievable, no hegemonic event could be possible and the political, far from being an ontological dimension of the social—an "existential" of the social— would just be an ontic dimension of the latter. Second, however, the hegemonic suture has to produce a retotalizing effect, without which no hegemonic articulation would be possible either. But, third, this re-totalization cannot have the character of a dialectical reintegration. It has, on the contrary, to maintain alive and visible the original and constitutive heterogeneity from which the hegemonic articulation started. How is a logic that can maintain these two contradictory requirements at the same time possible? Let us approach this question through the exploration of its possible presence in de Man's texts. We will start from the analysis of Pascal's *Réflexions sur la géométrie en général; De l'esprit géométrique et de l'Art de persuader* that de Man carries out in "Pascal's Allegory of Persuasion."[2]

Pascal starts his study of the *esprit géométrique* from the distinction between nominal and real definitions—the first resulting from convention and being thus exempt from contradiction, the second being axioms or propositions to be proved—and asserts that the confusion between the two is the main cause of philosophical difficulties. Maintaining the separation between the two—as the geometrician does—is the first rule of philosophical clarity. However, the argument runs quickly into difficulties, as geometrical discourse includes not only nominal definitions but also "primitive terms"—such as motion, number, and extension—which are undefinable but, nonetheless, fully intelligible. According to Pascal, these undefinable words find a universal reference not in the (impossible) fact that all men have the same idea concerning their essence, but instead, in the fact that there is a relation of reference between name and thing, "so that on hearing the expression *time,* all turn (or direct) the mind to the same entity" (56). But, as de Man shows, this brings back the real definition into the geometrical camp itself, for

> the word does not function as a sign or a name, as was the case in the nominal definition, but as a vector, as a directional motion that is manifest only as a turn, since the target toward which it turns remains unknown. In other words, the sign has become a trope, a substitutive relationship that has to posit a meaning whose existence cannot be verified, but that confers upon the sign an unavoidable signifying function. (56)

As the semantic function of the primitive terms has the structure of a trope, "it acquires a signifying function that it controls neither in its existence nor in its direction." Ergo, "[s]ince definition is now itself a primitive term, it follows that the definition of the nominal definition is itself a real, and not a nominal, definition" (57).

This contamination of the nominal by the real definition is still more visible when we move to the question of double infinitude, which is decisive in establishing the coherence and intelligibility of the relationship between mind and cosmos. Here, Pascal deals with the objections put to him by the Chevalier de Méré, according to whom—given the Pascalian principle of homogeneity between space and number—it is possible to conceive an extension formed by parts that are not themselves extended, since it is possible to have numbers made up of units that are devoid of number. With this, the principle of infinite smallness would be put into question. Pascal's answer has two steps. He asserts, in the first place, that which applies to the order of number does not apply to the order of space. *One* is not a number, there is no plurality in it; but at the same time it belongs to the order of number for, given the Euclidean principle of homogeneity ("magnitudes are said to be of the same kind or species when one magnitude can be made to exceed another by reiterated multiplication"), it is part of the infinity postulated by that principle. On that basis, Pascal can distinguish between number and extension, but only at the price of grounding the distinction in real and not nominal definitions. As de Man asserts:

> The synecdochal totalization of infinitude is possible because the unit of number, the *one*, functions as a nominal definition. But, for the argument to be valid, the nominally indivisible number must be distinguished from the *really* indivisible space, a demonstration that Pascal can accomplish easily, but only because the key words of the demonstration—indivisible, spatial extension *(étendue)*, species *(genre)*, and definition—function as real, and not as nominal, definitions. (58–59)

But—second step—if the order of number and the order of extension had to be separated to answer Méré's objection, the rift between the two had also to be healed if the principle of homogeneity between both was to be maintained. This homology is restored by appealing, as far as number is concerned, to the zero—which, on the difference with *one* is radically heterogeneous with the order of number—and by finding equivalences in the order of time and motion, such as "instant" and "stasis." This appeal to the zero, however, has dramatic consequences for the coherence of the system, which de Man describes in a passage worth quoting in full:

> the coherence of the system is now seen to be entirely dependent on the introduction of an element—the zero and its equivalences in time and motion—that is itself entirely heterogeneous with regard to the system

and is nowhere part of it. . . . Moreover, this rupture of the infinitesimal and the homogeneous does not occur on the transcendental level, but on the level of language, in the inability of a theory of language as sign or as name (nominal definition) to ground this homogeneity without having recourse to the signifying function, the real definition, that makes the zero of signification the necessary condition for grounded knowledge. . . . It is as sign that language is capable of engendering the principles of infinity, of genus, species, and homogeneity, which allow for synecdochal totalizations, but none of these tropes could come about without the systematic effacement of the zero and its reconversion into a name. There can be no *one* without zero, but the zero always appears in the guise of a *one*, of a (some)thing. The name is the trope of the zero. The zero is always *called* a one, when the zero is actually nameless, "innommable." In the French language, as used by Pascal and his interpreters, this happens concretely in the confusedly alternate use of the two terms *zéro* and *néant*. The verbal, predicative form *néant*, with its gerundive ending, indicates not the zero, but rather the one, as the *limit* of the infinitely small, the almost zero that is the one. (59)

It is important to give serious consideration to this remarkable passage—remarkable, among other things, because de Man does not pursue later in his essay all the implications of his own démarche—for it contains, *in nuce,* all the relevant dimensions of the problem we are exploring. Everything turns around the role of the zero. The zero is, we are told, something radically heterogeneous with the order of number. The order of number, however, cannot constitute itself without reference to the zero. It is, in this sense, a supplement to the system that, nonetheless, is necessary for constituting the latter. Vis-à-vis the system, the zero is in an undecidable tension between internality and externality—but an internality that does not exclude heterogeneity. The zero, in the second place is "innommable," nameless, but at the same time it produces effects, it closes the system, even at the price of making it hopelessly heterogeneous. It *retotalizes* the system, incurring, however, an inconsistency that cannot be overcome. The zero is nothing, but it is the nothing of the system itself, the impossibility of its consistent closure, which is signified by the zero and in that sense, paradoxically, the zero as empty place becomes the signifier of fullness, of systematicity as such, as that which is lacking. The semantic oscillation between *zéro* and *néant* that de Man observes is the result of this dual condition of the moment of closure: being an impossible object, but also a necessary one. Finally, if the zero as moment of closure is impossible as an object but also necessary, it will have to have access to the field of representation. But the means of representation will be constitutively inadequate. It will give to the "innommable" a body, a name, but this can be done only at the price of betraying its true "nonbeing"; thus the tropological movement that prolongs sine die the non-resolvable dialectics between the zero and the one. In the words of de Man just quoted: "There can be no *one* without zero, but the zero always appears in the guise of a *one*, of a (some)thing. The name is the trope of the zero. The zero is always *called* a one, when the zero is actually nameless, 'innommable.'"

Now, this succession of structural moments coincides, almost step by step, with the logic of hegemony that I have tried to describe in my work and which I see operating in the texts of Gramsci—to whom I will return later on. To start with, the condition of any hegemonic suture is the constitutive nonclosure of a system of political signification. The systemacity of a system, its closure—which is the condition of signification in a system, such as Saussure's, whose identities are merely differential—coincides with the determination of its limits. These limits, however, can only be dictated by something that is beyond them. But, as the system is a system of differences, of all actual differences, that "beyond"—which should be heterogeneous with the system in order to fulfill its function of truly closing it—lacks the condition of a true heterogeneity if it consists in one more difference. The latter would be, in some way, undecided, suspended between being internal and external to the system. This jeopardizes the role of the "beyond" as limit and, as a result, the possibility of constituting the differences as truly intrasystemic differences. It is only if the beyond the limit has the character of an exclusion that its role as limit is restored and with it the possibility of emergence of a full system of differences.[3]

However, this fullness of the system (obtained, it is true, at the price of a dialectical retrieval of its negation) has a shortcoming. For, vis-à-vis the excluded element, all differences within the system establish relations of equivalence between themselves. And equivalence is precisely that which subverts difference. So the "beyond" which is the condition of possibility of the system is also its condition of impossibility. All identity is constituted within the unsolvable tension between equivalence and difference.

So, as with the Pascalian zero, we arrive at an object that is at the same time impossible and necessary. As impossible, it is an empty place within the structure. But, as necessary, it is a "nothing" that will produce structural effects, and this requires that it has access to the field of representation. And, as in the dialectics between the zero and the one, this double condition of necessity and impossibility will be constitutively inadequate. The fullness of the system, its point of imaginary saturation, will be, as in the example of de Man, a nothing that becomes a something. What are the possible means of this distorted representation? Only the particular differences internal to the system. Now, this relationship by which a particular difference takes up the representation of an impossible totality entirely incommensurable with it is what I call a hegemonic relation.

There are only two differences between the hegemonic logic and the Pascalian dialectics between the zero and the *one* as described by de Man. The first is that—given the numerical nature of Pascal's case—the zero can only be embodied by the *one,* while in the case of the hegemonic logic *any* element within the system can be a bearer of a hegemonic function.[4] The second difference is that, given de Man's interests, the determination of the heterogeneous character of the tropological displacement from the zero to the *one* is the point of arrival of his analysis, whereas for a student of hegemonic logics the analysis of the exact nature of this tropological movement becomes imperative. In de Man's detotalizing discourse, what matters is to show the heterogeneity out of which the tropological movement operates. This is also a vital part of a hegemonic analysis. But what is decisive for the latter is the determination of the partial retotalizations that the tropological movement makes possible.[5] This is the dimension that we now have to take into account. I will do it through a reference to the opposition metaphor/metonymy as presented in de Man's essay on Proust in *Allegories of Reading.*[6]

## II

The text on Proust deals, as is well known, with the discourse of young Marcel on the pleasure of reading and with the way in which such pleasure is constructed through a set of metaphoric substitutions that are, however, persuasive only through the operation of a series of contingent metonymic movements. De Man asserts:

> The crossing of sensory attributes in synaesthesia is only a special case
> of a more general pattern of substitution that all tropes have in common.
> It is the result of an exchange of properties made possible by a

proximity or an analogy so close and intimate that it allows the one to substitute for the other without revealing the difference necessarily introduced by the substitution. The relational link between the two entities involved in the exchange then becomes so strong that it can be called necessary: there could be no summer without flies; no flies without summer. . . . The synecdoche that substitutes part for whole and whole for part is in fact a metaphor, powerful enough to transform a temporal contiguity into an infinite duration. . . . Compared to this compelling coherence, the contingency of a metonymy based only on a casual encounter of two entities that could very well exist in each other's absence would be entirely devoid of poetic power. . . . If metonymy is distinguished from metaphor in terms of necessity and contingency . . . then metonymy is per definition unable to create genuine links, whereas no one can doubt, thanks to the butterflies, the resonance of the crates, and especially the "chamber music" of the flies, of the presence of light and of warmth in the room. On the level of sensation, metaphor can reconcile night and day in a *chiaroscuro* that is entirely convincing. (62–63)

We see that this passage establishes the distinction between metaphor and metonymy on the basis of the two oppositions contiguity/analogy— the dominant opposition in classical rhetoric—and contingency/necessity. As far as the first opposition is concerned, the difficulty is that the distinction between analogy and contiguity is rather slippery. Contiguity, in rhetorical terms, cannot be equivalent to mere physical contiguity, for the latter can be the basis of a metaphoric relation. And analogy can depend on such a variety of criteria that we are actually faced with a continuum in which analogy fades into mere contiguity. De Man himself points out, for instance, that "Synecdoche is one of the borderline figures that creates an ambivalent zone between metaphor and metonymy and that, by its spatial nature, creates the illusion of a synthesis by totalization" (63). And in one of the essays included in *Blindness and Insight,* he asserts that it is notoriously difficult, logically as well as historically, to keep the various tropes and figures rigorously apart, to establish precisely when catachresis becomes metaphor and when metaphor turns into metonymy; to quote an apt water-metaphor to which an expert of the field (Lansberg) has to resort precisely in his discussion of metaphor: "the transition (of one figure to another, in this case, from metaphor to metonymy) is fluid."[7]

We could say that the frontiers between figures and tropes in classical rhetoric are ancillary to the main objective distinctions of ancient ontology. This is evident from Aristotle to Cicero and Quintilian. It is precisely the close character of this system of distinctions that is put into question by the deconstructive turn. Both de Man and Gérard Genette, for example, have shown how Proust, great defender of the creative role of metaphor, had to ground his own metaphors in a generalized system of metonymic transitions.[8]

The distinction between necessity and contingency is more promising. In this case, without being entirely able to avoid the continuum by which one figure fades into the other, we have at least a less ambiguous criterion of classification: a discourse will be more or less metaphoric depending on the degree of fixation that it establishes between its constitutive components. De Man attempts to show how all metaphorical totalization is based on a metonymic textual infrastructure that resists this totalizing movement. In *Hegemony and Socialist Strategy* we have asserted that hegemony is always metonymic.[9] In the light of our previous analysis we see why this has to be the case. What is constitutive of a hegemonic relation is that its component elements and dimensions are articulated by contingent links. A trade union or a peasant organization, for instance, can take up political tasks that are not related by necessary links to their own corporative specificity. The hegemonic links by which those political tasks become workers' or peasants' tasks are metonymic displacements based on relations of contiguity (on the simple availability of those forces in a certain context in which no other social force could take up those tasks—which involves no relation of analogic necessity existing between task and agent). In that sense, if there is going to be hegemony, the traces of the contingency of the articulation cannot be entirely effaced.

The type of relationship involved in a hegemonic link can be further clarified if we return for a moment to the Pascalian zero. As in the case of the hegemonic relation, the heterogeneous character of the element that brings about whatever totalization can exist—the zero—is a contingent remainder that cannot be eradicated. But there is a crucial difference between the latter and that inhabiting the tropological movement which is at the root of hegemony. Where in hegemony there is free variation as far as the element that occupies the hegemonic position is concerned, in the case of the zero we do not have such a latitude of maneuver: the zero can only be a *one*. In that case we are not dealing, properly speaking, with a metonymy but with a catachresis.[10] Now, in the field of rhetoric, catachresis occupies a very special position. At the time of the last codification of classical rhetoric in the early nine-teenth century, it was even denied the status of a figure. Thus, Fontanier defined it in the following way:

> *La Catachrèse, en général, consiste en ce qu'un signe déjà affecté à une première idée, la soit aussi à une idée nouvelle qui elle-même n'en avait point ou n'en a plus d'autre en propre dans la langue.* Elle est, par con-séquent, tout Trope d'un usage forcé et nécessaire, tout Trope d'où ré-sulte un *sens* purement *extensif*; ce sens propre de second origine, inter-médiaire entre le *sens propre primitif* et le *sens figuré*, mais qui par sa propre nature se rapproche plus du premier qui du second, bien qu'il ait pu être lui même *figuré* dans le principe.[11]

For instance, if I speak of the "wings of an airplane" or the "wings of the building," the expression was metaphoric at the beginning, but the difference with a proper metaphor that fully operates as a figure is that there is no proper designation of the referent. I am not free to call the "wing" in any other way.

So if the only defining feature of a catachresis is its being based in a figural name that has no counterpart in a proper one, it is clear that there is no specificity in the kind of figuration introduced by catachre-sis, and that it will repeat the figures of language sensu stricto with the only *differentia specifica* of there being no tropological movement from the proper to the figural. Thus Fontanier can speak of a cata-chresis of metonymy, of synecdoche and of metaphor. The difficulty is that the distinction between a catachresis of metonymy and a proper metonymy depends on the possibility of establishing an uncontaminat-ed frontier between the proper and the figural. As soon as some *sou-plesse* is introduced, the exchanges between these polar extremes be-come more complicated: the proper becomes the extreme, the reductio ad absurdum of a continuum that is figural through and through. With this, the possibility of a *radical* heterogeneity on which the sharp dis-tinction between catachresis and metonymy is grounded is consider-ably eroded. The only thing we can say is that the very possibility of a hegemonic relationship depends on this erosion, on keeping an unstable equilibrium between heterogeneity and contiguity, between catachresis and metonymy—an equilibrium whose conditions of ex-tinction would be either a heterogeneity without common measure be-tween the elements, or a contiguity that becomes total and, thus, ab-sorbs within an implicitly assumed space the contiguous positions as internal differences.[12] (These two conditions of extinction of the hegemonic link are, in fact, only one and the same: in order to be *radically* heterogeneous, two elements require a common ground out of which their heterogeneity can be thought.)

On the other hand, however, all hegemony tries to retotalize and to make as necessary as possible the contingent links on which its articulating power is based. In this sense, it tends to metaphorical totalization. This is what gives it its dimension of power. It is a power, however, that maintains the traces of its contingency, and is, in that sense, essentially metonymic. Hegemony is always suspended between two impossible poles: the first, that there would be no displacement, that contiguity becomes mere contiguity, and that all tropological movement ceases—this would be the case of what Gramsci called the "corporative class"; the second, that the metaphorical totalization becomes complete and that purely analogical relations fully saturate the social space—in which case we would have the "universal class" of the classical emancipatory discourse. Both poles are excluded by the hegemonic relation. It is only on the traces of (contingent) contiguity contaminating all analogy that a hegemonic relation can emerge.

III

I will now attempt to illustrate these propositions with a historical example showing an extreme attempt at metaphorical totalization, whose very failure shows the space in which the undecidable logic of hegemony operates. I am referring to the work of Georges Sorel.

Sorel's work is a product of that period of socialist thought that has been called, following the characterization of Thomas Masaryk, "the crisis of Marxism." The increasing gap between the classical Marxist dogma, as codified in the *Anti-Dühring*, and the actual turn of events opened a theoretical vacuum that various intellectual projects attempted to fill.

Two themes quite frequent at that time—the impossibility of unifying historical events by conceptual means, the grounding of historical action in conviction and will—are certainly present in Sorel, but he is going to give them a new twist and to invest them with a new meaning, as he is going to see them from the viewpoint of a far more radical historical possibility. Let us consider the following passage from the *Réflexions sur la violence,* which shows the deep gap separating Sorel's socialism from that of most of his contemporaries:

Dans une société aussi enfiévrée par la passion du succès à obtenir dans la concurrence, tous les acteurs marchent droit devant eux comme de véritables automates, sans se préoccuper des grandes idées des sociologues; ils sont soumis à des forces très simples et nul d'entre eux ne songe à se soustraire aux conditions de son état. C'est alors seulement que le développement du capitalisme se poursuit avec cette rigueur qui avait tant frappé Marx et qui lui semblait comparable à celle d'une loi naturelle. Si, au contraire, les bourgeois, égarés par les *blagues* des prédicateurs de morale ou de sociologie, reviennent à un *idéal de médiocrité conservatrice,* cherchent à corriger les *abus* de l'économie et veulent rompre avec la barbarie de leurs anciens, alors une partie des forces qui devaient produire la tendance du capitalisme est employée à l'enrayer, du hasard s'introduit et l'avenir du monde est complètement indéterminé.

Cette indétermination augmente encore si le prolétariat se convertit à la paix sociale en même temps que ses maîtres;—ou même simplement s'il considère toutes choses sous un aspect corporatif;—tandis que le socialisme donne à toutes les contestations économiques une couleur générale et révolutionnaire.[13]

Let us follow this argument closely. If the objective logic of historical change that Marx had presented depends for its full development on the bourgeoisie not being dominated by the ideal of a "médiocrité conservatrice"—because in the latter case "du hasard s'introduit et l'avenir du monde est complètement indéterminé"—everything turns on whether that ideal will prevail or not. That prevalence, however, cannot be the result of identifiable objective economic processes, given that the very possibility of those processes taking place depends, for Sorel, on the absence of the "médiocrité conservatrice." Here we find the cornerstone of Sorel's thought in its mature stage: social processes do not involve only displacements in the relationship of forces between classes, because a more radical and constitutive possibility is always haunting society: the dissolution of the social fabric and the implosion of society as a totality. So, society is not only suffering domination and exploitation: it is also threatened with decadence, with the only too real possibility of its radical not being. Let us see how in Sorel this distinctive possibility opens the way to a new and peculiar logic in the relation between groups. There are two capital moments in this logic.

The first, is that the opposition that dominates Sorel's vision of the social is not primarily the one between bourgeoisie and proletariat but, rather, that between decadence and full realization of society. If the proletariat as a social force receives historical priority, it is because it is seen as the main instrument in confronting decadence. But—and this is a crucial point—it is not the actual victory of the proletariat against the bourgeoisie that will bring about "grandeur" and will arrest decadence, but the very fact of the open confrontation between the two groups. Without confrontation there is no identity; social identities require conflict for their constitution. This explains Sorel's critique of democracy. If social identities require open conflict for their full constitution, any attempt to dilute, reduce, or even regulate that conflict can only be an instrument of decadence and corruption of those identities. Democratic participation in public institutions is the sure road leading to such corruption. So, Sorel had to see in Marxism not a scientific doctrine explaining the objective laws of capitalism, but a finalistic ideology of the proletariat, grounded in class struggle. Social relations, left to themselves, are just "mélange." Only the will of determined social forces gives a consistent shape to social relations, and the determination of that will depends on the violent confrontation with other wills.

But, second, if the historical justification of the action of the proletariat is given by its being the only force capable of opposing the decadence of civilization, that justification is indifferent to the *contents* of the proletarian program and depends entirely on the contingent ability of those contents to bring about an effect that is external to themselves. There is no ethical justification that is intrinsic to socialism. This has two capital consequences. The first, that all social identity or social demand is constitutively split. It is, on the one hand, a concrete demand; but, on the other hand, it can also be the bearer, the incarnation of social "grandeur" as opposed to decadence. "Grandeur" and "decadence" do not have intrinsic contents of their own, but are the empty signifiers of a fullness of society (or its opposite, its corruption or nonbeing) that can be actualized by the most different social forces. So—and this is the second consequence—it is enough that the working class shows itself as a limited historical actor, closed in its corporative demands and incapable of incarnating the will to fullness of society, for its claims to lose all legitimacy. And the political trajectory of Sorel is a living example of the contingency of this relation between working-class demands and "grandeur": he passed from being a theoretician of revolutionary syndicalism to ally himself with a fraction of the monarchist movement, and ended his career by being close to the Third International. The diffusion of Sorelian themes in antagonistic social movements, from bolshevism to fascism, is an even more telling example of the ambiguous possibilities that his démarche was opening. For Sorel, the action (violence) is increasingly separated from its own contents and exclusively judged by the effect the latter have on the identity of the actors.

Let us now translate these reflections on Sorel into our tropological argument. Any attempt by the proletariat to constitute its subjectivity through a variety of loosely related subject positions can only lead, according to Sorel, to corporative integration and to decadence; so all metonymic variation had to be eliminated. In that case, how to aggregate working-class struggles in such a way that the proletarian identity is maintained and reinforced? Through an education of the will grounded in the myth of the general strike. Each action of the workers— whether a strike, a demonstration, or a factory occupation—should be seen, not in its own specificity and particular objectives, but as one more event in the formation of the revolutionary will. That is, these actions are all analogous from the point of view of their ultimate deep aims and are, as a result, in a relation of metaphorical substitution with each other. Their mutual relations—as that between flies and summer in Proust's text—are necessary. The drawback of this vision is that, in that case, the myth that unifies the struggles beyond all specificity cannot be specific either. The reduction of all specificity to the repetition of something analogous can only be the metaphor of metaphoricity as such. We know what this involves: the interruption of any hegemonic operation. The metaphor of metaphoricity can only be a zero that is in no tropological relation with a one, or—at most—a zero that is in a catechretical relation with *only one* position. Only at that price can revolutionary closure be achieved. And this is precisely what Sorel attempts to achieve by making the general strike totally heterogeneous with the empirical world of limited and partial struggles. The general strike is presented as a myth and not a utopia—it has lost all the detailed descriptive features of the latter; it has no particular objectives; it is merely an empty image that galvanizes the consciousness of the masses; it is exhausted in this last function without possibly corresponding to any actual historical event. It is a radical nonevent that is, paradoxically, the condition of all events if there is going to be a "grandeur" in society.

In that case, why revolutionary general strike rather than anything else? Is there any ground to think that the general strike is the (necessary) catachresis of that radical nonevent which brings about "grandeur"?

Sorel cannot answer this question, and the oscillations of his political career are a clear indication that the question is unanswerable. The relationship between "grandeur" and general strike is a hegemonic incarnation, which involves all metaphoric aggregation being ultimately grounded in (reversible) metonymic displacements. The attempt to ground the revolutionary will in a metaphoric totalization that would avoid the particularism of hegemonic variations ends in failure. As Plato knew, perhaps better than Sorel—only protracted metonymic displacements between Athens and Siracusa can give some hope that the king agrees to become a philosopher.

Perhaps we could still make this point in a slightly different way: it is only through the pure, irreducible event that consists in a contingent displacement not retrievable by any metaphoric reaggregation that we can have a history, in the sense of both *Geschichte* and *Historie*. It is because there is hegemony (and metonymy) that there is history. Couldn't some deconstructive strategies, such as iteration, be seen as attempts at introducing metonymy at the heart of metaphor, displacement at the heart of analogy? Genette (following Blanchot) tries to show, in his analysis of Proust, how the latter moved from a structure of his novel conceived as a succession of poetic instants, of punctual moments, to a conception of his whole narrative in which anamnesis is inseparable from—it is actually governed by—the whole process of narration. As he points out:

> Sans métaphore, dit (à peu près) Proust, pas de véritables souvenirs; nous ajoutons pour lui (et pour tous): Sans métonymie, pas d'enchaînement de souvenirs, pas d'histoire, pas de roman. Car c'est la métaphore qui retrouve le Temps perdu, mais c'est la métonymie qui le ranime, et le remets en marche: qui le rend à lui-même et à sa véritable "essence", qui est sa propre fuite et sa propre Recherche. Ici donc, ici seulement—par la métaphore mais *dans* le métonymie—, ici commence le Récit.[14]

Perhaps this is, exactly, the intellectual displacement leading from Sorel to Gramsci. Whereas in the first the analogizing movement of the metaphor of metaphoricity led to a repetition that tried to eliminate the possibility of any *proper* event, Gramsci's notion of war of position, of a narrative-political displacement governed by a logic of pure events which always transcend any preconstituted identity, announces the beginning of a new vision of historicity—one governed by the ineradicable tension between metonymy (or synecdoche) and metaphor.

**I V**

We now arrive at a decisive point in our argument on hegemony. If hegemony means the representation, by a particular social sector, of an impossible totality with which it is incommensurable, then it is enough that we make the space of tropological substitutions fully visible, to enable the hegemonic logic to operate freely. If the fullness of society is unachievable, the attempts at reaching it will necessarily fail, although they will be able, in the search for that impossible object, to solve a variety of partial problems; that is, the particularism of the struggles, which was systematically demoted in Sorel's analysis, now becomes central. With this, the metonymic game occupies center stage, and politics—which was for Sorel the nemesis of proletarian action—takes the upper hand.

All this becomes more visible if we compare Sorel's discursive démarche with other socialist discourses of the time, which oriented themselves in the opposite direction. Let us clarify, however, an important point before engaging in that comparison. Both metaphor and metonymy are tropological movements, that is, forms of condensation and displacement whose effects are achieved on the basis of going beyond literal meaning. Now, from this point of view, classical Marxian discourse presented itself as the zero degree of tropology, as a scientific discourse describing the necessary laws of history, which did not need to go beyond the literality of their formulation in order to achieve the totalizing effects that they postulated. That this ideal of scientificity points to an impossible task, and that whatever totalizing effects Marxian discourse could have can only be achieved through putting into operation a whole arsenal of tropological movements, is well known; but the important point is that as an ideal that governed its own discursivity, literality is fully present in it and produces a whole set of concealing effects. Sorel had ceased to believe in objective, necessary laws of history and wanted to substitute them with an *artificial* necessity grounded in the power of the will; so he had, as we have seen, to have full recourse to the principle of analogy—which in a literal discourse of necessary, objective laws would have no incidence—and to install himself, fully conscious of the fact, in the terrain of metaphor. But, as we have also seen, metaphorical necessity was decisively contaminated by metonymic contingency. What were, in that case, the politico-discursive and strategic effects of accepting as inevitable the metonymic terrain?

Let us consider the discussions in Russian social democracy at the turn of the last century. The general view was that Russia was ripe for a bourgeois-democratic revolution in which the bourgeoisie, as in all major revolutions of the West, would carry on the tasks of sweeping away the remainders of feudalism and creating a new state along liberal-democratic lines. The drawback was that the Russian bourgeoisie arrived in the historical arena too late and was weak and incapable of carrying out its political tasks. The need for a democratic revolution was, however, still there. This led to the conclusion—drawn at least by some sections of the social democrats—that in that case those tasks had to be taken up by some other social sector *that was not its natural bearer*:—in this case, the working class. This relationship by which a sector takes up tasks that are not its own is what the Russian social democrats called *hegemony*. So we see how the political steps that this analysis took led in the opposite direction to Sorel's. Whereas the latter tried to close the working class around its own *natural* tasks through metaphoric totalizations, here we find the opening of a field of metonymic displacements in the relations between tasks and agents, an undecided terrain of contingent articulations in which the principle of contiguity prevails over that of analogy. It was only the contingent peculiarity of the Russian situation—the presence of a weak bourgeoisie and a strong working class—that was at the root of the working-class leadership in the democratic revolution.

This complicated dialectics between analogy and contiguity can be seen to expand in a plurality of directions. First, as the nontropological succession of programmed stages is interrupted, a space of logical indeterminacy arises: "Tsarism, having entered into complete contradiction with the demands of Russia's social development, continued to exist thanks to the power of its organisation, the political nullity of the Russian bourgeoisie and its growing fear of the proletariat."[15]

Second, this indeterminacy is the source of pure relations of contiguity that break the possibility of totalizations in terms of either syntagmatically retrievable differences or metaphorically "necessary" aggregations:

> Russian capitalism did not develop from artisanal trade via the manufacturing workshop to the factory for the reason that European capital, first in the form of trade capital and later in the form of financial and industrial capital, flooded the country at a time when most Russian artisanal trade had not yet separated itself from agriculture. Hence the

appearance in Russia of modern capitalist industry in a completely
primitive economic environment: for instance, a huge Belgian or American
industrial plant surrounded by dirty roads and villages built of straw
and wood, which burn down every year, etc. The most primitive beginnings and the most modern European endings. (339)

This gap, which interrupts any nontropological succession of *necessary
stages,* but also any metaphoric aggregation of events around a pre-
given *necessary* point, gives proletarian identity in Russia an open
character in which contingent displacements, *pure* events, assume a
constitutive role that no a prioristic logic can govern:

I remember an old friend, Korotkov, a cabinetmaker from Nikolayev,
who wrote a song back in 1897. It was called *The Proletarians' March*
and it began with the words: "We are the alpha and the omega, we are the
beginning and the end . . ." And that's the plain truth. The first letter is
there and so is the last, but all the middle of the alphabet is missing. Hence
the absence of conservative traditions, the absence of castes within the
proletariat, hence its revolutionary freshness, hence, as well as for other
reasons, the October Revolution and the first workers' government in the
world. But hence also the illiteracy, the absence of organisational know-
how, the lack of system, of cultural and technical education . . . (340)

And then the inevitable consequence:

From the viewpoint of that spurious Marxism which nourishes itself on
historical clichés and formal analogies . . . the slogan of the seizure of
power by the Russian working class was bound to appear as a monstrous denial of Marxism. . . . What then is the real substance of the
problem? Russia's incontestably and incontrovertibly backward development, under the pressure of the higher culture of the West, leads not
to a simple repetition of the Western European historical process but to a
set of fundamentally new features which requires independent study. . . .
Where there are no "special features", there is no history, but only a
sort of pseudo-materialistic geometry. Instead of studying the living and
changing matter of economic development it is enough to notice a few
outward symptoms and adapt them to a few ready-made clichés. (339)

Could it be clearer? Historicity is identified with "special features" un-
assimilable to any form of repetition. History is a field of contingent displacements that are not retrievable by any of the (analogical) figures of
the same.

Of course, this field of contingent variations can be more or less extended, depending on the width of the area in which the literal still prevails and arrests the tropological movement. Now what happened in socialist discourses, like those we are considering, was that what we have described as a tropological movement expanded ever more and covered wider and wider sections of political life. Let us consider a concept such as "combined and uneven development." It was introduced to refer to the experience of social struggles in Third World countries, in which—even more than in the case of Russia—a nonorthodox combination of developments that should have corresponded to successive stages makes more contingent and risky hegemonic interventions possible. In the 1930s, Trotsky drew the inevitable conclusion: an uneven development is the terrain of all social and political struggles in our time. The only thing we have is an unlimited tropological movement that is the very terrain in which society constitutes itself. And we see why metonymy is, in some sense, more "primordial" than metaphor (or, as in other of de Man's analyses, why allegory takes precedence over the symbol): because in a situation of radical contingency no criterion of analogy is stable; it is always governed by changing relations of contiguity that no metaphorical totalization can control. Metaphor—and analogy—is at most a "superstructural" effect of a partial stabilization in relations of contiguity that are not submitted to any literal principle of a priori determination.

This process of general rhetorization only takes place as far as none of the conditions in which each of the tropoi would become what it literally claims to be can be met. If metonymy were *just* a metonymy, its ground should be a contiguity that is not contaminated by analogy, and in that case the literal separations within a given discursive space would be fully in control of the limits of the metonymic movement. If analogy dominated unchallenged, a full totalization would have taken place that would make analogy collapse into identity—and the tropological movement would cease. If synecdoche was actually able to substitute the whole for the part, this would mean that the whole could have been apprehended independently of the part. If catachresis could be grounded in a tropological movement that started from total heterogeneity, it could only take place insofar as the distinction between the homogeneous and the heterogeneous would be established with entire precision. It is as if in some way the conditions for a rhetoric whose tropological movements are going to occupy the terrain of a ground that is not itself grounded are to be found in the impossibility of taking the definitions of each of the tropoi at face value, and in the need to stress the logics by which each tends to fade into the other. The same for hegemony: the conditions of its full success are the same as the conditions of its extinction.

This can be shown by a couple of historical examples. The first concerns Italy. At the end of World War II there was a confrontation of tendencies, within the Italian Communist Party, about the right strategy to be followed in the new democratic environment. There were two positions: one that asserted that the Communist Party, being the party of the working class and the latter being an enclave in the industrial north, had to limit its efforts mainly to creating forms of representation for that enclave; the second, more Gramscian, maintained that the party had to build up its hegemony by spreading its activities to a variety of areas, the agrarian Mezzoggiorno included. How was this possible, given the particularistic social and geographical location of the working class? Simply, by making the party and the unions the rallying point of a variety of democratic initiatives in a country moving away from fascist dictatorship. The democratic initiatives postulated by this approach were entirely contingent—their success was not guaranteed by any logic of history—and depending, thus, on the construction of a collective will; but, in a way different from the Sorelian will, they were not aiming for the reinforcement of a purely proletarian identity. They tended, instead, to the creation of a multifarious democratic identity, always spreading beyond itself in directions only graspable through a contingent narration. Togliatti wrote in 1957:

> A class may lead society insofar as it imposes its own rule, and to this end the force of arms can also be used. It becomes a national class, however, only insofar as it solves the problems of the whole of society. . . . The proletariat becomes a national class insofar as it takes on these problems as its own and thence comes to know, by the process of changing it, the whole reality of national life. In this way it produces the conditions of its own political rule, and the road to becoming an effective ruling class is opened. . . .
>
> We have to spread the activity of an organised vanguard over the whole area of society, into all aspects of national life. This activity must not be reduced to preaching propaganda, to phrase-making or clever tactics, but must stick closely to the conditions of collective life and give, therefore, a foundation, real possibilities and prospects to the movement of the popular masses. . . . Our struggle for the unity of popu-

lar, democratic forces is, therefore, not imposed by tactical skills, but is
an historical requirement, both to maintain conquests already achieved,
to defend and safeguard democracy, and to develop it.[16]

Here we have a tropological space in which each of the figures tends to
fade into the other. The different struggles and democratic initiatives
are not united to each other by necessary links—so we have metonymical relations of contiguity. The hegemonic operation tries, however, to
make the condensation of these struggles as strong as possible—so the
metonymics fade into metaphoric totalization. The hegemonic relation
is synecdochal, as far as a particular sector in society—the working-
class party, in this case—tends to represent a whole exceeding it. As,
however, this whole lacks any precisely defined limits, we are dealing
with an impure synecdoche: it consists in the undecidable movement
between a part attempting to incarnate an undefinable whole, and a
whole that can only be named through its alienation in one of its parts.
Finally, the heterogeneity can only be a relative one—with the result
that the line separating catachresis from metonymy becomes also undecidable. I think that all the main categories of Gramscian theory—
war of position, collective will, organic intellectuals, integral state, historical bloc, hegemony—could be read rhetorically: as circumscribing
the space of tropological movement that brings about new strategic
flexibility in political analysis.

A comparable discussion took place in the South African context, in
the years before the end of apartheid, between the so-called workers
and populist tendencies within the liberation movement. The first tendency, based largely in the trade-union movement, asserted the need
for an immediate socialist transformation constituted around a working class whose protagonist role resulted from its structural centrality
in capitalist society. Contingent and particularistic displacements in the
search for alliances were reduced to a minimum. The populist camp,
on the contrary, based on the principles of the Freedom Charter, made
contingent hegemonic articulations the cornerstone of its strategy. As
David Howarth and Aletta Norval have asserted,

> the Charterists have suggested that the formation of political conscious-
> ness cannot be exclusively attributed to factory floor experiences, or de-
> rived simply from the agent's location in the relations of production, but
> occurs in a much wider discursive context. Instead of positing an ab-
> stract working class persona analytically separable from the complex
> set of discourses in which the worker is situated, the working class is

regarded as a real social force forming an essential component of the na-
tionally oppressed people. . . . In this sense, the working class as a real
social force engaged in struggle is always to some extent marked by
struggles, identities and discourses which cannot simply be reduced to
its position in the relations of production; their leadership will only be
attained by means of actively introducing socialist discourses into the
struggle for national liberation.[17]

Although Howarth and Norval have pointed out the limited character
of the hegemonic opening that the populist camp was postulating, it is
clear that the strategic confrontation was taking place along lines similar to those that we have so far discussed: in one case a principle of
analogy by which the South African working class *repeats* a worker's
identity dictated by the abstract analysis of the capitalist relations of
production; in the other case, a succession of merely contiguous articulations that governs a predominantly contingent and contextualized
narrative.

This political argument could, obviously, be extended in a variety of
directions beyond the socialist discourses that we have considered
here. There is one, however, that I would like to stress. I see the history
of democracy as divided by one fundamental cleavage. On the one
hand, we have democracy as the attempt to construct the people as
*one,* a homogeneous social actor opposed either to "power" or to an
external enemy—or to a combination of both. This is the Jacobin conception of democracy, with its concomitant ideal of a transparent com-
munity unified—if necessary—by terror. This is the tradition that runs,
with very analogous structural features, from Robespierre to Pol Pot.
The discourses around which this democratic ideal is constructed are,
obviously, predominantly metaphoric—although, for reasons previously mentioned, they cannot conceal their metonymic foundations.
On the other hand, we have democracy as respect of difference, as
shown, for instance, in multiculturalism or in the new pluralism associated with contemporary social movements. Here we have discourses
that are predominantly metonymic, for although—given the impossibility of a pure differential, nontropological closure—some effect
of metaphoric aggregation is inevitable, it will be an aggregation that
always keeps the traces of its own contingency and incompleteness
visible. Within this basic polarity there are, obviously, all kinds of possible intermediate combinations that we can start exploring through
the variety of tropoi to be found in classical rhetoric.

Paul de Man's main contribution to this task lies not in anything that he had to say about politics—something his untimely death prevented him from doing—but rather, in two main accomplishments. The first is to have extended the field of rhetoric—or, rather, of rhetoricity— to the ensemble of language, to have made it a constitutive dimension of language as such. The second is to have deconstructed the dominant tropoi of the Romantic tradition—such as symbol and metaphor— showing the contingent infrastructure of more humble tropoi on which any totalizing effect is grounded. I have attempted in this essay to show the potential importance of both accomplishments for the elaboration of a theory of hegemony.

**NOTES**

A preliminary version of this essay was presented at the "Culture and Materiality" conference that took place at the University of California, Davis, on April 23–25, 1998. It was also discussed in the seminar on Ideology and Discourse Analysis, University of Essex, a month later. I want to thank those whose commentaries led me to introduce precisions in my text and, in some cases, partial reformulations of the argument: at Davis, Jacques Derrida, Fredrick Jameson, J. Hillis Miller, and Andrzej Warminski; at Essex, David Howarth and Aletta Norval.

1. Stefano Rosso, "An Interview with Paul de Man," in Paul de Man, *The Resistance to Theory* (Minneapolis: University of Minnesota Press, 1993), 121.

2. Paul de Man, "Pascal's Allegory of Persuasion," in *Aesthetic Ideology* (Minneapolis: University of Minnesota Press, 1996), 51–69. Subsequent page references are given in the text.

3. For the full development of this argument, see my *Emancipations(s)* (London: Verso, 1996), especially the essay "Why Do Empty Signifiers Matter to Politics?" 36–46.

4. Cf. the disagreement between de Man and Louis Maris, as presented by de Man in "Pascal's Allegory of Persuasion," 60.

5. What is important is to realize that these retotalizations do not operate through a simple and retrievable negation. As de Man asserts: "What is here called, for lack of a better term, a rupture or a disjunction is not to be thought of as a negation, however tragic it may be. Negation, in a mind as resilient as Pascal's, is always susceptible of being reinscribed in a system of intelligibility. . . . It is possible to find, in the terminology of rhetoric, terms that come close to designating such disruptions (e.g., *parabasis* or *anacoluthon*), which designate the interruption of a semantic continuum in a manner that lies beyond the power of reintegration" (ibid., p. 61). But the very fact that there are tropoi which make describable that which is beyond the power of reintegration clearly shows that we are not dealing with a simple collapse of the system but, rather, with an orderly drifting away from what would have otherwise been the conditions of its full closure. It is in the field of this drifting away that the hegemonic logics operate.

6. Paul de Man, "Reading (Proust)," in *Allegories of Reading Figural Language*

*in Rousseau, Nietzsche, Rilke and Proust* (New Haven: Yale University Press, 1979), 57–58.

7. Paul de Man, *Blindness and Insight: Essays in the Rhetoric of Contemporary Criticism* (Minneapolis: University of Minnesota Press, 1983), 284.

8. Gérard Genette, "Métonymie chez Proust," in *Figures III* (Paris, Éditions du Seuil, 1972), 41–43. Paul de Man finds the use by Genette of the category of diegetic metaphor limited as far as Proust is concerned. Both, however, agree in privileging the metonymic transitions in Proust's text.

9. Ernesto Laclau and Chantal Mouffe, *Hegemony and Socialist Strategy: Towards a Radical Democratic Politics* (London: Verso, 1985).

10. I thank J. Hillis Miller for having called my attention to the need for elaborating more the distinction between catachresis and metonymy—a distinction that, as will be seen, is crucial for my analysis.

11. Pierre Fontanier, *Les figures du discours* (Paris: Flammarion, 1968), 213. "*Generally speaking there is catachresis when a sign already linked to a first idea is also linked to a new idea which itself does not have or no longer has a literal meaning in language.* It is, as a result, any trope whose use is forced and necessary, any trope from which a purely *extended meaning* is derived; this literal meaning of second origin, mediating between the *original literal meaning* and the *figurative meaning,* but which by its own nature is closer to the first than to the second, even though it might have been *figurative* in the beginning.*"

12. With this, of course, the tropological movement would come to an end.

13. Georges Sorel, *Réflexions sur la violence* (Paris: Éditions du Seuil, 1990), 77. "In a society so enfevered by the passion of competitive success, all the actors march straight ahead like true automatons, unconcerned with the great ideas of the sociologists, and none of them considers extricating himself from that condition. It is only then that the development of capitalism is pursued with that rigor which so struck Marx and which seemed to him comparable to a natural law. If, on the contrary, the bourgeois, diverted by the *jokes* of moral or sociological preachers, return to the *ideal of conservative mediocrity,* seek to correct the *abuses* of the economy, and wish to break with the barbarity of their ancestors, then a part of the forces which should produce the dynamic of capitalism are employed in checking it, chance is introduced, and the future of the world becomes completely indeterminate.

"This indeterminacy further increases if the proletariat is converted to social peace at the same time as their masters—or even simply that it considers everything from a corporative perspective—while socialism gives to all economic struggles a general and revolutionary character."

14. Genette, "Métonymie chez Proust," 63. "Without metaphor, says Proust (more or less), there are no true memories; we can add for him (and for everybody): without metonymy, no linkage of memories, no history, no novel. Because it is metaphor that recovers lost Time, which reanimates and sets it in motion: which returns it to itself and its true 'essence,' which is in its own flight and its own Search. So here, here alone—through metaphor but *within* metonymy—Narration begins."

15. Leon Trotsky, *1905* (London: Allen Lane, 1971), 328. Subsequent page references are given in the text.

16. Palmiro Togliatti, *On Gramsci and Other Writings* (London: Lawrence and Wishart, 1979), 157–59.

17. David Howarth and Aletta Norval, "Subjectivity and Strategy in South African Resistance Politics: Prospects for a New Imaginary," *Essex Papers in Politics and Government,* Department of Government, University of Essex (May 1992): 9.

# How Can I Deny That These Hands
# and This Body Are Mine?

Judith Butler

I remember a sleepless night last year when I came into my living room and turned on the television set to discover that C-Span was offering a special session on feminist topics, and that the historian Elizabeth Fox-Genovese was making clear why she thought women's studies had continuing relevance, and why she opposed certain radical strains in feminist thinking. Among those positions she most disliked she included the feminist view that no stable distinction between the sexes could be drawn or known, a view that suggests that the difference between the sexes is itself culturally variable or, worse, discursively fabricated, as if it is all a matter of language. Of course, this did not help my project of falling asleep, and I became aware of being, as it were, a sleepless body in the world accused, at least obliquely, with having made the body less rather than more relevant. Indeed, I was not altogether sure that the bad dream from which I had awoken some hours earlier was not in some sense being further played out on the screen. Was I waking or was I dreaming? After all, it was no doubt the persecutory dimension of paranoia that hounded me from the bed. Was it still paranoia to think that she was talking about me, and was there really any way to know? If it was me, then how would I know that I am the one to whom she refers?

I relate this incident to you here today not only because it foreshadows the Cartesian dilemmas with which I will be preoccupied in the following paper, and not because I propose to answer the question of whether sexual difference is only produced in language. I will, for the moment, leave the question of sexual difference to be returned to another time.[1] The problem I do propose to address emerges every time we try to describe *the kind of action* that language exercises on the body or, indeed, in the production or maintenance of bodies. And we do tend to describe language as actively producing or crafting a body every time we use, implicitly or explicitly, the language of discursive construction.

In the consideration of Descartes's *Meditations* that follows, I propose to ask whether the way in which Descartes posits the irreality of his own body does not allegorize a more general problem of positing that is to be found in various forms of constructivism and various critical rejoinders to a constructivism that is sometimes less well understood than it ought to be. The name of this paper that I have already begun, but not yet begun, is: "How Can I Deny That These Hands and This Body Are Mine?" These are, of course, Descartes's words, but they could be ours or, indeed, mine, given the dilemmas posed by contemporary constructivism.

The language of discursive construction takes various forms in contemporary scholarship and sometimes it does seem as if the body is created ex nihilo from the resources of discourse. To claim, for instance, that the body is fabricated in discourse is not only to figure discourse as a fabricating kind of activity, but to sidestep the important questions of "in what way" and "to what extent." To say that the line between the sexes, for instance, must be drawn, and must be drawable, is to concede that at some level the stability of the distinction depends on a line being drawn. But to say that we must be able to draw a line in order to stabilize the distinction between the sexes may simply mean that we must first grasp this distinction in a way that allows us then to draw the line, and the drawing of the line confirms a distinction that is somehow already at hand. But it may mean, conversely, that there are certain conventions that govern how and where the line ought or ought not to be drawn, and that these conventions, as conventions, change through time, and produce a sense of anxiety and of unknowingness precisely at the moment in which we are compelled to draw a line in reference to the sexes. The line then lets us know what will and will not qualify as "sex"; the line works as a regulatory ideal, in Foucault's sense, or a normative criterion that permits and controls the appearance and knowability of sex. Then the question, which is not easily settled, becomes: do the conventions that demarcate sexual difference determine in part what we "see" and "comprehend" as sexual difference? It is, you might surmise, not a large leap from this claim to the notion that sexual difference is fabricated in language. But I think that we may need to look more carefully before either championing or reviling this conclusion.

The language of construction risks a certain form of linguisticism, the assumption that what is constructed by language is therefore also language, that the object of linguistic construction is nothing other than language itself. Moreover, the action of this construction is conveyed through verbal expressions that sometimes imply a simple and unilateral creation at work.

Language is said to fabricate or to figure the body, to produce or construct it, to constitute or to make it. Thus, language is said to act, which involves a tropological understanding of language as performing and performative. There is, of course, something quite scandalous involved in the strong version of construction that is sometimes at work when, for instance, the doctrine of construction implies that the body is not only made *by* language, but made *of* language, or that the body is somehow reducible to the linguistic coordinates by which it is identified and identifiable, as if there is no nonlinguistic stuff at issue. The result is not only an ontological realm understood as so many effects of linguistic monism, but the tropological functioning of language as action becomes strangely literalized in the description of what it does, and how it does what it does. And though de Man often argued that the tropological dimension of discourse works against the performative, it seems here that we see, as I believe we do in de Man's discussion of Nietzsche, the literalization of the trope of performativity.

I want to suggest another way of approaching this question that refuses the reduction of linguistic construction to linguistic monism, and which calls into question the figure of language acting unilaterally and unequivocally on the object of construction. It may be that the very term *construction* no longer makes sense in this context, that the term *deconstruction* is better suited to what I propose to describe, but I confess to not really caring about how or whether these terms are stabilized in relation to each other or, indeed, in relation to me. My concerns are of another order, perhaps in the very tension that emerges as the problem of discursive construction comes into tension with deconstruction.

For my purposes, I think it must be possible to claim that the body is not known or identifiable apart from the linguistic coordinates that establish the boundaries of the body *without* thereby claiming that the body is nothing other than the language by which it is known. This last claim seeks to make the body an ontological effect of the language that governs its knowability. But this view fails to note the incommensurability between the two domains, an incommensurability that is not precisely an opposition. Although one might accept the proposition that the body is only knowable through language, that *the body is given through language,* it is never fully given in that way, and to say that it is given partially can only be understood if we also acknowledge that it is given, when it is given, in parts; it is, as it were, given and withheld at the same time, and language might be said to perform both of these operations. Although the body depends on language to be known, the body also exceeds every possible linguistic effort of capture. It would be tempting to conclude that this means that the body exists outside of language, that it has an ontology separable from any linguistic one, and that we might be able to describe this separable ontology. But this is where I would hesitate, perhaps permanently, for as we begin that description of what is outside of language, the chiasm reappears: we have already contaminated, though not contained, the very body we seek to establish in its ontological purity. The body escapes its linguistic grasp, but so too does it escape the subsequent effort to determine ontologically that very escape. The very description of the extralinguistic body allegorizes the problem of the chiasmic relation between language and body and so fails to supply the distinction it seeks to articulate.

To say that the body is figured chiasmically is to say that the following logical relations hold simultaneously: the body is given through language but is not, for that reason, reducible to language. The language through which the body emerges helps to form and establish that body in its knowability, but the language that forms the body does not fully or exclusively form it. Indeed, the movement of language that appears to create what it names, its operation as a seamless performative of the illocutionary persuasion, covers over or dissimulates the substitution, the trope, by which language appears as transitive act, that is, by which language is mobilized as a performative that simultaneously does what it says. If language acts on the body in some way, if we want to speak, for instance, of a bodily inscription, as so much cultural theory does, it might be worth considering whether language literally acts on a body, and whether that body is an exterior surface for such action, or whether these are figures that we mobilize when we seek to establish the efficacy of language.

This leads to a converse problem, namely, the case in which language attempts to deny its own implication in the body, in which the case for the radical disembodiment of the soul is made within language. Here it is a question of the way in which the body emerges in the very language that seeks to deny it, which suggests that no operation of language can fully separate itself from the operation of the body.

Language itself cannot proceed without positing the body, and when it tries to proceed as if the body were not essential to its own operation, figures of the body reappear in spectral and partial form within the very language that seeks to perform their denial. Thus, language cannot escape the way in which it is implicated in bodily life, and when it attempts such an escape, the body returns in the form of spectral figures whose semantic implications undermine the explicit claims of disembodiment made within language itself. Thus, just as the effort to determine the body linguistically fails to grasp what it names, so the effort to establish that failure as definitive is undermined by the figural persistence of the body.

The way in which I propose to show this chiasmic relation is through a reconsideration of the opening *Meditations* of Descartes, the ones in which he seeks to bring the reality of the body into question. Descartes seeks to know whether he can deny the reality of his own body and, in particular, the reality of his limbs. Suspended and inscrutable limbs reemerge in de Man's essay "Phenomenality and Materiality in Kant" in ways that suggest a metonymic relation to the problem that Descartes poses. For de Man, the body within the third *Critique* is understood, if we can use that word, as prior to figuration and cognition. In Descartes, it emerges as a particular kind of figure, one that suspends the ontological status of the term, and this raises the question of any absolute separability between materiality and figuration, a distinction that de Man on some occasions tries to make as absolutely as possible. I hope to make this chiasmic relation between those two texts clear toward the end of my remarks.

For the moment, though, I want to suggest that Descartes's ability to doubt the body appears to prefigure the skeptical stance toward bodily reality that is often associated with contemporary constructionist positions. What happens in the course of Descartes's fabulous trajectory of doubt is that the very language through which he calls the body into question ends up reasserting the body as a condition of his own writing. Thus, the body that comes into question as an "object" that may be doubted surfaces in the text as a figural precondition of his writing.

But what is the status of Cartesian doubt understood as something that takes place in writing, in a writing that we read and that, in reading, we are compelled to reperform? Derrida raises the question of whether the Cartesian "I" is compatible with the method of doubt, if that method is understood as transposable, one that anyone might perform. A method must be repeatable or iterable: intuition (or self-inspection) requires the singularity of the mind under inspection. How can a method be made compatible with the requirements of introspection? Although Descartes's meditative method is an introspective one in which he seeks in an unmediated fashion to know himself, it is also one that is written, and that is apparently performed in the very temporality of writing. Significantly, he does not report in language the various introspective acts that he has performed prior to the writing: the writing appears as contemporaneous with this introspection, implying, contrary to his explicit claims, that meditation is not an unmediated relation at all, but one that must and does take place through language.

As I presume my readership knows, Descartes begins his *Meditations* by seeking to eradicate doubt. Indeed, he begins in an autobiographical mode, asking how long it has been that he sensed that many of his beliefs were false, these beliefs that he held in the past, that appeared to be part of his youth, that were part of his history; he then seeks to "rid himself" *(défaire)* of his former beliefs.[2] First, he claims, "I have delivered my mind from every care," and that he is, apparently luckily, "agitated by no passions," free to "address myself to the upheaval (destruction) of all my former opinions" (F:26).

His task is the dispassionate destruction of his own opinion, but also of his own past, and so we might understand the onset of *The Meditations* to require performing a destruction of one's own past, of memory. Thus, an "I" emerges, narratively, at a distance from its former opinions, shearing off its historicity, and inspecting and adjudicating its beliefs from a carefree position. Whatever the "I" is, it is from the start not the same as the beliefs that it holds and that it scrutinizes, or rather, the "I" appears to be able to maintain itself, at the level of grammar, while it calls such beliefs into question. To call such beliefs into question is apparently not to call the "I" into question. The one, the "I," is manifestly distinct from the beliefs that this "I" has held.

We must then, as readers, in order to follow this text, imagine an "I" who is detachable from the history of its beliefs. And the grammar asks us to do this prior to the official beginning of the method of doubt. Moreover, the very term that is generally translated as "belief" is "opinions" and so implies a kind of groundless knowing from the start, a form of knowing whose groundlessness will be exposed.

Descartes seeks the principles of those former beliefs, and finds that relying on the senses produces deception, and argues that nothing that once produced deception ought to be trusted again to furnish anything other than deception in the future. And yet, sometimes the senses furnish a certain indubitability, as when the narrator relays the following famous scene: "there is the fact that leads Descartes to say, I am here, seated by the fire, attired in a dressing gown, having this paper in my hands and other similar matters"(145/27). Let me call attention to the fact that the "I" is "here," "ici," because this term in this sentence is a deictic one, and it is a shifter, pointing to a "here" that could be any here, but that seems to be the term that helps to anchor the spatial coordinates of the scene and so to ground, at least, the spatial ground of its indubitability. When Descartes writes "here," he appears to refer to the place where he is, but this is a term that could refer to any "here" and so fails to anchor Descartes to his place in the way that we might expect it to. What does the writing of his place do to the indubitable referentiality of that "here"? Clearly, it is not here; the "here" works as an indexical that refers only by remaining indifferent to its occasion. Thus the word, precisely because it can refer promiscuously, introduces an equivocalness and, indeed, a dubitability that makes it quite impossible to say whether or not his being "here" is a fact as he claims that it is. Indeed, the very use of such an equivocal term makes it seem possibly untrue.

What I seek to underscore "here," as it were, is that Descartes's very language exceeds the perspective it seeks to affirm, permitting a narration of himself and a reflexive referentiality that distances the one who narrates from the "I" who is narrated by that one. The emergence of a narrative "I" in *The Meditations* has consequences for the philosophical argument Descartes seeks to make. The written status of the "I" splits the narrator from the very self he seeks to know and *not* to doubt. The "I" has, as it were, gotten out of his control by virtue of becoming written. Philosophically, we are asked to accept an "I" who is not the same as the history of its opinions, who can "undo" and "destroy" such opinions and still remain intact. Narratively, we have an "I" that is a textual phenomenon, exceeding the place and time in which it seeks to ground itself, whose very written character depends on this transposability from context to context.

But things have already become strange, for we were to have started, as Descartes maintains in the "preface," with reasons, ones that persuade, and that give us a clear and distinct idea of what cannot be doubted. We were about to distrust the senses, but instead we are drawn into the certainties that they provide, the fact that I sit here, am clothed, hold the paper that I do by the fire that is also here.

From this scene in which indubitability is asserted and withdrawn at once emerges the question of the body. Descartes asks, "how could I deny that these hands and this body here belong to me?" (F:27). Consider the very way in which he poses the question, the way in which the question becomes posable within language. The question takes, I believe, a strange grammar, one that affirms the separability of what it seeks to establish as necessarily joined. If one can pose the question whether one's hands and one's body are not one's own, then what has happened such that the question has become posable? In other words, how is it that my hands and my body became something other than me, or at least appeared to be other than me, such that the question could even be posed whether or not they belong to me? What is the status of the question, such that it can postulate a distinction between the I who asks and the bodily me, as it were, that it interrogates, and so performs grammatically precisely what it seeks to show *cannot* be performed?

Indeed, Descartes begins to ask a set of questions that perform what they claim cannot be performed: "how can I deny that these hands and this body are mine?" is one of them, and it is a strange, paraliptical question because he does give us the graphic contours of such a doubt, and so shows that such a doubt is possible. This is, of course, not to say that the doubt is finally sustainable, or that no indubitability emerges to put an end to such doubt. For Descartes to claim that the body is the basis of indubitability, as he does, is a strange consequence, if only because it appears to appeal to an empiricism that sustains an uneasy compatibility with the theological project at hand. These examples also seem to relate to the problem of clothing, knowing that one is clothed, for he claims to be sure that he was clothed in his nightgown next to the fire.

The surety of this claim is followed by a series of speculations, however, ones that he imagines others might make, but that, in his imagining, he himself makes: indeed, the writing becomes the occasion to posit and adopt narrative perspectives on himself that he claims not to be his own, but that, in adopting, are his own in the very mode of their projection and displacement. The other who appears is thus the "I" who, in paranoia, is circuited and deflected through alterity: what of those who think they are clothed in purple, but are really without covering, those others who are like me who think they are clothed, but whose thinking turns out to be an ungrounded imagining. Descartes, after all, is the one who is actively imagining others as nude, implying but not pursuing the implication that they might well think of him as nude as well. But why? Of course, he wants to get beneath the layers that cover the body, but this very occasion of radical exposure toward which *The Meditations* move is precisely what threatens him with a hallucinatory loss of self-certainty.

Indeed, it appears that the certainty he seeks of the body leads him into a proliferation of doubts. He is sure that he sits there clothed: his perspective, as sense perception and not pure intellection, is in that sense clothed or cloaked; thus this certainty depends on a certain dissimulation. The nudity he attributes to the hallucinatory certainty of others constantly threatens to return to him, to become his own hallucinatory certainty. Indeed, precisely as a sign of radical certainty, that nudity undermines his certainty. If he is clothed, he is certain of what is true, but if he is not, then the truth has been exposed, the body without dissimulation, which leads to the paradoxical conclusion that only if he is deluded about being clothed can his own utterances be taken as indubitable, in which case hallucination and certainty are no longer radically distinguishable from one another.

This is not any nude body, but one that belongs to someone who is deluded about his own nudity, one whom others see in his nudity and his delusion. And this is not simply any "one" with some characterological singularity, but a "one" who is produced precisely by the heuristic of doubt. This is one who calls the reality of his body into question only to suffer the hallucinatory spectrality of his act. When he sees others in such a state, nude and thinking themselves clothed, he knows them to be deluded, and so if others were to see him in such a state, they would know him to be deluded as well; thus, the exposure of his body would be the occasion for a loss of self-certainty. Thus, the insistence on the exposed body as an ultimate and indubitable fact in turn exposes the hallucinations of the one who is nude, nude and hallucinating that he or she is fully clothed. This figure of the indubitable body, one that only the mad might doubt, is made to represent the limit case of the *res extensa,* a body that cannot be doubted but that, comprised of the senses, will be held to be detachable from the soul and its quest for certainty.

If one were to imagine the body instead as an earthenware head or made of glass, as Descartes puts it, one would be doubting what is true. But notice that here the very act of doubting seems bound up with the possibility of figural substitutions, ones in which the living body is made synonomous with its artifactual simulation or, indeed, with glass, a figure for transparency itself. If the body is certain as *res extensa*, what is to distinguish the human body as *res extensa* from other such instances of substance? If it must, by definition, be separable from the soul, what is to guarantee its humanity? Apparently, nothing can or does.

After all, Descartes not only reports that others perform such hallucinations, the report constitutes the textualization of the hallucination; his writings perform them for us, through an alienation of perspective that is and is not exclusively his own. Thus, he conjures such possibilities precisely at the moment in which he also renounces such possibilities as mad, raising the question, is there a difference between the kind of conjuring that is a constitutive part of the meditative method, and those hallucinations that the method is supposed to refute? He remarks: "I should not be any the less insane were I to follow examples so extravagant [si je me reglais sur leurs exemples]." But what if he has already just ruled himself on these examples, followed these examples, asked us to follow them, in the sense that to write them is to follow them, and we are clearly following them as well in reading him as we do. The doubt he wants to overcome can only be reenacted within the treatise, which produces the textual occasion for an identification with those from whom he seeks to differentiate himself. These are his hands, no? but where are the hands that write the text itself, and is it not the case that they never actually show themselves as we read the marks that they leave? Can the text ever furnish a certain sense of the hands that write the text, or does the writing eclipse the hands that make it possible, such that the marks on the page erase the bodily origins from which they apparently emerge, and to emerge as tattered and ontologically suspended remains? Is this not the predicament of all writing in relation to its bodily origins? There is no writing without the body, but no body fully appears along with the writing that it produces. Where is the trace of Descartes's body in the text? Does it not resurface precisely as the figure of its own dubitability, a writing that must, as it were, make the body strange, if not hallucinatory, whose condition is an alienation of bodily perspective in a textual circuitry from which it cannot be delivered or returned? After all, the text quite literally leaves the authorial body behind, and yet there one is, on the page, strange to oneself.

At the end of *Meditation I,* he resolves to suppose that God is not good nor the fountain of truth, but some evil genius, that external things are illusions and dreams and, accordingly, he writes, "I shall consider myself as having no hands, no eyes, nor any senses, yet falsely believing myself to possess all these things." It would seem, then, that the task of the Meditation is to overcome this doubt in his own body, but it is that doubt that he also seeks to radicalize. After all, it is Descartes's ultimate project to understand himself as a soul, as a *res cogitans* and not as a body; in this way, he seeks to establish the ultimate dubitability of the body and so to ally himself with those who dream and hallucinate when they take the body to be the basis of certain knowledge. Thus, his effort to establish radical self-certainty as a rational being leads within the text to an identification with the irrational. Indeed, such dreams and hallucinations must be illimitable if he is to understand that certainty of himself as a thinking being will never be furnished by the body.

He writes that "the knowledge of myself does not depend on things not yet known to me." And it does not depend on "things that are *feigned* or *imagined* by my imagination [celles qui sont feintes et inventées par l'imagination]" (42).[3] The Latin term—*effingo*—can mean, ambiguously, "to form an image," but also, "to make a fact," which means that the knowledge of himself does not depend on forming an image or making a fact. Inadvertently, Descartes introduces an equivocation between an imagining of what is not a fact and an imagining or making of what is a fact. Has the same imagining wandered across the divide between delusion and reality such that it is at once what Descartes must exclude as the basis of self-knowledge and what he also must accommodate?

If knowledge does *not* depend on things that are feigned or imagined or facts that are made, then on what does it depend? And does his dismissal of imagining, invention, and factual making not undermine the very procedure of doubt that he uses to gauge the falsifiability of his theses? Indeed, at another moment in the text, he insists that imagination, even invention, serves a cognitive function, and that it can be used as the basis for making inferences about the indubitability of substance itself: "I would invent, in effect, when I am imagining something, since imagining is nothing other than contemplating the figure or image of a corporeal thing."[4]

The imagination is nothing other than the contemplation of the figure or image of a corporeal thing. The proposition foreshadows the claims that Husserl will make about the intentionality of the act of imagining, suggesting that objects appear to the imagination in some specific modality of their essence. If this is so, then the imagination does not merely invent bodies, but its inventiveness is also a form of referentiality, that is, of contemplating the figure or image of bodies in their essential possibility. The sense in which the imagination is inventive is not that it produces bodies where there were none. Just as referential suggestion of the term *effingo* complicates the problem, tying imagining to fact making, so Descartes's notion of the image as relaying the object in some specific way ties imagining to objects of perception, but in both cases the link is made not conceptually, but through a semantic equivocation. Indeed, if the method of doubt involves supposing or positing as true a set of conditions that he then seeks to doubt, it involves conjecturing what is counterintuitive, and so centrally engages the imagination.

"Je supposerai"—I suppose, I will suppose, I would suppose—this is the strange way that Descartes renders his doubt in language, where the term *supposer* carries the referential ambiguity that plagues his discussion. After all, *supposer* means to take for granted, to accept as a premise, but also to postulate or posit, to make or to produce. If the "I" is not a corporeal thing, then it cannot be imagined.

When he writes "I suppose," he offers appositions that suggest its interchangeability with the following formulations: I persuade myself, I posit, I think, I believe. Then the object of that supposing and thinking takes the form of a different fiction than the one he has just performed: what he supposes or believes is "that body, figure, extension . . . are nothing but fictions of my own spirit." Here there appears to be a doubling of the fictional going on, for he is supposing that the body, among other things, is a fiction of his own mind, but is that supposing not itself a fictionalizing of sorts? If so, is he then producing a fiction in which his body is the creation of a fiction? Does the method not allegorize the very problem of fictive making that he seeks to understand and dispute, and can he understand this fictive making if he continues to ask the question within the terms of the fiction from which he also seeks to escape?

Supposing, self-persuasion, thinking, believing, work by way of positing or, indeed, fabulating, but what is it that is fabulated? If the body is a fiction of one's own spirit, then this suggests that it is made or composed of one's own spirit. Thus, to posit is not merely to conjecture a false world or to make one up, but to invent and refer at the same

moment, thus confounding the possibility of a strict distinction between the two. In this way, "the fictions of the spirit" for Descartes are
not in opposition to the acts of thinking or persuasion, but the very
means by which they operate. "Positing" is a fiction of the spirit which
is not for that reason false or without referentiality. To deny the fictive
aspect of positing or supposing is to posit the denial, and in that sense
to reiterate the way that the fictive is implicated in the very act of positing. The very means by which Descartes seeks to falsify false belief involves a positing or fictionalizing that, homeopathically, recontracts
the very illness it seeks to cure. If the falsification of the untrue must
take place through a counterfactual positing, which is itself a form of
fiction, then falsification reintroduces fiction at the very moment in
which it seeks to refute it. Of course, if we could establish that what is
fictional in supposing is not the same as what is fictional in what is
being supposed, then we would avoid this contradiction, but Descartes
does not offer us any way of doing precisely that.

I hope that I have begun to show that, in imagining the body, Descartes is at once referring to the body through an image or figure—his
words—and conjuring or inventing that body at the same time, and
that the terms he uses to describe this act of supposing or imagining
carry that important double meaning. Hence, for Descartes, the language in which the body is conjectured does not quite imply that the
body is nothing other than an effect of language; it means that conjecturing and supposing have to be understood as fictional exercises that
are nevertheless not devoid of referentiality.

When we consider Descartes's efforts to think the mind apart from
the body, we see that he cannot help but use certain bodily figures in
describing that mind. The effort to excise the body fails because the
body returns, spectrally, as a figural dimension of the text. For instance, Descartes refers to God as one who inscribes or engraves on his
soul, when he writes, for instance, that he will never forget to refrain
from judgment of what he does not clearly and distinctly understand
"simply by [God's] engraving deeply in my memory the resolution
never to form a judgment on" such matters. Descartes's mind is here
figured as a slate or a blank page of sorts, and God is figured as an en-
graver. "God deeply engrave(s) [gravé] a resolution in memory not to
judge."

Similarly, Descartes appears to imprint a thought on his memory in
the same way that God engraves a resolution on the will: he refers to
his own human and frail capacity to "forcibly impress [imprimer]" a

thought on his memory, and so help in the process of building up a new memory where the old one had been destroyed.[5] Meditation now appears as a particular kind of action, one that, he claims, must be repeated, and that has as its goal the forcible imprinting *(imprimer)* of this same thought on the memory, an imprinting that is as apparently forceful as God's engraving is profound: indeed, both convey a certain formative violence, a rupture of surface, as the effect of writing.

Indeed, "the engraving" is thus the means by which God's will is transferred to Descartes, a peculiar form of transitivity that the trope of writing helps to effect. His memory becomes the object in which God engraves a resolution, as if Descartes's memory were a page, a surface, an extended substance. But this is clearly a problem, since the mind is supposed to be, as we know, *res cogitans* rather than *res extensa,* but is figured here precisely as an extended surface and substance. Hence, the memory in some ways becomes figured as a kind of body, extended substance and surface, and we might well read here the resurfacing of the lost and repudiated body within the text of Descartes, one on which God now so profoundly engraves a resolution; indeed, the metaphorical stage is now set for Kafka's "In the Penal Colony."

Indeed, it makes sense to ask whether the writing of *The Meditations* is precisely what guarantees this soldering of the memory to the will. The extended writing of *The Meditations* acts to imprint a new knowledge on his memory. To the extent that the page substitutes for memory, or becomes the figure through which memory is understood, then does that figure have philosophical consequences, namely, that introspection as method succeeds only to the extent that it is performed in writing on the page? Is writing not precisely the effort to solder a new memory to the will, and if so, then does it not require the very material surface and, indeed, the materiality of language itself that are hardly compatible with what Descartes seeks to separate from the introspective act of the mind? And does this writing not implicitly require the hand of the one who engraves and the body as surface on which to write, dispersing bodily figures throughout the explanation of the soul?

If it seems that Descartes's text cannot but figure the body, that it does not reduce the body to its figuration, and if that figuration turns out to be referential, that does not mean that the referent can somehow be extracted from its figuration. The act by which the body is supposed is precisely the act that posits and suspends the ontological status of the body, an act that does not create or form that body unilaterally (and thereby not an act in the service of linguisticism or linguistic monism), but one that posits and figures, one for which positing and figuring are not finally distinguishable.

If there is no act of positing that does not become implicated in figuration, then it follows that the heuristic of doubt not only entails figuration, but works fundamentally through the figures that compromise its own epistemological aspirations. But this conclusion is immediately impaired by another, namely, that the figuration of the body meets its necessary limit in a materiality that cannot finally be captured by the figure. Here is where proceeding by way of both grammar and figuration falters, though it is a telling faltering. If the body is not reducible to its figuration or, indeed, its conceptualization, and it cannot be said to be a mere effect of discourse, then what finally is it? The question stands, but just because there is a grammar of the question in which the ontological status of the body is posed does not mean that the answer, if there is one, can be accommodated within the grammatical terms that await that answer. In this case, the posability of the question does not imply its answerability within the terms in which it is posed. The body escapes the terms of the question by which it is approached. And even to make such a formulaic claim, relying on "The body" as the subject-noun of the sentence, domesticates precisely what it seeks to unleash. Indeed, the grammar itself exposes the limits of its own mimetic conceit, asserting a reality that is of necessity distorted through the terms of the assertion, a reality that can only appear, as it were, through distortion.[6]

Descartes makes this point perhaps unwittingly as he proceeds to dismember his own body in the course of his written meditation. We might rush in to say that this "dismemberment" is merely figural, but perhaps, Paul de Man suggests, it marks the very limits of figuration—its uncanny limits. Indeed, de Man makes his point in reference to Kant, centering on the problem that emerges in his third *Critique,* where the need for a bridge between conceptual and empirical discourses arises. He argues in favor of a "materiality" that eludes both kinds, and that also marks the conditions and limits of figuration itself.

The aesthetic is introduced as a "phenomenalized, empirically manifest principle of cognition on whose existence the possibility of such an articulation depends" (79). But, de Man notes, this articulation "depends on a linguistic structure (language as a performative as well as a cognitive system) that is not itself accessible to the powers of transcendental philosophy."

Although he has earlier insisted that the relationship between the transcendental and the empirical depends on a widening notion of language as both tropological and performative, he makes clear that what he is approaching is that which cannot be accounted for by either the performative or the tropological dimensions of language, and that this linguistic structure which is supposed to bridge the gap between the conceptual and empirical discourses will be instead a mode of disarticulation.

Isolating what is prior to figuration and cognition, de Man concentrates on the use of the apparent figure of the *Augenschein,* which is the eye itself, or rather, pure vision or ocularity. We broach here that which is, strictly speaking, neither figurable nor cognizable. It cannot be called literal, he tells us (99), for that would imply its possible conversion into figuration or symbolization. Materiality will be precisely that which is convertible into neither figuration nor cognition. This materiality characterizes an aesthetic vision in its irreducibility. The "eye," he writes, is here its own agent, and not the specular echo of the sun. The trope of the "sea," he writes, functions similarly; although Kant calls it "a mirror," it reflects nothing. And it seems that, for de Man, at this textual instance, the failure of these figures to reflect or to act mimetically disqualifies them as figures. This is no doubt a strange requirement to set upon figures, and I doubt that it is one that he has consistently applied. At any rate, in both cases, the effect of these figures is that they fail to perform their figural function and thus relapse into the material condition of figuration, one that is itself, strictly speaking, not convertible into any figure and not understood by its opposite, the literal, *and* not, strictly speaking, even a condition, since this materiality does not *support* figuration, but exercises a corrosive effect on all figuration. Whereas the phenomenality of the aesthetic rests on an adequate representation, the materiality of aesthetic vision is a pure materiality that makes no reference to adequate representation.

Toward the end of the essay, de Man turns to the chapter titled "The Architectonics of Pure Reason" in the third *Critique* in which he refers to the organic unity of systems, and this unity is conceived through "the recurring metaphor of the body, as a totality of limbs and parts." Because the aesthetic will involve the suspension of all reference to organic purposiveness, Kant admonishes that "we must not regard as the determining grounds of our judgment the concepts of the purposes which all our limbs serve . . . and we must not allow this unity of purpose to influence our aesthetic judgment."

If aesthetic judgment is to be separated from the understanding of natural unities of purpose, and there is an aesthetic judgment of the body, then it will be precisely of the limbs as severed from the unity of purposes (natural) that the body is. Assuming that this unity of purpose is expressed by the notion of substance, and that substance is understood as torso, it would appear that the aesthetic vision of the body would be one of dismemberment wherein the limbs are separated from the torso or the substance of the body. Thus, de Man writes, "we must, in other words, disarticulate, mutilate the body . . . : "we must consider the limbs . . . severed from any purpose or use."

He writes not only in the imperative, but identifies disarticulation with mutilation, and offers *mutilate* itself as a transitive verb—we must mutilate—although the following sentence amplifies this meaning by claiming that we must only "consider" the limbs as severed. Interestingly, the very formulation that gives us what is prior to figuration and cognition and, indeed, the performative, is one that figures our own "seeing" as a mutilating activity that works on the body. Indeed, de Man makes his pedagogical point by likening this dismembered body to the dismemberment of language. He writes: "To the dismemberment of the body corresponds a dismemberment of language, as meaning producing tropes are replaced by the fragmentation of sentences and propositions into discrete words, or the fragmentation of words into syllables or finally letters" (113). The use of "corresponds," however, in this last sentence seems to recall the very model of adequation from which materiality as dismemberment is supposed to differ. Here de Man is seeking to trace the relapse of a trope into the materiality of the letter, a materiality that grounds and exceeds the trope and that is never exhaustively convertible into the trope itself: the condition of the trope, but also the destiny of its disarticulation.

But why is this point about language introduced through a comparison or, indeed, a correspondence with the body? And what is the relation between materiality understood as bodily dismemberment and the fragmentation of words into letters and the so-called materiality of aesthetic vision? In what sense does the dismemberment of the body, which is one that takes place in or for vision, not precisely a figurative operation? If seeing effects this dismemberment, then seeing is figured as a performative, and both the figural and performative dimensions of language remain at work in the description of this materiality, a description that may well have to be fully catachrestic to make any sense at all. Indeed, if the body in pieces is neither figurative nor literal, but material, then it would still follow that the only way to convey that materiality is precisely through catachresis, as de Man actually does, and so through a figure. If the body is not literally dismembered, though the language figures that as its effect, in what sense is it dismembered? And if dismemberment is but a sign of a prefigural materiality, then that materiality has been converted into a trope through the very example that is said to illustrate that nonconvertibility. A figure can function as a substitution for that which is fundamentally irrecoverable within or by the figure itself: indeed, this is perhaps where Benjamin on allegory would, if he could, if I would let him, make his eery return. Such a figure is, however, no less a figure than a mimetic one, or one whose terms can be related through means of adequation. So is this body figurable or not? It depends, I would suggest, on how one approaches the question of figurality. If Descartes's body is not literally dismembered, though the language figures that as its effect, in what sense is it still dismembered? And if dismemberment is but a sign of a prefigural materiality, then that materiality has been converted into a trope through the very example that is said to illustrate that nonconvertibility. The body does not, then, imply the destruction of figurality if only because a figure can function as a substitution for that which is fundamentally irrecoverable within or by the figure itself.[7] Such a figure is, however, no less a figure than a mimetic one, and a figure need not be mimetic to sustain its status as figural.

Clearly, though, the final question here must be to consider this strange separation of the limbs from the body, this repeated scene of castration, the one that Descartes enacts through the grammar that conditions the question he poses of his body in which he is already separated from that which he calls into question, a separation at the level of grammar that prepares the philosophical question itself, in which the hand that writes the doubt and the hand that is doubted—is it mine?— is at once the hand that is left behind as the writing emerges in, we might say, its dismembering effect.[8]

There is no doubt a hand that writes Descartes's text, and a hand figured within that text as appearing at a distance from the one who looks upon it and asks after its reality. The hand is reflexively spectralized in the course of the writing it performs. It undoes its reality precisely at the moment in which it acts or, rather, becomes undone precisely by the traces of the act of writing it performs. If the body is what inaugurates the process of its own spectralization through writing, then it is and is not determined by the discourse it produces. If there is a materiality of the body that escapes from the figures it conditions and by which it is corroded and haunted, then this body is neither a surface nor a substance, but the linguistic occasion of the body's separation from itself, one that eludes its capture by the figure it compels.

**NOTES**

This essay was first presented as an invited lecture at the American Philosophical Association Meetings in December 1987 in Philadelphia. It was re-presented in revised version for the "Culture and Materiality" conference at the University of California at Davis in April 1998, and appeared in *Qui Parle* 11: 1 (1997).

1. Excellent work reconsidering the relationship of language and materiality in sexual difference is currently being done by Charles Shephardson, Debra Keates, and Katherine Rudolph.

2. "Il me fallait entreprendre sérieusement une fois en ma vie de me défaire de toutes les opinions que j'avais reçues . . . me défaire de toutes les opinions." The text was originally published in Latin in 1641 in France, although Descartes was living in Holland at the time. Descartes apparently had reasons to fear the Dutch ministers reading the text, and so he had a friend oversee its publication in France. It did, however, appear the following year, 1642, in Amsterdam, and the second edition includes the objections and replies. This second edition is usually referred to as the Adam and Tannery version, and it was the basis for the French translations. One of those took place that same year by the Duc de Luynes, and Descartes approved the translation, which is to say that he subjected it to various corrections and revisions. It appeared in revised form in 1647. Hence, we can to some degree think of the French text as one that Descartes approved, and in some instances, wrote, but nevertheless one to which he was willing to attach a signature.

Almost every English version of Descartes will be a translation of the second version of *The Meditations*. Two French translations were offered to Descartes for approval, one by the Duc de Luynes and another by Clerselier; he chose the one by the Duc de Luynes for *The Meditations* themselves, and the "objections and replies" translation by Clerselier.

In 1661, Clerselier republished his translation, making corrections, and abandoning the translation by the Duc de Luynes that Descartes had approved. Many scholarly editions take this to be a more exact and literal translation and have used it as the primary text. Some have complained that the Duc de Luynes's version was too liberal a translation, lacking Descartes's exactitude. And they have made excuses for why Descartes might have accepted the translation—politesse, politics, and the like.

The French that I follow here is that provided by the Duc de Luynes. The English is from *The Philosophical Works of Descartes,* trans. Elizabeth S. Haldane and G. R. T. Ross (Cambridge: Cambridge University Press, 1973).

3. In the French, he refers to what is "feintes et inventées par l'imagination," and this notion of "invented" is translated from the Latin: *effingo.* Knowledge of oneself does not depend on what is feigned or invented, but the Latin term casts doubt on the very denial that Descartes performs.

4. "Je feindrais en effet, si j'imaginais être quelque chose, puisque imaginer n'est autre chose que contempler la figure ou l'image d'une chose corporelle."

5. Descartes writes, "he has at least left within my power this resolution . . . for although I notice a certain weakness in my nature in that I cannot continually concentrate my mind on one single thought [je ne puis pas attacher continuellement mon esprit à une même pensée, I cannot continually attach my spirit to the same thought], I can yet, by attentive and frequent meditation, impress [*imprimer*] it so forcibly on my memory that I shall never fail to recollect it whenever I have need of it, and thus acquire the habit of never going astray" (178).

6. This view corresponds to Lacan's view of the mirror stage as that which permits a specular version of the body on the condition of distortion. The subsequent references to Paul de Man's essays are from *Aesthetic Ideology,* ed. Andrzej Warminski (Minneapolis: University of Minnesota Press, 1996).

7. One might usefully consult Walter Benjamin on the status of allegory for precisely such an approach to the figure.

8. See Jonathan Goldberg, *Writing Matter: From the Hands of the English Renaissance* (Stanford, Calif.: Stanford University Press, 1990).

# V. Materiality without Matter

# Typewriter Ribbon: Limited Ink (2) ("within such limits")

Jacques Derrida

Translated by Peggy Kamuf

Will this become possible? Will we one day be able, and in a single ges-ture, to join the thinking of the event to the thinking of the machine? Will we be able to think, what is called thinking, at one and the same time, *both* what is happening (we call that an event) *and* the calculable programming of an automatic repetition (we call that a machine)? Will we be able in the future (and there will be no future except on this condition) to think *both* the event *and* the machine as two com-patible or even indissociable concepts, although today they appear to us to be antinomic? Antinomic because we think that what happens ought to keep, so we think, some nonprogrammable and therefore in-calculable singularity. We think that an event worthy of the name ought not, so we think, to give in or be reduced to repetition. An event ought above all to happen to someone, to some living being who is thus affected by it, consciously or unconsciously. It is difficult, however, to conceive of a living being *to* whom or *through* whom something happens without an affection getting inscribed in a sensible, aesthetic manner right on some body or some organic matter.

Notice I say *organic*. No thinking of the event, therefore, without an aesthetic and some presumption of living organicity.

The machine, on the contrary, is thought to repeat impassively, im-perceptibly received commands. In a state of anesthesia, it obeys or commands a calculable program without affect or auto-affection, like an indifferent automaton. Its functioning, if not its production, does not need anyone. And it is difficult to conceive of a machine-like appa-ratus without inorganic matter.

Notice I say *inorganic*. Inorganic, that is, nonliving, sometimes dead

277

but always, in principle, unfeeling and inanimate, without desire, without intention, without spontaneity. The automaticity of the inorganic machine is not the spontaneity attributed to organic life.

This is at least how the event and the machine are generally conceived. Among all the incompatible traits that I have just briefly recalled, so as to suggest how difficult it is to think them together as the same "thing," I have underscored these two predicates that are most often attributed without hesitation to matter or to the material body: the *organic* and the *inorganic.*

These two commonly used words carry an obvious reference, either positive or negative, to the possibility of an internal principle that is proper and *totalizing,* to a total form of, precisely, *organization,* whether or not it be a beautiful form, an aesthetic form, this time in the sense of the fine arts. This organicity is thought to be lacking from so-called inorganic matter. If one day, with one and the same concept, these two incompatible concepts, the event and the machine, were to be thought together, you can bet that *not only* (and I insist on *not only*) will one have produced a new logic, an unheard-of conceptual form; against the background and at the horizon of our present possibilities, this new figure would resemble a monster (even more disturbing than what we see on the poster for our colloquium, which represents, I suppose, Shelley's "Chariot of Life"). Moreover, it is already necessary to correct this formulation: the new figure of an event-machine would no longer be even a figure and it would not resemble, it would resemble nothing, not even what we call, in a still-familiar way, a monster. But it would therefore be, by virtue of this very novelty, an event, the only and the first possible event, because im-possible. That is why I ventured to say that this thinking could belong only to the future—and even that it makes the future possible. An event does not come about unless its irruption interrupts the course of the possible, and, as the impossible itself, surprises any foreseeability. But such a supermonster of eventness would be, this time, for the first time, *also* produced by the machine.

*Not only,* I said. The thinking of this new concept will have changed the very essence and the very name of what we today call "thought," the "concept," "thinking thought," "thinking the thinkable," or "thinking the concept." Perhaps another thinking is heralded here. Perhaps it is heralded without announcing itself, without horizon of expectation, by means of this old word *thought,* this homonym or paleonym that has sheltered for such a long time the name still to come of a thinking that has not yet thought what it must think, namely, thought, namely, what is given to be thought with the name "thought," beyond knowledge, theory, philosophy, literature, the fine arts—and even technics.

As a still preliminary exercise, somewhat like musicians who listen to their instruments and tune them before beginning to play, we could try out another version of the same aporia. Such an aporia would not block or paralyze, but on the contrary would condition any event of thought that resembles somewhat the unrecognizable monster that has just passed in front of our eyes. What would this aporia be? One may say of a machine that it is productive, active, efficient, or as one says in French, *performante*. But a machine as such, however *performante* it may be, could never, according to the strict Austinian orthodoxy of speech acts, produce an event of the *performative* type. Performativity will never be reduced to technical performance. Pure performativity implies the presence of a living being, and of a living being speaking one time only, in its own name, in the first person. And speaking in a manner that is at once spontaneous, intentional, free, and irreplaceable. Performativity, therefore, excludes in principle, in its own moment, any machine-like *[machinale]* technicity. It is even the name given to this intentional exclusion. This foreclosure of the machine answers to the intentionality of intention itself. It is intentionality. If, then, some machinality (repetition, calculability, *inorganic* matter of the body) intervenes in a performative event, it is always as an accidental, extrinsic, and parasitical element, in truth a pathological, mutilating, or even mortal element. Here again, to think *both* the machine *and* the performative event together remains a monstrosity to come, an impossible event, and therefore the only possible event. But it would be an event that, this time, no longer happens without the machine. Rather, it would happen by the machine. To give up neither the event nor the machine, to subordinate neither one to the other, never to reduce one to the other: this is perhaps a concern of thinking that has kept a certain number of "us" working for the last few decades. But who is this "us"? Who would be this "us" whom I dare to speak of so carelessly? Perhaps it designates at bottom, and first of all, those who find themselves in the improbable place or in the uninhabitable habitat of this monster.

Having begun in this manner, as you can very well hear, I already owe you an excuse, many excuses, an incalculable number of excuses. *I should apologize,* as you say in English, *endlessly.* In a very limited space and time, "within such limits," I will no doubt fail, by my own fault, to negotiate among several necessary compromises and to honor several commitments that are sometimes difficult to reconcile.

There are at least three or four of these. The announced title for my contribution, "'Materiality'"—in quotation marks—"Archival Intervention, Virtual Futures," was not one I myself chose, as you might have supposed. Quite a while ago, Tom Cohen and I no doubt evoked this series of themes, but simply as abstract possibilities. Upon receiving the poster for the colloquium, I for the first time saw unfurl before my eyes this intimidating banner that I would never have dared to wave myself: "'Materiality'"—in quotation marks, and yes, I myself would certainly have wanted to add those quotation marks—"Archival Intervention, Virtual Futures." I nevertheless promised, promised myself, right away, to do everything to honor as best I could the impossible task that had thus been assigned to me. I will therefore attempt to approach in my own way all these formidable questions, even if I prefer to withdraw and beat a retreat toward the final title that I myself chose, namely: "Typewriter Ribbon: Limited Ink (2) ("within such limits"). This is the *first compromise.*

I owe you an apology for a *second compromise.* So as to save some time and energy at a moment when I have little of either to spare, I had to reorient in the direction of this colloquium certain sessions of the seminar that I am giving this year in Paris and at UC Irvine on *pardon* and *perjury.* By analyzing the filiations of these concepts (on the one hand, the Abrahamic inheritance—that is, Jewish, Christian, or Muslim—and the Greek inheritance, on the other), by formalizing the aporetic logic that torments this history, these concepts, this experience, their present-day mutation on a geo-juridico-political scale in a world where scenes of public repentance happen more and more frequently, I insist in this seminar on a certain irreducibility of the *work,* that is, *l'œuvre.* As a possible legacy from what is above all an event, *l'œuvre* has a virtual future only by surviving or cutting itself off from its presumed responsible signatory. It *thereby* supposes that a logic of the machine is in accordance, however improbable that may seem, with a logic of the event. Hence, there will remain some traces, dare I say visible archives, of this ongoing seminar and of its own context. This will not escape you and I do not wish to hide it. In a certain way, I will be speaking solely about pardon, forgiveness, excuse, betrayal, and perjury. You noticed that I began to do so already in order to attempt to excuse myself. But my speaking of forgiveness and so forth will not necessarily betray the general contract of our colloquium. And

I will speak neither of myself, nor of my texts on the scene of writing or archive fever, on the signature, event, context, nor on the spirit, the virtual revenants and other specters of Marx, nor even directly of my seminar on forgiveness and perjury. I will speak only of Paul de Man apropos of one or another of his works, for example, apropos of Rousseau and apropos of the announced themes for this colloquium.

These first two compromises were no doubt excessive and inexcusable. They became also unavoidable from the moment the title, program, or even the protocol of this colloquium defined implacable imperatives. To save time, I ought not to undertake to read in its entirety this title, which I hold to be a masterpiece. Nevertheless, I reread it in extenso, for one must register everything about it, including its play with quotation marks—the word *Materiality* having been freed from quotation marks whereas, in the subtitle, care was taken to put the word *materialist* in the expression "'materialist' thought" (rather than materialist philosophy or theory) under the strict surveillance of quotation marks. I underscore this fact now because, much later, I will wonder apropos of de Man, what might be a thinking of machinistic materiality without materialism and even perhaps without matter. The generalization of quotation marks that then becomes necessary would in that case no longer mean in the least that one is citing an ulterior author or text; rather, and quite on the contrary, it would mean that one is performatively instituting a new concept and a new contract with the word. One is thus inaugurating another word, in sum, a homonym that must be put forward cautiously between quotation marks. Another word-concept is thus staged whose event one causes to come about. The quotation marks signal in this case that one is citing only oneself at the moment of this invention or this convention in a gesture that is as inaugural as it is arbitrary. I now reread, as promised, the complete title: "Culture and Materiality: A post-millenarian conference—à propos of Paul de Man's *Aesthetic Ideology*—to consider trajectories for 'materialist' thought in the afterlife of theory, cultural studies, and Marxist critique." This is an impressive series of transactions that called for an equally impressive number of rhetorical performances or theoretical exploits: between culture and materiality, between a corpus or a proper name, Paul de Man, more precisely a very particular place of the posthumous corpus, *Aesthetic Ideology* ("—à propos of Paul de Man's *Aesthetic Ideology*—"). Here, then, is an inheritance that is also a posthumous work of Paul de Man's to which we are invited to refer, between dashes, in the mode of an "à-propos" that set me to wondering.

I wondered about this French idiom, which seems untranslatable and overdetermined enough that, I suppose, it was left like the foreign body it remains in your language. Moreover, and apropos, I had for a moment dreamed of entitling my lecture: "Apropos of apropos, apropos of all the meanings and all the uses of *à propos* and of the *à-propos* in French (*à propos*, as you know, can be an adverb, *à propos*, or a noun, the *à propos*). I had thus dreamed, but perhaps I will do it silently, of examining the modalities and figures of reference that are crossing in the inimitable and untranslatable expression *à propos*—which allies chance to necessity, contingency to obligation, machine-like association to the internal, intentional, organic link. When one says "*à propos*," "*à propos de* . . . ," there is from a pragmatic point of view always a mark of reference, a *reference to* . . . , but it is sometimes a direct reference, sometimes indirect, furtive, passing, oblique, accidental, machine-like, also in the mode of the quasi avoidance of the unavoidable, of repression, or of the lapsus, and so forth. When one says "*à propos*," it is because one is at least pretending to leap at the opportunity to speak, metonymically, of something else altogether, to change the subject without changing the subject, or else to underscore that between what is being talked about and what someone wants to talk about there is either a link of organic, internal, and essential necessity, or else, inversely, an insignificant and superficial association, a purely mechanical and metonymic association, the arbitrary or fortuitous comparison—"by accident"—of two signifiers. And yet it is clear that, at that very moment, one touches on the essential or the place of decision. That is where the thing happens, that is where it comes about. When Rousseau, after having stolen the ribbon, accuses Marion so as to excuse himself (and we will come back to this when we follow de Man's magisterial reading), it is because he denounced, he said, "the first object that presented itself *[le premier objet qui s'offrit]*."[1] Marion herself, or the name of Marion, being there by chance, by accident, it is as if he leaped on the opportunity and said with *à-propos*: "Apropos, it's Marion who gave it to me, I didn't steal it." The "esprit d'à-propos," in French, is the art, the genius, but also the technique that consists of knowing how to grab an opportunity, to make the best of it, the best economy of contingency, and to make of the *Khairos* or the *Chaos* a significant, archivable, necessary, or even ineffaceable event.

So many other things still remained enormous and enigmatic for me in the "*à-propos*" of this title—which says everything in advance, beginning with "post-millenarian" and "'materialist' thought" ("materialist" in quotation marks), not to mention everything that is put under the "umbrella" of some "afterlife" ("theory, cultural studies, and Marxist critique"). When I read this protocol, I asked myself which theoretical animal or which animal-machine of the third millennium could measure up to this inhuman program. If anyone could ever treat the subject in question, it will not be me, I said as I commanded myself to retreat: withdraw toward your own compromise on the subject of these untenable promises, but make every possible effort not to be too unworthy of the square you've landed on in this *jeu de l'oie* (a French board game that is something like a cross between Chinese checkers and Monopoly). On the poster, I said to myself, you find yourself fortunately immobilized in the company of Carla Freccero and Hillis Miller. Each time I look at this poster, it makes me think of a *jeu de l'oie* for a Californian science fiction. A throw of the dice that is incalculably well calculated has assigned all three of us, Carla Freccero, Hillis Miller, and me, three immigrants from Yale, the burden, and the word is well chosen, of "material events."

So I pray you to excuse me, but I will not treat the subject. In his article "Excuses *(Confessions)*," apropos of Rousseau, de Man refers in a note to Austin's "A Plea for Excuses." But he pays no attention to the fact that this text by Austin itself begins by presenting an excuse. It is thereby altogether enveloped, comprehended, included in the event of this first performative. Everything that Austin is going to say on the subject of the excuse will be at once comprehended and signed by the first gesture of the first sentence, by the performative event that is put to work, precisely, by the first words of "A Plea for Excuses." With the excuse that they implicitly present, these words of introduction make of this text an event, *une œuvre,* something other than a purely theoretical treatise: "The subject of this paper, *Excuses,* is one not to be treated, but only to be introduced, within such limits."[2] Everything happens as if the title, "A Plea for Excuses," designated first of all and solely Austin's performative gesture that itself presents excuses and alleges limits (time, urgency, situation, context, etc.: "within such limits," he says). The title, "A Plea for Excuses," would thus be the name or the description of this lecturer's gesture rather than and before being the announced subject, a theme or a problem to be treated in a theoretical, philosophical, constative, or metalinguistic mode, namely, the concept or the usage of the word *excuses.* This text constitutes a "Plea for Excuses," and it even does so in an exemplary fashion. So Austin excuses himself for not treating the excuse in a serious enough fashion.

He excuses himself for remaining or for leaving his audience in ignorance on the subject of what is meant by "to excuse oneself." And this at the moment when (performative contradiction or not), having begun by excusing himself, by pretending to do so, or rather by pretending to pretend to do so, he undertakes to excuse himself for not treating the subject of the excuse. He must, nevertheless, know enough about it, he must presuppose enough on the subject of what his audience knows and understands about it in advance, in so-called ordinary language (which is, moreover, the real subject of this essay), to declare that he will not treat it—even as he introduces it. Will he have treated it? Perhaps. It is for the reader to judge and for the addressee to decide. It is like the scene of writing of a postcard whose virtual addressee would in the future have to decide whether or not he or she will receive it and whether it is indeed to him or to her that it will have been addressed, in the singular or the plural. The signature is left to the initiative, to the responsibility, to the discretion of the other. Get to work. One will sign, if one signs, at the moment of arrival at destination, rather than at the origin, at the moment of reading rather than of writing. (As for the hypothesis according to which Austin as well and already would have allowed himself to get enclosed in a "performative contradiction," him without whom we would not even have been able to formulate a suspicion in this regard, permit us to smile at it along with his ghost. As if it were possible to escape all performative contradiction! And as if it were possible to exclude that an Austin would have had a little fun illustrating this inevitable trap!)

Now, it is not unthinkable that, in *Allegories of Reading* (a book published just before or even while the texts of *Aesthetic Ideology* were being prepared), de Man's title "Excuses *(Confessions)*" also presents the excuses and confessions of de Man himself, if I can put it that way, on some subject or another, and that he played at this scene without playing, that he pretended to play at it, apropos of Rousseau's *Confessions* and *Rêveries,* and perhaps, for example (this is only an example), inasmuch as he only "introduced" it, as Austin said, without really treating it—neither apropos of Rousseau nor in general.

I will add two subtitles to my title, namely, "machine" and "textual event." These are words de Man uses in "Excuses *(Confessions)*." I will thus propose that we interrogate together, at least obliquely, the use of these words, *machine* and *textual event,* in *Allegories of Reading.* Their use as well as their supposed meaning. My hypothesis is that de Man reinvents and signs these words, in a certain way, even as he leads us, if we can still put it that way, toward the "thinking of materiality" that comes to light in *Aesthetic Ideology*. The coherent use, the performative inaugurality of these words (*machine* and *textual event*), their conceptual effects and the formalization that will follow, in semantics and beyond semantics, this is what will affect in a necessary fashion all of de Man's writing and thus the destiny of all the other words he put to work. For example, but these are only examples, despite their frequent occurrence in this book from 1979, the words *deconstruction* and *dissemination*. My timid contribution would thus describe only a modest divergence in relation to the gigantic program proposed to us by Tom Cohen, Hillis Miller, and Andrzej Warminski. This displacement would remain discreet, micrological, infinitesimal—and literal. Perhaps it will be limited to underscoring "materiality," in place, so to speak, of "matter," then insisting on "thought of materiality," or even "material thought of materiality," in place, if I may put it this way, of "materialist" thought, even within quotation marks.

But we will see what happens when the moment comes.

I

There is a memory, a history, and an archive of confession, a genealogy of confessions: of the word *confession*, of the rather later Christian institution that bears this name, but also of the works that, in the West, are registered under this title and whose status as works of literature remains to be decided. Augustine and Rousseau, both authors of *Confessions,* speak more often the language of excuse rather than of pardon or forgiveness. Augustine speaks of the inexcusable *(inexcusabilis)*, Rousseau of "excusing himself." I must recall this even though or because, in this context, in the course of his exemplary and from now on canonical reading of Rousseau's *Confessions,* de Man never speaks of Augustine and of this Christian history.[3] I must make at least some minimal reference to this because the sedimentation in question forms an interior stratum of the very structure of Rousseau's text, of its "textual event." It is not certain that a purely internal reading can legitimately neglect it, even supposing that the concept of "textual event" (and I remind you that these are de Man's words) leaves standing the distinction between internal and external reading. For my part, I believe that if there is "textual event," this very border would have to be reconsidered.

I don't know if anyone has ever noticed, in this immense archive, that Augustine and Rousseau both confess a theft and both do so in book 2 of their *Confessions,* in a decisive or even determining and paradigmatic place. That is not all: in this archive that is also a confession, both of them confess that, although it was objectively trifling, this theft had the greatest psychical repercussions on their whole lives. Apropos, this apparently insignificant theft was committed by each of them at the precise age of sixteen; apropos, and on top of it all, each of them presents it as a useless theft. Their abusive appropriation did not take aim at the use value of the thing stolen: pears in the case of Saint Augustine, the famous ribbon in the case of Rousseau (presuming that one can know with certainty the use value of a fetishizable thing). Both of them insist on the fact that the use value was null or secondary. Augustine: "For I stole a thing of which I had plenty of my own and of much better quality. Nor did I wish to enjoy that thing which I desired to gain by theft, but rather to enjoy the actual theft and the sin of theft."[4] Rousseau will likewise speak of the trifling value, or even the insignificance, of the ribbon. We will see what fate de Man reserves for what he then calls the "free signifier" of a ribbon become available for a "system of symbolic substitutions (based on encoded significations arbitrarily attributed to a free signifier, the ribbon)."[5] Even though, at this point in his itinerary, de Man seems to expose, rather than countersign, a psychoanalytic or even self-analytic interpretation of the Lacanian type—he speaks of a "general economy of human affectivity, in a theory of desire, repression, and self-analyzing discourse" (ibid.)—everything seems to indicate that he does in fact consider the ribbon to be a "free signifier," thus indifferent as regards its meanings, like that purloined letter concerning which Lacan said that its content had no importance. I am less sure of this point myself in both cases, as I have shown elsewhere and I will return to it. As you know, the first title de Man thought of giving to this text was "The Purloined Ribbon."

No more than its immediate *use value,* Augustine and Rousseau likewise do not covet the *exchange value* of the stolen object, at least not in the banal sense of the term. It is the very act of stealing that becomes the object of desire, or the equivalent of its metonymic value for a desire that we are going to talk about. Augustine thus confesses, in book 2 (chapter 4, 9ff.), the theft of pears. But to whom does he address his confession? In the course of this long confession and the prayer on which it is carried, he addresses the theft itself: "What was it that I, a wretch, loved in you *[Quid ego miser in te amavi?]* oh my act of theft *[o furtum meum],* oh my deed of crime done by night in the sixteenth year of my life, *o facinus illud meum nocturnum sexti decimi anni aetatis meae?"* (chapter 6, 12). Augustine himself thus archives his age at the time of the theft. He registers the age he was at the moment of the sin and declares his age to the theft itself. His addressee, the destination of his addressee, his address and his addressee is the theft. He addresses the sin in order to tell it two things, which he thereby archives and consigns: *both* its date, the date of the event of the theft, *and* his own age, the age of the thief at the moment of the misdeed. Theft, o theft, my theft *(o furtum meum)*, know that I committed you, that I loved you, like a crime *(facinus)*, theft, I loved you and I perpetrated you that night when I was sixteen years old.

Rousseau also speaks of his age in direct reference to this theft, at the precise moment when he writes: "this ribbon alone tempted me. I stole it . . ." As always, he speaks of it *both* to clear himself *and* to add to his burden of guilt. "My age also should be taken into account. I was scarcely more than a child. Indeed I still was one" (89). That ought to clear him. But he right away adds: "In youth real crimes are even more reprehensible than in riper years." That ought to aggravate his fault. But he right away adds: "but what is no more than weakness is much less blameworthy, and really my crime amounted to no more than weakness." He does not say here that he was exactly sixteen years old at the time, but he had pointed it out earlier (I will cite this later) and, moreover, an easy calculation allowed me to deduce without any risk of error that he too was just sixteen years old when, in 1728, during the summer and fall, he spent three months as a lackey in the house of Mme de Vercellis where the affair of the ribbon took place. 1728: Jean-Jacques, son of Isaac Rousseau, was born in 1712; so he was sixteen years old. Exactly like Augustine. And this theft, which is also confessed in book 2 of the *Confessions*, was, by Rousseau's own admission, a determining event, a structuring theft, a wound (a *trauma*, to use the Yale and Cornell neologism), an endless scarring, the repeated access to the experience of guilt and to the writing of the *Confessions*. And this is true in both cases, even if the experience and the interpretation of guilt appear different, at first glance, in the two cases. As if, through a supplement of fiction in what remains a possible fiction, Rousseau had played at practicing an artifice of composition: he would have invented an intrigue, a narrative knot, as if to knot a ribbon around a basket of pears, a "plot," a dramaturgy destined to inscribe itself in the archive of a new quasi-literary genre, the history of confessions entitled *Confessions*, autobiographical stories inaugurated by a theft, each time the paradigmatic and paradisical theft of forbidden fruit or a forbidden pleasure. Augustine's *Confessions* were written before the Catholic sacrament of confession was instituted; those of Rousseau, the converted Protestant, were written after this institution and, moreover, after his abjuration of Calvinism. As if it were a matter for Jean-Jacques of inscribing himself into this great genealogical history of confessions entitled *Confessions*. The genealogical tree of a more or less literary lineage that would begin with the theft, from some tree, in the literal or the figural sense, of some forbidden fruit. A tree with leaves or a tree without leaves that produced so many leaves of paper, manuscript paper and typing paper. Rousseau would have inscribed his name in the archival economy of a palimpsest, by means of quasi quotations drawn from the palimpsestuous and ligneous thickness of a quasi-literary memory: a clandestine or encrypted lineage, a testamentary cryptography of confessional narration, the secret of an autobiography between Augustine and Rousseau, the simulacrum of a fiction right there where *both* Augustine *and* Rousseau claim truth, a veracity of testimony that never makes any concessions to the lies of literature (although fiction would not constitute a lie for Rousseau: he explains himself on this score with clarity and acuity in all his refined discourses on the lie, especially in the *Fourth Promenade,* precisely, where he confides to paper the story of the ribbon).

To be sure, before reaching the age of sixteen, Rousseau had already stolen, moreover, he had stolen forbidden fruit, just as Augustine had done. More orthodox than Augustine, he had already stolen apples, rather than pears. He confesses it with delight, lightheartedness, and abundance in book 1 of the *Confessions*. What is more, he stole constantly in his early youth: first asparagus, then apples. He's inexhaustible on the subject, and he insists on his good conscience, up until the theft of the ribbon: since he was punished for all these earlier thefts, he began, I quote, to "voler plus tranquillement qu'auparavant," "to thieve with an easier conscience than before, saying to myself, 'Well, what will happen? I shall be beaten. All right that's what I was made for'" (43) ("Je me disais: qu'en arrivera-t-il enfin? Je serai battu. Soit: je suis fait pour l'être"). As if corporal punishment, physical injury, the automatic and justly repaid sanction exonerated him from any guilt, thus from any remorse. He steals more and more, and not only things to eat but also tools, which confirms his feeling of innocence. Rousseau, as you know, will have spent his life protesting his innocence and thus excusing himself rather than seeking to be forgiven: "Really the theft of these trifles [the master's tools] was quite innocent,

since I only took them to use in his service" (43). The thefts predating
the theft of the ribbon when he was sixteen years old engender no feelings of guilt; they have no repercussions, there is no common measure
with the trauma of the story of the ribbon, at sixteen years old, an
episode that is like the credits or the matrix of the *Confessions*. As is
well known, the appropriation of the ribbon was less serious as a theft
than as a dissimulating lie. He allowed someone else to be accused, an
innocent girl who does not understand what is happening to her: he accused her in order to excuse himself.

I don't know whether there are any archives other than Rousseau's
writings (the second book of the *Confessions* and the *Fourth Promenade*) that give access to this story of the ribbon. If, as I believe,
Rousseau was the only testimonial source and the only archivist of the
event, every hypothesis is possible (although I will abstain here from
making any) regarding a pure and simple invention of the episode of the
theft out of a compositional concern (at sixteen years old and in the second book of his *Confessions* like the great ancestor of the *Confessions*,
Augustine, with whom, in the ligneous lineage of the same genealogical
tree bearing forbidden fruit, it would be a matter of sharing the titles of
nobility: the same tree, the same wood, the same paper pulp). A delicate
and abyssal problem of conscious or unconscious archivation. De Man
does not speak of Augustine. It is true that his project allows him legitimately, up to a certain point, to dispense with talking about him. But as
for Rousseau, he did read Augustine. And he talks about him. But he
does so also, as you will hear, to avoid him. He at least alludes to him,
precisely in the same book 2 of his own *Confessions*. Let us be more
precise, since it is a matter of the obscure relations between memory
(either mechanical or not), archive, consciousness, the unconscious,
and disavowal. Rousseau does not in truth admit that he had read
Augustine, Saint Augustine himself, in the text of his great corpus. He
recognizes merely that he had nevertheless, without having read it, retained many passages from this text. He did not read it but he knew
some passages by heart:

> "He [an old priest] thought he could floor me with Saint Augustine,
> Saint Gregory, and the other Fathers, but found to his utter surprise that
> I could handle all the Fathers as nimbly as he. It was not that I had ever
> read them. Nor perhaps had he. But I remembered a number of passages
> out of my Le Sueur [author of a *History of the Church and the Empire
> up to the Year 1000*] . . . (70)

The question remains as to what it means to "know by heart" certain passages cited from a secondary source, and whether the second book of Augustine's *Confessions* was included there. It all comes down to the faith one can put in a given word, be it a word of avowal or confession.

Another superficial reference to Saint Augustine appears at the end of the *Second Promenade*. Rousseau briefly names him at that point in order to oppose him. I will not do so here, but one could, "within such limits," reserve a structuring place for this objection and thus for this difference in the archive and the economy of a religious history of confession, but as well in the genealogy of autobiographies entitled *Confessions*. The place of the passage, at the end of the *Second Promenade*, is highly significant. Rousseau has just evoked humanity's "common plot" against him, what he calls the "universal conspiracy *[l'accord universel]*" of all men against him.[6] Here, then, is an agreement too universal and too "extraordinary to be a mere coincidence." Not a single accomplice has refused to cooperate with this plot, with this veritable *conjuration,* since the failure of just one accomplice would have caused it to fail. Rousseau evokes "human malevolence," a malevolence that is so universal that men themselves cannot be responsible for it, only God, only a divine secret: "I cannot help regarding as a divine secret beyond the reach of human reason the plot that I previously saw as nothing but the fruit of human malevolence" (45) ("Je ne puis m'empêcher de regarder désormais comme un de ces secrets du ciel impénétrables à la raison humaine la même *œuvre* que je n'envisageois jusqu'ici que comme un fruit de la méchanceté des hommes.") This *"œuvre"* (translated as "plot"), this fact, these crimes, this *conjuration,* this misdeed of men's *sworn* [conjurée] will would thus not depend on the will of men. It would be a trade secret of God, a secret impenetrable to human reason. For such a work of evil, only heaven can answer. But since one cannot accuse heaven any more than human malevolence of such an extraordinary work of evil, of this "universal conspiracy . . . too extraordinary to be a mere coincidence," thus of the necessity of a machination, Rousseau must then at the same time turn toward God and put blind trust in God, in the secret of God: beyond evil and beyond the machination of which he accuses him. It is at this point that he makes a brief allusion to Saint Augustine in order to oppose him. In this last paragraph of the *Second Promenade,* you will notice the at least *apparent* de-Christianization of Augustine and of Rousseau's *Confessions:*

I do not go so far as Saint Augustine, who would have been content to be damned if such had been the will of God. My resignation is of a less disinterested kind perhaps [Rousseau thus confesses that his confessions obey an economy, however subtle or sublime it may be], but its origin is no less pure and I believe it is more worthy of the perfect Being whom I adore. God is just; his will is that I should suffer, and he knows my innocence [this takes us to the other extreme from Augustine, whose *Confessions* are made, in principle, so as to beg pardon for a confessed fault—God knows I am a sinner—whereas Rousseau confesses everything only so as to excuse himself and proclaim his radical innocence; at least at first glance, this will already mark the difference between the theft of the pears and the theft of the ribbon]. That is what gives me confidence. My heart and my reason cry out that I shall not be disappointed. Let men and fate do their worst, we must learn to suffer in silence, everything will find its proper place in the end and my turn will come sooner or later. (45)

This "sooner or later," which signs the last words of the *Second Promenade,* is extraordinary—like other "last words" that are waiting for us: "everything will find its proper place in the end and my turn will come sooner or later." "Sooner or later": this patience of the virtual stretches time beyond death. It promises the survival of the work, but also survival *by* the work as self-justification and faith in redemption— not only my justification but the justification of men and of heaven, of God whose order and indisputable justice will return. This act of faith, this patience, this passion of faith comes to seal in some way the virtual time of the work, of *une œuvre* that will operate by itself. The work will accomplish its work of work, *son œuvre d'oeuvre* beyond its signatory and without his living assistance, whatever may be the time required, whatever may be the time to come; for time itself no longer counts in the survival of this "sooner or later." It little matters the time that this will take, time is given, thus it no longer exists, it no longer costs anything, and since it no longer costs anything, it is graciously given in exchange for the labor of the work that operates all by itself, in a quasi-machine-like fashion, virtually, and thus without the author's work: as if, contrary to what is commonly thought, there were a secret affinity between grace and machine, between the heart and the automatism of the marionette, as if the excusing machine as writing machine and machine for establishing innocence worked all by itself. This would be Rousseau's grace but also his machine whereby he pardons himself in advance. He excuses himself by giving himself in advance the time needed and that he therefore annuls in a "sooner or later" that the work bears like a machine for killing time and redeeming the fault, a fault that seems therefore only apparent, whether this appearance be the malevolence of men or the secret of heaven. Sooner or later, grace will operate in the work, by the work of the work at work, in a machine-like fashion. Rousseau's innocence will shine forth. Not only will he be forgiven, like his enemies themselves, but there will have been no fault [il n'y aura pas eu de mal]. Not only will he excuse himself, but he will have been excused. And he will have excused.

Apropos of this extraordinary machine of the future (namely, a machine that by itself, in a machine-like fashion, overturns the machination, the conjuration of all those who would have conspired against Rousseau, of all those enemies who would have universally sworn his demise), apropos also of this allusion to Augustine at the end of the *Second Promenade,* in a context that de Man no doubt, and perhaps rightly, considered "hors de propos," extrinsic to his "propos," I would like to evoke the beginning of the *Fourth Promenade.* Allusion is made there to the theft of the ribbon, to the lie that followed it, and to the story of the one whom he will later call, in the same *Promenade,* "poor Marion." But I would also like to recognize or see get put in place there a kind of machine that articulates among themselves events of a kind that ought to resist any mechanization, any economy of the machine, namely, oaths, acts of sworn faith: *jurer, conjurer, abjurer,* to swear, to conjure, to abjure or forswear.

I will first underscore the act of swearing (swearing before heaven in order to proclaim his innocence). Very close by, the word *"délire"* (folly, "irresponsible folly") will have the charge of naming above all the extraordinary coincidence between, on the one hand, the irrationality of the machine that is irresponsible or beyond my control, the mechanism that caused me to do evil, and, on the other hand, the absolute sincerity, the authentic innocence of my intentions. On the one hand, the extreme self-accusation for an infinite crime, which is incalculable in its actual and virtual effects (the "sooner or later" of these effects, conscious or unconscious, known or unknown), the coincidence or the unheard-of compatibility between this feeling of properly infinite guilt, which is confessed as such, and, on the other hand, the just as unshakable certainty in the absolute, virgin, intact innocence, which will "sooner or later" appear, the declared absence of any "repentance," of any "regret," of any "remorse" for the fault, the theft, and the lie.

"Repentance," "regret," "remorse" *(repentir, regret, remord)* are Rousseau's words, on the same page, when he speaks of what he himself calls an "incredible contradiction" between his infinite guilt and the absence of any guilty conscience. It is as if he still had to confess the guilt that there is, and that remains, in not feeling guilty, or better yet, in saying he is innocent, in swearing his innocence in the very place where he confesses the worst. As if Rousseau still had to ask forgiveness for feeling innocent. (Think of the scene where Hamlet asks his mother to forgive him his own virtue, to forgive him in sum for having nothing to forgive him for, to forgive Hamlet the fact that he has nothing to be forgiven for: pardon me my virtue, he says in sum to Gertrude; and perhaps it is also on Rousseau's part another address of the same discourse of innocence to his mother.)

When I set out the next day to put this resolution into practice [the resolution to examine the subject of falsehood], my first thought on beginning to reflect was of a terrible lie I had told in my early youth, a lie the memory of which has troubled me all my life and even now, in my old age, adds sorrow to a heart already suffering in so many other ways. This lie, which was a great crime in itself, was doubtless still more evil in its effects; these have remained unknown to me, but remorse has painted them to me in the cruelest possible colors. Yet, if one were to consider only my state of mind at the time, this lie was simply the product of false shame, and far from its being the result of a desire to harm the girl who was its victim, I can swear to Heaven that at the very moment when this invincible shame dragged it from me, I would joyfully have given my life's blood to deflect the blow on to myself alone. It was a moment of irresponsible folly which I can only explain by saying what I feel to be true, that all the wishes of my heart were conquered by my innate timidity.

The memory of this deplorable act and the undying remorse it left me, instilled in me a horror of falsehood that ought to have preserved my heart from this vice for the rest of my life. . . .

What surprised me most was that when I recalled these fabrications I felt no real repentance. I, whose horror of falsehood outweighs all my other feelings, who would willingly face torture rather than tell a lie, by what strange inconsistency could I lie so cheerfully without compulsion or profit, and by what incredible contradiction could I do so without the slightest twinge of regret, when remorse for a lie has continually tormented me these fifty years? I have never hardened myself against my faults; my moral sense has always been a faithful guide to me, my conscience has retained its original integrity, and even if it might be corrupted and swayed by my personal interests, how could I explain that, remaining firm and unmoved on those occasions when a man can at least excuse himself by his weakness in the face of passion, it loses its integrity precisely over those unimportant matters where vice has no excuse? (63–65)

"I can swear to Heaven," "Je puis jurer à la face du ciel," says the *Fourth Promenade*. But he had abjured many years earlier. At the age of sixteen, a few months before the theft of the ribbon (a theft and a lie, a perjury confessed more than a decade earlier in book 2 of the *Confessions* but committed at the age of sixteen), Rousseau, then, abjures. At sixteen, he abjures Protestantism and converts to Catholicism. A few pages earlier, before the recital of the theft, he had recounted how he was "led in procession to the metropolitan Church of Saint John to make a solemn abjuration" (73). This debate between Protestantism and Catholicism tormented the whole life of this citizen of Geneva who shared, as he tells us in the same book of the *Confessions*, "that aversion to Catholicism which is peculiar to our city. It was represented to us as the blackest idolatry and its clergy were depicted in the most sordid colors" (67). Then, noting that "I did not exactly resolve to turn Catholic," he writes:

> Protestants are generally better instructed than Catholics, and necessarily so, for their doctrine requires discussion, where the Roman faith demands submission. A Catholic must accept a decision imposed on him; a Protestant must learn to decide for himself. They were aware of this but they did not expect from my age and circumstances that I should present any great difficulty to men of experience. (69)

Couldn't one say that Catholicism is more machine-like, machinistic, mechanistic, and therefore more literalist, whereas the Protestantism that Rousseau abjures is freer, more intentionalist, more decisionist, less mechanistic, less literalist, and therefore more spiritualist? Rousseau abjures and converts therefore mechanically to the Catholic mechanism; he abjures without having had the intention to abjure, he becomes a renegade without having resolved to do so, and what is more, and this is another mechanism, without being of an age to do so. Like an immature child, he mechanically pretends to abjure intentionalist and decisionist Protestantism; he feigns this event of rupture so as

to convert to mechanistic and authoritarian Catholicism. He feigns mechanically to become mechanistic. But nothing happens in his heart;
nothing happens. He converted mechanically, as if by chance, but op-
portunistically, for the circumstance, with *à-propos*, to a literalist and
mechanistic religion of the *à-propos*.

Apropos, remaining still on the edge of these things, on the barely
preliminary threshold of what is going to interest us, since we have
begun to wander or to rave deliriously apropos the kind of notations
that seemed to me unavoidable upon a first rereading of these scenes,
I also noticed something else, apropos of Catholicism and the debate,
within Rousseau himself, between the Catholicism of his conversion and his originary Protestantism (the Catholicism of his conversion
and of confession—since one-on-one confession to a confessor and
Protestantism are mutually exclusive; the word *confession,* which
means both the confession of sin and the profession of faith—and
which has an enormous textual, semantic, and social history in the
Bible—did not come to designate a Catholic, rather than Protestant,
institution until well after Augustine's time). It so happens in fact that
the recital of the theft of the ribbon begins right after the recital of the
death of Mme de Vercellis, the Catholic woman in whose home the
young Rousseau was both housed and employed, his "principal occupation" being, as he himself puts it, to "write [letters] at her dictation." Paul de Man, in "Excuses *(Confessions),*" devotes a note to this
situation of the two accounts, to this linking of the two accounts (the
death of Mme de Vercellis, then the theft of the ribbon). At the point at
which de Man is seeking, as he puts it, "another form of desire than
the desire of possession" with which to explain "the latter part of the
story," the part that "bears the main performative burden of the excuse and in which the crime is no longer that of theft," but rather of
lying—and we will see in which sense, in particular for de Man, this
crime excludes two forms of desire, the simple desire or love for Marion
and a hidden desire of the Oedipal type—at this point, then, de Man
adds the following note: "The embarrassing story of Rousseau's rejection by Mme de Vercellis, who is dying of a cancer of the breast, immediately precedes the story of Marion, but *nothing in the text* suggests a
concatenation that would allow one to substitute Marion for Mme de
Vercellis in a scene of rejection" (285; emphasis added).

I have underscored the phrase "nothing in the text."

No doubt de Man is right to beware a grossly Oedipal scheme (but
there are more refined Oedipal schemes) and I am not about to plunge

headfirst into such a scheme in my turn; he is also no doubt right to say that *"nothing in the text* suggests a concatenation that would allow one to substitute Marion for Mme de Vercellis in a scene of rejection."* But what does "nothing" mean here? "Nothing in the text"? How can one be sure of "nothing" suggested in a text? Of a "nothing in a text"? And if really "nothing" suggested this Oedipal substitution, how does one explain that de Man thought of it? And that he devotes a footnote to it? (Apropos, I might ask moreover, for the fun of it, whether every footnote is not Oedipal. In pure apropos logic, is not a footnote a symptomatic swelling, the swollen foot of a text hindered in its step-by-step advance?) How does one explain that de Man devotes an embarrassed footnote to all this in which he excludes that the "embarrassing story," as he puts it, suggests an Oedipal substitution of Marion for Mme de Vercellis, that is to say, first of all of Mme de Vercellis for Maman? For Mme de Vercellis immediately succeeds Maman in the narrative, the same year, the year he turns sixteen. She succeeds Mme de Warens, whose acquaintance Rousseau had made several months earlier—and who had also recently converted to Catholicism, like the Calvinist Jean-Jacques.

It is, moreover, soon after this meeting that he travels on foot to Turin and finds shelter at the hospice of the Holy Spirit where he abjures. (This episode is told at the beginning of the *Creed of a Priest of Savoy*—a text that we ought to reread closely, in particular because it contains, at the end of its seventh chapter, an interesting comparison between the respective deaths of Socrates and Jesus, who both grant, but differently according to Rousseau, the first his blessing and the second his forgiveness to their executioners, the first conducting himself as a man, the other as a God. The conclusion of the book recommends the wager of remaining in the religion of one's birth. Yes, the wager, in the quasi-Pascalian sense of the machine, because it is the best calculation, in case of error, with which to obtain the excuse or the forgiveness of God. Here is the argument, in which I underscore the lexicon of *excuse* and of *pardon* or forgiveness:

> You will feel that, in the uncertainty in which we find ourselves, it is an *inexcusable* presumption to profess another religion than the one in which you were born, and a falsehood not to practice sincerely the one you profess. If you wander from it, you deprive yourself of a great *excuse* before the throne of the sovereign judge. Will he not rather *pardon* the error in which you were reared than one which you dared choose yourself?[7]

I return now to my question concerning the substitution among all these women, who are more or less mothers and Catholics by more or less recent confession.)

If one supposes that there is nothing, as de Man notes, "nothing" positive in the text to suggest positively this substitution, "nothing" in the content of the accounts, what is the meaning of the mere juxtaposition, the absolute proximity in the time of the narration, the simple linking of places, there where de Man says that "nothing in the text [what does "in" the text mean here?] suggests a concatenation that would allow one to substitute Marion for Mme de Vercellis in a scene of rejection" (moreover, I don't see the reason to speak here of rejection: there is no more a simple rejection of one than of the other)? The mere concatenation of places, the sequential juxtaposition of the two accounts is not nothing, if one wanted to psychoanalyze things. The juxtaposition of the two accounts, even if nothing but chronological succession seems to justify it, is not "nothing in the text," it is not a textual nothing even if there is nothing, nothing else, *in* the text. Even if there were nothing else that was posed, nothing positive, this topology of sequential juxtaposition can have by itself a metonymic force, the very force that will have suggested to de Man's mind the hypothesis of the substitution that he nevertheless excludes. In order to exclude it, it still has to present itself to the mind with some seduction. It still has to be tempting. And the temptation suffices. We are talking here only about temptation and forbidden fruit. So even if there were nothing *in* the text of these two accounts, the simple topographic or sequential juxtaposition is "in the text," it constitutes the text itself and can be *interpreted*: it is interpretable, I don't say necessarily in an Oedipal fashion, but it is interpretable. One must and one cannot not interpret it; it cannot be simply insignificant.

Two series of arguments could confirm this interpretability. One concerns this time the *content* of the two accounts; the other, once again, their *form* and their place, their situation, their localization. I will not insist on the content; however, a very large number of traits that you would not fail to recognize, stretching over many pages, describe the at once amorous and filial attachment that Rousseau feels for Mme de Vercellis, whose appearance succeeds the meeting with Mme de Warens in the second book of the *Confessions*. Mme de Vercellis, a widow without children, as he repeats several times, suffered from a "cancer of the breast," which he also comes back to innumerable times. This illness of the maternal breast, "which gave her great pain," he writes, "prevented her from writing herself." Jean-Jacques becomes, by reason of this infirmity, her penholder; he holds her pen like a secretary, he writes in her place; he becomes her pen, her hand, or her arm, for "she liked writing letters." On the scenes of letters and testaments that follow, we could offer infinite glosses, before coming back to a topography of the border, of border substitution at the border, of parergonal composition in which we find once again in passing *both* the memory of the abjuration (thus the frontier "Protestantism-Catholicism" as passage from childhood to adulthood in a sort of internal history of the confessions, of the confession) *and* what I will entitle the last word of the other and of self, the double silence on which the double episode closes: that of the theft-lie that wrongs Marion and that of the death of the stepmother, the childless widow, the death of Mme de Vercellis. Rousseau praises Mme de Vercellis even as he speaks ill of her. He also criticizes her insensitivity, her indifference, and more precisely her lack of mercy *[miséricorde]*, of "commiseration": as if she had no mercy, no heart, or, for a mother, no breast. She is, moreover, going to die from that, from the illness called, and that Rousseau also calls literally, "cancer of the breast" and that will have eaten away her breast. What good she does, she does mechanically, automatically, out of duty and not from the heart ("She always seemed to me to have as little feeling for others as for herself; and when she did a kindness to anyone in misfortune, it was in order to do something good on principle, rather than out of true commiseration" [84]). Moreover, the breast is the heart and the place of commiseration, especially for Rousseau. A few pages after these allusions to the "cancer of the breast" and to the double expiration of Mme de Vercellis, who lacks commiseration, Rousseau writes this, in which I underline a certain "not even":

> Nevertheless I have never been able to bring myself to relieve my heart by revealing this in private to a friend. Not with the most intimate friend, *not even* with Mme de Warens, has this been possible. The most that I could do was to confess that I had a terrible deed on my conscience, but I have never said in what it consisted. The burden, therefore, has rested till this day on my conscience without any relief; and I can affirm that the desire to some extent to rid myself of it has greatly contributed to my resolution of writing these *Confessions*. (88)

Twice a last word, I said. A double silence comes to seal irreversibly an end. Here, first of all, is the first last word:

She liked writing letters, which diverted her mind from her illness. But they put her against the habit, and got the doctor to make her give it up, on the plea that it was too tiring for her. On the pretense that I did not understand my duties, two great louts of chairmen were put in my place. In the end they were so successful that when she made her will I had not entered her room for a week. It is true that after that I went in as before. Indeed I was more attentive to her than anyone else, for the poor woman's suffering tore my heart, and the fortitude with which she bore it inspired me with the greatest respect and affection for her. Many were the genuine tears I shed in her room without her or anyone else noticing it.

Finally we lost her. I watched her die. She had lived like a woman of talents and intelligence; she died like a philosopher. I may say that she made the Catholic religion seem beautiful to me, by the serenity of heart with which she fulfilled its instructions, without either carelessness or affectation. She was of a serious nature. Towards the end of her illness she displayed a sort of gaiety too unbroken to be assumed, which was merely a counterpoise to her melancholy condition, the gift of her reason. She only kept her bed for the last two days, and continued to converse quietly with everyone to the last. Finally when she could no longer talk and was already in her death agony, she broke wind loudly. "Good," she said, turning over, "a woman who can fart is not dead." Those were the last words she spoke. (85-86)

Here now the second and last last word. After this fart, this last breath, this agony, and these "last words she spoke" like a double expiration, a fart and a testamentary metalanguage on a next-to-the-last breath, here is the last last word, right at the end of the account of the ribbon that itself follows without transition the double expiration of Mme de Vercellis. After it was said of her "Finally . . . she could no longer talk," she still farts and adds a living, surviving gloss, the fart, to this after-the-last word. Here, then, is the absolute last word, after the respect due to Marion will have been, like the young girl herself, violated both by the theft and by the lie, that is, by the perjury, by the false testimony accusing Marion to excuse himself. I read this conclusion beginning with the allusion to age, which shows clearly that, even if Rousseau, at least at this point, does not say, like Augustine, "I was sixteen years old," he underscores the element of his age as an essential feature of the story, a feature that both accuses *and* excuses him, accuses and charges him, condemns him all the more *but* clears him of guilt by the same token, automatically.

My age also should be taken into account. I was scarcely more than a child. Indeed I still was one. In youth real crimes are even more reprehensible than in riper years; but what is no more than weakness is much less blameworthy, and really my crime amounted to no more than weakness. So the memory tortures me less on account of the crime itself than because of its possible evil consequences. But I have derived some benefit from the terrible impression left with me by the sole offense I have committed. For it has secured me for the rest of my life against any act that might prove criminal in its results. I think also that my loathing of untruth derives to a large extent from my having told that one wicked lie. If this is a crime that can be expiated, as I venture to believe, it must have been atoned for by all the misfortunes that have crowded the end of my life, by forty years of honest and upright behavior under difficult circumstances. Poor Marion finds so many avengers in this world that, however great my offense against her may have been, I have little fear of carrying the sin on my conscience at death. That is all I have to say on the subject. May I never have to speak of it again.

He will speak of it again, of course, as if he had gotten a second wind in his turn in the *Rêveries*. And there again, he will call Marion "poor Marion" (74).

On the subject still of this age of sixteen years, what must one say? Although, of course, Rousseau does not indicate his age at the moment of the story of the ribbon, he proliferates to a really obsessive degree remarks about his age in the first two books of the *Confessions*. Apropos, since we are talking about substitutions (Marion for Mme de Vercellis, Mme de Vercellis who succeeds Mme de Warens—and the logic of the *à-propos* is also a logic of substitution), some months earlier in the same year, 1728, in April, a few months before the death of Mme de Vercellis, therefore before the theft and the lie of the ribbon, Rousseau meets Mme de Warens. This is the beginning, as you know, of his singular passion for the one he called Maman. Well, almost in the very sentence in which he notes the first meeting with Mme de Warens, like Saint Augustine he makes note of his age, sixteen years:

"Finally I arrived and saw Mme de Warens. This stage in my life has been decisive in the formation of my character, and I cannot make up my mind to pass lightly over it. I was half way through my sixteenth year and, without being what is called a handsome youth, I was well-made for my modest size, had a pretty foot, a fine leg . . . (54–55)

The same year, the year he was sixteen, decides his life twice. And in the same second book of the *Confessions,* this decision is distributed over a single sequence of metonymic transitions; one sees the succession there, all along the same chain of quasi substitutions, before "poor Marion," the Catholic Mme de Warens, and the no less Catholic Mme de Vercellis, Marion and the theft-lie of the ribbon. I will not exploit this Marial chain of three women to whom a desire without desire links him as to the breast of a virgin mother. I will not exploit the name of poor Marion so as to recognize the diminutive figure in a scene of passion and martyrdom. But who could deny that Jean-Jacques puts himself on a cross, even as he seems to de-Christianize the Augustinian confession? "Sooner or later," "dans les siècles des siècles," as one says in Christian rhetoric, people will know he has suffered and expiated as an innocent martyr for all men, and at the hands of the wicked men who do not know what they do. And God the father is not to be accused of it.[8]

**II**

Over three pages, toward the end, the second book of the *Confessions* multiplies the ends, its own ends. It divides them and doubles them. Two ends, and two times a last word: first, the double expiration of Mme de Vercellis ("Those were the last words she spoke"), then the very last word of the chapter, the end of the story of the ribbon ("May I never have to speak of it again").

The first "last words," attributed to the dying woman, belong to a sentence in the constative form, in the past: this is what she said. The last last word, however, forms a performative sentence, at once a wish, a promise, a commitment, or a prayer in the first person: this is what I myself say, now, for the future. Although its grammar is such that, at least in French, the first person is not a subject, the "I" reappears in the English translation ("Qu'il me soit permis de n'en reparler jamais"; "May I never have to speak of it again").

These two occurrences of a last word sink into the abyssal depths of a palimpsest. "Within such limits," we will not have time to reinscribe them in the endless archive of last words that are not words of the end: from Socrates' last word in an apologetic scene in the *Hippias Minor* to Blanchot's *Le dernier mot,* passing by way of Austin's "A Plea for Excuses"—this address that speaks to us also of machines and of a "complicated internal machinery," even as it explains in passing that, although ordinary language is not the last word, it is in any case the first ("ordinary language is *not* the last word: in principle it can be supplemented and improved upon and superseded. Only remember, it *is* the *first* word"; the question of "ordinary language" is perhaps, apropos, the real question of "A Plea for Excuses").[9] At a certain moment, Blanchot's *Le dernier mot* (1935) takes the figure of the French expression "il y a." I would have been tempted to relate this moment to the long meditation by Levinas on the "il y a." For this problematic of the "il y a" (in ordinary, which is to say untranslatable, French) has a pertinence for our conference. But I must leave this for another time.

One could also reread the whole de Manian interpretation of the purloined ribbon as the displacement of a "last word." The last word of the *Confessions* on this subject, the ultimate decision which he would like never to have to go back on ("May I never have to speak of it again," "Qu'il me soit permis de n'en reparler jamais"), was, according to de Man, only the next-to-last. Rousseau will have to reiterate this confession many years later, in the *Rêveries,* which delivers the last last word. One of the many interesting and original things about the de Manian analysis is that it takes into account this difference between the very last word and the next-to-last, and it mobilizes what seems necessary in order to explain the history and the mechanism that transforms the last into the next-to-last.

If I insist on this paradoxical instance of the "last word," it is because forgiveness or pardon, the excuse, and the remission of sin, absolute absolution are always proposed in the figure, so to speak, of the "last word." A pardon that is not granted with the assurance, the promise, or in any case the meaning of a last word, or an end of history (even if it is according to the virtualizing logic of the "sooner or later"), would that still be a pardon? Hence the disturbing proximity the pardon maintains with the last judgment—which nevertheless it is not. A pardon does not judge; it transcends all judgment, whether penal or not. Foreign to the courtroom, it nevertheless remains as close as possible to the verdict, to the "veridictum," by the irresistible and irreversible force it has as, precisely, "last word." *I forgive you* has the structure of the last word, hence its apocalyptic and millenarian aura; hence the sign it makes in the direction of the end of time and the end of history. We will later get around to this concept of history that de Man wants to link not to time ("History is therefore not a temporal notion," as he will say in "Kant and Schiller")[10] but to "power," to the "event," and to the "occurrence." I have tried to show elsewhere that what I call "le mal d'archive" has to do with the fact that the archive, which is always finite and therefore selective, interpretive, filtering, and filtered, censuring, and repressive, always figures a place and an instance of power.[11] Destined to the virtuality of the "sooner or later," the archive produces the event no less than it records or consigns it.

After having analyzed two long series of possible readings, de Man explains, then, these two times of the end: after a certain failure of the confession in the *Confessions* (begun in 1764–65, the second part completed at the latest in 1767 and the whole in 1770), after this first last word, Rousseau was to write the *Fourth Promenade* (in 1777, therefore at least ten years later). The last word of the *Confessions* would thus have marked a failure. After the avowal, the vow ("May I never have to speak of it again") does not succeed in sealing an authentic last word signing the end of the story or of history. According to de Man, this failure, this becoming next-to-last of the last is what motivated, compulsively, the writing of the *Fourth Promenade* and the return, let us not say the repentance, the rewriting of the confession in the form of excuse.

> But the text offers further possibilities. The analysis of shame as excuse makes evident the strong link between the performance of excuses and the act of understanding. It has led to the problematics of hiding and revealing, which are clearly problematics of cognition. Excuse occurs within an epistemological twilight zone between knowing and not-knowing; this is also why it has to be centered on the crime of lying and why Rousseau can excuse himself for everything provided he can be excused for lying. When this turns out not to have been the case, when his claim to have lived for the sake of truth *(vitam impendere vero)* is being contested from the outside, the closure of excuse ("qu'il me soit permis de n'en reparler jamais") becomes a delusion and the *Fourth Rêverie* has to be written. (286)

How is one to understand this incessant passage that transports and deports beyond the last word of excuse, from the *Confessions* to the *Rêveries,* for example? De Man himself here calls upon a logic of *supplementarity* to explain the relation between excuse and guilt. Far from effacing guilt, far from leading to the "without-fault" or the "without-defect," excuses add to it, they engender and augment the fault. The "plus de faute," "no more fault" (innocence), becomes right away the "plus de faute," all the more fault (endless guilt).[12] The more one excuses oneself, the more one admits that one is guilty and the more one feels guilt. Guilty of excusing oneself. By excusing oneself. The more one excuses oneself, the less one clears oneself. Guilt is thus an *in-effaceable* inscription, inexorable because inexonerable (this will be de Man's lexicon). The *written* excuse produces guilt. The inscription of the work, *l'œuvre*, the event of a written text generates and capitalizes a sort of interest (I won't be so bold as to say surplus value) of guilt. It overproduces this shame, it archives it instead of effacing it. I under-score *effacing* or *exonerating*, and *inexonerable* guilt, for two reasons of unequal importance. Here first is the passage where all of these threads are knotted together in the most visible and tightly wound fashion:

> Excuses generate the very guilt they *exonerate*, though always in excess or by default. At the end of the *Rêverie* there is a lot more guilt around than we had at the start: Rousseau's indulgence in what he calls, in an-other bodily metaphor, "*le plaisir* d'écrire" [the phrase occurs at the end of the *Fourth Promenade*], leaves him guiltier than ever. . . . Additional guilt means additional excuse. . . . No excuse can ever hope to catch up with such a proliferation of guilt. On the other hand, any guilt, includ-ing the guilty pleasure of writing the *Fourth Rêverie*, can always be dis-missed as the gratuitous product of a textual grammar or a radical fic-tion: there can never be enough guilt around to match the text-machine's infinite power to excuse. (Ibid.)

The "text-machine" has just arrived on stage. We will let it wait for a moment.

I announced two unequal reasons for underscoring the verb *exoner-ate* (which is translated in French by *effacer,* to efface or erase), but also the figure of an ineffaceable guilt that the excuse, instead of effac-ing, aggravated, tattooed in a more and more indelible fashion onto the body of the archive. The first reason is *objective*; the other is in some way, for de Man and for me, if I may say, *autobiographical.* The objective reason first: de Man will have wanted to show that from the *Confessions* to the *Rêveries,* the guilt (with regard to one and the same event, of course, the theft of the ribbon) has been displaced from the written *thing* to the *writing* of the thing, from the referent of the narrative writing (the theft and the lie) to the act of writing the ac-count, from the written confession to the inscription of the confession. The second time it is no longer the theft or the lie, as the thing itself, the fault itself, the perjury itself, that becomes guilty; it is the writing or the account of the thing, the pleasure taken in inscribing this memory, in archiving it, setting it down in ink on paper. The sin of this pleasure cannot be effaced because it is reprinted and rewritten while it is being confessed. It is aggravated and capitalized, it overproduces itself, it becomes pregnant with itself by confessing itself. De Man writes: "The question takes us to the *Fourth Rêverie* and its implicit shift from reported guilt to the guilt of reporting, since here the lie is no longer connected with some former misdeed but specifically with the act of writing the *Confessions* and, by extension, with all writing" (290). The excuse does not merely accuse; it carries out the verdict: "Excuses not only accuse but they carry out the verdict implicit in their accusation" (293).

One must hear the weight of this sentence as carried by the "carry out," this execution of the verdict, this performance of the judgment and its application, its "enforcement." There is not only accusation and judgment in the confession or in the excuse itself; there is already the executioner, the carrying out of the sentence—but here of the sentence endured in the very pleasure of writing, in the ambiguous enjoyment, the terrible and severe jubilation of the inscription—of the trace left now for the "sooner or later," but enjoying now already, virtually, the retrospection of the "sooner or later." One steps up to the cashier right away to collect interest on a capital that will assume value only "sooner or later," perhaps after my death, in any case, in my absence.

Structurally, ineffaceable guilt no longer has to do with this or that misdeed, but with the confession itself, with confessional writing. The first and last fault would be the public *mise en œuvre* of the self-justification, of the self-disculpation, and of the shameful pleasure that the body finds there—still or already. Guilt is no longer effaced because it has to do with the body of the confession, with its literal inscription, with that which is meant to confess the fault in writing—contradicting or disavowing thereby the avowal at the heart of the avowal.[13]

The second (minor and autobiographical) reason for which I underscore the lexicon of the inexorable as ineffaceable is the archive of a dedication, of an "inscription," if I dare to cite it, of *Allegories of Reading,* dated November 1979: "Pour Jacques, en ineffaçable amitié, Paul" ("For Jacques, in ineffaceable friendship, Paul"). This "inscription" in ink was followed, in pencil, by two last words: "lettre suit." Yes, "letter follows." You know at least something of the rest, the posthumous continuation. De Man dies four years later, in 1983, leaving us with the now-notorious legacies for a virtually indeterminable "sooner or later." Letter follows: this was also the continuation of a history in which certain people believed they could reproach de Man, not so much for having done this or that, but especially, or even solely, for having dissimulated, for not having admitted what he ought to have admitted, for not having publicly confessed what he had one day written, precisely, during the war. For his fault will have also consisted in writing. This is enough to make one dream aloud—about the "sooner or later" of archives, about machines in general, and about confession machines. We know quite well that there are machines for making people confess. And there are those who like these things. The police, the Inquisition, and torturers throughout history are very familiar with these machines for extracting confessions. They also know the jubilatory pleasure to be had in the handling of these machines, in the forced confession, in the forcing of the confession more than in knowing what is true, more than in knowing to what the confession, or so one supposes, refers. In this familiar and ageless tradition, those that manipulate these confessing machines care less about the fault committed than about the pleasure they take in requiring or extracting the confession. What they realize only rarely, however, and what de Man in any case knew (it is one of the themes of his text), is that confession, for the addresser as well as the addressee, is always in itself, in the act of its inscription, guilty—more *and* less, more *or* less guilty than the fault being confessed. The confession, in a word, on both sides, is never innocent. This is a first machine, the implacable and repetitive law of an undeniable program; this is the economy of a calculation inscribed in advance and that one can only disavow.

A moment ago, we met up with the expression "text-machine." The whole of this demonstration is played out around the text-machine, around the work, the *œuvre* of a writing-machine. The concept of a textual machine is both produced by de Man and, as it were, found, discovered, *invented* by him in Rousseau's text. (One also speaks of the invention of the body of Christ to designate the experience that consists in discovering, in an inaugural fashion, to be sure, but all the same a body that was already there, in some place or other, and that had to be found, discovered, *invented*. Even though it unveils the body of what was already there, this invention is an event.) De Man invents the text-machine by discovering and citing, so as to justify his expression, a certain passage of the *Fourth Rêverie* that speaks in fact of a "machine-like effect," an "effet machinal." But there are also, in Rousseau, many other examples of machines—both prosthetic and mutilating machines. We will keep them waiting as well.

All this must be placed in a network of relations with the whole work of de Man, with his style, and with the axioms of what he calls, after "Blindness and Insight," in the essay "Excuses" and elsewhere, while insisting on it more and more, a "deconstruction." The latter always implies the reference to a certain mechanicity or rather machinality, to the automaticity of the body or of the automaton corpus. The allusion, in this same essay, to Kleist's marionettes refers us back to other references to Kleist (for example, in "Phenomenality and Materiality in Kant," in *Aesthetic Ideology*). "Excuses *(Confessions)*" is also the theater of Rousseau's marionettes:

> By saying that the excuse is not only a fiction but also a machine one adds to the connotation of referential detachment, of gratuitous improvisation, that of the implacable repetition of a preordained pattern. Like Kleist's marionettes, the machine is both "anti-grav," the anamorphosis of a form detached from meaning [somewhat like the neutral, anonymous, and insignificant "il y a" in Blanchot and Levinas] and capable of taking on any structure whatever, yet entirely *ruthless* in its inability to modify its own structural design for nonstructural reasons. The machine *is like* the grammar of the text when it is isolated from its rhetoric, the merely formal element without which no text can be generated. There can be no use of language which is not, within a certain perspective thus radically formal, i.e. mechanical, no matter how deeply this aspect may be concealed by aesthetic, formalistic delusions. (294; emphasis added)

Why this resemblance ("is like")? And why "ruthless"? Why would a text-machine be ruthless? Not mean but ruthless in its effects, in the suffering it inflicts? What relation is there between the ruthlessness of this "text-machine" and what de Man calls, at the end of the trajectory, the "textual event"? This is another way of repeating my initial question: how is one to think together the machine *and* the event, a machinelike repetition *and* what happens? What happens to what? To whom?

De Man speaks only of excuse, never, or almost never, of "pardon" or "forgiveness." He seems to exclude the specific problem of forgiveness from his field of analysis (and first of all because both Rousseau and Austin, who are here the guiding references, also speak massively of excuse rather than forgiveness). Unless he considers, perhaps like Rousseau and like Austin, that whatever one says about the excuse is valid as well for forgiveness. That remains to be seen. I have two hypotheses in this regard.

First hypothesis: de Man sees no essential difference between forgiveness and excuse. This argument can be made but it leaves aside enormous historical and semantic stakes. The very possibility of this distinction is not problematized. I therefore set it aside.

The other hypothesis would concern as much Austin as de Man: the only pragmatic or performative modality that interests them is what happens on the side of the one who has committed the misdeed, never on the other side, the side of the victim. What they want to analyze is the act that consists in saying "I apologize" rather than "I ask forgiveness," "I beg your pardon," and, above all, "I forgive" or "I pardon." Rather than the possibility of forgiving or even of excusing, both of them are interested only in what one *does* when one *says*, in the performative mode, "excuse me" and more precisely "I apologize." They believe they can consider only the modality of the excuse and that the rest is beyond the limit of the field of their analysis.

So, unless I am mistaken, de Man almost never speaks of forgiveness, except in passing, as if it were no big deal, in two passages. One concerns what is, he says, "easy to forgive" since "the motivation for the theft becomes understandable." But here as well, de Man keeps to the side of the one who excuses himself and thinks that it's "easy to forgive":

> The allegory of this metaphor, revealed in the "confession" of Rousseau's desire for Marion, functions as an excuse if we are willing to take the desire at face value. If it is granted that Marion is desirable, or Rousseau ardent to such an extent, then the motivation for the theft becomes understandable and easy to forgive. He did it all out of love for her, and who would be a dour enough literalist to let a little property stand in the way of young love? (284)

The other occurrence of the word *forgiveness* is found in a passage that carries the only reference to Heidegger, whose designation of truth as revelation-dissimulation remains determinant in this whole strategy. De Man inscribes in fact his deconstructive gesture and his interpretation of dissemination—these two insistent words, *deconstruction* and *dissemination,* are everywhere and foregrounded in this essay—in a highly ambiguous double proximity: proximity to a certain Lacanianism, readable in what is said both about repression as "one speech act among others," and about desire and language, and even in the recourse to the truth according to Heidegger. But there is the proximity as well, despite this Lacanianism, to a certain Deleuzianism from the period of the *Anti-Oedipus,* in what links desire to the machine, I would almost say to a desiring machine. How is one to sort out all these threads (disseminal deconstruction, Lacanianism, and Deleuzianism) in de Man's original signature? That is what I would like to be able to do, without being sure in the least that I will manage it today. Here is the allusion to the guilt that is "forgiven":

Promise is proleptic, but excuse is belated and always occurs after the crime; since the crime is exposure, the excuse consists in recapitulating the exposure in the guise of concealment. The excuse is a ruse which permits exposure in the name of hiding, not unlike Being, in the later Heidegger, reveals itself by hiding. Or, put differently, shame used as excuse permits repression to function as revelation, and thus to make pleasure and guilt interchangeable. Guilt is forgiven because it allows for the pleasure of revealing its repression. It follows that repression is in fact an excuse, one speech act among others. (286)

Unless I missed something, these are the only borrowings from the lexicon of forgiveness, in what is a strong genealogy of excuse and forgiveness (here put in the same boat) as economic ruse, as stratagem and calculation, either conscious or unconscious, in view of the greatest pleasure at the service of the greatest desire. We will later get around to the complication of this desire, of its writing machine as a mutilating machine.

If there is also a proper eventness and of a performative type in the moment of the avowal but also in the moment of the excuse, can one distinguish the avowal from the excuse, as de Man attempts to do? Can one distinguish between, on the one hand, the confession as avowal (namely, a truth revealed-dissimulated according to the revisited Heideggerian scheme) and, on the other, the confession as excuse? For, at the beginning of his text, he proposes clearly isolating from each other the two structures and the two moments, with regard to referentiality, that is, their reference to an event—extraverbal or verbal. The distinction that is thereby proposed is alone capable of accounting for, in his view, the divergence, within the repetition, between the two texts, the *Confessions* and the *Fourth Rêverie,* which, with a ten-year interval, refer to the same event, the theft of the ribbon and the lie that followed it. But they refer to it differently. The avowal "stated in the mode of revealed truth" has recourse to "evidence" that is, according to de Man, "referential (the ribbon)," whereas the "evidence" for the avowal "stated in the mode of excuse" could only be "verbal." This is the beginning of a difficult analysis, which often leaves me perplexed. I am not sure, for example, that, if there is reference to an avowal that admits a misdeed, this reference consists here, as de Man asserts very quickly, in "the ribbon": "the evidence . . . is referential (the ribbon)," he says (280). The reference of the avowal, the fault, is the theft of the ribbon and not the ribbon, and above all, above all, more gravely, the lie that followed, and the verbal act that accused "poor Marion." Even if de Man is right to recall that "To steal is to act and includes no necessary verbal elements" (281), the reference of the avowal is not only to the theft but to the lie that followed.

De Man thus proposes here a distinction that is at once subtle, necessary, and problematic, by which I mean fragile, in a process that, at any rate, is of the order of event, doubly or triply so: *first,* by reference to an irreversible event that has already happened; *second,* as productive of event and archivation, inscription, consignment of the event; *third,* in a mode that is each time performative and that we must clarify. The distinction proposed by de Man is useful but also problematic. For if there is indeed an allegation of truth to be revealed, to be made known, thus a gesture of the theoretical type, a cognitive or, as de Man says, epistemological dimension in the confession, the confession is not a confession or avowal except to the extent that it in no case allows itself to be determined by this dimension, reduced to it, or even analyzed into two dissociable elements (the one de Man calls the cognitive and the other, the apologetic). *To make* known does not come down to knowing and, above all, to make known a *fault* does not come down to making known anything whatsoever; it is *already* to accuse oneself and to engage in a performative process of excuse and forgiveness. A declaration that would bring forward some knowledge, a piece of information, a thing to be known, would in no case be a confession, even if the thing to be known, even if the cognitive referent were otherwise defined as a fault (e.g., I can inform someone that I have killed, stolen, or lied without that being at all an avowal or a confession). For there to be a confessional declaration or avowal, it is necessary, indissociably, that I recognize that I am guilty in a mode of recognition that is not of the order of cognition, and it is therefore necessary that, at least implicitly, I begin to accuse myself—and thus to excuse myself or to present my apologies, or even to ask for forgiveness. There is doubtless an irreducible element of "truth" in this process but this truth, precisely, is not a truth to be known or, as de Man puts it so frequently, revealed. Rather, as Augustine says, it is a truth to be "made," to be "verified," if you will, and this order of truth (which is to be totally rethought) is not of a cognitive order. It is not a revelation. In any case, this revelation, if one insists on that term, does not consist only in lifting a veil so as to present something to be seen in a neutral, cognitive, or theoretical fashion. A more probing and patient discussion (for I admit that I don't see things clearly enough here) would therefore have to focus on what de Man calls "verification," which allows him, if I have understood correctly, to dissociate the confession of the *Confessions* from the excuses of the *Rêveries*:

> The difference between the verbal excuse and the referential crime is not a simple opposition between an action and a mere utterance about an action. To steal is to act and includes no necessary verbal element. To confess is discursive, but the discourse is governed by a principle of referential verification that includes an extraverbal moment: even if we confess that we *said* something (as opposed to *did*) [and this is also what happens with Rousseau, as I recalled a moment ago: he confessed what he *said* as well as what he *did*], the verification of this verbal event, the decision about the truth or falsehood of its occurrence, is not verbal but factual, the knowledge that the utterance actually took place. No such possibility of verification exists for the excuse, which is verbal in its utterance, in its effects and in its authority: its purpose is not to state but to convince, itself an "inner" process [this is an allusion to Rousseau's "inner feeling"] to which only words can bear witness. As is well known at least since Austin, excuses are a complex instance of what he termed performative utterances, a variety of speech acts. (281–82)

This series of affirmations does not seem to me always clear and convincing. The "inner process" can also be, it is even always the object of a reference, even in testimony; and testimony is never simply verbal. Inversely, the determination of the "factual" and of the factual occurrence of something that has actually taken place always passes by way of an act of testimony, whether verbal or not.

I am all the more troubled by these passages inasmuch as de Man seems to insist firmly on a distinction that he will later have to suspend, at least as regards the example he considers, Rousseau, but in my opinion throughout. The distinction is in fact suspended, thus interrupted, by the "as well" ("performatively as well as cognitively") that describes, de Man says, "the interest of Rousseau's text"—I would say the interest of Rousseau period, and even, by radicalizing the thing, all "interest" in general: "The interest of Rousseau's text is that it explicitly functions performatively as well as cognitively, and thus gives indications about the structure of performative rhetoric; this is already established in this text when the confession fails to close off a discourse which feels compelled to modulate from the confessional into the apologetic mode" (282). Yes, but I wonder if the confessional mode is not *already,* always, an apologetic mode. In truth, I believe there are not here two dissociable modes and two different times, which create the possibility of modulating from the one to the other. I don't believe even that what de Man names "the interest of Rousseau's text," there-fore its originality, consists in having to "modulate" from the confessional mode to the apologetic mode. Every confessional text is already apologetic, every avowal begins by offering apologies or by excusing itself.

Let's leave this difficulty in place. It is going to haunt everything that we will say from here on. For what de Man calls "the distinction between the confession stated in the mode of revealed truth and the confession stated in the mode of excuse" (280) organizes, it seems to me, his whole demonstration, whereas I find this distinction impos-sible, in truth undecidable. This undecidability, moreover, is what would make for all the interest, the obscurity, the nondecomposable specificity of what is called a confession, an avowal, an excuse, or an asked-for forgiveness. But if one went still further in this direction by leaving behind the context and the element of the de Manian interpre-tation, it would be because we are touching here on the equivocation of an originary or pre-originary synthesis without which there would be neither trace nor inscription, neither experience of the body nor ma-teriality. It would be a question of the equivocation between, *on the one hand,* the truth to be known, revealed, or asserted, the truth that, according to de Man, concerns the order of the pure and simple con-fessional, and, *on the other,* the truth of the pure performative of the excuse, to which de Man gives the name of the apologetic, two orders that are analogous, in sum, to the constative and the performative. By reason of this equivocation itself, which invades language and action at their source, we are always already in the process of excusing our-selves, or even asking forgiveness, precisely in this ambiguous and per-juring mode.

Following a path whose necessity neither Austin nor de Man failed to perceive, we may say that every constative is rooted in the presuppo-sition of an at least implicit performative. Every theoretical, cognitive utterance, every truth to be revealed, and so forth, assumes a testimo-nial form, an "I myself think," "I myself say," "I myself believe," or "I myself have the inner feeling that," and so forth, a relation to self to which you never have immediate access and for which you must believe me by taking my word for it (which is why I can always lie and bear false witness, right there where I say to you "I am speaking to you, me, to you," "I take you as my witness," "I promise you," or "I confess to you," "I tell you the truth"). This radical and general form of testimoniality means that wherever someone speaks, the false witness is always possible, as well as the equivocation between the two orders. In my address to another, I must always ask for faith or confidence, beg to be believed at my word, there where the equivocation is ineffaceable and perjury always possible, precisely unverifiable. This necessity is nothing other than the solitude, the singularity, the inaccessibility of the "as for me," the impossibility of having an originary and internal intuition of the proper experience of the other ego, of the alter ego. This same necessity is necessarily felt on both sides of the address or the destination (on the side of the addresser and of the addressee) as the place of a violence and an always possible abuse for which the apologetic confession (to use these two de Manian notions that are here indissociable, always indissociable) is already at work, à l'œuvre. And not only in Rousseau. But this is also why Rousseau is interesting, as the one who endured in an exemplary fashion this common fatality, a common fatality that is not only a misfortune, a trap, or a curse of the gods; for it is also the only possibility of speaking to the other, of blessing, saying, or making the truth, and so forth. Since I can always lie and since the other can always be the victim of this lie, since he or she never has the same access that I do to what I myself think or mean to say, I always begin, at least implicitly, by confessing a possible fault, abuse, or violence. I always begin by asking forgiveness when I address myself to the other and precisely in this equivocal mode, even if it is in order to say to him or her things that are as constative as, for example: "you know, it's raining."

Which is why, in the last phase of his interpretation, the one that is most important to him and that concerns the leap from the *Confessions* to the *Fourth Rêverie,* when de Man evokes at that point a "twilight zone between knowing and not-knowing," I feel so much in agreement with him that I believe such a twilight does not obscure only an initial clarity or cover only the passage from the *Confessions* to the *Rêveries.* This twilight seems to me consubstantial, already at the origin, with confession even in that element that de Man would like to identify as purely cognitive, epistemological, as a moment of revealed truth. De Man argues, in the following lines, for the necessity of the passage from the *Confessions* to the *Fourth Rêverie*. But this seems to me already valid for the *Confessions*. If I am right, that would make it difficult to maintain the allegation of a change of register between the two, at least in this regard.

> But the text offers further possibilities. The analysis of shame as excuse makes evident the strong link between the performance of excuses and the act of understanding. It has led to the problematics of hiding and revealing, which are clearly problematics of cognition. Excuse occurs within an epistemological twilight zone between knowing and not-knowing; this is also why it has to be centered on the crime of lying and why Rousseau can excuse himself for everything provided he can be excused for lying. When this turns out not to have been the case, when his claim to have lived for the sake of truth *(vitam impendere vero)* is being contested from the outside, the closure of excuse ("qu'il me soit permis de n'en reparler jamais") becomes a delusion and the *Fourth Rêverie* has to be written. (286)

If "the closure of excuse," at the end of the avowal in the *Confessions,* later "becomes a delusion," it is indeed because it already is there, in the *Confessions*. And it will remain a delusion after the *Fourth Rêverie*. But let us leave all that.

### III

Let us return to the value of event, of affection by the event that affects and changes things, and especially the past event, inscribed or archived. Irreducible eventness, to be sure. The event in question, which, then, must be retained, inscribed, traced, and so forth, can be the thing itself that is thus archived, but it can also be the event of the inscription. Even as it consigns, inscription produces a new event, thereby affecting the presumed primary event it is supposed to retain, engram, consign, archive. There is the event one archives, the *archived* event (and there is no archive without a body—I prefer to say "body" rather than "matter" for reasons that I will try to justify later) and there is the *archiving* event, the archivation. The latter is not the same thing, structurally, as the archived event even if, in certain cases, it is indissociable from it or even contemporary with it.

In his reading of Rousseau, de Man is concerned with what he himself calls a "textual event." An admirable reading, in fact a paradigmatic interpretation of a text that it poses as paradigmatic, namely, Rousseau's confession and excuse, whether one considers them to be successive, as de Man wants to do, or as simultaneous and indissociable in both their moment and their structure. A double paradigm, therefore, paradigm on paradigm. For if de Man's reading is exemplary, and from now on canonical, because of its inaugural character as the first rigorous elaboration, with regard to this famous passage, of certain theoretical protocols of reading (in particular, although not only, of a theory of the performative whose Austinian complications I had followed and aggravated elsewhere), such a reading itself declares that it bears on a "paradigmatic event" (these are de Man's terms) in the work of Rousseau:

> We are invited to believe that the episode [of the stolen ribbon] was never revealed to anyone prior to the privileged reader of the *Confessions* [this privileged reader, this original addressee of the confession and of the scene of excuse would thus be neither Marion nor any other living person, neither a priest nor God but an anonymous reader and still to come] "and . . . that the desire to free myself, so to speak, from this weight has greatly contributed to my resolve to write my confessions." When Rousseau returns to the *Confessions* in the later *Fourth Rêverie,* he again singles out this same episode as a paradigmatic event, the core of his autobiographical narrative. (278–79)

Right away, in the second paragraph of his introduction, de Man uses the expression "textual event," an expression that will reappear on the last page of the same essay. He continues: "The selection [of the theft of the ribbon and the lie that followed as paradigmatic episode] is, in itself, as arbitrary as it is suspicious, but it provides us with a *textual event* of undeniable exegetic interest: the juxtaposition of two confessional texts linked together by an explicit repetition, the confession, as it were, of a confession" (279; emphasis added).

That this selection is held by de Man to be "as arbitrary as it is suspicious" is a hypothesis that must be taken seriously, even if one is not prepared to subscribe to it unreservedly. For it subtends in a definitive way de Man's whole interpretation, notably his concepts of grammar and machine. At the end of the text, he will speak of the "gratuitous product of a textual grammar" (299), or yet again, still apropos of this structure of machine-like repetition, of "a system that is both entirely arbitrary and entirely repeatable, *like* a grammar" (300). Once again I underscore this "like."

The expression "textual event" is found again in conclusion, very close to the final word—not only of the chapter but of the book since this is, in de Man's corpus, the last chapter of the last book he will have published and reread during his lifetime. Now, it both is and is not the same "textual event" in question at the beginning of the text. It is the same, to be sure, because it is still a matter of what happens with the paradigmatic passage of the *Confessions*; but now it has been analyzed, determined, interpreted, localized within a certain mechanism, namely—and we will come back to this later—an anacoluthon or a parabasis, a discontinuity, or, to quote de Man's conclusion, "a sudden revelation of the discontinuity between two rhetorical codes. This isolated textual event, as the reading of the *Fourth Rêverie* shows, is disseminated throughout the entire text and the anacoluthon is extended over all the points of the figural line or allegory" (300).

How does this "textual event" inscribe itself? What is the operation of its inscription? What is the writing machine, the typewriter, that both produces it and archives it? What is the body, or even the materiality that confers on this inscription both a support and a resistance? And, above all, what essential relation does this textual event maintain with a scene of confession and excuse?

Since we are getting ready to speak of matter, or more precisely of the body, I note in the first place, and, as it were, between brackets, that de Man, very curiously, pays almost no attention (for reasons he doubtless considers justified and that in my view are only partially so) either to the matter and body of the ribbon itself, or to its use, because he holds it to be "devoid of meaning and function," circulating "symbolically as a pure signifier" (283), like the purloined letter, at least as it is interpreted by Lacan—to whom I objected that if the content of the letter appeared indifferent, it is because each of the protagonists, and each reader, knew that it signified at least perjury and betrayal of a sworn faith, just as I would observe here that the ribbon is not such a free or undetermined signifier: it has at least the sexualizable signification of ornament and fetish; and by the same token it has perhaps several others.

De Man is not interested either in the intermediary paragraph between the account of the death of Mme de Vercellis from a cancer of the breast (her double expiration, her last word) and the beginning of the confession of the misdeed that afflicts Rousseau with the "unbearable weight of a remorse" from which he cannot recover any more than he can ever console himself for it. The paragraph neglected by de Man describes nothing less than a scene of inheritance. It is a question of the will left by Mme de Vercellis, of whom de Man nevertheless says, as you recall, that there is no reason to "substitute" Marion for her ("nothing in the text," he says, suggests such a "concatenation") and thus a fortiori no reason to replace her with Mme de Warens—of whom de Man speaks only once in this context, and concerning whom I recall that Rousseau had met her for the first time the same year, a few months earlier, their meeting coinciding more or less with their common abjuration, their almost simultaneous conversion to Catholicism. This scene of inheritance seems to me significant, in this place, for countless reasons that I will not develop because they are too obvious. By essence or par excellence, and like every scene of inheritance, this one is a scene of *substitution* (and thus of responsibility, guilt, and forgiveness): substitution of persons and things, in the domains of the law governing persons and the law governing things. For one must not forget that the ribbon belongs more or less clearly to this scene and to the patrimony of things and valuables left as legacies. Even if it is a thing without value, as we will see, an old and used thing, its exchange value is caught up in the logic of substitution constituted by the inheritance. And we will once again have to reckon with more than one substitution—those of which de Man speaks and those of which he says nothing.

So that this may be more concrete in your eyes, here are the lines that seem not to interest de Man:

> She had left one year's wages to each of the under-servants. But not having been entered on the strength of her household I received nothing. . . . It is almost inevitable that the breaking up of an establishment should cause some confusion in the house, and that various things should be mislaid. But so honest were the servants and so vigilant were M. and Mme Lorenzi that nothing was found missing when the inventory was taken. Only Mlle Pontal lost a little pink and silver-colored ribbon, which was quite old [un petit ruban de couleur de rose et argent déjà vieux]. (86)

These two little words "quite old," "déjà vieux," are also omitted by de Man, I don't know why, in his quotation of this phrase, which he extracts therefore from its context and without having cited the preceding paragraph that I would call testamentary. No doubt the inventory in the course of which the disappearance of the ribbon was remarked is not the moment of the inheritance itself, but it is something like its inseparable continuation; and Mlle Portal, who "lost" *(perdit)* the "little ribbon," had received six hundred *livres* in inheritance, twenty times more than all the servants who had each received, in addition, individual legacies. Rousseau inherited nothing and he complains about it. These scenes of inheritance and inventory, which de Man does not evoke, are not the scenes that Rousseau describes before recounting the death of Mme de Vercellis, in a passage where it is already a question of legacies (the entourage of Mme de Vercellis, already thinking about the legacy, had done everything to get Rousseau out of the way and "banish [him] from her sight," as he puts it). No doubt it is to this paragraph preceding the account that de Man refers in the note that had surprised me somewhat ("The embarrassing story of Rousseau's rejection by Mme de Vercellis, who is dying of a cancer of the breast, immediately precedes the story of Marion, but nothing in the text suggests a concatenation that would allow one to substitute Marion for Mme. de Vercellis in a scene of rejection"). It is this substitution that de Man curiously does not believe should be credited. Curiously because, inversely, his whole text will put to work in a decisive fashion a logic of substitution. In a later passage, which is not, it is true, his last word on the subject, he talks abundantly of a substitution between Rousseau and Marion and even of "two levels of substitution (or displacement) taking place: the ribbon substituting for a desire which is itself a desire for substitution" (284). Summing up the facts, he writes: "The episode itself is one in a series of stories of petty larceny, but with an added twist. While employed as a servant in an aristocratic Turin household, Rousseau has stolen a 'pink and silver-colored ribbon'" (279).

Why does he cut the sentence, mutilating it or dismembering it in this way, and in such an apparently arbitrary fashion? Why does he amputate two of its own little words before the period: "quite old," "déjà vieux"? I have no answer to this question. I say mutilation, amputation, or dismemberment, or even arbitrary cut to qualify the operation by which a phrase is thus deprived of two of its little words and interrupted in its organic syntax. I do so both because, first of all, that's the way it is, no doubt, and the phenomenon is as strange as it is remarkable (it is indeed an apparently arbitrary amputation and dissociation),[14] but also because the general interpretation by de Man of the "textual event" in question will put to work, in a determinant fashion, these motifs (mutilation and dismemberment) as well as the operation of a machinery, as we will see. Moreover, and so as to anticipate things at a somewhat greater distance, among the significations that will later structure the de Manian concept of materiality or material inscription—

although the words *matter* and especially *materialism* never occur in
"Excuses *(Confessions),*" a certain lodging seems to be made ready for
the welcome de Man will extend to them later)—one finds once again,
besides the significations of mute literality and body, those of discontinuity, caesura, division, mutilation, and dismemberment or, as de Man
often says here, dissemination. Whether one is talking about the body
in general, the body proper, or, as in the example of Kleist's *Marionettentheater* read by de Man, of the linguistic body of phrases and words in
syllables and letters (for example, from *Fall* as case or fall to *Falle* as
trap),[15] these figures of dismemberment, fragmentation, mutilation,
and "material disarticulation" play an essential role in a certain "materialist" signature (I leave the word *materialist* in quotation marks)
that insists in the last texts of de Man. How does the concept of materiality or the associated concept of "materialism" get elaborated in
the later texts ("Phenomenality and Materiality in Kant" and "Kant's
Materialism," both in *Aesthetic Ideology*)? This is a question we can
keep in view in the interpretation of Rousseau. We can also keep in
view a certain concept of *history,* of the historicity of history, so as to
trace its intersection with this logic of the textual event as material inscription. When it is a matter of this structure of the text, the concept
of historicity will no longer be regulated by the scheme of progression
or of regression, thus by a scheme of teleological process, but rather by
that of the event, or occurrence, thus by the singularity of the "one
time only." This value of occurrence links historicity not to time, as is
usually thought, nor to the temporal process but, according to de Man,
to power, to the language *of* power, and to language *as* power. Hence
the necessity to take into account performativity, which defines precisely the power *of* language and power *as* language, the excess of the
language of power or of the power of language over constative or cognitive language. In "Kant and Schiller" (a lecture delivered at Cornell
the year of his death, in 1983, and collected in *Aesthetic Ideology* on
the basis of audiotapes), de Man speaks of thinking history as *event*
and not as *process,* progress, or regression. He then adds:

> There is history from the moment that words such as "power" and
> "battle" and so on emerge on the scene. At that moment things *happen,*
> there is *occurrence,* there is *event.* History is therefore not a temporal
> notion, it has nothing to do with temporality [this hyperbolic provo-
> cation, in the style of de Man, certainly does not negate all temporality
> of history; it merely recalls that time, temporal unfolding, is not the

essential predicate of the concept of history: time is not enough to make history], but it is the emergence of a language of power out of a language of cognition. (133)

De Man distinguishes the eventness of events from a dialectical process or from any continuum accessible to a process of knowledge, such as the Hegelian dialectic. No doubt he would have said the same thing of the Marxist dialectic, I presume, if at least the heritage and the thought of Marx could be reduced to that of the dialectic. He also specifies that the performative (the language of power beyond the language of knowledge) is not the negation of the tropological but remains separated from the tropological by a *discontinuity* that tolerates no mediation and no temporal scheme. It remains the case that the performative, however foreign and excessive it may be in relation to the cognitive, can always be reinscribed, *recuperated* is de Man's word, in a cognitive system. This discontinuity, this event as discontinuity, is important for us if only because it will allow us to go beyond the excuse and come closer to the event of forgiveness, which always supposes irreversible interruption, revolutionary caesura, or even the end of history, at least of history as teleological process. Moreover, one may note with equal interest that, in the same text ("Kant and Schiller"), de Man constructs his concept of event, of history as the eventness of events rather than as temporal process, on the basis of two determinations that are equally important for us: that of irreversibility (forgiveness and excuse suppose precisely that what has happened is irreversible) and that of inscription or material trace:

When I speak of irreversibility, and insist on irreversibility, this is because in all those texts and those juxtapositions of texts, we have been aware of something which one could call a progression—though it shouldn't be—a movement, from cognition, from acts of knowledge, from states of cognition, to something which is no longer a cognition but which is to some extent an *occurrence,* which has the materiality of something that actually happens, that actually occurs. And there, the thought of material occurrence, something that occurs materially, that leaves a trace on the world, that does something to the world as such— that notion of occurrence is not opposed in any sense to the notion of writing. But it is opposed to some extent to the notion of cognition. I'm reminded of a quotation in Hölderlin—if you don't quote Pascal you can always quote Hölderlin, that's about equally useful—which says: "Lang ist die Zeit, es ereignet sich aber das Wahre." Long is time, but—

not truth, not *Wahrheit*, but *das Wahre*, that which is true, will occur, will take place, will eventually take place, will eventually occur. And the characteristic of truth is the fact that it occurs, not the truth, but that which is true. The occurrence is true because it occurs; by the fact that it occurs it has truth, truth value, it is true. (132)

Why did de Man forget, omit, or efface those two words ("quite old," "déjà vieux") that qualify also a certain materiality of the enigmatic thing called a ribbon? Was it to save space, as one sometimes does by not citing a text integrally, by omitting passages that are less pertinent for the demonstration under way? Perhaps, but it is difficult to justify doing so for two little words ("quite old") that come just after the words quoted and before the final period. I recall the sentence and underscore certain words: "La seule Mlle Portal *perdit* un petit ruban couleur de rose et argent *déjà vieux*" ("Only Mlle Portal lost a little pink and silver-colored ribbon, which was quite old"). I underscore in passing that Rousseau says of this ribbon that she "lost it," "le perdit." On the preceding page, it was said of Mme de Vercellis: "Nous la *perdîmes* enfin. Je la vis expirer" ("Finally we lost her. I watched her die").

Might there be a relation of substitution between these two losses signified by the same verb in the same tense, the *passé simple* or historic past that says—but what does it thereby say and mean to say?—*nous la perdîmes, elle perdit*? I would not swear to such a relation of substitution, but we'll leave it at that.

Excluding a concern for economy and the possibly inconsequential abbreviation of two little words, can one speak of a pure and simple omission by mechanical distraction? If one supposes that such a thing exists, it is all the more puzzling why it would have struck these two words from which de Man, instead of letting them drop, could have drawn an argument or with which he could have reinforced his own argument. To lend coherence to his hypothesis of substitution (between Rousseau and Marion, the desire of Rousseau and Marion, desire and the desire of substitution), the ribbon had itself to be a "free signifier," a simple exchange value without use value. Moreover, if indeed theft is a sin, then no one ever steals anything but exchange values, not use values. If I steal in order to eat, my theft is not really a crime, an evil for the sake of evil. In order to speak of misdeed, the profit must not be located in the usefulness of the fault, the crime, the theft, or the lie, but in a certain uselessness. One has to have loved the crime for itself, for the shame that it procures, and that supposes some "beyond-use" of the immediate or apparent object of the fault. But, in relation to immediate use, the beyond-use does not mean absolute insignificance and uselessness. Augustine and Rousseau understood that very well. They both emphasize that they stole something for which they had no need and no use. And, moreover, a little further on (and this explains my astonishment), de Man does make allusion to the fact that the ribbon must be beyond use, "devoid," as he puts it, "of meaning and function," in order to play the role it plays. In the first stage of his analysis, at the level he himself calls elementary, when he is describing one of the ways the text functions (among others, which he will exhibit later), de Man specifies forcefully that the desire for gift and possession, the movement of representation, exchange, and substitution of the ribbon supposes that it not be, I would say, a "use value" but an exchange value, or even, I would say again (but this is not de Man's term), already a fetish, an exchange value whose body is fetishizable; one never steals the thing itself, which, moreover, never presents itself. Let us read:

> Once it is removed from its legitimate owner, the ribbon, being in itself devoid of meaning and function, can circulate symbolically as a pure signifier and become the articulating hinge in a chain of exchanges and possessions. As the ribbon changes hands it traces a circuit leading to the exposure of a hidden, censored desire. Rousseau identifies the desire as his desire for Marion: "it was my intention to give her the ribbon," i.e., to "possess" her. At this point in the reading suggested by Rousseau, the proper meaning of the trope is clear enough: the ribbon "stands for" Rousseau's desire for Marion or, what amounts to the same thing, for Marion herself.
>
> Or, rather, it stands for the free circulation of the desire between Rousseau and Marion, for the reciprocity which, as we know from *Julie,* is for Rousseau the very condition of love; it stands for the substitutability of Rousseau for Marion and vice versa. Rousseau desires Marion as Marion desires Rousseau. . . . The system works: "I accused Marion of having done what I wanted to do and of having given me the ribbon because it was my intention to give it to her." The substitutions have taken place without destroying the cohesion of the system, reflected in the balanced syntax of the sentence and now understandable exactly as we comprehend the ribbon to signify desire. Specular figures of this kind are metaphors and it should be noted that on this still elemen-

tary level of understanding, the introduction of the figural dimension in
the text occurs first by ways of metaphor. (283–84)

Now think of the word *ribbon,* but also of this figure of a narrow
band of silk, velvet, or satin, which one wears on one's head, in one's
hair, or like a necklace around the neck. The uncertain origin of the
word *ribbon* probably links the motifs of the *ring,* thus the circular
link, the annular, or even the wedding band, and *band,* namely, once
again the link, as *bind* or *Bund* (in Middle Dutch the word, it seems, is
*ringhband*). The ribbon thus seems to be, in itself, doubly enribboned,
*ring* and *band,* twice knotted, banded, or banding, *bandé* or *bandant,*
as I might say in French. A ribbon perhaps figures therefore the double
bind *en soie,* in itself, its own silky self.[16] By thus renaming the ribbon
of the *Confessions,* I've been led to associate, without doing it on purpose, without expecting it but no doubt not fortuitously, Marion's ribbon with the typewriter ribbon. De Man has little interest in the material of the ribbon, as we have just seen, for he takes the thing "ribbon"
to be a "free signifier." But he is also not interested in the verbal signifier or the word *ribbon.* Yet this lost piece of finery from the eighteenth
century, the ribbon that Mlle Portal "lost" after we "lost" Mme de
Vercellis, was also, once stolen and passed from hand to hand, a formidable writing machine, a ribbon of ink along which so many signs
transited so irresistibly, a skin on which or under which so many words
will have been printed, a phantasmatic body through which waves of
ink will have been made to flow. An affluence or confluence of limited
ink, to be sure, because a typewriter ribbon, like a computer printer,
has only a finite reserve of coloring substance. The material potenti-
ality of this ink remains modest, that is true, but it capitalizes, virtually,
for the sooner or later, an impressive quantity of text: not only a great
flux of liquid, good for writing, but a growing flux at the rhythm of a
capital—on a day when speculation goes crazy in the capitals of the
stock markets. And when one makes ink flow, figuratively or not, one
can also figure that one *causes* to flow or *lets* flow all that which, by
spilling itself this way, can invade or fertilize some cloth or tissue. Poor
Marion's ribbon (which Mlle Portal, who lost it, will not have worn up
till the end) will have supplied the body and the tissue and the ink and
the surface of an immense bibliography. A virtual library. I would have
been tempted, but I will not have the time, to sketch other itineraries
apropos of this ink flow: for example, to pass from the figural ink of this
ink ribbon across a text of Austin's that I treated elsewhere, precisely

in *Limited Inc* (and it is also a text on excuse and responsibility, an analysis that is, moreover, complementary with "A Plea for Excuses"). Austin analyzes there the possibilities of a bad thing one does intentionally or unintentionally, deliberately or by accident, by inadvertence (which one can always claim in order to excuse oneself), and so forth. This text is titled "Three Ways of Spilling Ink," by reason of the *à-propos* of a first example: a child spills some ink and the schoolmaster asks him "Did you do that intentionally?" or "Did you do that deliberately?" or "Did you do that on purpose (purposely)?"[17]

This ribbon will have been more or less than a subject. It was already at the origin a material support, at once a subjectile on which one writes and the piece of a machine thanks to which one will never have done with inscribing: discourse upon discourse, exegesis on top of exegesis, beginning with those of Rousseau. In the universal *doxa,* this typewriter ribbon has become by substitution the ribbon of "poor Marion" whose property it never was and to whom it was therefore never given or returned. Imagine what she might have thought if someone had told her what was going to happen sooner or later to her ghost, that is to say, *to* her name and *in* her name over centuries, thanks to Rousseau or by "Rousseau's fault," on the basis of the act to which she was perhaps one day (will one ever know? could one know it without the archive of the violent writing machine?) barely the witness, an act of which she was only the poor victim who understands nothing of what is happening, the innocent girl who is perhaps as virginal as Mary. For, with or without annunciation, she will have been fertilized with ink through the ribbon of a terrible and tireless writing machine that is now relayed, in this floating sea of characters, by the apparently liquid element of computer screens and from time to time by ink cartridges for an Apple printer, just the thing to recall the forbidden fruit and the apples stolen by the young Jean-Jacques. Almost everything here will have passed by way of a written confession, without living addressee and within the writing of Rousseau, between the *Confessions* and the *Rêveries* dreaming the virtual history of their "sooner or later."

As piece of a tireless writing machine, this ribbon gave rise—which is why I began by the event, by the event that is archivable as much as it is archiving—to what de Man twice calls, at the beginning and the end of his text, a "textual event." The second time it is in order to recognize there, as you heard, a dissemination of the textual event called anacoluthon; the first time it is to recall that this event has already the structure of a repetitive substitution, a repetition of the confession in the confession.

Among all the remarkable merits of de Man's great reading, there is first of all this reckoning with the works of Austin. I say purposely, and vaguely, the "works" of Austin because one value of these works is to have not only resisted but marked the line of resistance to the systematic work, to philosophy as formalizing theorization, absolute and closed, freed of its adherences to ordinary language and to so-called natural languages. There is also, and this is another of de Man's merits, an elaboration and an original complication of Austinian concepts. De Man cites "Performative Utterances" and "A Plea for Excuses" precisely at the point at which he writes: "As is well known at least since Austin, excuses are a complex instance of what he termed performative utterances, a variety of speech acts" (281–82). To illustrate the complexity of this "complex example," he specifies right away that "The interest of Rousseau's text is that it explicitly functions performatively as well as cognitively, and thus gives indications about the structure of performative rhetoric" (282). Now, the opposition between "performative" and "cognitive" was evoked in the first lines of the chapter, which apparently mark the passage from temporality to historicity, a passage that is all the more paradoxical in that it goes from a more political text, the *Social Contract*, to a less political one, the *Confessions* or the *Rêveries*. But it is the phenomenon of this appearance that must be analyzed. If, de Man says, "the relationship between cognition and performance is relatively easy to grasp in the case of a temporal speech act such as a *promise*— which, in Rousseau's work, is the model for the *Social Contract*—it is more complex in the confessional mode of his autobiographies" (278).

In other words, the performative mode of the promise would be simpler than that of the confession or the excuse, notably as regards this distinction cognition/performance. In the preceding chapter, de Man had treated the promise by setting out from the *Social Contract*. He thus goes from the *Social Contract* to the *Confessions* and to the *Rêveries,* from the simpler to the more complex (where, precisely, the complexity can no longer be undone, and the distinction can no longer operate—at least as I see it, because de Man wants to maintain this distinction even when it seems difficult to do so). In the preceding chapters on Rousseau, and in particular in the chapter on the *Social Contract*, one finds the premises of the chapter we are now reading on "Excuses *(Confessions)."* I retain at least three of these premises:

1. A concept or an operation of *deconstruction*: "a deconstruction

always has for its target to reveal the existence of hidden articulations and fragmentations within assumedly monadic totalities" (249), within a binary system, or in "metaphorical patterns based on binary models" (255). Nature becoming a "self-deconstructive term" (249), one will always be dealing with a series of deconstructions of figures.

2. A concept of "machine": a text whose grammaticality is a logical code obeys a machine. No text is conceivable without grammar and no grammar (thus no machine) is conceivable without the "suspension of referential meaning." In the order of the law (and this is valid for any law, it is the law of the law), this means that "Just as no law can ever be written unless one suspends any consideration of applicability to a particular entity including, of course, oneself, grammatical logic can function only if its referential consequences are disregarded. On the other hand, no law is a law unless it also applies to particular individuals. It cannot be left hanging in the air, in the abstraction of its generality" (269).

3. De Man interprets this contradiction or this incompatibility (the law suspends referential application even as it requires it as verification) in a striking fashion, in particular in the passage from the *Social Contract* (read here from the point of view of the promise) to the *Confessions* or to the *Rêveries* (read here from the point of view of the excuse). One can overcome this contradiction or this incompatibility only by an *act of deceit*. This deception is a *theft*, a theft in language, the theft of a word, the abusive appropriation of the meaning of a word. This theft is not the appropriation of just any word whatsoever: it is the theft of the subject, more precisely of the word *chacun*, "each one," inasmuch as it says at once the "I," the singularity and the generality of every "I." Nothing is in fact more irreducibly singular than "I" and yet nothing is more universal, anonymous, and substitutable. This deception and this theft consist in appropriating the word *chacun* (to appropriate the words *each one* [s'approprier le mot *chacun*] are Rousseau's terms; deceit and theft are de Manian translations, which are at once brutal and faithful: when one appropriates, one always steals, and when one steals, one deceives, one lies, especially when one denies it). This deceit and this theft, therefore, are constitutive of justice (which is both without reference and applicable, thus with a reference: *without and with* reference). De Man is then led to say that "justice is unjust," a formula that I must have retained while forgetting it, while forgetting that I stole it in this way because afterwards, and very recently, I took it up on my own account and ventured it in another

context, without making reference to de Man. The context was an interpretation of Levinas, of the logic of the third party and of perjury, namely, that all justice is unjust and begins in perjury.[18] Having confessed this involuntary theft, so as to excuse myself for it, I underscore the reference to theft in the chapter preceding the one we are concerned with at present on the excuse, and which thus serves as a premise for it.

Here are several lines, but, to be just, one would have to reconstitute the whole context:

> The preceding passage makes clear that the incompatibility between the elaboration of the law and its application (or justice) can only be bridged by an act of deceit. "S'approprier en secret ce mot *chacun*" is to steal from the text the very meaning to which, according to this text, we are not entitled, the particular *I* which destroys its generality; hence the deceitful, covert gesture "en secret," in the foolish hope that the theft will go unnoticed. Justice is unjust; no wonder that the language of justice is also the language of guilt and that, as we know from the *Confessions,* we never lie as much as when we want to do full justice to ourselves, especially in self-accusation. (268)

The substitution of the "I" for the "I" is also the root of perjury: I (the I) can always, by addressing myself/itself to (a) you, each one to each one, substitute the other same "I" for this here "I" and change the destination. (An) "I" can always change the address in secret at the last moment. Since every "I" is an "I" (the same and altogether other: *tout autre est tout autre,* every other is altogether other as the same), since every other is altogether other, (the) I can betray, without the least appearance becoming manifest, by substituting the address of one for the address of the other, up to the last moment—in ecstasy or in death.

Apropos of "Performative Utterances" and "A Plea for Excuses," I call your attention to several strategic and, in my view, important gestures. I remark on them, although de Man does not, because they cross with the paths we are following in an amusing way.

First of all, just for laughs, a strange association: the second example of "performative utterances," in the text with that title, is "I apologize" when you step on someone's toes. Now, how does this example come up? Is it symptomatic (a question one must always ask when Englishmen seem to exercise their wit by choosing at random arbitrary, insignificant, joking, or trivial examples)? The text had begun, as always with Austin, in an amusing way when, in what is precisely a deciding and performative fashion, he baptizes "performative" what will be defined as performative. Why this word, "performative"? Beyond the theoretical or semantic justifications for this terminological choice of an expression consecrated to a regulated use, the choice includes a performative dimension: I decide to propose that utterances of this type be called *performatives*. Austin has decided thus—and it has worked, it has been imprinted on all typewriter ribbons (more or less correctly, because the rigorous definition of the performative is infinitely problematic; but the word is now ineffaceable).

So Austin begins his text as follows:

> You are more than entitled not to know what the word "performative" means. It is a new word and an ugly word, and perhaps it does not mean anything very much. But at any rate there is one thing in its favor, it is not a profound word. I remember once when I had been talking on this subject that somebody afterwards said: "You know, I haven't the least idea what he means, unless it could be that he simply means what he says." Well, that is what I should like to mean. (233)

(This reminds me of my experience with the "ugly" and "new" words *deconstruction* and *differance* in 1967 at Oxford; whenever I have misadventures at Oxford, where Austin taught, or at Cambridge, I always think of him.)

The second major example of "performative utterance" will thus be "I apologize" when I step on someone's toes. This example comes up right after the example of the "I do" in the marriage ceremony, the "I do" that marks clearly that I do what I say by saying what I do. Austin has just said that with certain utterances, one says that the person is in the process of doing something rather than saying something: "Suppose for example, that in the course of a marriage ceremony I say, as people will, 'I do' (sc. take this woman to be my lawful wedded wife). Or again [this "Or again" is sublime] suppose that I tread on your toe and say 'I apologize.' Or again . . ." (235). This linking by additive contiguity, without transition ("Or again") from the marriage ceremony to the excuse when I tread on another's toes makes me think irresistibly of an Algerian Jewish rite. According to a more or less superstitious custom, the wedded couple is advised, at the precise moment when their marriage is consecrated in the synagogue, to hurry up and place a foot on the other's foot so as to guarantee for himself or herself power in their conjugal life. One has to hurry and take the other by surprise. One must create the event. The first one who places his or her foot on the other's will have the upper hand during the rest of their life together, until the end of history: history as occurrence and power. As if, right after the paradigmatic "I do" of the wedding ceremony, one had to excuse oneself or ask forgiveness from the other for this first *coup d'état,* for the power that is thus violently appropriated by a *coup de force.* "I do take you for husband (or wife), oh, excuse me, sorry," followed perhaps by an "It's nothing," "no problem," *"y a pas d'mal."* At any rate, whatever the response might be to a marriage proposal, it would be necessary to excuse oneself or ask forgiveness. "Marry me, I want to marry you." Response: "Yes, I beg your pardon" or "No, I beg your pardon." In either case, there is fault and thus forgiveness to be asked—and it is always as if one had tread on the toes of the other.

By excusing himself for not treating it "within such limits," Austin wonders what the subject of his paper is. He uses the word *Excuses,* but, he says, one must not be rigid about this noun and this verb. For a while, he had used the word *extenuation.* The word *excuse* now seems to him more convenient in this field, even though he includes others there, just as important, such as *plea, defence, justification.*

I will now propose that we make a detour. For a time and then from time to time, we are going to stop referring to *Allegories of Reading,* but will come back to it in conclusion. However, even though the Rousseau I am going to talk about is not always very present in *Allegories of Reading,* one may always try to reconstitute a possible reading of it by de Man.

**I V**

*As if . . .*

Not *it was* as if, but *I was* as if. How can one say "I was as if . . ."?

For example: "I was as if I had committed incest." Not *it was* as if, but *I was* as if. The "I" comes to be, as the other used to say, there where it was, there where the neutral, impersonal "it," the *"ce,"* the *"ça,"* ought to have been—or stay what it will have been.

More than thirty years ago, I inscribed this phrase, "J'étais comme si j'avais commis un inceste" (in the translation, it reads: "I felt as if I had committed incest"), as epigraph to the whole second part of *Of Grammatology* devoted to Rousseau. Signed Rousseau, the "I was as if . . ." comes from the *Confessions* (book 5, 189). Rousseau describes himself with these words in a passage around the famous and scabrous sexual initiation by Maman. At the beginning of the paragraph, the account (constative, therefore) of a (performative) commitment, a promise and, as always, a profession of veracity: "The day came at last, more dreaded than desired. I promised all and did not break my word" (189) ("Ce jour-là, plustot redouté qu'attendu, vint enfin. Je promis tout, et je ne mentis pas" [197]). Further in the same paragraph: "No, I tasted pleasure, but I knew not what invincible sadness poisoned its charm. I was as if I had committed incest . . ." ("Non, je goûtai le plaisir. Je ne sais quelle invincible tristesse en empoisonnait le charme. J'étois comme si j'avais commis un inceste"). He notes that Maman knew no remorse: "As she was not at all sensual and had not sought for gratification, she neither received sexual pleasure nor knew the remorse that follows" ("Comme elle était peu sensuelle et n'avoit point recherché la volupté, elle n'en eut pas les délices, et n'en a jamais eu les remords"). She did not come, so there was no fault, no remorse for her. Not only did she know no remorse, but she had, like God, the virtue of mercy [miséricorde], forgiving without even thinking that there was some merit in forgiveness. So Maman never knew any remorse about this quasi incest, and Rousseau justifies her in every regard, he excuses her with all his well-known eloquence. Now, you know, and Rousseau knew better than we do, how many lovers the lady he called Maman had had. He nevertheless wrote, as if he were speaking of himself: "All her faults, I repeat, came from her lack of judgment, never from her passions. She was of gentle birth, her heart was pure . . ." (190). Several pages later, he is still speaking of her as if he were speaking of himself: "She loathed duplicity and lying; she was just, equitable, humane, disinterested, true to her word, her friends, and what she recognized as her duties, incapable of hatred or vengeance and not even imagining that there was the slightest merit in forgiveness" (191). So she forgave graciously, without difficulty, without forcing herself. She was mercy itself and forgiveness itself. The following sentence, however, still attempts to excuse the least excusable: "Finally, to return to her less excusable qualities, though she did not rate her favors at their true worth, she never made a common trade in them; she conferred them lavishly but she did not sell them, though continually reduced to expedients in order to live; and I would venture to say that if Socrates could esteem Aspasia, he would have respected Mme de Warens."

Maman forgives infinitely, like God. As to her faults, she may be excused, which is what the son sets about to do. One could follow the occurrences of the word forgive, "first jouissance," that of the quasi incest, and this oath: "I can swear that I never loved her more tenderly than when I so little desired to possess her" (189).

Several weeks ago, in Picardy, a prodigious archive was exhumed and then deciphered. In layers of fauna and flora were found, protected in amber, some animal or other, some insect or other (which is nothing new) but also the intact cadaver of another insect surprised by death, in an instant, by a geological or geothermal catastrophe, at the moment at which it was sucking the blood of another insect, 54 million years before humans appeared on Earth. Fifty-four million years before humans appeared on Earth, there was once upon a time an insect that died, its cadaver still visible and intact, the cadaver of someone who was surprised by death at the instant it was sucking the blood of another! But it would suffice that it be but two hours before the appearance of any living being or other, of whoever would be capable of referring to this archive as such, that is, to the archive of a singular event at which this living being will not have been, itself, present, yesterday, an hour ago—or 54 million years before humans appeared, sooner or later, on Earth.

It is one thing to know the sediments, rocks, plants that can be dated to a period when nothing human or even living signaled its presence on Earth. It is another thing to refer to a singular event, to what took place one time, one time only, in a nonrepeatable instant, like that animal surprised by catastrophe at the moment, at some instant, at some stigmatic point of time in which it was in the process of taking its pleasure sucking the blood of another animal, just as it could have taken it in some other way, moreover. For there is also a report of two midges immobilized in amber the color of honey when they were surprised by death as they made love: 54 million years before humans appeared on earth, a *jouissance* took place whose archive we preserve. We have there, set down, consigned to a support, protected by the body of an amber coffin, the trace, which is itself corporeal, of an event that took place only once and that, as a one-time-only event, is not at all reducible to the permanence of elements from the same period that have endured through time and come down to us, for example, amber in general. There are many things on Earth that have been there since 54 million years before humans. We can identify them and analyze them, but rarely in the form of the archive of a singular event and, what is more, of an event that happened to some living being, affecting an organized living being, already endowed with a kind of memory, with project, need, desire, pleasure, *jouissance,* and aptitude to retain traces.

I don't know why I am telling you this. Perhaps because I'm planning to talk about *cutting* and *mutilations,* and "insect," like "sex," refers to cutting and means uncut or uncuttable, in French, *non-coupable,* allergic to section and to segmentation.[19] Perhaps because this discovery is itself an event, an event having to do with another event that is thus archived. Perhaps because we are in the process of interrogating the relation between, on the one hand, impassive but fragile matter, the material depository, the support, the subjectile, the document and, on the other hand, singularity, semelfactivity (that is, the concept of what happens just once), the "one time only" of the event that is thus consigned, to be confided without guarantee other than an aleatory one, incalculably, to some resistant matter, here to amber.

Perhaps one begins to think, to know and to know how to think, to know how to think knowing, only by taking the measure of this scale: for example, 54 million years before humans appeared on Earth. Or yesterday, when I was not there, when an "I" and above all an "I" saying "me, a man" was not there—or, tomorrow, sooner or later, will not be there any longer. On this scale, what happens to our interest for archives that are as human, recent, micrological but just as fragile as confessions or excuses, as some "I apologize" and some asked-for pardons in a history of literature that, even on the very small scale of human history, is barely a child born yesterday, being only a few centuries old or young, namely, a few fractions of a second in the history of life, Earth, and the rest?

Let us now recall the two beginnings of the *Confessions,* for there are two of them. Let us go back toward the duplicity of these two beginnings, of the first word and the before-the-first word. These two beginnings begin, both of them, by saying that what is beginning there begins for the first and last time in the history of humanity. No true archive of man in his truth before the *Confessions.* Unique event, without precedent and without sequel, event that is its own archivation: "This is the only portrait of a man, drawn precisely from nature and in all its truth, that exists and that will probably ever exist [Voici le seul portrait d'homme, peint exactement d'après nature et dans toute sa vérité. Qui existe et qui probablement existera jamais]" (15; 3). This is found in the preamble, which has a strange status that I will talk about in a moment. On the following page, with the opening of the first book and therefore with what one may call the first word of the *Confessions,* Rousseau repeats more or less the same thing: "I have resolved on an enterprise that has no precedent, and which, once complete, will have no imitator. My purpose is to display to my kind a portrait in every way true to nature, and the man I shall portray will be myself [Je forme une entreprise qui n'eut jamais d'exemple, et dont l'exécution n'aura point d'imitateur. Je veux montrer à mes semblables un homme dans toute la vérité de la nature; et cet homme ce sera moi]" (17; 5).

As if, after 54 million years, one were witnessing in nature, and according to nature, the first pictorial archive of man worthy of that name and in its truth: the birth if not of man, at least of the exhibition of the natural truth of man.

I didn't know, a moment ago, why I was telling you these stories of an archive: archives of a vampire insect, archives of insects in the process of making love 54 million years ago—and archives as *Confessions*. But yes, I think I remember now, even though it was first of all unconscious and came back to me only after the fact. It is because, in a moment, I am going to talk to you about the effacement and mutilation of texts, about the falsification of the letter, about prosthesis, and so forth. Now—and here you'll just have to believe me because I am telling you the truth, as always—when I quoted Rousseau, in *Of Grammatology*, in 1967, and wrote as an epigraph for the whole section, almost the whole book, that I devoted to Rousseau, "J'étois comme si j'avais commis un inceste," "I was as if I had committed incest," well, the first proofs of the book came back to me with a typographical error that I was tempted not to correct. The printer in fact had written: "J'étois comme si j'avais commis un *insecte*," "I was as if I had committed an *insect*." Perhaps the typo was meant to protect from incest, but to protect whom or what? A perfect anagram *(inceste/insecte)* that, in order to respect the grammatical machine, I had to resolve to rectify and to normalize, so as to return from insect to incest, retracing the whole path, the 54 million years that lead from the insect sucking blood to the first man of the *Confessions*, an Oedipal man as first man (Hegel) or as last man (Nietzsche), Oedipus dictating there the first, here the last word of man.

We are seeking in this way to advance our research on the subject of that which, in forgiveness, excuse, or perjury, *comes to pass, is done, comes about, happens,* and thus that which, as event, requires not only an operation, an act, a performance, a praxis, but an *œuvre,* that is, at the same time the result and the trace left by a supposed operation, an *œuvre* that survives its supposed operation and its supposed operator. Surviving it, being destined to this sur-vival, to this excess over present life, the *œuvre* as trace implies from the outset the structure of this sur-vival, that is, what *cuts* the *œuvre* off from the operation. This *cut* assures it a sort of archival independence or autonomy that is quasi-machine-like (not machine-like but *quasi-machine-like*), a power of repetition, repeatability, iterability, serial and prosthetic substitution of self for self. This cut is not so much effected by the machine (even though the machine can in fact cut and repeat the cut in its turn) as it is the condition of production of a machine. The machine is *cut* as well as *cutting* with regard to the living present of life or of the living body: it is an *effect of the cut* as much as it is a *cause of the cut*. And that is one of the difficulties in handling this concept of machine, which always and by definition structurally resembles a *causa sui*.

Forgiveness and excuse are possible, are called upon to go into effect only there where this relative, quasi-machine-like survival of the *œuvre* (or of the archive as *oeuvre*) *takes place*—where it constitutes and institutes an event, in some manner taking charge of the forgiveness or the excuse. To say in this way that the *œuvre* institutes and constitutes an event is to register in a confused way an ambiguous thing. An *œuvre* is an event, to be sure, there is no *œuvre* without singular event, without textual event, if one can agree to enlarge this notion beyond its verbal or discursive limits. But is the *œuvre* the trace of an event, the name of the trace of the event that will have instituted it as *œuvre*? Or is it the institution of this event itself?

I would be tempted to respond, and not only so as to avoid the question: both at the same time. Every surviving *œuvre* keeps the trace of this ambiguity. It keeps the memory of the present that instituted it but, in this present, there was *already*, if not the project, at least the essential possibility of this cut—of this cut in view of leaving a trace, of this cut whose purpose is survival, of this cut that sometimes assures survival even if there is not the purpose of survival. This cut (both a wounding and an opening, the chance of a respiration) was in some way already there at work, *à l'œuvre*. It marked, like a scar, the originary living present of this institution—*as if* the machine, the *quasi* machine, were already operating, even before being produced in the world, if I can put it that way, in the vivid experience of the living present.

This is already a terrifying aporia (but why *terrifying* and for whom? this question will continue to haunt us). A terrifying aporia because this fatal necessity engenders automatically a situation in which forgiveness and excuse are both automatic (they cannot not take place, in some way independently of the presumed living "subjects" that they are supposed to involve) and therefore null and void, since they are in contradiction with what we, as inheritors of these values, either

Abrahamic or not, think about forgiveness and excuse: automatic and mechanical pardons or excuses cannot have the value of pardon and excuse. Or, if you prefer, one of the formidable effects of this machine-like automaticity would be to reduce every scene of forgiveness not only to a process of excuse but to the automatic and null efficacy of an a priori "I apologize," I disculpate myself and justify myself a priori or a posteriori, with an a posteriori that is a priori programmed, and in which, moreover, the "I" itself would be the "I" of anyone at all, according to that law of "deceit" or "theft" we have discussed: usurpation of the singular *I* by the universal *I*, ineluctable substitution and subterfuge that makes all "justice" "unjust."

Why would this self-destructive and automatic neutralization, which both is *produced by* and *produces* the scene of forgiveness or the apologetic scene, why would it be terrifying and its effects fearsome? One could use other words, more or less grave. In any case, it would be a matter of naming a negative affect, the feeling of threat, but of a threat at the heart of the promise. For what threatens is also what makes possible the expectation or the promise (for example, of a forgiveness or an excuse that I could not even desire, expect, or anticipate without this cut, this survival, this beyond-the-living-present). Right there where automaticity is effective and disculpates "me" a priori, it threatens me, therefore. Right there where it reassures me, I can fear it. Because it cuts me off from my own initiative, from my own origin, from my originary life, therefore from the present of my life, but also from the authenticity of the forgiveness and the excuse, from their very meaning, and finally from the eventness of the event, that of the fault or its confession, that of the forgiveness or the excuse. As a result and by reason of this quasi automaticity or quasi-machine-like quality of the sur-viving *œuvre,* one has the impression that one is dealing only with quasi events, quasi faults, quasi excuses, or quasi pardons. Before any other possible suffering or any other possible passion, there is the wound, which is at once infinite and unfelt, anesthetized, of this neutralization by the "as if," by the "as if" of this *quasi,* by the limitless risk of becoming a simulacrum or a virtuality without consistency—of everything. Is it necessary and is it possible to give an account of this wound, of this trauma, that is, of the desire, of the living movement, of the proper body, and so forth, given that the desire in question is not only injured or threatened with injury by the machine, but produced by the very possibility of the machine, of the machine-like expropriation? Giving an account becomes impossible once the condition of possibility *is* the condition of impossibility, and so forth. This is, it seems to me, the place of a thinking that ought to be devoted to the virtualization of the event by the machine, to a virtuality that exceeds the philosophical determination of the possibility of the possible (*dynamis, power, Möglichkeit*), the classical opposition of the possible and the impossible.

One of our greatest difficulties, then, would be to reconcile with the machine a thinking of the event (the real, undeniable, inscribed, singular event, of an always essentially traumatic type, even when it is a happy event, inasmuch as its singularity interrupts an order and rips apart, like every decision worthy of the name, the normal tissue of temporality or history). How is one to reconcile, *on the one hand,* a thinking of the event, which I propose withdrawing, despite the apparent paradox, from an ontology or a metaphysics of presence (it would be a matter of thinking an event that is undeniable but without pure presence), and, *on the other hand,* a certain concept of machine-ness *[machinalité]*? The latter would imply at least the following predicates: a certain materiality (which is not necessarily a corporeality), technicity, programming, repetition, or iterability; a cutting off from or independence from the subject—the psychological, sociological, transcendental, or even human subject, and so forth. In two words, how is one to think the event *and* the machine, the event *with* the machine, this here event *with* this here machine? In a word and repeating myself in a quasi-machine-like fashion, how is one to think together the machine *and* the event, a machine-like repetition *and* that which happens?

**V**

In the perspective opened by this repetitive series of questions, we have begun to read what de Man wrote one day, what he inscribed one day, apparently apropos of Rousseau—who was perhaps only an "excuse me" for de Man, just as we read an "excuse me" for Austin at the moment he was getting ready to talk about the excuse in general and excused himself for not doing so, contenting himself apparently with excusing himself, "within such limits."

I say indeed an "excuse me" of Rousseau. Instead of the excuse in general, or even some generality in general, de Man apparently intends this *here* "excuse me" of this *here* Rousseau, even if, as we will see, with the example or the index of this *here* "excuse me," he appeals to what he himself says he "calls text" ("What we call text," he will have written, a phrase that is followed by a definition of the text in general that places the word *definition* in quotation marks). There is, to be sure, a general thematics or problematics in play in these very rich texts. But at the point of the reference, what is at stake, in my opinion, is the singularity of a certain "excuse me" by Rousseau that is, moreover, double, according to the at once ordinary and ambiguous French grammar of this verb that appears at least twice in Rousseau, in strategic places, in the same paragraph of the *Confessions* concerning the theft of the ribbon.

The two occurrences are the object of a very active interpretation by de Man. One of the reasons the use of *s'excuser* is sometimes deemed improper in French culture is that it can mean either to "offer apologies" or else to clear oneself in advance, to wash one's hands of the confessed fault, which, in truth, since it was not a fault, does not even have to be confessed, still less excused or forgiven. Thus, all this becomes, as event itself, simulacrum or feint, fiction or scene of quasi excuse. And the machine-ness of this *s'excuser* draws in like a magnet the whole field of the de Manian analysis.

These two occurrences fall within the space of three sentences, in the paragraph that concludes the second book of the *Confessions* and the episode of the ribbon. In a fashion somewhat analogous to the scene, at once naive and perverse, in which Austin seems, in "A Plea for Excuses," to excuse himself in advance for not being able to treat the announced subject, namely, the "excuse," Rousseau begins, in a passage that does not appear to interest de Man, by excusing himself for having not even succeeded in excusing himself. He excuses himself for having been unable to exonerate himself of his crime. As if, at bottom, one had always to excuse oneself for failing to excuse oneself. But once one excuses oneself for failing, one may deem oneself to be, as one says in French, *d'avance tout excusé* or, on the contrary, condemned forever, irremediably, irreparably. It is the madness of this machine that interests us.

A. Here is the first occurrence of the *s'excuser* in this last paragraph:

> I have been absolutely frank in the account I have just given, and no one will accuse me, I am certain, of palliating the heinousness of my offense [thus, I have surely not convinced you that I was in no way at fault or that my fault was minor, and this is my fault: I have failed, and I am at fault; but—for there is a "but" and it is the "but" that is going to interest us—but, as Rousseau is going to explain to us right away, I believe I must explain to you, while justifying myself, why I believed I must do

it, that is, excuse myself, excuse myself for excusing myself for excusing myself]. But I should not fulfill the aim of this book if I did not at the same time reveal my inner feelings and hesitated to put up such excuses for myself as I honestly could. [Mais je ne remplirois pas le but de ce livre si je n'exposois en même tems mes dispositions intérieures, et que je craignisse de m'excuser en ce qui est conforme à la vérité].

De Man quotes this latter sentence in the original French *and* in translation. But he then undertakes a surprising operation, which, moreover, has been pointed out by his French translator and for which I can find neither the justification nor the necessity. He adds within brackets a word to the text, an expletive *ne*. An expletive *ne* in French is a pleonastic *ne*. One may either inscribe it or not inscribe it in a sentence as one wishes. For example (and this example, which is given in all the dictionaries, is all the more interesting in that it uses a verb found in Rousseau's sentence as changed or augmented by the useless expletive prosthesis that de Man nevertheless utilizes), I can say "il craint que je sois trop jeune" or, just as well and with the same meaning, "il craint que je *ne* sois trop jeune." These two sentences are strictly equivalent in French. Now, what does de Man do? Where Rousseau writes: "Mais je ne remplirois pas le but de ce livre si je n'exposois en même tems mes dispositions intérieures, et que je craignisse de m'excuser en ce qui est conforme à la vérité" (which is perfectly clear for a French ear and means "if I feared to excuse myself," and so forth), de Man adds a *ne* between brackets in his quotation of the French—which is not at all serious and can always be done, pleonastically, without changing the meaning, all the more so in that the brackets signal clearly de Man's intervention. But what he also does, and what seems disturbing to me because more serious, because it even risks inducing or translating a misinterpretation in the mind of the reader or in de Man's own mind, is that he then translates, so to speak, this expletive *ne* into English but without brackets, and he translates it as a "not" that is no longer at all expletive. As a result one reads, in de Man's own translation: "But I would not fulfill the purpose of this book if I did not reveal my inner sentiments as well, and if I did *not* fear" (here, de Man neither underscores nor brackets the second "not" that he adds even before he quotes the French in parentheses; he assumes only the fact of having himself italicized the French *excuser* and "excuse" in English) "to excuse myself by means of what conforms to the truth." This confusion, which I do not know how to interpret, risks making the text say exactly the opposite of what its grammar, its grammatical machine says, namely, that Rousseau does not fear, he does not want to fear, he does not want to have to fear to excuse himself. He would not fulfill the aim of his book if he did not reveal his inner feelings and if he feared to excuse himself with what conforms to the truth. So the correct translation would be exactly the opposite of the one proposed by de Man: "But I would not fulfill the purpose of this book if I did not reveal my inner sentiments as well and if I did fear [or "if I feared" and not as de Man writes, "if I did *not* fear"] to excuse myself by means of what conforms to the truth." Naturally, de Man might claim, and this is perhaps what he has in mind when he proceeds to comment at length on this motive of fear, that Rousseau says he does not fear or he must not fear *because* in fact he does fear, and all of this is disavowal by means of an expletive ruse.[20]

Well, let's leave this aside. But, apropos, as it has been and will often be a question of what *happens* to texts, injuring them, mutilating them, adding prostheses to them (de Man himself mentions the word prosthesis at one point),[21] I point out this little thing, just as I pointed out, apropos, de Man's omission of the two little words "déjà vieux" in relation to the ribbon. As if, to take up again the example of the dictionary I quoted a moment ago, de Man feared that the ribbon "*ne* fusse (ou fusse) déjà vieux ou qu'il craignisse au contraire qu'il fût ou *ne* fût 'trop jeune'" (as if de Man feared that the ribbon were too old or on the contrary as if he feared that it were "too young").

Apropos of this first occurrence of *m'excuser*: the imperative to which Rousseau here seems to submit everything so as to justify the gesture that consists in excusing himself, in not fearing to excuse himself, even if he does not succeed in doing so in a convincing way, this imperative is, not just the truth itself, not just the truth in itself, but his *promise* before the truth, more precisely, his sworn promise to write in a truthful and sincere fashion. What counts here is less the truth in itself than the oath, namely, the written promise to write this book in such and such a way, to sign it in conformity with a promise, not to betray, not to perjure the promise made at the beginning of the *Confessions* or in any case at the beginning of the first book of the *Confessions*, which is not, as we will see right away, the absolute beginning of the work. I will recall only these few lines (which de Man, of course, supposes are familiar to everyone, but which he does not reinscribe in their necessity of principle that determines the general structure and the whole chain of the *Confessions*), but I refer you to this whole first page of book 1, a page that is at once canonical and extraordinary and whose first version was much longer. This immense little page would call for centuries of reading by itself alone, as would the reactions that it has incited. The scene of the oath not to betray, of the performative promise not to perjure or abjure, seems to me more important than the theoretical or constative dimension of a truth to be revealed or known. I underscore this point so as to mark once again that the criterion by which de Man distinguishes confession from excuse, as well as an epistemic moment from an apologetic moment, seems to me problematic. At any rate, the moment said to be epistemic, the moment of knowledge, truth, or revelation, *already* depends, from the first line of the book, on a performative promise, the promise to tell the truth, including the truth of the faults and indignities that are going to be mentioned right after, the indignities of someone who declares "I may not be better, but at least I am different" ("si je ne vaux pas mieux, au moins je suis autre") and adds that he does not know "whether nature did well or ill in breaking the mold in which she formed me" ("si la nature a bien ou mal fait de briser le moule dans lequel elle m'a jetté"), that is, left his example without possible imitation or reproduction. He does not know, but as for the reader, he or she, sooner or later, will judge:

> I have resolved on an enterprise which has no precedent, and which, once completed, will have no imitator. My purpose is to display to my kind a portrait in every way true to nature, and the man I shall portray will be myself.
>
> Myself alone. . . . Let the last trumpet sound when it will [here is the call to appear before the last word], I shall come forward with this book in my hand, to present myself before the sovereign judge, and proclaim aloud: "Here is what I have done, what I have thought, what I have been." (17)

Commitment to the future, toward the future, promise, sworn faith (at the risk of perjury, promising never to commit perjury), these gestures present themselves as exemplary. The signatory wants to be, he declares himself to be at once singular, unique, *and* exemplary, in a manner analogous to what Augustine did with a more explicitly Christian gesture. Rousseau also addresses God, he invokes God, like Augustine he uses the familiar *tu* form of address. He addresses his fellow men through the intermediary of God, he apostrophizes them as brothers: sons of God. The scene of this virtual "sooner or later" remains fundamentally Christian.

But taken for myself alone ("Moi seul": Rousseau insists on both his solitude and his isolation, forever, without example, without precedent or sequel, without imitator), the same oath also commits, beginning at the origin, all others yet to come. It is a "without example" that, as always, aims to be exemplary and therefore repeatable. It will not be long before Rousseau apostrophizes others: in a defiant tone, he calls them to imitation, to compassion, to community, to sharing what cannot be shared, as if he were appealing to them not only to judge whether nature did well in breaking the mold in which she formed him, but also to see to it that this mold be not forever broken. This appeal to others and to the future belongs to the same time, to the same moment as the "myself alone," the only portrait "that exists and that will *probably* ever exist." This is what the pre-beginning will have said, as we will see in a moment. "This is the only portrait of a man, drawn precisely from nature and in all its truth, that exists and that will probably ever exist." This "probably" says the aleatory, the nonprobable, improbable space or time, thus delivered over to uncertainty or to the wager, virtual space or time, the incalculability of the absolute *perhaps* in which the contradiction between the *without example* and the exemplary will be able to insinuate itself, worm itself, and survive, not surmount itself but survive and endure as such, without solution but without disappearing right away:

> Eternal Being, let the numberless legion of my fellow men gather round me, and hear my confessions. Let them groan at my depravities, and blush for my misdeeds. [So everyone should be ashamed and confess with him, for him, like him, provided that one read and understand him.] Let each of them in turn reveal his heart at the foot of Thy throne with equal sincerity [what counts, therefore, is not the objective truth, referred to the outside, but veracity referred to the inside, to the internal feeling, to the adequation between what I say and what I think, even if what I think is false] and then let any man say if he dares: "I was better than he" ["je fus meilleur que cet homme-là," a formula one finds very frequently in Rousseau].

Apropos of this act of sworn faith, in the final form of the work this beginning is only a *quasi* opening. It is preceded by another little page, still shorter and without title, something like an *avant-propos*, a before-the-first-word that would also call for an infinite analysis. I will have to be content, within such limits, with signaling one or two little things. This before-the-first-word of the *Confessions* is found only in the

Geneva manuscript, as it is called, and it is in a different handwriting than that of the *Confessions* (the handwriting is larger and looser says the editor of the Pléiade edition in a note that in effect concerns the material body of the archive or the ribbon of textual events). This before-the-first-word announces, repeats, or anticipates the first words of the *Confessions,* to be sure. One reads there in fact, right away with the first words, the challenge whose hubris I have just recalled: "This is the only portrait of a man, drawn precisely from nature and in all its truth, that exists and that will probably ever exist." But in the logic of this challenge, the little phrase is followed by something else altogether that will not appear on the actual first page, which resembles it in many other ways. The following sentence makes an appeal to every reader to come, sooner or later. It asks whoever might be in a situation to do so *not to destroy* this document, this archive, this subjectile, the support of this confession—literally a notebook, a "cahier."

Here, then, for once, one time only, is something that precedes and conditions the confession. Here is something that comes before the virtually infinite oath that assures the performative condition of truth. What precedes and conditions the performative condition of the *Confessions* is thus another performative oath or rather another performative appeal *conjuring, beseeching* others to swear an oath, but this time regarding a body, a "cahier," this *here* "cahier" of this *here* body in a single copy, a single *exemplaire*: unique and authentic. This copy or *exemplaire* can be reproduced, of course, but it is first of all reducible to a single original and authentic copy, without other example. This body of paper, this body of destructible, effaceable, vulnerable paper, is exposed to accident, mutilation, falsification, or revenge. Rousseau is going to *conjure* (that is his word, for this appeal is another performative, another recourse to sworn faith, in the name "of my misfortunes," "by my misfortunes," Rousseau says), but he is going to conjure also "in the name of all humankind." He is going to conjure, that is, beseech men unknown to him, men of the present and of the future, not to "annihilate," sooner or later, his work. This "cahier," which he confides to future generations, is at once "unique" and, in that it is an original archive, it is the "one certain *monument.*" This document, this "cahier" is a "monument" (a sign destined to warn and to recall in the form of a thing exposed in the world, a thing that is *at the same time* natural and artifactual, a stone, amber, or another substance). Here is this appeal. It comes just after the first sentence, the one that is more or less equivalent to the first paragraph of the *Confessions*:

Whoever you are whom my destiny or my confidence has made the arbiter of the fate of *this "cahier"* [I underscore the deictic, "this here *cahier,*" which functions only if the "cahier" in question has not been destroyed, *already* destroyed], I beseech you *[je vous conjure]* by *my* misfortunes, by *your* entrails [it would be necessary to analyze this series of things in the name of which he swears and guarantees this act of swearing and conjuring: he adjures, he swears by calling upon others to swear with him, he conjures/beseeches them], and in the name of the whole human race [here, the guarantor in the name of which Rousseau swears, conjures, adjures, and calls on others not to abjure is almost infinite: after my misfortunes and your entrails, it is the "sooner of later" of the whole human race, past, present, and to come] not to annihilate an unique and useful work, which can serve as the first piece of comparison for the study of men, a study that is certainly yet to be begun [so, although it is unique and concerns me alone, it is exemplary for the study of men in general, a study to come for which this document will be the instituting arche-archive, something like the first man caught in absolute amber], and not to remove from the honor of my memory the *only* certain document [I underscore "only" because if this monumental document is vulnerable, it is because it is the only one and irreplaceable] of my character that has not been disfigured by my enemies. (3)[22]

This page was published only in 1850, based on a copy of the Moultou manuscript, as it is called, that was made by Du Peyrou in 1780. By its inspiration, it is comparable to the many analogous and well-known things Rousseau wrote when he began to fear that *Émile* had fallen into the hands of the Jesuits, who would have sought to mutilate it. What is very quickly termed his persecution complex was fixated, as you know and as many texts attest, on the fate of the manuscripts or the original copies, on the authentic arche-archive, in some fashion (*Rousseau Juge de Jean Jaques, 1772, Histoire du précédent écrit,* 1776). Concerning this whole problematic, I refer you to the splendid and well-known chapters that Peggy Kamuf devoted to Rousseau, to this Rousseau, in her *Signature Pieces.*[23]

The end of this adjuration explicitly announces the time when, sooner or later, none of those who are called upon to swear, adjure, conjure in this way will still be alive: "Finally, if you yourself are one of these implacable enemies, cease being so with regard to my ashes and do not carry over your cruel injustice to the time when neither you nor I will any longer be alive."

The logic of the argument consists, to be sure, in calling on others to save this "cahier," to promise not to destroy it, but not only for the future; rather, in truth and first of all, so that they may now bear witness to themselves, in the present, of their generosity, more precisely, so that they may bear witness that they have been able to forswear vengeance—thus that they have been able to substitute a movement of understanding, compassion, reconciliation, or even of forgiveness for a logic of retaliation and revenge. Even though, Rousseau suggests, everything is still to be decided for the future, in the future when neither you nor I will still be there, you can nevertheless right away *today* have the advantage, realize a benefit, a profit *at present,* from the anticipation *now* of this future perfect; you could right now look yourself in the eye, love yourself, and honor yourself, beginning at this very instant, for what you will have done tomorrow for the future—that is, for me, for this here "cahier" that by itself tells the first truth of man. That is the present chance offered to you already today, if you read me and understand me, if you watch over this manuscript, this "cahier": you will thus be able to honor yourself, love yourself, bear witness to yourself that you will have been good "at least once." This offered chance is also a wager, a logic and an economy of the wager: by wagering on the future, for the future of this "cahier," you will win at every throw, since you draw an immediate benefit, that of bearing witness in your own eyes as to your goodness, that of having thereby a good image of yourself right away, without waiting, and of enjoying it no matter what happens in the future. Logic and economy of a wager whose import cannot be exaggerated for all our calculations and our whole relation to time, to the future and to survival, to the work *[l'œuvre]* and to the work of time. De Man does not analyze this logic of the wager in Rousseau. He did so, mutatis mutandis, apropos of Pascal, in "Pascal's Allegory of Persuasion" (I take advantage of this remark to recall the superb essay that Geoffrey Bennington has devoted to this reading, precisely around a certain machine: "Aberrations: De Man [and] the Machine").[24]

A least once, launches Rousseau's apostrophe, here is the chance I offer you. I beseech you to seize it. For once at least, you will not have been guilty, you will be able to forgive yourself. Better than that, for once at least, you will not even have virtually to excuse yourself or ask for forgiveness for having done wrong, for having been "wicked and vindictive." This end of the before-the-first-word is sculpted by the multiplicity of these temporal modes (almost all of them are there) and by all the possible blows of this "at least once" that plays on all these virtualities of time, of the "sooner or later" of yesterday and tomorrow: ". . . *to the time* when neither you nor I will any longer be alive; so that you *may* at least once bear the noble witness to yourself of *having been* generous and good when you *could have been* wicked and vindictive— if it *is* the case that the evil one *bears* a man who *has never done any* [myself] *can be called* vengeance."

Apropos of this *avant-propos,* we could have devoted an abyssal development to this archivation, to the exceptional treatment that this before-the-first-word, this little page of the Geneva manuscript, will have undergone. *On the one hand,* the sheet was *cut* (the editors of the *Confessions* in the Pléiade edition write: "the sheet has been imperfectly cut about halfway up" [1230]). *On the other hand,* right on the cut sheet, one can see "traces" (once again, this is the editors' term) of a dozen additional lines that have been effaced, but that remain as vestiges of the effacement. They remain, but as illegible traces ("The page must have had another dozen lines whose traces can be seen, but the sheet has been imperfectly cut about halfway up"). This confirms the vulnerability of the effaceable document. The archive is as precarious as it is artificial, and precisely in that very place where the signatory puts on guard, appeals, beseeches, warns against the risk of whatever might come along, as he says, "to annihilate this work." Even if he is the one who erased this dozen additional lines and cut the sheet, this demonstrates a priori that he was right to worry: the archive document is transformable, alterable, even destructible or, in a word, falsifiable. The authentic integrity is, in its very body, in its proper and unique body, threatened in advance. Sooner or later, virtually, the worse can happen to it. Although it is presented as the only "certain monument," the little document could have not been there. After these contingent ups and downs, these *après-coups,* these recompositions, here it is now at the head of the *Confessions,* before the exordium and the self-presentation in the form of the exemplary promise addressed at once to you, "Eternal Being," and to all of you, "the crowd of my fellow men." The "I beseech you" not to "annihilate" this "cahier" is not only a before-the-first-word; it is the performative eve of the first performative, an arche-performative before the performative. Younger or older than all the others, it concerns the support and the archive of the confession, the very body of the event, the archival and auto-deictic body that will have to consign all the textual events engendered *as* and *by* the *Confessions,* the *Rêveries, Rousseau Juge de Jean Jaques,* or other writings in the same vein. Arche-performative, the arche-event of this sequence adjures one to save the body of the inscriptions, the "cahier" without which the revelation of the truth itself, however unconditional, truthful, sincere it may be in its promised manifestation, would have no chance of coming about and would be in its turn compromised. Perhaps we have here, apropos (but this would deserve long and careful analyses), a historical difference between Augustine's *Confessions* and those of Rousseau, whatever Christian filiation they no doubt share, but in a quite different way. Why is it so difficult to imagine this archival protocol at the beginning of Augustine's *Confessions*? This question would require that we articulate many problematics of different styles among themselves.

B. We were in the process of reciting the two occurrences of Rousseau's *s'excuser* in the last paragraph of the second book of the *Confessions*. The second occurrence of the "I excused myself" comes several lines after the first. After having said "I would not fulfill the purpose of this book if I did not reveal my inner sentiments as well, and if I feared *to excuse myself* by means of what conforms to the truth," he continues:

> Never was deliberate wickedness further from my intention than at that cruel moment. When I accused that poor girl, it is strange but true that my friendship for her was the cause. She was present in my thoughts, and I *excused myself* on the first object that presented *itself [je m'excusai sur le premier objet qui s'offrit]. I accused her* of having done what I intended to do myself. I said that she had given the ribbon to me because I meant to give it to her. (88)

Despite the proximity in the text, despite the semantic or grammatical analogy, this "I excused myself" does not refer to the same object or the same time as the first occurrence ("if I feared to excuse myself"). The first occurrence refers to an ulterior event, the last in time since it is a matter of excusing oneself *by writing* or *while writing* the *Confessions*. The second occurrence refers to an earlier time: what Rousseau did, that day, by accusing Marion. In other words, Rousseau does not want to fear to excuse himself in the *Confessions* by telling how and why he already excused himself, so many years earlier, at the time of the theft of the ribbon. Without forcing things too much, one could perhaps say that the first "excuse oneself" (the first event in the order of the text and according to the time of the *Confessions*) is a first "excuse oneself" on the subject of the second "excuse oneself," even though this second "excuse oneself" refers, in the order of real events, as we say, to an anterior or first moment. Unlike the first, the second "excuse oneself" recalls a past anterior to the writing of the *Confessions*. Rousseau first of all excused himself by means of the first object that offered itself and he must now, and in the future, without fear, excuse himself on the subject of this past excuse. He must not fear to excuse himself on the subject of a fault that consisted in excusing himself by lying. And he has, moreover, just recognized that he risks being less convincing with excuse number two (in the *Confessions*) than excuse number one (at the moment of the crime).

**V I**

Having arrived at this point, I submit to you in conclusion a few hypotheses or interpretations whose performative imprudence I assume, apropos of the extraordinary event constituted by de Man's reading of Rousseau, a reading to which I above all wanted to pay tribute by recognizing everything I owe to it. It is as a testimony of gratitude that I believe I should offer here a few supplementary footnotes.

De Man does not treat this couple of excuses, this excuse on the subject of an excuse, as I am in the process of doing. I will nevertheless venture to assert, while attempting to demonstrate (and I am not sure of being able to do this today), that his whole interpretation fits between these two times, which are also two events and two regimes of the "excuse oneself." Not, as seems to be the most manifest appearance and as he says and wants to say himself, between the excuses of the *Confessions* and those of the *Rêveries*, but between the two times of the excuse already in the *Confessions* itself. Approaching the second phase of his reading, the one that interests him the most, he declares, moreover:

> We have, of course, omitted from the reading the other sentence in which the verb "excuser" is explicitly being used, again in a somewhat unusual construction; the oddity of "que je craignisse de m'excuser" is repeated in the even more unusual locution: "Je m'excusai sur le premier objet qui s'offrit" ("I excused myself upon the first thing that offered itself," as one would say "je me vengeai" or "je m'acharnai sur le premier objet qui s'offrit." . . . )[25] Because Rousseau desires Marion, she haunts his mind and her name is pronounced almost unconsciously, as if it were a slip, a segment of the discourse of the other . . . the sentence is phrased in such a way as to allow for a complete disjunction between

Rousseau's desires and interests and the selection of this particular name. . . . She [Marion] is a free signifier, metonymically related to the part she is made to play in the subsequent system of exchanges and substitutions. She is, however, in an entirely different situation than the other free signifier, the ribbon, which also just happened to be ready-at-hand, but which is not in any way itself the object of a desire [I mentioned my reservations on this subject earlier, but de Man goes a little further]. . . . But if her nominal presence is a mere coincidence, then we are entering an entirely different system in which such terms as desire, shame, guilt, exposure, and repression no longer have any place.

In the spirit of the text, one should resist any temptation to give any significance whatever to the sound "Marion." For it is only if the act that initiated the entire chain, the utterance of the sound "Marion," is truly without any conceivable motive that the total arbitrariness of the action becomes the most effective, the most efficaciously performative excuse of all. (288–89)

Here is a disarticulatable articulation of allusions to contingency, to the "almost unconscious," not only to the discourse of the other, but to the "fragment of the discourse of the other," to the discourse of the other as fragmented discourse, therefore mutilated, half-effaced, redistributed, deconstructed, and disseminated as if by a machine. This disarticulated articulation of allusions is relayed, in the whole text, by a number of analogous motifs: the machine, the arbitrary, mutilation, prosthesis, and so forth.

I do not find Rousseau's constructions as "strange" as de Man twice says they are; I have explained why on the subject of the expletive added by de Man in French and transmuted in advance into a pure and simple negation in English. As for "sur le premier objet qui s'offrit," the thing is very clear in French even if de Man is right to say that this *may* in fact make one think of "je me vengeai" or "je m'acharnai sur le premier objet"—yes, or as well, I would say, one might think of "à propos, je me précipitais sur le premier objet qui s'offrit," "à-propos, I leaped on the first object that presented itself," "je me jetai sur le premier objet qui s'offrit à propos," "I threw myself on the first object that presented itself apropos."

It would be necessary to reread together, step by step, de Man's whole text. Since that is not possible, here are some hypotheses or interpretations.

In the first place, de Man also analyzes Rousseau's text as "the first object that offered itself." He constantly supposes (a number of his for-mulations show this clearly) that the text (here apropos of *s'excuser*) is exemplary, that is, at once singular (therefore an irreplaceable event) and yet, according to the very machine described here, valid for every text—and thus, as de Man said in the preceding chapter on the *Social Contract,* for everything that "we call text." The performative formu-lation of this "we call text" is assumed as such—and I want to reread it. The phrase appears just after the passage in which it is a question of the "theft," of stealing "from the text the very meaning to which, ac-cording to this text, we are not entitled":

> We call *text* any entity that can be considered from such a double per-spective: as a generative, open-ended, non-referential grammatical sys-tem and as a figural system closed off by a transcendental signification that subverts the grammatical code to which the text owes its existence. The "definition" of the text also states the impossibility of its existence and prefigures the allegorical narratives of this impossibility. (270)

I commented on and interpreted these words "We call *text*" (*text* in italics) and these quotation marks around *definition* in *Mémoires for Paul de Man.*[26] If what is said here about what we "call" text (fol-lowed by a "definition" in quotation marks) is valid for every text, ex-emplarily and metonymically (*metonymically* is my addition; in any case it is not metaphorically, for de Man is explaining here the dis-placement of the metaphor, including the metaphor of the text, espe-cially of the text as body, into something else), then it is valid as well for de Man's text, which includes itself, and by itself, in what he "calls" and "defines" in this fashion. I do not think de Man would have rejected this consequence: his writings can and should be read as also politico-autobiographical texts, a long, machine-like performa-tive, at once confessional and apologetic, with all the traits that he himself, in an exemplary way, trains on this object that offers itself and that is called, for example, and apropos, Rousseau. (It is true that even if there were, for de Man as for Rousseau, other objects on other stages, one may wonder why Rousseau gave such emphasis and privi-lege to this theft and this perjury, when he was sixteen years old, in the genesis of the *Confessions*; and why de Man hounds him, *s'acharne sur lui,* so lovingly, as if he were *after him* in this trace.)

Without any doubt, many passages would demonstrate, in their very letter, that Rousseau's text, however singular it may be, serves here as exemplary index. Of what? Of the text *in general,* or more rigorously (and this makes a difference that counts here) of "what we call *text*," as de Man says playing with the italics and with the "definition" that he gives by putting the word *definition* in quotation marks. These are literal artifices that mark at the same time (1) that de Man assumes the performative and decisional character of the responsibility he takes in this appellation and this "definition" and (2) that one must be attentive to every detail of the letter, the literality of the letter defining here the place of what de Man will call materiality. The literality of the letter situates in fact this materiality not so much because it would be a physical or sensible (aesthetic) substance, or even matter, but because it is the place of prosaic resistance (cf. "Phenomenality and Materiality in Kant" in *Aesthetic Ideology,* where de Man concludes with these words: "prosaic materiality of the letter") to any organic and aesthetic totalization, to any aesthetic form. And first of all, I would say for my part, a resistance to every possible reappropriation. Perhaps in a fashion that is analogous (notice I do not say identical) to that "fonction référentielle" whose "trap" would be "inevitable," according to the phrase of de Man's that Andrzej Warminski inscribes in epigraph to his luminous introduction to *Aesthetic Ideology.* The materiality in question—and one must gauge the importance of this irony or paradox—is not a thing; it is not something (sensible or intelligible); it is not even the matter of a body. As it is not something, as it is nothing and yet it works, *cela œuvre,* this nothing therefore operates, it forces, but as a force of resistance. It resists both beautiful form and matter as substantial and organic totality. This is one of the reasons that de Man never says, it seems to me, *matter,* but *materiality.* Assuming the risk of this formula, although de Man does not do so himself, I would say that it is a materiality without matter, which, moreover, allies itself very well with a formality without form (in the sense of the beautiful synthetic and totalizing form) and without formalism. De Man, it seems to me, in his thinking of materiality, is no more materialist than he is formalist. To be sure, on occasion he uses these two words to accentuate and accompany a Kantian movement, an original reading of Kant. At the end of "Kant's Materialism," he speaks of an "absolute, radical formalism," and while taking all possible precautions regarding this performative nomination and appellation, regarding this act of calling, he adds: "To parody Kant's stylistic procedure of dictionary definition: the radical formalism that animates aesthetic judgment in the dynamics of the sublime is *what is called* materialism" (128). I have added emphasis to suggest that this "what is called" gives a good measure of the audacity in this materialist interpretation of the sublime. But de Man does not himself assume, it seems to me, a philosophical or metaphysical position that one might complacently call materialism. This force of resistance without material substance derives from the dissociative, dismembering, fracturing, disarticulating, and even disseminal power that de Man attributes to the letter.[27] To a letter whose dissociative and inorganic, disorganizing, disarticulating force affects not only nature but the body itself—as organic and organized totality. From this point of view, even though the word *matter* is not pronounced, nor even the word *materiality*, this thinking of the materiality of the letter already silently marks the chapter of *Allegories of Reading* that we are in the process of reading and that attributes a determinant role to dismemberment, mutilation, disfigurations, and so forth, as well as to the contingency of literal signifiers. The textual event is inseparable from this formal materiality of the letter. I say formal materiality or literality because what one might call in quotation marks or italics "materialism"—it would be better to say the re-noun, the re-nomination, the re-calling of materiality—requires a consequent reckoning with formality. You heard it at the end of the text "Kant's Materialism."

Valid for what de Man calls text, this becomes just as pertinent for *his* text itself, this very text of his—which thus becomes a case of what he is talking about and does not fail to present itself in that fashion, more or less ironically. Just one example. It says something about the values of machine, mechanicity, and formality toward which I will then turn, after having left under construction, an endless task, the project not only of showing the politico-performative autobiographicity of this text of de Man's, but of reapplying to it in a quasi-machine-like way what he himself writes on one of the first objects that offered itself, namely, the text of Rousseau—and the texts of a few others. If the confession of the *Confessions*, even after one distinguishes it as a moment of truth from the apologetic text of the *Rêveries*, cannot be a text of pure knowledge, if it includes an irresistible and irreducible performativity in its cognitive structure, well then, likewise, the performativity of the de Manian text prohibits one from reducing it to an operation of pure knowledge. Here, then, is an exemplary passage: apropos of Rousseau's text, its object is the text and language *in general*, in its law, in a law that is itself without individual reference or application (as grammar of political law—the notion of *grammar* is to be understood with reference to the trivium and the quadrivium, as Warminski shows very clearly in his indispensable study). This grammar of the law is a machine of the letter *(gramma)*, a letter machine, a writing machine, a typewriter. Exemplarity in general is this difficult marriage between the event and the typewriter. De Man writes: "The machine is *like* [I would be tempted to insist heavily, perhaps beyond what de Man would himself have wanted, on this word *like* that marks an analogy, the "like" of a resemblance or of an "as if," rather than an "as"] the grammar of the text when it is isolated from its rhetoric, the merely formal element without which no text can be generated" (294).

It is not said that the machine *is* a grammar of the text. Nor that the grammar of the text *is* a machine. One is *like* the other once grammar is isolated from rhetoric (performative rhetoric or cognitive rhetoric, the rhetoric of tropes, according to another distinction). The machine is determined on the basis of grammar and vice versa. Isolated from its rhetoric, as suspension of reference, grammar is purely formal. This is valid in general: no text can be produced without this formal, grammatical, or machine-like element. No text and no language. De Man right away adds, speaking of *language* after having spoken of *text*, and here they amount to the same thing: "There can be no use of language which is not, within a certain perspective, thus radically formal, i.e. mechanical, no matter how deeply this aspect may be concealed by aesthetic, formalistic delusions. The machine not only generates, but also suppresses, and not always in an innocent or balanced way" (ibid.)

We see here, already (but dare I say *already* without teleological illusion?), the insistence on the formal, on formality, in truth on grammatical or machine-like formality, in opposition to aesthetic illusions but also formalist illusions in the philosophy of art or the theory of literature. This is a gesture and a strategy that de Man deploys in a systematic way in *Aesthetic Ideology*.

My only ambition would thus be, on the basis of this text from *Allegories of Reading*, to sketch out a kind of deduction, in the quasi-philosophical sense, of the concept of materiality (without matter). It is not present here in that name but I believe one can recognize all its traits. However, in the texts gathered under the title *Aesthetic Ideology*, this concept will occupy in that name a thematic place.

Despite the association of materiality and the machine, why are we not dealing here with a mechanistic materialism? No more than with a dialectical materialism? It is because the de Manian concept of materiality is not, dare I say to his credit, a *philosophical* concept, the *metaphysical concept of matter*; it is, it seems to me, the name, the artifactual nomination of an artifactual figure that I will not dissociate from the performative signature I spoke of a moment ago. It is a sort of invention by de Man, one could say, almost a fiction produced in the movement of a strategy that is at once theoretical and autobiographical and that would need to be analyzed at length. To say it is a fiction (in the de Manian sense) does not mean that it is without theoretical value or philosophical effect, or that it is totally arbitrary; but the choice of the word *materiality* to designate "this" is in part arbitrary, in part necessary in relation to an entire historical space (the history of philosophy and, for example, of the diverse possibilities of philosophies of matter, the history of literary theory, political history, ideological camps, and so forth), in short, to a contextualized world, to a worldwide context in which de Man is calculating his strategy. And placing his bets.

To attempt the deduction I've just described on the basis of this text, I will take (too quickly) into account the different predicates (which are so many *predicaments,* de Man might say, who liked this word a lot), the different predicating traits that constitute inseparably and irreducibly this concept of materiality. Without having yet been named, this *concept of materiality,* in *Allegories of Reading* and no doubt in *The Rhetoric of Romanticism,* plays a role that I will not call organizing, for obvious reasons, but rather trenchant, decisive. (I am insisting on the concept of materiality and not of matter. This is not easily said and I leave intact the problem of the choice of this word *materiality* that brings with it a high essentializing risk where it should exclude, in its interpretation, any semantic implication of matter, of substratum or instance called "matter" and any reference to some content named matter; it risks thereby meaning only "effect of matter" without matter.) This concept of materiality determines the concept of textual event that, as you recall, is named as such at least twice, and twice associated with what de Man, for his part, *calls* in his fashion, but literally and often in this text, "deconstruction" and "dissemination."

I will cut out several motifs that are finally indissociable in what is at bottom one and the same perspective, one and the same performative strategy.

1. First of all, the inscription of the textual event—and this will later be one of the traits of the materiality of matter—is a machine-like deconstruction of the body proper. This is why I said, using a formulation that is not de Man's, that *materiality* becomes a very useful generic name for all that resists appropriation. De Man writes, moreover, from another point of view, in "Promises *(Social Contract)*": "There is nothing legitimate about property, but the rhetoric of property confers

the illusion of legitimacy" (262). He also analyzes the "fascination of . . . *proper* names" in Proust (ibid.). Materiality is not the body, at least the body proper as organic totality. This machine-like deconstruction is also a deconstruction of metaphor, of the totalizing metaphorical model, by a dissociative metonymic structure (a gesture that, I suggested, has some affinity with a certain Lacanianism allied with a certain Deleuzianism). The preceding essay on the *Social Contract* called for "the deconstruction of metaphorical patterns" (255), there where "the attribute of naturalness shifts from the metaphorical totality to the metonymic aggregate" (259). This movement becomes more precise in the essay on the *Confessions*. In the context of an analysis of the *Fourth Promenade*, de Man writes, for example: "But precisely because, in all these instances, the metaphor for the text is still the metaphor of text as body (from which a more or less vital part, including the head, is being severed), the *threat* [my emphasis] remains sheltered behind its metaphoricity" (297). When Rousseau is concerned no longer with the text of Tasso or Montesquieu but with the *Confessions*, then "the metaphor of text as body make[s] way for the more directly *threatening* alternative of the text as machine" (ibid.). I underscore *threatening*: from the preceding text to this one, one passes from the promise to the excuse, to be sure, as from one performative to another, but also from the promise to the threat (fear in the face of a cruel menace). As I have tried to show elsewhere,[28] this threat is also and already constitutive of any promise, and is not at all, as common sense and the theorists of speech acts would have it, irreducibly opposed to the promise (which, to common sense, may in fact seem to be able to promise only something good: one does not promise something threatening; this is what I contest, but we'll not pursue the point here).

On the following page, de Man raises the stakes. To the same menacing machination of the body proper and its metaphor he adds the "loss of the illusion of meaning":

> But in what way are these narratives threatening? As instances of Rousseau's generosity they are . . . more inept than convincing. They seem to exist primarily for the sake of the mutilations they describe. But these actual, bodily mutilations seem, in their turn, to be there more for the sake of allowing the evocation of the machine that causes them than for their own shock value; Rousseau lingers complacently over the description of the machine that seduces him into dangerously close contact: "I looked at the metal rolls, my eyes were attracted by their polish. I

was tempted to touch them with my fingers and I moved them with pleasure over the polished surface of the cylinder" (1036). In the general
economy of the *Rêverie,* the machine displaces all other significations
and becomes the raison d'être of the text. Its power of suggestion reaches far beyond its illustrative purpose, especially if one bears in mind the
previous characterization of unmotivated fictional language as "machinal." The underlying structural patterns of addition and suppression as
well as the figural system of the text all converge towards it. Barely concealed by its peripheral function, the text here stages the textual machine
of its own constitution *and* performance, its own textual allegory. The
threatening element in these incidents then becomes more apparent. The
text as body, with all its implications of substitutive tropes ultimately
always retraceable to metaphor, is displaced by the text as machine and,
in the process, it suffers the loss of the illusion of meaning. (298)

This loss of the illusion of meaning is also sometimes, as passage from
metaphor to metonymy and as fiction, the loss of the illusion of reference: "In fiction thus conceived the 'necessary link' of the metaphor
has been metonymized beyond the point of catachresis, and the fiction
becomes the disruption of the narrative's referential illusion" (292).

2. The word *machine* is here singled out, apparently, in the text of
Rousseau: "It is certain that neither my judgment, nor my will dictated
my reply, but that it was the automatic result *[l'effet machinal]* of my
embarrassment" (1034; quoted by de Man, 294). But the word and
the concept of machine are found again, re-elaborated, and redistributed everywhere: in Kleist, Pascal, and already in the *Social Contract*
when Rousseau speaks of what there is "in the wheels of the State"
*[dans les ressorts de l'État],* namely an "equivalent of the principle of
inertia in machines" (272). This word-concept *machine* is thus inseparable from motifs of suspended reference, repetition, the threat of mutilation, and so forth—and interpretation as the de Manian practice of
deconstruction-dissemination.

3. This deconstruction implies a process of de-metaphorization and
also, by the same token, of machine-like dis-figuration. Another example allows one to deduce a third motif of this concept of materiality,
namely, a mechanical, machine-like, automatic independence in relation
to any subject, any subject of desire and its unconscious, and therefore,
de Man doubtless thinks, any psychology or psychoanalysis as such.
(This point remains to be discussed: Where is one then to situate the affect of desire and especially of threat and cruelty? Is there not a force of

nondesire in desire, a law of desubjectivation in and as the subject itself? These are so many questions that I would have liked to deploy before this magnificent text, which I find sometimes too Lacanian, sometimes insufficiently Lacanian, in any case insufficiently "psychoanalytic.")

> The deconstruction of the figural dimension is a process that takes place independently of any desire; as such it is not unconscious but mechanical, systematic in its performance but *arbitrary* in its principle, *like a grammar.* This threatens the autobiographical subject not as the loss of something that once was present and that it once possessed, but as a radical estrangement between the meaning and the performance of any text. (298; emphasis added)

Once again, the term *like* in the phrase "like a grammar," the status of which phrase can be as difficult to pin down as Lacan's "like a language": "The unconscious is structured like a language." As difficult and no doubt very close, even in its implicit protest against psychology—or against psychoanalysis as psychology, be it that of desire.

Because this deconstruction *should be,* according to him, independent of any desire (which, although I can only say it quickly, seems to me both defensible and indefensible, depending on the concept of desire one puts to work), de Man goes beyond his first attempts at interpretation of the purloined ribbon (the logic of Rousseau's desire for Marion, substitution between Rousseau and Marion, symbolic circulation of the ribbon that, as "pure signifier," is substituted for a desire that is itself "desire for substitution," both desires being "governed by the same desire for specular symmetry" and so forth). But because this logic of desire seems to him to be, if not without pertinence, at least unable to account for the textual event, de Man wants to go further. On two occasions, within an interval of two pages, he declares: "This is not the only way, however, in which the text functions" (284) or "But the text offers further possibilities" (286). He then goes from the *Confessions* to the *Rêveries,* from the excuse for what happened to the excuse for the writing of the excuse, for the pleasure taken in writing what happened and thus for the pleasure taken in excusing himself. And in fact, Rousseau clearly suspects what he calls his "pleasure in writing" at the end of the *Fourth Promenade.*

4. Beyond this logic and this necessity of desire, materiality implies the effect of *arbitrariness.* The systematic recourse to this machine-like value of the arbitrary (which is relayed by a series of equivalents, notably the *gratuitous,* the *contingent,* the *random,* or the *fortuitous*),

whether one is talking about "the gratuitous product of a textual grammar" (299), the "random lie in the Marion episode" (291), the "absolute randomness of language," the "arbitrary power play of the signifier" (296), the "gratuitous improvisation, that of the implacable repetition of a preordained pattern. Like Kleist's marionettes . . ." (294), the fortuitous proximity of the ribbon and Marion (293), the "excuse of randomness in the *Confessions*" (291), the "total arbitrariness" (291) of "the sound 'Marion'" (289)—a name that, despite its alleged contingency and even though de Man makes no remark to this effect, we can now no longer separate from either Marie/Mary or marionette. The Marion of the ribbon will have been the instant, the blink of an eye of a fictive generation, just the time of a literary Passion and Pietà, the intercessor in a marriage of reason between the Virgin Mary and all her marionettes. Or, if you prefer, Marion the intercessor remains also in the literary archives of Christian Europe like the sister-in-law of all the automatic virgins that still amble about between the Gospels and Kleist.

Even though de Man does not say it, at least not in this way, the eventness of the event requires, if one wants to think it, this insistence on the arbitrary, fortuitous, contingent, aleatory, unforeseeable. An event held to be necessary and thus programmed, foreseeable, and so forth, would that be an event? De Man associates this feeling of arbitrariness with the experience of threat, cruelty, suffering in dismemberment, decapitation, disfiguration, or castration (the abundance of whose figures he isolates in Rousseau). What conclusions should be drawn from this?

There is the conclusion that de Man himself draws, namely, that this suffering is in fact what happens and is lived, but "from the point of view of the subject": "This more than warrants the anxiety with which Rousseau acknowledges the lethal quality of writing. Writing always includes the moment of dispossession in favor of the arbitrary power of the play of the signifier and *from the point of view of the subject* [my emphasis], this can only be experienced as a dismemberment, a beheading, or a castration" (296).

De Man therefore wishes to describe what it is in deconstruction-dissemination (that which "disseminates," he says, as "textual event" and as anacoluthon "throughout the entire text" [300]) that operates independently of and beyond any desire. The materiality of this event as textual event is what is or makes itself independent of any subject or any desire.

It is a logic that has something irrefutable about it. If, on the one hand, the event supposes surprise, contingency, or the arbitrary, as I emphasized a moment ago, it also supposes, on the other hand, this exteriority or this irreducibility to desire. And therefore it supposes that which makes it radically inappropriable, nonreappropriable, radically resistant to the logic of the proper. Moreover, what elsewhere I have called *exappropriation* concerns this work of the inappropriable in desire and in the process of appropriation.

Without being able to develop it here, I would draw another consequence that no doubt goes beyond what de Man himself says or would say. It is this: By reason of this unforeseeability, this irreducible and inappropriable exteriority for the subject of experience, every event as such is *traumatic*. Even an event experienced as a "happy" one. This does, I concede, confer on the word *trauma* a generality that is as fearsome as it is extenuating. But perhaps we have here a double consequence that must be drawn in the face of the speculative inflation to which the word is today subject. Understood in this sense, trauma is that which makes precarious any distinction between the point of view of the subject and what is produced independently of desire. It makes precarious even the use and the sense of all these words. An event is traumatic or it does not happen. It injures desire, whether or not desire desires or does not desire what happens. It is that which, within desire, constitutes it as possible and insists there while resisting it, as the impossible: some outside, irreducibly, as some nondesire, some death, and something inorganic, the becoming possible of the impossible as im-possible.

It is on this stage no doubt that arise the questions of the unforgivable, the unpardonable, the inexcusable—and of perjury.

There you are, pardon me for having spoken too long. I cut things off here, arbitrarily.

But not without saluting once again the spirit, I mean the ghost, of my friend. One day, de Man wrote this: "whatever happens in Derrida, it happens between him and his own text. He doesn't need Rousseau, he doesn't need anybody else."[29] As you have seen quite well, this is of course not true. De Man was wrong. I needed Paul de Man. But I needed him no doubt in order to show in my turn, many years later, that he, Paul de Man, perhaps had no need of Rousseau in order to show and to demonstrate, himself, what he thought he ought to confide in us. That is what I was suggesting by insisting on the exemplarity, and for example, the exemplarity of de Man's autobiographico-political texts apropos of Rousseau, materiality, and other similar things.

I am so sad that Paul de Man is not here himself to answer me and to object. But I can hear him already—and sooner or later his text will answer for him. That is what we all call a machine. But a spectral machine. By telling me I am right, it will tell him he is right. And sooner or later, our common innocence will not fail to appear to everyone's eyes, as the best intentioned of all our machinations. Sooner or later and virtually already, always, here now.

**NOTES**

1. Jean-Jacques Rousseau, *The Confessions,* trans. J. M. Cohen (New York: Penguin, 1953), 88; the translation, as here, will often be modified to remain closer to the literality of Rousseau's text. Page references to the French are to: Jean-Jacques Rousseau, *Oeuvres complètes,* ed. Bernard Gagnebin and Marcel Raymond, vol. 1, *Les confessions: Autres textes autobiographiques,* Bibliothèques de la Pléiade (Paris: Gallimard, 1959).

2. J. L. Austin, "A Plea for Excuses," in *Philosophical Papers,* 3d ed. (Oxford: Oxford University Press, 1979), 175. Since delivering this lecture, I have published a text titled "Comme si c'était possible—'within such limits,'" in *Revue Internationale de Philosophie* 3 (1998).

3. The brief allusions de Man makes (pp. 10, 68, 101, 102) in *The Rhetoric of Romanticism* (New York: Columbia University Press, 1984), do not touch at all on this history.

4. *The Confessions of St. Augustine,* trans. John K. Ryan (New York: Doubleday, 1960), book 2, chapter 4, 70.

5. Paul de Man, *Allegories of Reading: Figural Language in Rousseau, Nietzsche, Rilke, and Proust* (New Haven: Yale University Press, 1979), 287.

6. Jean-Jacques Rousseau, *Reveries of the Solitary Walker,* trans. Peter France (London: Penguin, 1979), 44.

7. Jean-Jacques Rousseau, *The Creed of a Priest of Savoy,* trans. Arthur H. Beattie (New York: Frederick Ungar, 1956), 80.

8. If I had the time, I would have liked to demonstrate that where the two authors of *Confessions* speak the language of the excuse, the one of the "inexcusable" *(inexcusabilis),* the other of "excusing himself," they inscribe their utterances in the thickness of an immense Christian, and first of all Paulinian, archive, in a palimpsest of quotations and quasi quotations, which, moreover, Augustine exhibits as such, notably in his borrowings from the *Epistle to the Romans* (I, ii, 20).

9. Austin, "A Plea for Excuses," 185.

10. Paul de Man, "Kant and Schiller," in *Aesthetic Ideology,* ed. Andrzej Warminski (Minneapolis: University of Minnesota Press, 1996), 133.

11. See Jacques Derrida, *Archive Fever,* trans. Eric Prenowitz (Chicago: University of Chicago Press, 1996).

12. Derrida is exploiting here, as he has often done, the opposite meanings of the homonymic expressions: *plus de,* no more, and *plus de,* more.—Trans.

13. It would be necessary, of course, to mobilize other readings de Man undertook around the motifs of the materiality of inscription and effacement (cf. "Shelley Disfigured," where it is a question of the materiality of inscription; and "Autobiography as Defacement," both in *The Rhetoric of Romanticism*).

14. On arbitrariness and gratuitousness, see *Allegories of Reading*, 357.

15. De Man, *Aesthetic Ideology*, 89; "Aesthetic Formalization: Kleist's 'Über das Marionettentheater,'" in *The Rhetoric of Romanticism*.

16. Derrida is exploiting the homonymic possibilities of *soie* (silk), *soi* (self), and the expression *en soi* (in itself).—*Trans.*

17. Austin, *Philosophical Papers*, 274.

18. See Derrida, *Adieu à Emmanuel Lévinas* (Paris: Galilée, 1997).

19. The term *non-coupable*, in addition to the meaning being adduced here, commonly signifies: not guilty.—*Trans.*

20. When this lecture was delivered, I did not know, I confess, that Ortwin de Graef had already pointed out what he calls in quotation marks "the 'mistake' in de Man's translation," or again "de Man's erratic anacoluthonic translation" ("Silence to Be Observed: A Trial for Paul de Man's Inexcusable Confessions," *Yale Journal of Criticism* 3: 2 [1990]: 214–15; also in *Postmodern Studies* 2 [1989]). I thank Erin Ferris for having brought this publication to my attention.

21. "The mutilation seems to be incurable and the prothesis *[sic]* only serves to mark this fact more strongly" (295–96).

22. The paragraph from the Geneva manuscript is not included in the translation of the *Confessions.*—*Trans.*

23. Peggy Kamuf, *Signature Pieces: On the Institution of Authorship* (Ithaca, N.Y.: Cornell University Press, 1988).

24. Geoffrey Bennington, "Aberrations: De Man (and) the Machine," in *Legislations: The Politics of Deconstruction* (London and New York: Verso, 1994).

25. These two common expressions, which use the same construction as "je m'excusai sur," mean "I took my revenge on . . . ," "I took it out on the first thing that presented itself."—*Trans.*

26. Jacques Derrida, *Mémoires for Paul de Man*, trans. Cecile Lindsay, Jonathan Culler, and Eduardo Cadava (New York: Columbia University Press, 1986), 143.

27. "We must, in other words, disarticulate, mutilate the body in a way that is much closer to Kleist than to Winckelmann . . . material disarticulation not only of nature but of the body. . . . To the dismemberment of the body corresponds a dismemberment of language, as meaning-producing tropes are replaced by the fragmentation of sentences and propositions into discrete words, or the fragmentation of words into syllables or finally letters. In Kleist's text, one would isolate the dissemination of the word *Fall* . . ." (*Aesthetic Ideology*, 88–89).

28. In "Avances," preface to Serge Margel, *Le Tombeau du dieu artisan* (Paris: Minuit, 1995).

29. "An Interview with Paul de Man," in Paul de Man, *The Resistance to Theory* (Minneapolis: University of Minnesota Press, 1986), 118.

# Contributors

JUDITH BUTLER is Maxine Elliot Professor in the departments of rhetoric and comparative literature at the University of California at Berkeley. She is the author of *Subjects of Desire: Hegelian Reflections in Twentieth-Century France*; *Gender Trouble: Feminism and the Subversion of Identity*; *Bodies That Matter: On the Discursive Limits of "Sex"*; *The Psychic Life of Power: Theories of Subjection*; and *Excitable Speech*, as well as numerous articles and contributions on philosophy, feminist theory, and queer theory. Her most recent work on Antigone and the politics of kinship, *Antigone's Claim: Kinship between Life and Death*, is forthcoming.

T. J. CLARK is George C. and Helen N. Pardee Professor of art history at the University of California at Berkeley. He is the author of *The Absolute Bourgeois: Artists and Politics in France, 1848–51*; *Image of the People: Gustave Courbet and the 1848 Revolution*; *The Painting of Modern Life: Paris in the Art of Manet and His Followers*; and *Farewell to an Idea: Episodes from a History of Modernism*.

BARBARA COHEN is senior editor and director of HumaniTech, a center for the application of technology to humanities research and teaching at the University of California, Irvine. She previously taught French and art and has written several articles on the dynamics of art education in the public schools.

TOM COHEN is the author of *Anti-Mimesis (from Plato to Hitchcock)* and *Ideology and Inscription: "Cultural Studies" after Benjamin*, *de Man, and Bakhtin.* He is currently completing *Re-Marking Hitchcock,* editing *The Cambridge Companion to Derrida,* and coediting a volume titled *Technicity, "Life," the Animal.* He is currently chair of the English department at the University of Albany, SUNY.

JACQUES DERRIDA is director of studies of the École des Hautes Études in France and professor of English at the University of California, Irvine. He has published numerous books, including *Memoirs for Paul de Man, Specters of Marx, Politics of Friendship, Monolingualism of the Other,* and *Archive Fever.*

BARBARA JOHNSON teaches at Harvard University in the departments of English and comparative literature, where she holds the title of Fredric Wertham Professor of Law and Psychiatry in Society. She is author of *The Critical Difference; A World of Difference; The Wake of Deconstruction;* and *The Feminist Difference.* She has edited several volumes and is the translator of Jacques Derrida's *Dissemination.*

ERNESTO LACLAU is professor of political theory and director of the doctoral program in Ideology and Discourse Analysis at the University of Essex. He is author of *Politics and Ideology in Marxist Theory: Capitalism, Fascism, Populism; Hegemony and Socialist Strategy: Towards a Radical Democratic Politics* (with Chantal Mouffe); *New Reflections on the Revolution of Our Time;* and *Emancipation(s).*

J. HILLIS MILLER is Distinguished Professor of English and Comparative Literature at the University of California, Irvine. He previously taught at Johns Hopkins and Yale universities. He is the author of many books and articles on literature and literary theory, most recently *Reading Narrative* and *Black Holes.*

ARKADY PLOTNITSKY is professor of English and the director of the theory and cultural studies program at Purdue University. He has written extensively on English and European romanticism, critical theory, continental philosophy, and the relationships among literature, philosophy, and science. His books include *In the Shadow of Hegel; Complementarity: Antiepistemology after Bohr and Derrida;* a coedited volume (with Barbara H. Smith), *Mathematics, Science, and*

*Postclassical Theory*; and a forthcoming study, *The Invisible and the Unknowable: Modern Science and Nonclassical Thought.*

LAURENCE A. RICKELS, professor of German and comparative literature at the University of California, Santa Barbara, is the author of *The Vampire Lectures* (Minnesota, 1999); *The Case of California*; and *Aberrations of Mourning*; and editor of *Acting Out in Groups* (Minnesota, 1999). His three-volume study *Nazi Psychoanalysis* is forthcoming (Minnesota). He also works as a psychotherapist in Los Angeles.

MICHAEL SPRINKER was a member of the editorial committee of *New Left Review.* His books include *Imagining Relations: Aesthetics and Ideology in the Theory of Historical Materialism* and *History and Ideology in Proust.*

ANDRZEJ WARMINSKI is professor of comparative literature at the University of California, Irvine. He is author of *Readings in Interpretation: Hölderlin, Hegel, Heidegger* (Minnesota, 1987) and editor of Paul de Man's *Aesthetic Ideology* (Minnesota, 1996). His *Material Inscriptions* is forthcoming.

# Index

Compiled by Geoffrey Manaugh, University of Chicago